Exam Ref 70-484:
Essentials of Developing
Windows Store Apps
Using C#

Indrajit Chakrabarty

Published with the authorization of Microsoft Corporation by:

O'Reilly Media, Inc.
1005 Gravenstein Highway North
Sebastopol, California 95472

ISBN: 978-0-7356-7684-8

1 2 3 4 5 6 7 8 9 QG 8 7 6 5 4 3

Printed and bound in the United States of America.

Microsoft Press books are available through booksellers and distributors worldwide. If you need support related to this book, email Microsoft Press Book Support at *mspinput@microsoft.com*. Please tell us what you think of this book at *http://www.microsoft.com/learning/booksurvey*.

Microsoft and the trademarks listed at *http://www.microsoft.com/about/legal/en/us/Intellectual-Property/Trademarks/EN-US.aspx* are trademarks of the Microsoft group of companies. All other marks are property of their respective owners.

The example companies, organizations, products, domain names, email addresses, logos, people, places, and events depicted herein are fictitious. No association with any real company, organization, product, domain name, email address, logo, person, place, or event is intended or should be inferred.

This book expresses the author's views and opinions. The information contained in this book is provided without any express, statutory, or implied warranties. Neither the authors, O'Reilly Media, Inc., Microsoft Corporation, nor its resellers, or distributors will be held liable for any damages caused or alleged to be caused either directly or indirectly by this book.

Acquisitions Editor: Russell Jones
Developmental Editor: Box Twelve Communications, Inc.
Production Editor: Kristen Borg
Editorial Production: Box Twelve Communications, Inc.
Technical Reviewer: Damien Foggon
Copyeditor: Box Twelve Communications, Inc.
Indexer: Box Twelve Communications, Inc.
Cover Design: Twist Creative • Seattle
Cover Composition: Ellie Volckhausen
Illustrator: Rebecca Demarest

This book is dedicated to Tiya and Liana, the best gifts of my life.

Contents at a glance

Contents

What do you think of this book? We want to hear from you!

Microsoft is interested in hearing your feedback so we can continually improve our
books and learning resources for you. To participate in a brief online survey, please visit:

www.microsoft.com/learning/booksurvey/

Chapter 4   Program the user interaction   225

Chapter 5   Manage security and data   305

What do you think of this book? We want to hear from you!

Microsoft is interested in hearing your feedback so we can continually improve our
books and learning resources for you. To participate in a brief online survey, please visit:

www.microsoft.com/learning/booksurvey/

Introduction

The Microsoft 70-484 certification exam tests your knowledge of designing and develop-ing Windows Store apps. Readers are assumed to be experienced Microsoft Windows-based application developers, including two or more years creating and modifying touch-enabled interfaces.

The exam expects you to be familiar with the high-level concepts required to build such apps, including C# and the Microsoft Visual Studio 2012 environment. Therefore, this book adopts a high-level approach to teaching application design, and provides numerous code samples that illustrate concepts without step-by-step details of building a Windows Store app in Visual Studio. You should be able to design and build Windows Store apps on your own, while using this book to study for the exam.

Success on the 70-484 exam will prove your knowledge and experience in designing and developing Windows Store apps using Microsoft technologies. This exam guide reviews the concepts described in the exam objectives, such as:

- Designing Windows Store apps
- Developing Windows Store apps
- Creating the user interface
- Programming the user interaction
- Managing security and data

This book covers every exam objective, but it does not cover every exam question. Only the Microsoft exam team has access to the exam questions themselves and Microsoft regu-larly adds new questions to the exam, making it impossible to cover specific questions. You should consider this book a supplement to your relevant real-world experience and other study materials. If you encounter a topic in this book that you do not feel completely com-fortable with, use the links you'll find in text to find more information and take the time to research and study the topic. Great information is available on MSDN, TechNet, and in blogs and forums.

Microsoft certifications

Microsoft certifications distinguish you by proving your command of a broad set of skills and experience with current Microsoft products and technologies. The exams and corresponding certifications are developed to validate your mastery of critical competencies as you design and develop, or implement and support, solutions with Microsoft products and technologies both on-premise and in the cloud. Certification brings a variety of benefits to the individual and to employers and organizations.

> **MORE INFO** **ALL MICROSOFT CERTIFICATIONS**
>
> For information about Microsoft certifications, including a full list of available certifications, go to *http://www.microsoft.com/learning/en/us/certification/cert-default.aspx.*

Acknowledgments

I would like to thank Jeff Riley, Box Twelve Communications, for choosing me to write this book, and Kim Lindros for her work as the developmental editor. Kim's thorough reviews immensely improved the quality of the book. I would like to thank Damien Foggon, the technical reviewer, for his comments and attention to detail while reviewing the book.

I would also like to thank Carole Jelen, Waterside Publications, for the initial discussions and help in setting up the project, and David Wall (*www.davidwall.com*) for introducing me to Carole and for helping me complete other projects while this book was under way.

Finally, I must thank Tiya and Liana for their understanding and support while I was writing the book through the summer holidays.

Errata & book support

We've made every effort to ensure the accuracy of this book and its companion content. Any errors that have been reported since this book was published are listed on our Microsoft Press site at oreilly.com:

> *http://aka.ms/ER70-484/errata*

If you find an error that is not already listed, you can report it to us through the same page.

If you need additional support, email Microsoft Press Book Support at *mspinput@micro-soft.com.*

Please note that product support for Microsoft software is not offered through the addresses above.

We want to hear from you

At Microsoft Press, your satisfaction is our top priority, and your feedback our most valuable asset. Please tell us what you think of this book at:

http://www.microsoft.com/learning/booksurvey

The survey is short, and we read every one of your comments and ideas. Thanks in advance for your input!

Stay in touch

Let's keep the conversation going! We're on Twitter: *http://twitter.com/MicrosoftPress*.

Preparing for the exam

Microsoft certification exams are a great way to build your resume and let the world know about your level of expertise. Certification exams validate your on-the-job experience and product knowledge. While there is no substitution for on-the-job experience, preparation through study and hands-on practice can help you prepare for the exam. We recommend that you round out your exam preparation plan by using a combination of available study materials and courses. For example, you might use this *Exam Ref* and another study guide for your "at home" preparation, and take a Microsoft Official Curriculum course for the classroom experience. Choose the combination that you think works best for you.

Note that this *Exam Ref* is based on publically available information about the exam and the author's experience. To safeguard the integrity of the exam, authors do not have access to the live exam.

CHAPTER 1

Design Windows Store apps

The launch of Windows 8 was accompanied with the introduction of Windows Runtime (WinRT), a new framework for building touch-friendly user interfaces (UIs) for Windows Store applications (apps). With WinRT, Windows Presentation Foundation (WPF) and Silverlight developers could leverage their existing XAML and C#/VB.NET skills to build Windows Store apps. In addition to the new framework and an accompanying toolset, Microsoft introduced a new design language called "Microsoft design style."

The conceptual design of an application is the first stage of designing an application. In the conceptual design, you focus on a set of ideas and concepts about what your app should do, how it will behave when users interact with it, and what it should look like. A well-designed application has logical layers loosely coupled with a UI, which is used for presenting the data. Separating logic from presentation enables the application to be enhanced or updated without changing the conceptual design.

You can use design patterns such as Model-View-ViewModel (MVVM) to develop maintainable and extensible applications. Data and state preservation across various states of an application is important in providing a great user experience. After you build and test your application, you need to prepare the app for Windows Store certification. Microsoft provides a set of requirements to help you during the app certification process and deployment in the Windows Store.

Objectives in this chapter:

- Objective 1.1: Design the UI layout and structure
- Objective 1.2: Design for separation of concerns (SOC)
- Objective 1.3: Apply the MVVM pattern to your app design
- Objective 1.4: Design and implement Process Lifetime Management (PLM)
- Objective 1.5: Plan for an app deployment

Objective 1.1: Design the UI layout and structure

The primary form of interaction with a Windows Store app by its users is through the user interface (UI). Microsoft design style consists of a set of principles that provide a consistent, elegant, and compelling user experience in Windows Store apps. You should plan and design Windows Store app UIs with these principles as a reference. The UI should be composed of visual elements and controls, with a clear hierarchy in their layout. You should also consider users with disabilities and preferences, and design your app for accessibility. Reusing UI code in multiple applications will help you to rapidly build Windows Store apps; therefore, you should consider building custom controls and using them in your apps.

This objective covers how to:

- Evaluate the conceptual design and decide how the UI will be composed
- Design for the inheritance and re-use of visual elements
- Design for accessibility
- Decide when custom controls are needed

Evaluating the conceptual design and deciding how the UI will be composed

Windows Store apps provide Windows 8 users with a unique way of interacting with their PCs and devices. The apps are unique in their design and functionality; they share a set of important characteristics that are fundamental in their design. To design a compelling user experience in your app with an attractive user interface, it is important to plan your app well. Microsoft provides Windows Store app developers with a set of guidelines to help them in planning their app. The steps you should follow to plan and design your Windows Store app are described in the following sections.

Decide which features will make your app great

You might have an idea to create a blog reader or a weather app. When you check the Windows Store, you might find several dozen such apps, but none of them satisfies your needs. Although some apps may be simple to use, they are perhaps lacking in fundamental features such as sharing data with friends. You need to determine which features you think will make your app great and make it stand out from the rest of the apps in the Windows Store. Then, because it's sometimes difficult to incorporate every feature you want in the first release of your app, prepare a list of must-have features for the first release. Your focus should be on your users and the scenarios in which they will use your app.

Assess user scenarios

Users will interact with your app in a variety of ways and you need to anticipate as many of them as possible. For example, in the case of a blog reader app, users might open the app if they see an interesting post when it appears in the app's tile. This is one scenario you need to include when assessing the various scenarios your app will support. Then you visualize them by using sketches, prototypes, and storyboards. Remember that your app needs to perform well for such scenarios, and your design should accommodate any necessary requirements.

You might prioritize these scenarios and implement only a few of them in the first release of your application, adding other scenarios in future updates.

Decide on your app's features

After you decide on a set of scenarios to implement in your app, explore the Windows platform and investigate features to associate with your app's needs. To provide users with the best experience while using your app, follow the User Experience (UX) guidelines for each feature.

- **Use the right contracts in your app**   Contracts are agreements between apps that enable your app to interact with other apps. Complex interactions such as sharing content from within your app with your friends or searching with your app are easier to implement with contracts. If your app is a source of media, the Play To contract enables your app to stream media to devices such as televisions.

- **Touch-first design**   Windows 8 has promoted touch and gestures as the primary form of interaction with Windows Store apps, leaving the keyboard and mouse as alternative methods of interaction. Therefore, you should consider using touch interactions, such as rotate, pan, swipe, cross-slide and others, to provide a more visual and informative way to interact with content in your app.

- **Engaging experience**   Animations, toast notifications, live tiles, and secondary tiles can help users feel deeply immersed and engaged with your app.

- **Use device capabilities whenever possible**   Modern devices have proximity sensors, cameras, accelerometers, and geolocation capabilities that you should consider using in your app.

> **MORE INFO**   **USER EXPERIENCE (UX) GUIDELINES**
>
> See *http://msdn.microsoft.com/en-US/library/windows/apps/hh465424* for more information on UX guidelines.

Design a great user interface for your app

After you establish the features you want to implement in your app, you should start working on the fundamentals of designing the UI. Remember that the UI is the main gateway to your app, enabling users to be immersed and engaged with your app's features. Microsoft design style provides designers and developers with a set of simple principles to follow while designing the UI of Windows Store apps:

- **Showcase your content**   You should strive to adapt a clean and open layout. Minimize distractions by removing unnecessary lines, boxes, blurs, and gradients; and use open space to frame your app's content. Remember to put "content over chrome." You should provide a clear and simple information hierarchy in your app with an emphasis on typography. Remember to support landscape, portrait, snapped, and fill views. Your app should look and work appropriately in any of these views.

- **Interact with content**   Whenever possible, let your users interact with your app's content directly, without using controls such as tabs for navigation and buttons for actions. Use Semantic Zoom and the app bar instead. Show commands contextually and use charms, which are shown on demand.

- **Be fast and fluid in actions**   Using touch as the primary form of interaction with app content, design the UI to use gestures such as swipe, pinch-and-zoom, and so on. Provide visual feedback using animations and notifications whenever possible. Design for accessibility as well as for mouse and keyboard actions. Use built-in controls and their touch-optimized behaviors in your UI design. Note that built-in controls are accessible by default, so they lower the challenges and cost in building an accessible app.

- **Snap and scale beautifully**   Your app will be downloaded and installed in devices and PCs with a variety of resolutions and form factors. Using the Microsoft Visual Studio simulator, test how your app looks and behaves on different form factors. The platform provides automatic scaling based on screen size and resolution. Use Scalable Vector Graphics (SVG) and three resolutions of your app's assets to provide a crisp and polished UI to support screens with various pixel densities.

- **Make your app feel alive**   The app tile is the entrance to your application. The app tile can be updated with fresh content regularly, which will draw the attention of the user. Time-sensitive notifications delivered in a live tile enable the user who opts in to receive them a way to feel engaged with your app. Secondary tiles help people bookmark interesting content from your application.

Designing the UI of a Windows Store app can be challenging. You should refer to the design guidelines provided by Microsoft to help you design your app. The guidelines can help you choose the app's navigation pattern, which commands to use for common interactions such as copy and paste, how to include app branding, as well as how to create a great user experience. In the conceptual design stage, it is useful to create a prototype of the UI. The prototype can be used to validate your app's design against the design guidelines.

> **MORE INFO**   **DESIGN GUIDANCE FOR WINDOWS STORE APPS**
>
> Microsoft provides designers and developers with a set of design guidelines for Windows Store apps, which are available at *http://msdn.microsoft.com/en-us/library/windows/apps/ hh770552.aspx*.

Designing for the inheritance and reuse of visual elements

The Extensible Application Markup Language (XAML) platform in Windows 8 enables developers to customize controls that ship with the WinRT framework through styles, templates, and visual states. Existing controls retain their functionality when customized; however, their rendered appearance can change, and new properties and methods can be added. This helps you reuse controls within your Windows Store app.

In your app, you can add input validation to a text box or add autocomplete support. The following example shows how to create a control by customizing the *TextBox* class:

Sample of C# code

```csharp
using Windows.UI.Xaml.Controls;
namespace ContosoApp
{
    public class ExtendedTextBox : TextBox
    {
        // Implement your customization here
    }
}
```

Instead of extending a control, you might need to customize its visual appearance to meet the requirements of your application. Restyling a control in XAML is similar to using Cascading Style Sheets (CSS) with HTML pages. Styles are used to update the appearance of standard XAML controls. A style is represented by the *Windows.UI.Xaml.Style* class. A style is used to group together property values you would set individually. The style could then be used on multiple elements in the same page as well as different pages. Styles are declared in resources, in most cases. A style uses a collection of setters to set the target properties of the element. A setter uses a key and sets a value for the key. The following is a sample style for the *TextBlock* UI element:

Sample of XAML code

```xml
<Style x:Key="TextBlockHeaderStyle" TargetType="TextBlock">
    <Setter Property="Foreground" Value="White" />
    <Setter Property="FontSize" Value="44" />
    <Setter Property="TextTrimming" Value="WordEllipsis" />
    <Setter Property="TextWrapping" Value="Wrap" />
</Style>
```

Styles can be extended through inheritance, which avoids code duplication and (often) mistakes. You can extend a style and override setters in the parent style as follows:

```xml
<Style x:Key="TextBlockSubheaderStyle" TargetType="TextBlock"
        BasedOn="{StaticResource TextBlockHeaderStyle}">
    <!-- Extending a style -->
    <Setter Property="FontStyle" Value="Italic" />
    <!-- Overriding a setter in the parent style -->
    <Setter Property="FontSize" Value="32" />
</Style>
```

Note that the parent style is referred as a *StaticResource* in the extended style. To apply these styles on any text block in an app, their keys are explicitly used to refer them. Such styles are called *explicit styles*.

Some styles can affect UI elements even if they are not explicitly applied on them. Such styles are called *implicit styles*. They are automatically applied to any instance of a type they are targeted for within the scope of the style. Here is an example of an implicit style:

```
<Style TargetType="Button">
    <Setter Property="Background" Value="Red" />
</Style>
```

UI elements defined in XAML can contain a collection of resources used by themselves and their children. *Resources* are dictionaries that contain reusable values, and each value is provided with a unique key that is used to reference the value.

A resource is declared either at the app level, at the page level, or at a specific UI element—it cannot be declared multiple times in your application. This is because a resource is considered a visual element, and a visual element can be declared only once. Resources are generally reused; therefore, declaring them multiple times will result in an error. If a resource is declared at the app level, it can be used anywhere within the app. If it is declared in a page, it can be used only by the UI elements declared in the page. A resource can be scoped to a UI element, in which case it is available for use within the element by its children.

You can group all the resources you want to share across multiple pages in your application in a *resource dictionary*. One or more resource dictionaries declared in their own files are included in the App.xaml file, as follows:

```
<Application.Resources>
    <ResourceDictionary>
        <ResourceDictionary.MergedDictionaries>
            <ResourceDictionary Source="Common/StandardStyles.xaml" />
            <ResourceDictionary Source="Common/ControlStyles.xaml" />
        </ResourceDictionary.MergedDictionaries>
    </ResourceDictionary>
</Application.Resources>
```

Designing for accessibility

When designing your Windows Store app, you should consider app accessibility to serve various scenarios. This ensures that your application is usable by people with disabilities or other limitations such as mobility, vision, color perception, hearing, speech, cognition, and literacy, which might prevent them from using conventional UIs. Legal requirements might make it mandatory for your application to implement an accessible interface.

To implement accessibility in the design of your Windows Store app, you should follow these guidelines:

- **Screen reading** You can expose information such as name, role, and description about the visual elements in your UI. This helps blind or visually impaired users understand and access all UI elements and invoke available functionality.

- **Keyboard accessibility** Many users prefer to use the Tab key on the keyboard to navigate and use the UI, such as moving the focus on visual elements, and navigating through grids and lists. Users might also prefer to activate functionality using the Enter or Space key and common shortcuts such as Ctrl+P to print content.

- **Accessible visual experience**   Visually impaired users require sufficient contrast in the UI. You should use high-contrast themes to accommodate such requirements. You should also consider colorblind users when using colors to convey information through the UI of your application. The Windows Store requires visually accessible UIs to have a minimum text contrast ratio of 4.5:1 against the background.

Consider providing options for your users to select themes that suit their preferences, adjust the font size and color, and adjust the dots per inch (dpi) setting. You can also allow users to select alternative controls and turn off nonessential elements and animations. Keep in mind the Narrator, Magnifier, and Touch Keyboard accessibility features that enable users to interact more comfortably with apps. If you use a custom control in your app, you should provide basic accessibility information for the control. You need to ensure that the control is fully accessible by keyboard, and that the UI meets requirements for visual accessibility.

The Microsoft UI Automation framework is an accessibility framework for Windows. It is integrated within the base classes and the built-in behavior of UI control classes in Windows Store apps built with C#, C++, and Visual Basic. The Windows Store app is treated as a top-level window by UI Automation, and all the content within the app window is reported to and available to a UI Automation client. This enables UI Automation to obtain information about the UI and send input to controls. For example, UI Automation enables screen readers to provide information about the UI to the users, and enables users to manipulate the UI through ways other than standard input.

Before you submit your application to the Windows Store, you should test your app for accessibility. A good test for keyboard accessibility is to disconnect the mouse from your PC and test your app with only the keyboard. You should be able to cycle through all UI elements by using the Tab key. Composite UI elements should be navigable with the arrow keys. You should ensure that interactive UI elements can be invoked by pressing the Enter or Space key. You should also verify that your app uses the contrast ratio properly, and that when a high-contrast theme is used, all the UI elements display correctly. Users can turn on the *Make everything on your screen bigger* setting in *PC Settings*, *Ease of Access*. In such a case, you should ensure that all the controls in the UI are accessible, all text is visible, and no UI elements overlap.

The screen reading experience of your application's UI can be tested using Narrator. You can start Narrator while your app is running by pressing the Windows logo key and Enter button. Narrator automatically enters touch mode on devices that support more than four contacts. You can navigate through your UI by using single finger flick gestures, a three-finger swipe to the right or left to navigate like using Tab and Shift+Tab, and a three-finger swipe up to read the contents of the entire windows. To have Narrator read items under your finger, drag a single finger up and down or left and right.

The Windows Software Development Kit (SDK) for Windows 8 provides accessibility tools such as Inspect and UI Accessibility Checker to help you test your app for accessibility. Inspect enables you to select any UI element and view the element's accessibility data. Figure 1-1 shows the Inspect tool being used to check an element's accessibility information.

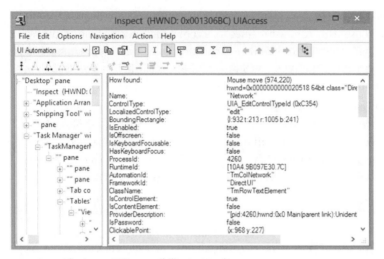

FIGURE 1-1 The Inspect UI accessibility test tool

The UI Accessibility Checker helps you identify problems with your UI at runtime. When you finish developing the UI of your app, use the UI Accessibility Checker to test various usage scenarios, verify that the runtime accessibility information is correct, and find any issues. Figure 1-2 shows the UI Accessibility Checker being set up to test the accessibility information in an app.

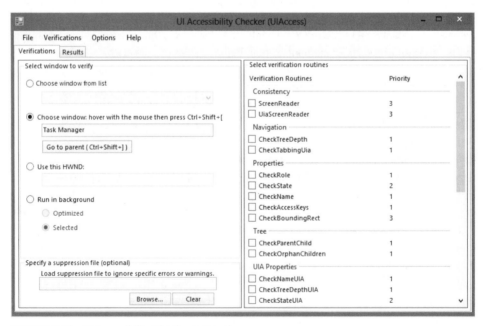

FIGURE 1-2 The UI Accessibility Checker test tool

After you have implemented an accessible design for your app, you can mark your app as accessible in the Windows Store, which makes it easier for users with disabilities to discover your app. Windows Store provides an Accessible filter to let users search for apps that have an accessible UI. When you declare your app as accessible, the Accessible tag is added to the description of your app.

> **MORE INFO**   **MAKING YOUR APP ACCESSIBLE**
>
> Read more about accessibility in Windows Store apps at *http://msdn.microsoft.com/en-us/library/windows/apps/xaml/hh452678.aspx*.

EXAM TIP

Although you are not expected to explain how a particular tool used for testing accessibility works, it is important to know the various ways of testing accessibility in a Windows Store app.

Deciding when custom controls are needed

Custom controls provide you with an option to create UI elements with a unique appearance that are often reusable across multiple apps. As a Windows Store app developer, you might consider building a user control or customize a control such as *GridView* using a template to extend its visual design. Therefore, you need to consider one of three options when building a control:

- Custom control
- User control
- Create a template and apply it to control element

In most cases, you will create a user control in the application where you will use it and add other control elements to it. For example, you might need a watermarked *TextBox* control at multiple places in your app, but you are not sure whether you will need this control in other apps that you build. Therefore, it is best to create a user control in your application project itself. Visual Studio provides developers with a template to create a user control, as shown in Figure 1-3.

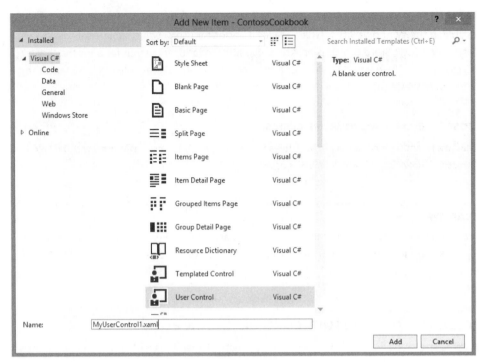

FIGURE 1-3 Creating a user control with Visual Studio

When you add a new user control to your project, an XAML file is added to your project along with a C# code-behind file. The visual representation of the user control is defined in the XAML, and the code-behind file is used to implement the functionality of the control.

A *custom control* is a reusable UI component you can use in multiple Windows Store projects. You can restyle and re-template a custom control as needed, and package it into its own assembly that can be distributed as a Nuget package, for example. Using custom controls enables the flexibility to create a new visual element with custom code that implements various features of the element. Custom controls are derived from either core controls such as *Button* or control primitives such as *Control* and *Panel*.

In Visual Studio, you can add a custom control to your project by using the Templated Control item template in the Add New Item dialog box. This will create an XAML file— themes\generic.xaml—and a class file. The XAML file contains the default styles and templates for your custom control. The location of Generic.xaml is important because the XAML framework loads your custom control automatically.

You are expected to implement your control logic in the class file. You must set the *Default-StyleKey* to the *Type* of your control in the constructor of the class; this tells the framework which style and template to apply to this *Type* when it is used in your application. A custom control is used in a way similar to how you use a user control: You declare a namespace and put it in the XAML wherever you need it.

Objective summary

- Evaluate the conceptual design of your application with an emphasis on how users will use your app.
- Compose the UI so it showcases content in your app.
- Use styles and resources to design the UI so that visual elements can be reused within your app.
- Consider users with disabilities and impairments when designing and building the UI of your app.
- Consider using custom controls whenever you find a need to reuse components across multiple Windows Store apps.

Objective review

Answer the following questions to test your knowledge of the information in this objective. You can find the answers to these questions and explanations of why each answer choice is correct or incorrect in the "Answers" section at the end of this chapter.

1. You have been asked to implement the UI of a Windows Store app. The application requirements make it essential for the app to be fast and fluid, and provide visual feedback to users for their actions at the same time. The designer of the user interface has recommended using animations. How should you implement animations while ensuring app requirements are met?

    A. Convince the designer that animations will make the UI complex and unintuitive.

    B. Use animations in the controls provided by the platform and in the animation library.

    C. Implement your own animations and add them to the UI.

    D. Build custom controls and add animations in them. Use these custom controls to build the UI.

2. You have created an application that aggregates news feeds from multiple sources. You have been asked to ensure your application is accessible by users with disabilities and visual impairments. Which tests should be carried out to ensure the app is accessible? (Choose all that apply.)

   A. Run the Inspect tool on your application.

   B. Run the UI Accessibility Checker on your application.

   C. Let the Windows Store run all the relevant tests on accessibility.

   D. Test your app with only the keyboard.

   E. Install and test your app on as many PCs and devices as possible.

3. Your organization produces a number of Windows Store apps every year. Designers and developers are located in separate geographical locations. They have to collaborate on a number of apps for a particular client, ensuring that branding in the apps is consistent and that functionality, such as authentication, is uniform across all apps. As the lead developer, what are your recommendations to ensure consistency in the design and functionality of the apps for the client? (Choose all that apply.)

   A. There should be only one project shared between designers and developers. Code in this project can be modified based on the applications' requirements for the UI.

   B. Wherever possible, visual elements specific to the brand should be implemented in styles that are defined in resources in the app level.

   C. Components with similar functionality should be developed as custom controls. These controls should be used in the apps.

   D. There is no easy way to share code within apps and between designers and developers. No recommendations can be made.

   E. Use UX design resources provided by Microsoft for creating the conceptual design of the app.

Objective 1.2: Design for separation of concerns (SOC)

Separation of concerns (SOC) is a concept in software design and development that helps to remove dependencies between various parts of an application, allowing for maintainability and testability of the application. SOC involves planning the logical layers of your solution and designing them to be loosely coupled with interfaces. The implementation of any layer is independent of the implementation of others, allowing for loose coupling between them. It is often useful to develop layers of a solution as WinRT components called Windows Metadata (WinMD) components so that they can be used to develop Windows Store apps with C#, Visual Basic, C++, or JavaScript.

Planning the logical layers of your solution to meet app requirements

You should design a Windows Store app with maintainability and extensibility in mind. After you finalize the conceptual design of your app, the next step is to plan the logical layers based on your app's requirements. Traditional software applications employ logical grouping of components into separate layers that communicate with each other and with other applications. Layers can be considered as logical divisions of components and functionality; they do not take into account physical location of components. Layers help to identify different kinds of tasks performed by components, thereby making it easier to create a design that supports the reuse of components.

In a logical layered design, a set of components performing similar tasks is grouped into a layer. Identifying logical layers in a design supports reusability of components as well as maintainability of your application. Figure 1-4 shows the architectural view of a logical layered system.

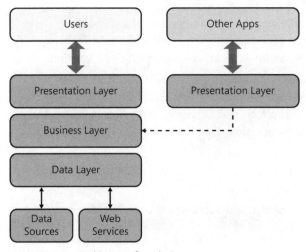

FIGURE 1-4 Logical layers of a solution

The three-layer architecture shown in Figure 1-4 consists of the following:

- **Presentation layer**   This layer is the UI of your application and is responsible for your application's layout and formatting. You will use XAML with core controls, user controls, and custom controls to implement this layer.

- **Business layer**   This layer is where you implement your application's core logic or business logic, and your application's business rules. Other Windows Store apps interact with your application via this layer. For example, the business layer can use contracts provided by Windows for integration with the platform and other apps to share data.

- **Data layer**   This layer provides the data repository required by the business layer of your application for storage and retrieval of data. It defines the interface used by the business layer for accessing a database, local settings, or remote web services.

These layers might be located in the same physical tier or they might be separated by physical boundaries. You should consider these layers as loosely coupled, with clearly defined interfaces that aid in the interaction between the layers. Loose coupling between the layers ensures your solution is maintainable and extensible, and is robust to any changes in implementation required in future updates. In addition, loose coupling helps with testing the different layers of a solution independent of each other.

Designing loosely coupled layers

When you design the layers of your solution, you should start by focusing on identifying and grouping functionality into layers. At the same time, you should identify the interfaces that help in the interaction between the various layers. After you define the layers and interfaces of your solution, you must consider how your solution will be deployed. At the final stage, you should choose the communication mechanism between various layers of your solution.

While designing loosely coupled layers for a solution, you should have a clear plan to group related functionalities into layers. Having too many layers adds to the complexity of the design, whereas having too few layers affects maintainability and extensibility. You should find a balance between reusability and loose coupling, and consider their impact on performance and complexity.

> **IMPORTANT   BENEFITS OF A LOOSELY COUPLED DESIGN**
>
> In general, the benefits of a loosely coupled design outweigh any degradation of performance of your solution.

You must define rules for the various layers to interact with each other. This helps eliminate dependencies and circular references among the layers. A common rule is to allow only one-way interaction between the presentation and business layers, thereby enforcing a strict separation of concerns. You can use events to notify other layers of any changes in a layer, avoiding dependencies between the layers.

After you have defined the layers of your solution, you should identify the functionality that spans across layers. Logging, caching of data, data validation, authentication, and authorization are some *crosscutting concerns* that require implementation in separate components. Functionality implemented in such components must be available across multiple layers; therefore, you should ensure these components are available across different physical tiers.

When you define the interface between various layers of your solution, your aim should be to enforce loose coupling between layers. This means that a layer in the solution must not expose its internal implementation to any other layer. A public interface that hides the details of implementation of the layer should be sufficient for other layers to communicate with it.

Communication between various layers of your solution should consider how your solution is deployed. If all the layers of your solution reside in one physical tier, you should choose the communication protocol between the layers accordingly. If your solution interacts with remote web services for data or application logic, you should consider implementing security and encryption in the interfaces that are involved in such communication.

EXAM TIP

You should be comfortable with designing your application and implementing requirements in the various layers. You should understand the primary function of each layer and where a particular requirement can be implemented in an app.

Incorporating WinMD components

The WinRT platform provides developers with a new way to build reusable software components—as WinRT types packaged in a WinRT component, also called a WinMD component. In traditional .NET application development, you could create a dynamic-link library (DLL) as a managed class library and use it in one or more applications. This option is still available in Visual Studio. However, you can change the output type of a library project from class library to WinRT component, and the output of such a project is a WinMD file. The main difference between the two types of libraries is that a class library can be accessed only from (managed) C# and Visual Basic applications. A WinRT component can be additionally accessed from Windows Store apps developed with C++ and JavaScript. Thus, a WinRT component allows for language-agnostic software development for Windows Store apps.

WinRT imposes some restrictions on the design and implementation of a WinMD component. For example, public classes must be sealed, public fields are not allowed, and public data members must be declared as properties. In addition, there are restrictions on the data types passed from within the WinMD component to applications that use the component. You can only pass WinRT-compatible data types when returning values from methods defined in a WinMD component to a consuming application.

You might want to develop a WinMD component in C++ to get the performance advantage of C++ in complex and computationally intensive operations such as image processing and transformations. Legacy code written in C++ can be reused in Windows Store apps by using it in a WinMD component. A WinMD component developed in C++ must have at least one activatable or ref class, a class that can be instantiated from any other language such as C#, Visual Basic, or JavaScript. It can contain more than one activatable class as well as other internal classes implementing the functionality per the application's requirements. An activatable class must be declared as *public ref class sealed*. If you choose not to expose a C++ type or a class that is not sealed, you should use the *[WebHostHidden]* attribute to prevent it from being exposed to consuming JavaScript applications. Note that an activatable class name and namespace name must not contain Unicode characters.

When you call methods implemented in a WinMD component developed in C++ in a JavaScript Windows Store app, you must use camel case in your JavaScript code. For example, for a method *CalculateAverageOfNumbers* implemented in a WinMD component, you will invoke it as *calculateAverageOfNumbers* in JavaScript. When you reference C++ namespaces and classes in JavaScript, you should use the same casing as in the C++ implementation. C# and Visual Basic follow their normal casing rules. The following code shows a C++ class definition in a WinMD component and how it is used in JavaScript and C#:

Sample of C++ code

```
// ref class definition in C++
public ref class Multiplier sealed
{
    // Class members
    public:
        double MultiplyAndAdd(double inputA, double inputB)
        {
            return (input A + inputB + (inputA * inputB));
        }
};
```

Sample of JavaScript code

```
// Create an instance of the WinMD class and invoke the method
var nativeObject = new CppComponent.Multiplier();
var result = nativeObject.multiplyAndAdd(22.2, 30.1););
```

Sample of C# code

```
// Create an instance of the WinMD class and invoke the method
var nativeObject = new CppComponent.Multiplier();
var result = nativeObject.MultiplyAndAdd(22.2, 30.1);
```

If you are creating a component that is meant for use in Windows Store apps developed with Visual Basic or C#, and the component does not contain Windows Store controls, you should consider developing your component as a class library instead of a WinMD component because the former has fewer restrictions.

When you create a WinMD component in C#, you can return a managed type created in managed code to JavaScript in a way similar to the corresponding WinRT type. Note that when a managed type implements multiple interfaces, JavaScript uses the interface that appears first in the list.

You can declare events by using the event pattern provided in the Microsoft .NET Framework or other patterns available in WinRT. You can implement an event handler in a C# WinMD component by using the *System.EventHandler<TEventArgs>* delegate and the WinRT *EventHandler<T>* delegate. If you declare custom event accessors, you must use the WinRT event pattern.

> ***MORE INFO*** **MAPPINGS BETWEEN .NET FRAMEWORK AND WINRT TYPES, AND WINRT EVENT PATTERNS**
>
> A table of .NET Framework mappings of WinRT types is available at *http://msdn.microsoft.com/en-us/library/windows/apps/hh995050.aspx*. You can read more about the WinRT event pattern at *http://msdn.microsoft.com/en-us/library/windows/apps/hh972883.aspx*.

Thought experiment
Creating a Windows Store app from an existing desktop app

In this thought experiment, apply what you've learned about this objective. You can find answers to these questions in the "Answers" section at the end of this chapter.

A popular media publishing company has developed a desktop application that uses a number of C++ components. These components use proprietary algorithms that will need significant amounts of time and effort to re-implement in a Windows Store app.

What are your recommendations for the organization interested in building a Windows Store app and make it available for consumers?

Objective summary

- Plan the logical layers of your solution with maintainability and extensibility of your app in mind.
- Loosely coupled layers in a solution ensure flexibility of your solution to adapt to any change of requirements over time.
- Consider incorporating WinMD components in your solution to harness the power of platform-specific features.

Objective review

Answer the following questions to test your knowledge of the information in this objective. You can find the answers to these questions and explanations of why each answer choice is correct or incorrect in the "Answers" section at the end of this chapter.

1. You have been asked to recommend an option for implementing logging in your app. The logging component should log events in an Extensible Markup Language (XML) file that resides in the local data store of the app and periodically uploads it to a remote web service. It should log events from the business layer as well as the data layer. Where should you implement the logging mechanism?

   A. Business layer

   B. Data layer

   C. Presentation layer

   D. As a separate component to maximize reuse

2. One of the requirements of the app you are implementing is to support contracts provided by the platform to exchange data between your app and the platform as well as with other apps. In which logical layer of your solution should you implement this feature?

   A. Presentation layer

   B. Data layer

   C. Business layer

   D. Application manifest

3. You have been given software that performs bit-rate manipulation of audio streams recorded using a microphone. The software is complex and is written in C++. Your organization does not have the budget to have the software rewritten for a Windows Store app. What are your recommendations for the conceptual design of a Windows Store app that does bit-rate manipulation? (Choose all that apply.)

   A. Develop a WinMD component in C++ incorporating the existing software.

   B. Develop a Windows Store app and use the C++/WinMD component for bit-rate manipulation.

   C. Such an application is impossible to build unless the C++ component is rewritten in C#.

   D. Use WinRT APIs (application programming interfaces) to implement the bit-rate manipulation algorithm.

   E. Use the existing test procedures for the C++ component to test the C++/WinMD component.

Objective 1.3: Apply the MVVM pattern to your app design

It is challenging to develop the UI of a modern application while considering code and visual element reuse, separation of concerns, and maintainability. UI design patterns are reusable solutions that can help developers build UIs. You can use the MVVM design pattern to develop Windows Store apps that are maintainable, testable, and extensible.

This objective covers how to:

- Design and implement the appropriate data model to support business entities
- Design your viewmodel to support your view based on your model
- Develop a view to meet data-binding requirements
- Create viewmodels using *INotifyPropertyChanged*, *ObservableCollection*, and *CollectionViewSource*

Designing and implementing the appropriate data model to support business entities

The data model in a Windows Store app implements the business logic and the mechanism for data access. It is responsible for notifying the viewmodel whenever data changes in the source and for persisting changes from the view in the data source. The model of the MVVM pattern is where the data model for the application is implemented.

Model-View-ViewModel pattern

The Model-View-ViewModel (MVVM) design pattern was introduced by John Gossman in 2005 as a variation of the popular Model-View-Controller (MVC) design pattern. The MVVM pattern helps you build your application with a clean separation of the business and presentation logic from the UI. It provides opportunities for code reuse, and encourages developers and UI designers to collaborate on developing various parts of the application.

> **MORE INFO** **MODEL-VIEW-VIEWMODEL PATTERN**
>
> For an introduction to the Model-View-ViewModel pattern for building WPF apps, go to *http://blogs.msdn.com/b/johngossman/archive/2005/10/08/478683.aspx*.

With the MVVM pattern, you can compose the design of your application using three loosely coupled layers or classes: the view, viewmodel, and model. Business logic in a Windows Store app is encapsulated in the model, including any services to fetch and store data from local or remote storage (that is, the data layer). The viewmodel encapsulates the presentation logic, and the view encapsulates the UI and UI logic. Figure 1-5 illustrates the MVVM pattern and the function of its various layers.

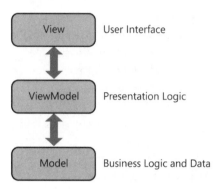

FIGURE 1-5 MVVM layers and their functions

THE VIEW

The *view* is the visual interface of the application. It comprises a visual element, such as a page or a window, and controls provided by the framework. The layout and styling of the controls is defined in the view. In addition, the view can define animations that are triggered when there is a change in the state of the viewmodel (for example, when there is new data) or when the user interacts with the view. The code-behind of the view can contain the UI logic to present data through the controls in the view or code to directly manipulate the visual elements in the view. In some situations, complex animations that are otherwise difficult to set up in XAML can be expressed in the code-behind. It is recommended that you do not put business or presentation logic in the code-behind of the view; otherwise, UI testing becomes difficult.

The view references the viewmodel through a property called *DataContext*. This property can be set through XAML or the code-behind of the view. The controls in the view are data-bound to the properties and commands in the viewmodel. For views that do not require any UI logic, data templates can be used to specify the UI elements that will represent an object in the viewmodel. This enables visual designers to define and easily update the visual representation without changing the object the view bound to or the behavior of the control that is used to display the object.

THE VIEWMODEL

The *viewmodel* encapsulates the presentation logic of the application. It does not have any knowledge of the view's design, layout, style, and so on. The viewmodel implements the properties and commands that the view binds to and notifies the view of state change through events. Although the viewmodel provides the properties and commands required by the view, the view determines how these properties will be rendered on the interface and how it will integrate the commands with actions for the user.

The viewmodel acts as the glue between the view and one or more model classes. In a complex view, you can require more than one model class to provide data. The viewmodel can transform the data so that it can be represented in the view. The viewmodel can combine multiple fields from models in a property that is then bound to a visual element in the view. This helps where a new requirement adds a new field in the data model that is to be combined with an existing field. It requires an update in the viewmodel code, but the view does not require a change.

Actions invoked by the user in a view such as tapping a button are typically defined as commands in the viewmodel. Commands provide a clean way to encapsulate user actions so that they are separate from the UI. The *ICommand* interface provides the mechanism to connect the UI with commands that are defined in the viewmodel.

THE MODEL

Business logic and data are encapsulated in the model. A model class defines the data structures based on the application's data model. The business logic as well as data validation rules are often implemented in the model, although a separate repository for data access, caching, and storage can be used. The model classes are often generated as part of the data access layer or remote service that provides the data for the application.

The model usually implements the *INotifyPropertyChanged* interface that enables it to be bound to the view. The model can also implement the *INotifyDataErrorInfo* interface to provide support for data validation. In some cases, when the model doesn't implement these interfaces, the viewmodel defines the model and implements these interfaces.

Data binding

Data binding is the mechanism that establishes a connection between the application's UI and business logic. If the model implements the data binding interface, when the data changes its value, it is reflected in the UI element that is bound to the data. Data binding also implies that any changes in the representation of the data in the UI can be used to update the underlying data.

Data binding in the MVVM pattern provides a clean and simple way of connecting UI elements with data. A binding consists of the following:

- A binding source that provides the data for the visual element in the view. A binding source can be a common language runtime (CLR) object such as a class defined in C# or any WinRT object of a type that has *[BindableAttribute]* or implements the *ICustomPropertyProvider* interface. To meet the app requirements, you can bind a property of a UI element with the value of a property of another UI element.

- A binding target that is a visual element for presenting the data in the view. A visual element is an object of the type *FrameworkElement*. It provides one or more properties of the type *DependencyProperty*, which is used as the binding target. Most *FrameworkElement* properties (except the read-only properties) are dependency properties. *FrameworkElement* properties support data binding by default.

- A binding object that defines the connection between the binding source and binding target and moves the data between them.

The binding object shown in Figure 1-6 provides the following information to the binding mechanism:

- The source and target objects.

- The direction of data flow, specified by setting the *Binding.Mode* property to one of the *BindingMode* enumeration values.

- The value converter, if the data used in the binding needs to be formatted or modified before it is presented in the UI. A value converter is specified by setting the Converter property of the *FrameworkElement* to an instance of a class that implements the *IValueConverter* interface.

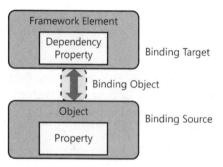

FIGURE 1-6 Data binding between source and target

The *BindingMode* enumeration describes how the data propagates in a binding. Its members are *OneWay*, *OneTime*, and *TwoWay*. In a *TwoWay* binding, changes to the target propagate to the source, except if the binding target is the *Text* property of a *FrameworkElement*. In such a case, the change is propagated only when the *TextBox* loses focus. In *OneWay* binding, the target is updated when data is available in the binding source and changes in the source are propagated to the target. In *OneTime* binding, the target is updated only once: when the binding is created.

Listing 1-1 shows how to set up binding in XAML and set up the *DataContext* property for the target in the code-behind file.

LISTING 1-1 Setting up binding (in XAML) and the *DataContext* property (in C#)

Sample of XAML code

```
<TextBox x:Name="FirstNameTextBox" Text="{Binding FirstName, Mode=OneWay}" />
```

Sample of C# code

```
// Create an instance of the Person
// class that implements INotifyPropertyChanged
Person person = new Person();
person.FirstName = "Joseph";
person.LastName = "Samuel";

// Set the DataContext of the TextBox FirstNameTextBox
FirstNameTextBox.DataContext = person;
```

The binding target is created in the XAML by using the *{Binding...}* syntax. The binding source is set in the code through the *DataContext* property of the *TextBox* in the code shown in Listing 1-1. You can use the *ElementName* property or the *RelativeSource* property to specify the binding source. If you need to bind a property of a UI element to a property of another UI element, the *ElementName* property is useful (for example, when you are changing the diameter of a circle using a slider). The *RelativeSource* property is commonly used to bind one property of an object to another property of the same object, or to define a binding in a style or template.

Design and implement the model

The model in the MVVM pattern is the entity responsible for moving data to and from the data store and implementing the business logic. Although the implementation of the model can vary based on the app requirements, the interface from the model to the viewmodel does not change. In the case of a simple application, the model can contain the implementation for retrieval and storage of data from the file system, in plain text. If the application needs to retrieve data from a remote web service or data store, you can create a repository class to implement the web service client. In that case, the model defines the data structures required to extract the data obtained from the remote web service. The repository can additionally support user authentication and authorization.

Model objects are either exposed through viewmodels or defined in a viewmodel. When model objects are exposed via viewmodels, they need to implement the *INotifyProperty Changed* interface and (optionally) the *INotifyDataErrorInfo* interface if it supports validation.

A single-page Windows Store app does not require more than one model class. For more complex applications, multiple models are required to support the business logic. Consider the design of a Windows Store app that enables user to search for photographs from a popular website using their web service. Amateurs and enthusiasts upload photographs and use a simple rating system to mark the photographs in order of popularity. A search term can be provided a string to query the web service. The web service returns the result of such a query as XML or JavaScript Object Notation (JSON) items in an array. Therefore, the model in this case is a data structure that can be used to extract the data from the raw XML or JSON response from the web service.

Listing 1-2 shows the C# code for a model class representing an individual item in the result of the query to the web service.

LISTING 1-2 Using a model class

```csharp
public class SearchResultItem
{
    public SearchResultItem(XElement elmt)
    {
        Id = elmt.Element("Id").Value;
        Name = elmt.Element("Name").Value;
        Description = elmt.Element("Name").Value;
        ImageUri = new Uri(elmt.Element("Url").Value);
        Votes = elmt.Element("Votes").Value;
    }
    public long Id { get; private set; }
    public string Name { get; private set; }
    public string Description { get; private set; }
    public Uri ImageUri { get; private set; }
    public int Votes { get; private set; }
}
```

The C# code in Listing 1-3 implements the logic to query the remote web service and parse the result into a list in a separate class. The result is sorted so that the photograph with the most number of votes is the first element in the list.

LISTING 1-3 Querying a web service and parsing the results

```csharp
public static class ContosoImageSearchService
{
    public static async Task<List<SearchResultItem>> SearchImagesAsync(string
searchTerm)
    {
        HttpClient httpClient = new HttpClient();
        Uri searchUri = new Uri("http://ws.contoso.com/?search=" + searchTerm);
        List<SearchResultItem> searchResults = new List<SearchResultItem>();

        using (HttpResponseMessage response = await
                httpClient.GetAsync(searchUri.ToString()))
        {
            if (response.IsSuccessStatusCode)
            {
                using (Stream strm = await response.Content.ReadAsStreamAsync())
                {
                    XElement elmnt = XElement.Load(strm);
                    searchResults = (from p in elmnt.DescendantsAndSelf("Photo")
                                     select new SearchResultItem(p)
                                    ).OrderByDescending(r => r.Votes). ToList();
                }
            }
        }

        return searchResults;
    }
}
```

You might notice that the query is executed asynchronously on the remote web service. Asynchronous execution of such requests is fundamental for the fast and fluid UI requirement in Windows Store apps. The viewmodel invokes the method to carry out the search through a command implemented with the *ICommand* interface, which facilitates binding the command with the view.

Designing a viewmodel to support the view based on your model

The classic definition of the viewmodel is that it is the model for the view. However, this definition is an oversimplification of the role a viewmodel plays in an application. The main features of a viewmodel are these:

- It provides data that is represented in the view. This data can include properties that are required in the view but are not part of the model.
- It provides commands that are connected to events of UI elements and are used to invoke an action. The commands are implementations of the *ICommand* interface.
- It implements the *INotifyPropertyChanged* interface, thereby keeping the UI in synchronization with the data model.
- It optionally implements the *INotifyDataErrorInfo* interface, which enables the viewmodel to provide feedback through the UI on issues with the data entered by the user.

You need to keep these features of a viewmodel in mind while designing your model, and you might have to simplify the complex object model that represents the data returned from a remote service. You might also need to transform model properties to allow binding in the view; for example, transforming an enumeration into a Boolean that can be used to set the visibility of a UI element. Instead of implementing the logic to carry out the transformation in the viewmodel, you can implement it in a value converter and use in the data binding.

A single-page Windows Store app requires the following presentation logic implemented in the viewmodel:

- A property that is a list of photographs for the search term.
- A property that is the search term inserted by the user. It is bound to a text box in the UI.
- A property that is a command bound to the search button in the user interface.

Developing a view to meet data-binding requirements

In the MVVM pattern, the role of the view is to present the data and enable the user to interact with it. In a Windows Store app, the view can be a *UserControl* or a *Page*. The relationship between the view and its data is set up through data binding. The simplest way to set this up is to add a reference to the viewmodel in the *DataContext* property of the view. You can bind the properties and commands of the viewmodel to the corresponding UI elements in the view.

For the single page discussed so far, there are five steps you need to carry out to set up data binding in the XAML:

1. Set up binding for a *TextBox* to *SearchTerm* property in the viewmodel and a button's command property to the *SearchPhotosCommand* in the viewmodel.

2. Define a *CollectionViewSource* in the XAML with the source set to the *ObservableCollection* member in the viewmodel.

3. Define a *DataTemplate* to represent the data in the *ObservableCollection* and name it *SearchItemTemplate*.

4. Declare a *GridView* and set its *ItemsSource* to the *CollectionViewSource*.

5. Set the *ItemTemplate* property of the *GridView* to the *SearchItemTemplate*.

These steps are shown in Listing 1-4.

LISTING 1-4 Setting up data binding in XAML

```xml
<Page.Resources>
    <!-- Define a CollectionViewSource -->
    <CollectionViewSource x:Name="SearchResultsCollection"
                          Source="{Binding SearchResultItems}" />

    <!-- Declare a DataTemplate for the GridView -->
    <DataTemplate x:Key="SearchItemTemplate">
        <StackPanel VerticalAlignment="Top" Margin="0,0,0,10">
            <Image Width="300" Height="150" Source="{Binding ImageUri}" />
            <TextBlock Padding="0,15,0,10" Text="{Binding Name}" />
        </StackPanel>
    </DataTemplate>

</Page.Resources>
<!-- Set up the data binding for the search text box and the search button -->
<TextBox x:Name="SearchTermTextBox" Text="{Binding Path=SearchTerm, Mode=TwoWay}" />
<Button x:Name="SearchPhotosButton" Content="Search"
        Command="{Binding SearchPhotosCommand}" />

<!-- Declare a GridView and set its ItemsSource to the CollectionViewSource -->
<GridView x:Name="SearchResultsGridView"
          SelectionMode="None"
          IsItemClickEnabled="False"
          ItemsSource="{Binding Source={StaticResource SearchResultsCollection}}"
          ItemTemplate="{StaticResource SearchItemTemplate}" />
```

In the code-behind of the page, you need to set up the *DataContext* of the page as an instance of the *SearchResultsViewModel* class:

Sample of C# code

```csharp
// Create an instance of the SearchResultsViewModel
SearchResultsViewModel viewModel = new SearchResultsViewModel();

// Setup the DataContext
this.DataContext = viewModel;
```

Creating viewmodels using *NotifyPropertyChanged*, *ObservableCollection*, and *CollectionViewSource*

The viewmodel implements the *INotifyPropertyChanged* interface. The result of the search query is a list of items. You use the *ObservableCollection* class to represent the result returned by the search query. This class represents a data collection and provides notifications when items are added or removed, or when the collection is refreshed. The data source of the *CollectionViewSource* is the *ObservableCollection* property of the viewmodel.

Before implementing the viewmodel, implement the *RelayCommand* class that is used in the viewmodel as a property bound to the search button. The *RelayCommand* class implements the *ICommand* interface, shown in Listing 1-5, and it can be used as a member in the viewmodel, thereby allowing it access private members of the viewmodel.

LISTING 1-5 Implementing the *RelayCommand* class

Sample of C# code

```csharp
public class RelayCommand : ICommand
{
    Action _TargetExecuteMethod;
    Func<bool> _TargetCanExecuteMethod;
    public RelayCommand(Action executeMethod)
    {
        _TargetExecuteMethod = executeMethod;
    }

    public RelayCommand(Action executeMethod, Func<bool> canExecuteMethod)
    {
        _TargetExecuteMethod = executeMethod;
        _TargetCanExecuteMethod = canExecuteMethod;
    }

    public void RaiseCanExecuteChanged()
    {
        CanExecuteChanged(this, EventArgs.Empty);
    }

    bool ICommand.CanExecute(object parameter)
    {
        if (_TargetCanExecuteMethod != null)
        {
            return _TargetCanExecuteMethod();
        }

        if (_TargetExecuteMethod != null)
        {
            return true;
        }
        return false;
    }
```

```
    public event EventHandler CanExecuteChanged = delegate { };

    void ICommand.Execute(object parameter)
    {
        if (_TargetExecuteMethod != null)
        {
            _TargetExecuteMethod();
        }
    }
}
```

The presentation logic for the single-page Windows Store app is the following:

- The *INotifyPropertyChanged* interface and the *PropertyChangedEventHandler* event.

- A member variable that is an *ObservableCollection* of the items returned in the search result.

- A command that is used to fire the image search query. The *ICommand* interface is implemented in a separate class (*RelayCommand*) and defined as a member in the viewmodel.

Listing 1-6 shows the implementation of the viewmodel of the single-page Windows Store app.

LISTING 1-6 Implementing the viewmodel for a single-page Windows Store app

```
public class SearchResultsViewModel : INotifyPropertyChanged
{
    public event PropertyChangedEventHandler PropertyChanged;
    ObservableCollection<SearchResultItem> _searchResultItems;
    string _searchTerm = string.Empty;

    public SearchResultsViewModel()
    {
        SearchPhotosCommand = new RelayCommand(SearchPhotos);
    }

    public string SearchTerm
    {
        get { return _searchTerm; }
        set
        {
            if (_searchTerm != value)
            {
                _searchTerm = value;
                if (PropertyChanged != null)
                    PropertyChanged(this, new PropertyChangedEventArgs("SearchTerm"));
            }
        }
    }
```

```
public ObservableCollection<SearchResultItem> SearchResultItems
{
    get { return _searchResultItems; }
    set
    {
        if (_searchResultItems != value)
        {
            _searchResultItems = value;
            if (PropertyChanged != null)
                PropertyChanged(this,
                    new PropertyChangedEventArgs("SearchResultItems"));
        }
    }
}

// Command bound to search button
public RelayCommand SearchPhotosCommand { get; private set; }
public async void SearchPhotos()
{

    SearchResultItems = new ObservableCollection<SearchResultItem>(
            await ContosoImageSearchService.SearchImagesAsync(_searchTerm));
}
}
```

When set, each property raises the *RaisePropertyChanged* event. This event is raised for simple properties such as the search term as well as for the collection property that represents the search results. You can put the code used to implement the *INotifyPropertyChanged* interface in viewmodels in an abstract class, which is then used as the base class for all your viewmodels. The Grid App and Split App XAML templates in Visual Studio provide developers with an abstract base class that helps refactor the code seen in the viewmodel class properties. Code for the *BindableBase* class is shown in Listing 1-7.

LISTING 1-7 Implementing the *INotifyPropertyChanged* interface through *BindableBase*

```
public abstract class BindableBase : INotifyPropertyChanged
{
    public event PropertyChangedEventHandler PropertyChanged;
    protected bool SetProperty<T>(ref T storage, T value,
                            [CallerMemberName] String propertyName = null)
    {
        if (object.Equals(storage, value)) return false;
        storage = value;
        this.OnPropertyChanged(propertyName);
        return true;
    }
    protected void OnPropertyChanged([CallerMemberName] string propertyName = null)
    {
        var eventHandler = this.PropertyChanged;
        if (eventHandler != null)
        {
            eventHandler(this, new PropertyChangedEventArgs(propertyName));
        }
    }
}
```

Note that the implementation of *OnPropertyChanged* in the *BindableBase* class uses the caller member attribute, removing the requirement of specifying the property name. The property name is passed automatically to the *[CallerMemberName]* attribute, so there is no need to specify it. Using *BindableBase* as the base class, a viewmodel can be implemented with the properties in Listing 1-8.

LISTING 1-8 Implementing a viewmodel through *BindableBase*

```
public abstract class SearchResultsViewModel : BindableBase
{
    private ObservableCollection<SearchResultItem> _searchResultItems;
    private string _searchTerm;

    public SearchResultsViewModel()
    {
        SearchPhotosCommand = new RelayCommand(SearchPhotos);
    }
    public ObservableCollection<SearchResultItem> SearchResultItems
    {
        get { return this._searchResultItems; }
        set { this.SetProperty(ref this._searchResultItems, value); }
    }
    public string SearchTerm
    {
        get { return this._searchTerm; }
        set { this.SetProperty(ref this._searchTerm, value); }
    }
    // Command bound to search button
    public RelayCommand SearchPhotosCommand { get; private set; }
    public async void SearchPhotos()
    {
        SearchResultItems = new ObservableCollection<SearchResultItem>(
                await ContosoImageSearchService.SearchImagesAsync(_searchTerm));
    }
}
```

EXAM TIP

You will not be asked to write XAML or C# code to illustrate how various interfaces and data binding work. However, it is important to understand the various interfaces, how they are used in data binding, and so on.

Objective summary

- A loosely coupled design for a Windows Store app can be prepared with the MVVM pattern.
- The view contains UI elements, the view model contains presentation logic, and the model contains business logic and is responsible for moving data to and from the data store.
- When designing an application, try to place as much code as possible in the business logic typically implemented in the model class and often in a repository class.
- The viewmodel should contain the presentation logic and should be designed based on the model. Its design should not be influenced by the view and UI requirements.

Objective review

Answer the following questions to test your knowledge of the information in this objective. You can find the answers to these questions and explanations of why each answer choice is correct or incorrect in the "Answers" section at the end of this chapter.

1. You are designing your Windows Store app with the MVVM design pattern. In the data access layer, you use an XML file to store and retrieve data. To maximize reuse of code across Windows Store, WPF, and Silverlight applications, how should you implement data access layer in your application?

   A. Implement the logic to read the XML file when the page loads and display data from the XML file.

   B. Create a viewmodel and populate its properties from the XML file in its constructor. Data-bind the viewmodel to the page.

C. Create a file helper class to read the XML file. Use this file to populate the data model. Data-bind the viewmodel with the page.

D. Implement the logic to read the XML file when the page loads and populate the viewmodel. After the data is loaded, data-bind the viewmodel with the page.

2. You are creating an application that enables the user to review data in a database and save changes to a separate file, but not to save changes to the database. What is the correct way to implement this requirement?

   A. Set the *Mode* property of the binding to *OneTime*.

   B. Set the *Mode* property of the binding to *OneWay*.

   C. Set the *Mode* property of the binding to *TwoWay*.

   D. Create a new command to save the changes.

3. You are developing an application in which a collection of objects is returned by a web service when the user carries out a search. You need to bind a *GridView* control with the results from the web service. How should you set up the data source of the *Grid-View* so that when the UI is updated, the result from the search is returned?

   A. Enumerate the members of the collection of objects from the search result. Add these members to a list and set the *DataContext* of the *GridView* to this list.

   B. Create a *CollectionViewSource* and set its source to the collection returned by the web service. Set the *ItemsSource* property of the *GridView* to the *CollectionView-Source*.

   C. Set the *ItemsSource* property of the *GridView* to the collection returned by the web service.

   D. Create a custom control and data-bind the custom control with the collection returned by the web service.

Objective 1.4: Design and implement Process Lifetime Management (PLM)

One of the key features of Windows Store apps is their fast and fluid behavior. The user has the ability to switch between multiple Windows Store apps. At any time, the focus is on a single application that occupies the full screen. (Apps in a snapped state are considered to be in the foreground.) A Windows Store app is running only when it is visible on the user's screen. At all other times, it is either suspended or not running. It is the application's responsibility to preserve its state, such as the scroll position in a page, when it is suspended and use this information when it is resumed. Process Lifetime Management (PLM) is the mechanism of managing the state of Windows Store apps.

This objective covers how to:

- Choose a state management strategy
- Handle the *Suspending* event and prepare for app termination
- Handle the *Resuming* event
- Handle the *OnActivated* event
- Check the *ActivationKind* and previous state

Choosing a state management strategy

PLM is an important concept you must understand and apply when designing and developing Windows Store apps. Because Windows Store apps execute only when they are in the foreground, you need to ensure that your application saves the current state of the application when the user switches to another application.

A user launches a Windows Store app whenever the user activates the app by tapping its tile or through the Search contract or a share operation, for example. When an app launches, a splash screen displays to the user.

> **MORE INFO** **CONTRACTS AND TILE**
>
> See Chapter 2, "Develop Windows Store Apps" for detailed information on contracts and Chapter 3, "Create the user interface" for tiles.

The app registers event handlers and prepares the UI before it enters the *Running* state and occupies the full screen. The user can send the app to the background by swapping with another app that is already running. The first app enters the *Suspended* state when it is sent to the background by the user. The app can remain in the *Suspended* state until the user brings it in the foreground by swapping with an app in the foreground, or it may be terminated by Windows if the operating system determines the app is consuming a lot of resources while in the background. Figure 1-7 illustrates various states of an application's lifetime.

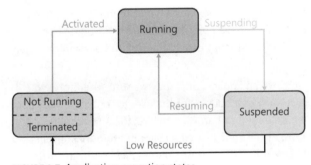

FIGURE 1-7 Application execution states

When Windows terminates your app, all state information that has not been saved is lost. Users will be disappointed when they restart the application and find all their unsaved work is gone. This is particularly relevant in applications that provide the user with multiple ways to interact, for example, navigating them through a number of pages, allowing them to save data in forms, and so on.

To provide users with an optimal experience while running your application, you need to implement a state management strategy. The key points while implementing such a strategy are the following:

- If your application has multiple pages and a navigation scheme, save the navigation steps and visual artifacts of each page while the user navigates through the app. Consider a page that uses horizontal scrolling to display form fields for data entry. If the user decides to leave your application and later return to it after checking email, for example, you need to preserve both the form content as well as the scroll position. When the user switches back to your application, he or she will be presented with the unsaved data and can carry on using your application.

- Windows can terminate your application while in the *Suspended* state if it finds the device is running low on resources. Therefore, as soon as your application is suspended, you should save the state of your application without waiting for your application to be terminated.

- When your application is being suspended, it should release any resources and file handles so that other apps can access them while your application is suspended.

- You can provide the user with an option to either resume from where they left your application or start afresh. This is relevant for applications such as games and media players.

- You do not need to restore the state of your application if it is launched via a contract, such as the Search contract, or if your app is launched because of a file association.

- If your application fetches data from a remote service on the Internet, you can check the time when it was suspended (and terminated if Windows ran out of resources) and refresh the UI instead of showing old content. This is relevant for applications that display the weather or news, for example.

- If your app needs to run even when Windows suspends it, you can implement such application logic as a background task. For example, if users start a file upload or download task from within your application, they expect the task to be complete when they are back in your application.

Windows provides a way for users to close an application if they want to. Therefore, you should not provide any options in the UI, such as a button, for the user to terminate your app. If your application terminates due to an exception or hardware failure, the app should not try to resume from a previous state and instead start afresh. In the event of abnormal termination, state saved by your app might be corrupt, and restoring your application from corrupt data can cause further crashes and termination. You should never consider overriding the application lifetime management provided by Windows in your app. This helps with your applications' performance and reduces power consumption in the device.

Handling the *Suspending* event and preparing for app termination

When a user suspends an app, explicitly saving the user's data and page navigation state enables the user to resume from where the app was suspended, even when the app is terminated by Windows. Suspended apps do not receive any notification because they are terminated; therefore, you should implement the mechanism to save your application's state in the *Suspending* event.

There are two kinds of data your app needs to manage: app data and session state. *App data* is persistent across sessions and must be available within the app to the user. *Session state* is temporary data that is relevant to a user's current session with your application. To save the data and session state when your application is suspended, you must subscribe to the *Suspending* event. You save app data and session state using the event handler, shown in Listing 1-9.

LISTING 1-9 Using the *Suspending* event to save app data and session state

```
using System;
using Windows.ApplicationModel;
using Windows.ApplicationModel.Activation;
using Windows.UI.Xaml;
public sealed partial class App : Application
{
    public App()
    {
        InitializeComponent();
        this.Suspending += OnSuspending;
    }

    private async void OnSuspending(object sender, SuspendingEventArgs e)
    {
        // Save your applications' state and data here
    }
}
```

Windows allows 10 seconds for your application to suspend, so you must ensure that saving data and state information in the *Suspending* event handler does not take longer than 10 seconds. If the app takes longer than 10 seconds in the event handler, Windows assumes your app is not responding and terminates it. If your app needs to complete any task when the app is being suspended, you need to defer completion of the suspend operation until the task is complete. You must use the *GetDeferral* method of the *SuspendingOperation* object (from the *SuspendingEventArgs* object) to delay completion of the suspend operation. After the task is complete, you can call the *Complete* method on the *SuspendingDeferral* object. The following C# code shows how to defer the suspend operation:

```
private void OnSuspending(object sender, SuspendingEventArgs e)
{
    SuspendingDeferral deferral = e.SuspendingOperation.GetDeferral();
    // Save your applications' state and data
    deferral.Complete();
}
```

Although your application can use the *Suspending* event to save app data and its state, Visual Studio adds a *SuspensionManager* class when you create a Windows Store app with one of the templates. It is a helper class that simplifies the lifetime management in your app. It saves and restores the navigation state of your application's pages that are hosted in the root *Frame*. It also provides every page in your application the opportunity to save and restore its state. *SuspensionManager* serializes app data and page state into an XML file that resides in your app's local storage.

When you create a new Windows Store project in Visual Studio, the Grid App and Split App templates already include the *SuspensionManager* class in the Common folder, as shown in Figure 1-8.

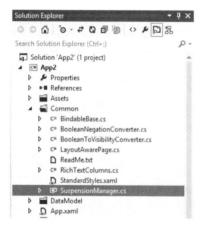

FIGURE 1-8 *SuspensionManager* class in a Visual Studio project

You have to register the app's *Frame* object with the *SuspensionManager* class. *SuspensionManager* is then aware of every page in your app and can save and restore the navigation state. The *Frame* of your app is registered in the *OnLaunched* method immediately after it is created. This is shown in the following example:

```
protected override async void OnLaunched(LaunchActivatedEventArgs e)
{
    var rootFrame = new Frame();

    // Associate with the SuspensionManager
    SuspensionManager.RegisterFrame(rootFrame, "AppFrame");
}
```

When your app is suspended, you need to save app data as well as session state. Because app data is not dependent on the device on which your application is running, you should consider using a data container that it is available to the user across multiple devices. The *Windows.Storage.ApplicationData* object has a *RoamingSettings* property that returns an *ApplicationDataContainer*. You can use the *ApplicationDataContainer* to store app data that persists across sessions. If your application requires storage of device-specific data, you should use the *LocalSettings* property. In the sample application discussed in the previous objective, you might want to save the search term entered by the user. This can be done in the *TextChanged* event of the *TextBox*, as shown in the following example:

```
private void SearchTermTextBox_TextChanged(object sender, TextChangedEventArgs e)
{
    Windows.Storage.ApplicationDataContainer roamingSettings =
        Windows.Storage.ApplicationData.Current.RoamingSettings;
    RoamingSettings.Values["SearchTerm"] = SearchTermTextBox.Text;
}
```

As mentioned previously, the session state of your application can be saved in the *Suspending* event. The *SuspensionManager* class makes it very easy to save the state of your application. All you need to implement is a single line of code to save your application's state:

```
private async void OnSuspending(object sender, SuspendingEventArgs e)
{
    SuspendingDeferral deferral = e.SuspendingOperation.GetDeferral();

    // Save the applications' state
    await SuspensionManager.SaveAsync();
    deferral.Complete();
}
```

You can test your application for suspension and termination using the Visual Studio debugger. If the debugger isn't available on the Visual Studio menu, ensure Debug Location is checked in the list of menu items. When you debug your application using Visual Studio, you can click the Suspend drop-down menu and test your application for various states, as shown in Figure 1-9.

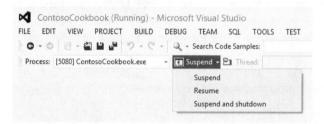

FIGURE 1-9 Visual Studio debugger with PLM testing support

Handling the *Resuming* event

A suspended Windows Store app resumes when the user switches it into view or when the device comes out of a low power state. Your application can subscribe to the *Resuming* event and refresh any content that is displayed in the page in view. This event is not raised in the UI thread, so a dispatcher must be used to update the UI. If your application does not have any displayed content that requires a refresh, there is no need for it to handle the *Resuming* event.

You can handle the *Resuming* event by providing an event handler, as shown in the following code:

```
partial class MainPage()
{
    public MainPage()
    {
        InitializeComponent();
        Application.Current.Resuming += OnResuming;
    }
    private void OnResuming(object sender, object e)
    {
        // Refresh the displayed contents in your app
    }
}
```

When you handle the *Resuming* event in your app, you must remember that your application's UI should be visible within 15 seconds. Ideally, you should add an extended splash screen in your application to provide continuous feedback to the user while your app refreshes the data.

Handling the *OnActivated* events

The *OnLaunched* and *OnActivated* events are used in Windows Store apps to check the kind of activation, obtain the previous state of execution of the application, and perform initialization of the application.

When your app is launched from its tile, in the *OnLaunched* event, a new *Frame* is created if the *Window* does not have content and the *Frame* navigates the user to your application's startup page. The *Frame* is then set as the content for your application's *Window*, and the *Activate* method is called to bring the application to the foreground, as shown in Listing 1-10.

LISTING 1-10 Handling the *OnLaunched* event

```
protected async override void OnLaunched(LaunchActivatedEventArgs e)
{
    Frame rootFrame = Window.Current.Content as Frame;
    if (rootFrame == null)
    {
        rootFrame = new Frame();
        SuspensionManager.RegisterFrame(rootFrame, "AppFrame");
        Window.Current.Content = rootFrame;
    }
    if (rootFrame.Content == null)
```

```
    {
        if (!rootFrame.Navigate(typeof(MainPage))
        {
            throw new Exception("Failed to create initial page");
        }
    }

    // Ensure the current Window is active
    Window.Current.Activate();
}
```

Your application does not require initialization if it is launched from a running state. There-fore, before initialization, it is important to see whether the previous state of your application is *Running*. The *OnLaunched* event needs an update, as shown in Listing 1-11.

LISTING 1-11 Updating the *OnLaunched* event

```
protected async override void OnLaunched(LaunchActivatedEventArgs e)
{
    // Do not repeat app initialization when already running, just ensure that
    // the window is active
    if (args.PreviousExecutionState == ApplicationExecutionState.Running)
    {
        Window.Current.Activate();
        return;
    }

    Frame rootFrame = Window.Current.Content as Frame;
    if (rootFrame == null)
    {
        rootFrame = new Frame();
        SuspensionManager.RegisterFrame(rootFrame, "AppFrame");
        Window.Current.Content = rootFrame;
    }
    if (rootFrame.Content == null)
    {
        if (!rootFrame.Navigate(typeof(MainPage))
        {
            throw new Exception("Failed to create initial page");
        }
    }

    // Ensure the current Window is active
    Window.Current.Activate();
}
```

If your app is activated from the *Terminated* state, it needs to restore its app state and app data that was saved when the app transitioned into the *Suspended* state. In the *OnLaunched* event, you can use the *SuspensionManager* to restore the navigation state of the *Frame* and provide the *Page* the opportunity to restore its content, as shown in Listing 1-12.

```
protected async override void OnLaunched(LaunchActivatedEventArgs e)
{
    // Do not repeat app initialization when already running, just ensure that
    // the window is active
    if (args.PreviousExecutionState == ApplicationExecutionState.Running)
    {
        Window.Current.Activate();
        return;
    }

    Frame rootFrame = Window.Current.Content as Frame;
    if (rootFrame == null)
    {
        rootFrame = new Frame();
        SuspensionManager.RegisterFrame(rootFrame, "AppFrame");
        // Restore the saved navigation state and application content
        if (args.PreviousExecutionState == ApplicationExecutionState.Terminated)
        {
            try
            {
                await SuspensionManager.RestoreAsync();
            }
            catch (SuspensionManagerException)
            {
                // Something went wrong, assume there is no state and continue.
            }
        }
        Window.Current.Content = rootFrame;
    }
    if (rootFrame.Content == null)
    {
        if (!rootFrame.Navigate(typeof(MainPage))
        {
            throw new Exception("Failed to create initial page");
        }
    }

    // Ensure the current Window is active
    Window.Current.Activate();
}
```

To restore the application data, you need to use the *LoadState* method in the page that is activated. In an example discussed previously, the search term entered by the user was saved in the *RoamingSettings* property of the *ApplicationDataContainer*. You need to load the search term from *RoamingSettings*, as shown in the following code:

```
protected override void LoadState(Object navigationParameter, Dictionary<String, Object>
pageState)
{
    Windows.Storage.ApplicationDataContainer roamingSettings =
        Windows.Storage.ApplicationData.Current.RoamingSettings;
    if (RoamingSettings.Values.ContainsKey("SearchTerm"))
    {
```

```
        SearchTermTextBox.Text = RoamingSettings.Values["SearchTerm"].ToString();
    }
}
```

When a Windows Store app uses a contract such as Search or Share from another app, the *Launched* event is sent to the app. The *LaunchActivatedEventArgs* parameter passed in the event contains a *Kind* property that has a value of type *ActivationKind*. This value tells you why the application was activated.

As an alternative to checking the *ActivationKind* in the *OnLaunched* method and performing the initialization for the activation kind, you can perform initialization specific to the activation type by overriding one of the following methods instead of the *OnLaunched* method:

- **OnFileActivated**   This event is fired when a Windows Store app is activated through a file-open action. The application needs to register as the default handler for a certain file type to receive this event.

- **OnSearchActivated**   This event is fired when a Windows Store app is activated through a search association.

- **OnShareTargetActivated**   This event is fired when a Windows Store app is activated through a sharing association; that is, the app receives content from other Windows Store apps.

- **OnFileOpenPickerActivated**   This event is fired when a Windows Store app is activated when it provides files that are opened by another application.

- **OnFileSavePickerActivated**   This event is fired when a Windows Store app is activated when it supports saving files created by another application.

- **OnCachedFileUpdaterActivated**   This event is fired when the user saves or opens a file that is updated by an app.

Checking the *ActivationKind* and previous state

A Windows Store app can be activated in a variety of ways by the user. A specific type of *Activated* event is fired in your application if it implements a contract such as the Search contract. Alternatively, in your application, you might want to implement a check of the activation kind to set up the UI. In the *OnLaunched* event, you can check for the activation type, as shown in the following example:

```
protected override void OnLaunched(LaunchActivatedEventArgs e)
{
    if (args.Kind == ActivationKind.Launch)
    {
        // The application has been launched by the user through its tile
    }
    else if (args.Kind == ActivationKind.ShareTarget)
    {
        // The application has been launched as a share target
    }
}
```

Table 1-1 lists members for ActivationKind enumeration.

TABLE 1-1 *ActivationKind enumeration members*

MEMBER	VALUE	DESCRIPTION
Launch	0	The user launched the app or tapped a content tile.
Search	1	The user is about to search with the app.
ShareTarget	2	The app is activated as a target for share operations.
File	3	An app launched a file whose file type the current app is registered to handle.
Protocol	4	An app launched a URL whose protocol the current app is registered to handle.
FileOpenPicker	5	The user wants to pick files that are provided by the app.
FileSavePicker	6	The user wants to save a file and selected the app as the location.
CachedFileUpdater	7	The user wants to save a file that the app provides content management for.
ContactPicker	8	The user wants to pick contacts using the app.
Device	9	The app handles AutoPlay.
PrintTaskSettings	10	The app handles print tasks.
CameraSettings	11	The app captures photos or videos from an attached camera.

* Source: Adapted from http://msdn.microsoft.com/en-au/library/windows/apps/windows.applicationmodel. activation.activationkind

When an app is activated, if the *PreviousExecutionState* property is *NotRunning*, the application failed to save its application data successfully and the app should start as if it was launched for the first time. In the *OnLaunched* event handler of your application, you can check the *PreviousExecutionState* property of the *LaunchActivatedEventArgs* parameter. The value of the *PreviousExecutionState* property is a member of the *ApplicationExecutionState* enumeration as listed in Table 1-2.

TABLE 1-2 *ApplicationExecutionState enumeration members*

MEMBER	VALUE	DESCRIPTION
NotRunning	0	The app is not running.
Running	1	The app is running.
Suspended	2	The app is suspended.
Terminated	3	The app was terminated after being suspended.
ClosedByUser	4	The app was closed by the user.

* Source: Adapted from http://msdn.microsoft.com/en-au/library/windows/apps/windows.applicationmodel. activation.applicationexecutionstate

The *NotRunning* execution state of a Windows Store app is seen in the following scenarios:

- After the app is installed from the Windows Store.
- When the app is closed with the Task Manager when it is running.
- After rebooting the device.
- After logging off a user and logging back on.
- After the user closes through the close gesture or Alt+F4 and activates it within about 10 seconds of closing it. Note that if the user closes the app and launches it after 10 seconds of closing it, the system sets the execution state to *ClosedByUser*.

The *Suspended* state of the app is seen when the app is activated using a secondary tile or using a contract or extension it is registered for while Windows is suspending it or after Windows has suspended it.

EXAM TIP

You are not expected to remember the various enumerations for the exam. However, you should be familiar with the values of properties commonly used for finding out the previous execution state, activation kind, and so on.

Thought experiment
Enhancing a photo editor Windows Store app

In this thought experiment, apply what you've learned about this objective. You can find answers to these questions in the "Answers" section at the end of this chapter.

Your organization has developed a photo editor app as a prototype for obtaining feedback and exploring interest among users of other apps developed previously. The three most common problems reported by the users of the prototype app are listed below. Suggest a solution for each problem with the concepts you have learned in this chapter.

1. Users have reported they cannot search for photos they have edited and saved previously.

2. Users have reported that after bringing another app to the foreground, the prototype app lost all their changes in photos that were open and being edited.

3. Users have reported they do not have an option to see a list of most recently edited photos in the app when it is launched.

Objective summary

- When you are implementing a state management strategy in your app, it is important to save the UI specific state as well as data in the app.

- Your application can be terminated by Windows while it is suspended. Therefore, any long-running tasks still being executed when the app is suspended need to be implemented as background tasks.

- When you design an app to support contracts and charms, you must ensure the respective *Activated* events are implemented and used in your app.

- Your application should check its previous state of execution before initializing the UI.

Objective review

Answer the following questions to test your knowledge of the information in this objective. You can find the answers to these questions and explanations of why each answer choice is correct or incorrect in the "Answers" section at the end of this chapter.

1. You are designing a Windows Store app that implements the Search contract and integrates with the Search charm. Which event should you implement to handle activation of your app?

   A. *OnLaunched*

   B. *OnActivated*

   C. *OnSearchActivated*

   D. *LoadState*

2. A Windows Store app is closed by the user using the Alt+F4 shortcut. Which app state will the app be in after it is closed?

   A. *ClosedByUser*

   B. *Terminated*

   C. *Suspended*

   D. *NotRunning*

3. You need to ensure that when your app resumes, it displays the information partially saved by the user. Which *ApplicationExecutionState* should you check to restore the state of the UI and the unsaved data?

   A. *ClosedByUser*

   B. *Running*

   C. *Suspended*

   D. *Terminated*

Objective 1.5: Plan for an app deployment

The Windows Store was originally launched to a restricted set of developers who had their apps evaluated by experienced Microsoft engineers. This process was implemented to ensure the application certification requirements were tested properly. During this phase, Microsoft used the feedback from developers around the world to refine requirements. Today, Microsoft provides a set of application certification requirements, guidance, and tools for developers to sign and test their applications before submitting them to the Windows Store.

This objective covers how to:

- Plan a deployment based on Windows Store app certification requirements
- Prepare an app manifest
- Sign an app
- Plan the requirements for an enterprise deployment

Planning a deployment based on Windows Store app certification requirements

The Windows Store is the primary source from where applications are downloaded and installed on a Windows device or a PC. The Windows Store provides a unique way to sell and distribute your apps and their updates, interact with users of your apps, and make money with them. The Windows Store acts as an entity that maintains the quality and reliability of Windows Store apps for all users. Your application's quality is evaluated by a testing process at Microsoft using a standard set of criteria, before the app is made available for download.

Your application must satisfy a basic set of requirements, as follows:

- **Application failures**   Your app should not crash or become unresponsive while running. If your app crashes, it should gracefully exit without requiring users to restart their system. This provides your customers with a better user experience.
- **Security**   Your app must use Windows security features. It should not compromise the security of the system under any circumstances.
- **Performance**   Your app should have a fast and responsive startup and suspend experience. It should release resources while suspended and consume only a reasonable amount of system resources such as central processing unit (CPU), memory, and disk input/output (I/O).
- **App packaging**   Your app manifest must contain all required attributes and must have valid resources defined as a Package Resource Index (PRI) file called Resources.pri. The app manifest is defined in the Package.appxmanifest file.

- **Platform application programming interfaces (APIs)**   Your app must only use APIs from the Windows 8 SDK. If you use an undocumented platform feature, your app will fail certification. Your app must use .NET 4.5 or later APIs.

It is important for your app to follow the Microsoft design style guidelines and its fundamental principles as well as the key features of Windows Store apps discussed previously. The Windows Store app certification requirements define a set of criteria your app should satisfy. To summarize, Windows Store apps:

- Should be creative, unique and provide value to the customer.
- Can display ads, but must not display only ads. The ads in your app must conform to the content and age rating guidelines.
- Should be responsive and perform reasonably well on any device, and updates should not remove functionality from your app.
- Should enable the customer to control data shared by the app, security, notifications, data transfers, and similar features.
- Should not contain offensive content and must conform to the content and age rating guidelines.
- Should have a unique name that helps with their identification in the Windows Store and their brand.

> *MORE INFO*   WINDOWS STORE APP CERTIFICATION REQUIREMENTS
>
> **You can read about the Windows Store app certification criteria at *http://msdn.microsoft.com/en-us/library/windows/apps/hh694083.aspx*.**

You can use Visual Studio to deploy your app on your local PC, on a remote PC on your network, or in the local simulator. The simulator is helpful when testing your app during development; however, it is not suitable for testing prior to distribution.

When you are ready to distribute your app for testing among other developers and testers, you have to create an app package. You have the option of creating either an .appx file or an .appxupload file. You can upload either file to the Windows Store when you are ready to submit your app. The .appxupload file contains two files: .appx and .appxsym. The .appxsym file contains the public symbols from your app. It provides useful information if your application crashes when it is running.

The .appx packages are ZIP-based container files that contain the app's payload files with information needed to validate, deploy, manage, and update the app. There are two ways to create an app package:

- **Use Visual Studio**   In Visual Studio, under the PROJECT menu, choose Store and then Create App Packages. You can choose the location in which the app package will be created, set a version number for the package, and choose the solution configuration. You can also choose to include public symbols that help with analyzing crashes in your app.

- **Use the command prompt** You can build an app package by opening a Visual Studio command prompt and then running MSBuild or by using Team Foundation Build. By default, the app package is created in the same location as other build output. However, you can override this behavior by specifying */p:GenerateProjectSpecificOutputFolder=false* as an argument for MSBuild.

After your application's app package is ready, you should review the app submission checklist, test your app with the Windows App Certification Kit (ACK), have your app tested by some volunteers, and take some screenshots to submit with your app. Make sure you have included a privacy statement or license terms if your app collects personal information.

> **MORE INFO** **APP SUBMISSION CHECKLIST**
>
> Information about the app submission checklist is at *http://msdn.microsoft.com/en-us/library/windows/apps/hh694062.aspx*.

Windows ACK is a free tool available for download from Microsoft. Windows ACK ensures that your application meets the basic requirements of a Windows Store app. Your app has to be installed on the PC where you plan to run Windows ACK. The kit launches your app a few times; tests it for startup and suspends performance; and checks the build version of your package, its dependencies, app capabilities, and so on. At the end of the testing process, Windows ACK creates an XML file you can open in Microsoft Internet Explorer and examine the results. A snippet from the XML file is shown in Figure 1-10.

> **MORE INFO** **WINDOWS APP CERTIFICATION KIT**
>
> The Windows ACK download is at *http://msdn.microsoft.com/en-US/windows/apps/jj572486*.

FIGURE 1-10 Windows ACK test results

Preparing an application manifest

A Windows Store app needs to be packaged before it is submitted to the Windows Store. When you create a new Windows Store project or item using Visual Studio, your application is set up for an app package to be created at a later stage of development. Visual Studio creates a source file for the app package (Package.appxmanifest) and adds it to your solution. When you build your project for the first time, Visual Studio transforms this file into the manifest file (AppxManifest.xml) and puts it in the output folder of the app. This is shown in Figure 1-11.

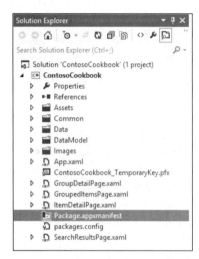

FIGURE 1-11 The application manifest file in Visual Studio

Your application's manifest file describes your app, including its name, description, start page, splash screen, and logos. In addition, you can use the manifest file to add capabilities and declarations, such as the ability to access a webcam or a microphone, and if your app supports search or acts as a share target, for example.

You can create the package manifest file manually using a text editor. Listing 1-13 shows the code for a package manifest.

LISTING 1-13 Package manifest example

```xml
<?xml version="1.0" encoding="utf-8"?>
<Package xmlns="http://schemas.microsoft.com/appx/2010/manifest">
  <Identity Name=""
            Version=""
            Publisher="" />
  <Properties>
   <DisplayName></DisplayName>
   <PublisherDisplayName></PublisherDisplayName>
   <Logo></Logo>
  </Properties>
  <Prerequisites>
   <OSMinVersion></OSMinVersion>
   <OSMaxVersionTested></OSMaxVersionTested>
  </Prerequisites>
  <Resources>
   <Resource Language="" />
  </Resources>
  <Applications>
    <Application Id="" StartPage="">
      <VisualElements DisplayName="" Description=""
          Logo="" SmallLogo=""
          ForegroundText="" BackgroundColor="">
        <SplashScreen Image="" />
      </VisualElements>
      <Extensions>
        <Extension Category="windows.search" />
      </Extensions>
    </Application>
  </Applications>
  <Capabilities>
    <Capability Name="internetClient" />
    <DeviceCapability="webcam" />
    <DeviceCapability="microphone" />
  </Capabilities>
</Package>
```

You should prepare your application's manifest using Visual Studio's app manifest designer. When you double-click the manifest file (or use the PROJECT|Store|Edit App Manifest option in Visual Studio), the manifest designer with the Application UI tab is the active tab. The Capabilities tab shown in Figure 1-12 shows a portion of the capabilities a Windows Store app can use.

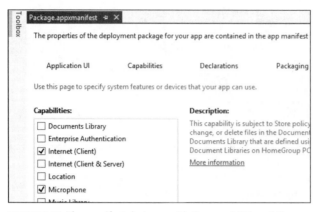

FIGURE 1-12 The manifest designer with the capabilities of the app

Table 1-3 lists the capabilities available to a Windows Store app.

TABLE 1-3 Windows Store app capabilities

CAPABILITY	DESCRIPTION
Documents Library	Provides programmatic access to the user's Documents library.
Enterprise Authentication	Typically used in line-of-business apps to access corporate resources.
Internet (Client)	Provides outbound access to the Internet and public networks through the firewall.
Internet (Client & Server)	Used in peer-to-peer (P2P) scenarios in apps that use file shares and voice over IP (VoIP).
Location	Provides access to the location functionality.
Microphone	Provides access to the microphone's audio feed; enables the app to record audio from connected microphones.
Music Library	Provides programmatic access to the user's Music library.
Pictures Library	Provides programmatic access to the user's Pictures library.
Private Networks (Client & Server)	Provides inbound and outbound access to home and work networks though the firewall, typically used for games that communicate across the local area network (LAN).
Proximity	Enables multiple devices in close proximity to communicate with each other.
Removable Storage	Provides programmatic access to files on removable store such as USB keys and external hard drives.
Shared User Certificates	Enables an app to access software and hardware certificates, such as certificates stored on a smart card.
Videos Library	Provides programmatic access to the user's Videos library.
Webcam	Provides access to the webcam's video feed, which enables the app to capture screenshots and movies from a connected webcam. You need to add microphone capability to grant access to the audio stream as well.

Windows Store apps use contracts and extensions to declare their interaction with other apps. To use the WinRT APIs to communicate with other Windows Store apps, you must add the required declarations in your app's manifest file. Visual Studio's manifest designer provides a number of declarations for various contracts and extensions (see Figure 1-13).

FIGURE 1-13 The manifest designer with the declarations available

Table 1-4 lists the declarations available for Windows Store apps.

TABLE 1-4 Windows Store app declarations

CAPABILITY	DESCRIPTION
Account Picture Provider	If your app takes pictures, you can use this extension to list your app in the Account Picture Settings control panel.
AutoPlay Content	This extension enables your app to be listed as an AutoPlay choice.
AutoPlay Device	This declaration registers your app for device events such as attaching a camera. Multiple instances of this declaration is allowed in an app.
Background Tasks	This declaration enables your app to register a background task that runs even when the app is suspended. Multiple instances of this declaration are allowed in an app.
Cached File Updater	This declaration enables users to use your app as a central repository to track and maintain files.
Camera Settings	This declaration provides a custom UI for selecting camera options.
Certificates	This extension enables you to install a digital certificate in your app, useful to authenticate a user to remote web services over SSL.

CAPABILITY	DESCRIPTION
Contact Picker	This extension enables your app to register to provide contact data.
File Open Picker	This declaration registers your app as a file open picker, making the content available in other apps.
File Save Picker	This declaration registers your app as a file save picker, making the app available as a save location for other Windows Store apps.
File Type Associations	This declaration registers file type associations with your app. Multiple instances of this declaration are allowed in this app.
Game Explorer	This declaration enables your app to register with the Windows Parental Controls system as a game.
Print Task Settings	This declaration enables your app to display a custom print-related UI and communicate directly with a print device.
Protocol	This declaration registers your app for existing or a custom uniform resource identifier (URI) scheme. Multiple instances of this declaration are allowed in this app.
Search	This declaration enables your app's content to be searchable by other apps and present search results from other apps in your app.
Share Target	This declaration sets up your app as a share target for other apps to share content with your app.

Visual Studio provides developers with an easy way to add a File Open Picker contract, Search contract, and/or Share Target contract in Windows Store apps. Just right-click your project in Visual Studio and select the Add New Item option. The window shown in Figure 1-14 displays.

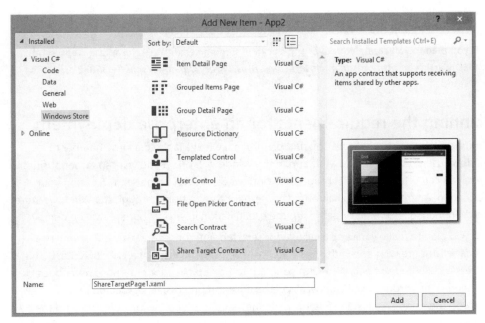

FIGURE 1-14 Adding a contract using Visual Studio

If you choose to implement one of these three contracts, the relevant declaration is automatically added to your app's manifest. In addition, the *Activated* event for the contract is also added to the app. For the File Open Picker contract, the *OnFileOpenPickerActivated* event is added; for the Search contract, the *OnSearchActivated* event is added; and for the Share Target contract, the *OnShareTargetActivated* contract is added.

Signing an application

When you create an app package using Visual Studio, it is signed with a test certificate. The app package resides in a folder called AppPackages within the package directory; this folder is created by Visual Studio. The certificate (.cer) file present in the folder contains the public key used to sign the package. This key must be installed before the app package is installed.

Visual Studio generates and adds the certificate file (with a .pfx extension) to your project. This certificate is valid for one year after creation. You can generate a new certificate using Visual Studio through the Packaging tab in the app manifest designer. Click the Choose Certificate button to open the Choose Certificate dialog box. Expand the Configure Certificate list, choose Create test certificate, and click OK. You will then add the Publisher Common Name and a password for the certificate file. Visual Studio regenerates the certificate with a new expiration date.

Planning the requirements for an enterprise deployment

If you develop a Windows Store app and plan to make it available to a large number of Windows users, you should list your app in the Windows Store. If you want to target business users, you can offer your app through the Windows Store with each user purchasing your application. Alternatively, you can offer your app for free to users through the Windows Store and then manage licensing directly with the organization in which your app will be deployed.

If you plan to make your app available for selected enterprises and users, IT administrators can distribute your app within the enterprise without involving the Windows Store. This process is called *sideloading*. Although your app to be deployed for enterprise users does not need to go through the Windows Store certification process, it is expected that you have followed the Windows design style UI guidelines and your app has been tested with the Windows ACK.

The following steps describe how to distribute a Windows Store app within an enterprise:

1. Use the Windows ACK to test your application. You should also test your app on Windows RT with the Windows ACK for Windows RT if you plan to support Windows RT. Testing your app with the ACK helps identify issues before deployment to users.

2. Your app must be signed with a certificate issued by a certificate authority (CA) trusted by the target PCs. The publisher name in your application's manifest must match the publisher name in the certificate used to sign the app. If you use a certificate from one of the many CAs trusted by Windows, you do not need to deploy and manage additional certificates on the targeted Windows 8 devices. If you choose to use your own CA to sign the app, IT administrators must ensure that the certificate is installed in the target Windows 8 devices because your CA might be untrusted.

3. When your app is tested and signed, give the signed app package and any app dependencies to the IT administrators.

4. IT administrators prepare the target Windows 8 PCs and deploy your app. Windows Server 2012 and Windows 8 Enterprise editions are enterprise sideloading ready, this means they are ready for your app to be installed. For such PCs, IT administrators should ensure they are joined in the domain and the Group Policy is set to *Allow Trusted Apps To Install*. IT administrators deploying your app to Windows 8 Pro, Windows RT, and Windows Enterprise devices should configure them by activating the product key for enterprise sideloading for each device and setting the Group Policy to *Allow Trusted Apps To Install*.

5. IT administrators can deploy your app to prepared PCs and devices by using a Windows image or at runtime.

Enterprise deployment of Windows Store apps does not stop users from installing business-related apps from the Windows Store. IT administrators might want to ensure that users in the enterprise network can access the Windows Store and the rich variety of apps. In a regulated environment, IT administrators can use a Group Policy to turn off access to the Windows Store for the users and their devices.

> **MORE INFO**   **WINDOWS STORE APP DEVELOPMENT FOR WINDOWS RT HARDWARE**
>
> You can read more about developing Windows Store apps targeting Windows RT hardware in the white paper at *http://www.microsoft.com/en-us/download/details.aspx?id=30703*.

Thought experiment

Maintaining a separate, custom version of a Windows Store app

In this thought experiment, apply what you've learned about this objective. You can find answers to these questions in the "Answers" section at the end of this chapter.

You have developed a Windows Store app and made it available for users through the Windows Store. The app has received positive feedback, and you are satisfied with the popularity of the app. An organization with a global presence has expressed interest in deploying your app internally with its own branding.

In your discussions with the organization, you have been told that your app can continue to be available in the Windows Store. However, you are expected to develop, deploy, and maintain a custom version of the app for the organization. How can you satisfy the requirements of the organization with your new app?

Objective summary

- Test a Windows Store app to ensure it meets Windows Store app certification requirements before making the app available to users through the Windows Store.
- Visual Studio provides a streamlined process to create your app package after you have edited and updated the package manifest file in which you set up your app's capabilities and declarations.
- You can use your own certificate to sign your app package.
- You can build Windows Store apps that target businesses and select a way to distribute them to users without submitting your app to the Windows Store.

Objective review

Answer the following questions to test your knowledge of the information in this objective. You can find the answers to these questions and explanations of why each answer choice is correct or incorrect in the "Answers" section at the end of this chapter.

1. You plan to send your application for testing to a small group of Windows 8 users. What is the best approach for deploying your app on the PCs of these users and obtain their feedback?

    A. Request the users to send their PCs or devices to you so you can install the app.

    B. Ask your users to install Visual Studio, send them your source code, and request them to compile the code and run your app.

    C. Prepare an app package and send them a copy of the app package. Request the users to install your app using the Windows PowerShell script in the package and test your app.

    D. Prepare an installer using one of the commercially available tools. Send the installer to your users.

2. You have prepared an app package and submitted it to the Windows Store. You have been informed that your app has passed certification and will be available in the Windows Store soon. You realize there are a few bugs that you should fix soon. What should be your approach in such a case?

    A. Create a new app from the code used to build the original app. Submit the new app and withdraw the original app.

    B. Bug fixes are not accepted in the Windows Store. You have to withdraw the app and you cannot submit updates to your app.

    C. You prepare an update for your app, test it with Windows ACK, and submit it to the Windows Store for certification. After it is certified, it will be available to your users.

    D. You can email a copy of your app with the bug fixes to your users.

3. You have completed the development of a Windows Store app that will be deployed in a few businesses. You choose to distribute the app yourself instead of using the Windows Store. What are the requirements for your app to be loaded onto PCs and devices in these organizations? (Choose all that apply.)

    A. Your app must be signed with a certificate from a CA trusted by the target PCs and devices.

    B. You should give your signed app and its dependencies to IT administrators in the organizations.

    C. You should send your app by email to the users who want to install and run your app.

    D. IT administrators can deploy your app using a Windows image or when the PC is in use.

    E. You should ask the users to send you their PCs and devices so that you can install your app.

Chapter summary

- Windows Store apps are unique in their appearance and behavior. The emphasis in these applications is on users and the way they interact with your application. You should following the principle of Microsoft design style and available guidance to design your app.

- Consider separation of concerns, reusability, and maintainability of your application when planning the logical layers of your solution. Divide your application into three main loosely coupled layers: presentation layer, business layer, and data layer. Wherever you have the requirement to integrate legacy software, consider using WinMD components in your Windows Store app.

- Use the MVVM pattern to implement the logical layers of your solution. The MVVM pattern is helpful for defining the interfaces for communication among the layers of your solution. Use the *INotifyPropertyChanged* interface to implement your viewmodels and employ data binding in your views to bind viewmodels. Use native controls such as *GridView* to render data collections in views using the *CollectionViewSource* and *ObservableCollection* classes.

- Plan and implement a sound state management strategy, one that preserves the state and app data when your app is suspended. Use the *OnLaunched* and *OnActivated* events to provide the user with a way to resume using your app. Check for the *PreviousExecutionState* and *ActivationKind* when your app is launched; restore the state and data if necessary.

- After development is complete, go through the Windows Store certification criteria to ensure your app meets all the requirements. Test your app with the Windows ACK and pay attention to the dependencies in your app. Prepare an app manifest ensuring all capabilities and declarations required by your app are included in the manifest. If you are planning to distribute your app directly, contact the IT administrators and give them the app package for deployment.

Answers

This section contains the solutions to the thought experiments and the answers to the lesson review questions in this chapter.

Objective 1.1: Thought experiment

1. **Design for re-use of visual elements**   Design and develop the app to maximize reuse of code, styles, and UI elements. This will be helpful if the app is re-branded for other businesses.

2. **Design for accessibility**   Use controls provided by the WinRT platform to compose the UI. These controls have built-in support for accessibility. Use the Inspect and UI Accessibility Checker tools to test for accessibility.

3. **Design a unique user experience**   Design the app for compelling UX with a UI that is easy and intuitive to use. Wherever possible, use device capabilities such as location sensors in the app.

Objective 1.1: Review

1. **Correct answer:** B

   A. **Incorrect:** Animations make the UI intuitive and appealing to use.

   B. **Correct:** Most controls have built-in animations. In addition, the Windows Animation library makes it easy to add animations.

   C. **Incorrect:** It is often a time-consuming exercise to create your own animations when you already have them in standard controls and in the Windows Animation library.

   D. **Incorrect:** It is best to use standard controls whenever possible.

2. **Correct answers:** A, B, D

   A. **Correct:** The Inspect tool enables you to select any UI element and view its accessibility data.

   B. **Correct:** The UI Accessibility Checker verifies that UI accessibility requirements are met in the design and implementation of UI Automation, regardless of the underlying UI framework.

   C. **Incorrect:** You shouldn't skip the accessibility tests and hope your application passes certification.

   D. **Correct:** Disconnecting the mouse and using only the keyboard to operate your app is a good test of a real-life scenario.

   E. **Incorrect:** Installing and testing your app on multiple PCs and devices is a time-consuming process and you are not guaranteed results that validate accessibility of the app.

3. **Correct answers:** B, C, E

   A. **Incorrect:** Using a single version or copy of code among designers and developers could result in serious problems with version conflict, missing requirements, and so on.

   B. **Correct:** Styles enable the reuse of visual elements.

   C. **Correct:** Custom controls can be reused in multiple apps.

   D. **Incorrect:** Tools provided by Microsoft such as Visual Studio facilitate collaboration between designers and developers.

   E. **Correct:** UX design resources provided by Microsoft consist of templates that can be used to create the conceptual design of an app.

Objective 1.2: Thought experiment

1. **Design and implement loosely coupled layers**   The app should be designed with loosely coupled layers to avoid dependencies between the layers that prevent the app from being enhanced in the future.

2. **Use C++/WinMD components**   In order to minimize the investment of time and other resources, the organization should consider reusing the C++ code through C++/WinMD components. Test infrastructure that exists for the C++ code can be reused with some modifications for testing the WinMD components.

Objective 1.2: Review

1. **Correct answer:** D

   A. **Incorrect:** The business layer is meant for the implementation of application logic.

   B. **Incorrect:** The data layer is meant for data access.

   C. **Incorrect:** The presentation layer is meant for implementing the UI.

   D. **Correct:** Implementing logging in a separate component enables for SOC and maximizes code reuse.

2. **Correct answer:** C

   A. **Incorrect:** The presentation layer is for implementing the UI.

   B. **Incorrect:** The data layer is meant for data access.

   C. **Correct:** Application logic is implemented in the business layer; this is the layer that interacts with other applications.

   D. **Incorrect:** The application manifest is to declare the capabilities and declarations only.

3. **Correct answers:** A, B, E

   A. **Correct:** It is easy to build a WinMD component in C++ using Visual Studio; the legacy code can be adapted easily.

   B. **Correct:** Windows Store apps can use WinMD components to incorporate functionality in their application layer.

   C. **Incorrect:** C# can impose limitations that could prevent the algorithm from being implemented.

   D. **Incorrect:** The WinRT data types and APIs available might not be adequate to implement the algorithm.

   E. **Correct:** Unit tests written in C++ for the existing software can be used as is or with minimal change to test the C++/WinMD component.

Objective 1.3: Thought experiment

1. **Reuse the data access code**   The prototype app has code that has been used to access the remote web service provided by the client. You should reuse the code in the data layer as the model of the MVVM pattern.

2. **Use the presentation layer**   The UI of the application should be designed and implemented so that styles and other UI components available in the prototype are reused in the view of the MVVM pattern.

3. **Implement business logic**   The business logic for the app should be implemented in the viewmodel of the application. The viewmodel can be data bound with the view to enable loose coupling.

Objective 1.3: Review

1. **Correct answer:** C

   A. **Incorrect:** The MVVM pattern encourages you to minimize code-behind to avoid strong coupling.

   B. **Incorrect:** It is not a good idea to implement business logic in the constructor of a viewmodel.

   C. **Correct:** The file helper class can be used on other platforms.

   D. **Incorrect:** The data is loaded in the data model, and the viewmodel is responsible for providing the data for data binding in the view. Data should not be loaded when the page loads.

2. **Correct answer:** B

   A. **Incorrect:** *OneTime* binding binds data when the binding is created; there are no updates possible after the binding has been constructed.

   B. **Correct:** *OneWay* binding from the database to the view and then from the view to a property in the viewmodel fulfills the requirements.

   C. **Incorrect:** *TwoWay* binding updates the database if any change is made by the user, thereby violating the requirements.

   D. **Incorrect:** A command is used with an element in the UI such as a button to invoke an action (for example, to load a new photo).

3. **Correct answer:** B

   A. **Incorrect:** Data binding should be used to bind collections with controls.

   B. **Correct:** The *ItemsSource* property should be used to set the data context for the *GridView* control.

   C. **Incorrect:** You need to create a *CollectionViewSource* using the data returned by the web service.

   D. **Incorrect:** There is no need to create a custom control; *GridView* supports data binding.

Objective 1.4: Thought experiment

1. **Search edited photos**   You should implement the Search contract and the *OnSearchActivated* event to present the user with the photos that they have edited previously.

2. **Use the *Suspending* and *Resuming* events**   You should use the *Suspending* event to save the state of the application and restore it through the *Resuming* event. This will help preserve the state the app was in when the application was sent to the background by the user.

3. **Save a list of most recently edited photos**   A list of most recently edited photos can be saved in the application data store when the application is suspended or closed by the user. This list can be displayed when the app is launched or resumed.

Objective 1.4: Review

1. **Correct answer:** C

   A. **Incorrect:** *OnSearchActivated* is the correct event for search activation of an app.

   B. **Incorrect:** You can check for the *ActivationKind* in *OnActivated* and react accordingly, but *OnSearchActivated* should be used.

   C. **Correct:** *OnSearchActivated* is the correct event for search activation of an app.

   D. **Incorrect:** The *LoadState* event is used in a page of a Windows Store app to restore data from the application settings or the application data store.

2. **Correct answer:** A

   A. **Correct:** *ClosedByUser* is a valid state of an app when it is closed by the user.

   B. **Incorrect:** An app is in the *Terminated* state when the operating system terminates it due to lack of resources.

   C. **Incorrect:** An app is in the *Suspended* state when it is no longer occupies the screen.

   D. **Incorrect:** An app is in the *NotRunning* state when it is yet to be launched.

3. **Correct answer:** D

   A. **Incorrect:** You shouldn't restore your app if it was closed by the user.

   B. **Incorrect:** You do not need to restore your app if it is already running.

   C. **Incorrect:** You shouldn't restore your app if it is resumed from suspension.

   D. **Correct:** An app is terminated when it is in the *Suspended* state when the system runs low on resources. You should restore your app if it was in the *Terminated* state before being resumed.

Objective 1.5: Thought experiment

1. **Create a custom version of the app**   Because the organization requires a custom version of your app, you should create one. In the custom version, you should implement the requirements that are specific for the organization.

2. **Test your app with the Windows ACK**   After you finish development of your app, you should test your app's app package with the Windows ACK.

3. **Sign your app with a certificate**   You should sign your app with a certificate from a known CA. This will enable the app to be sideloaded in the PCs and devices of the organization.

4. **Give the app package to the IT administrators**   You should give the app to the IT administrators for deployment in the PCs and devices in the organization.

Objective 1.5: Review

1. **Correct answer:** C

   A. **Incorrect:** Testers of your app would not send their PCs or devices to you for installation of the app.

   B. **Incorrect:** Users need not have the skills to install Visual Studio, compile your app's source code, and test it.

   C. **Correct:** An app package is the best way to distribute your app.

   D. **Incorrect:** Windows Store apps cannot be installed using an installer prepared with a commercial tool.

2. **Correct answer:** C

   A. **Incorrect:** Although you can withdraw your app, you might not be able to use the same name and publish a new version of your app.

   B. **Incorrect:** Bug fixes should be incorporated in an update and submitted to the Windows Store for certification and approval.

   C. **Correct:** Updates of your app go through the same approval process as your app. After approval, they are distributed through the app store.

   D. **Incorrect:** This is not allowed by the Windows Store.

3. **Correct answers:** A, B, D

   A. **Correct:** You must sign your app with a certificate whose certificate authority is trusted by the target PCs.

   B. **Correct:** IT administrators are responsible for deploying apps in their organizations.

   C. **Incorrect:** Sending your app by email to users is neither recommended nor permitted.

   D. **Correct:** IT administrators can prepare a Windows image that includes your app or deploy your app in the runtime. A similar procedure should be used to distribute updates to your app.

   E. **Incorrect:** Users will not want to part with their PCs and devices for you to install your app. Installing the app manually on every PC or device is a time-consuming and inefficient process.

CHAPTER 2

Develop Windows Store apps

One of the unique characteristics of a great Windows Store app is its capability to interact with other apps and Windows 8 through extensions and contracts. Extensions provide a way to extend or customize capabilities of Windows features within Windows Store apps. Contracts ensure that diverse apps present features, such as sharing an item through another app, using the same interface.

An extension enables an app to integrate with Windows and extend features provided by the operating system. Developers can extend features such as picking contacts and associating specific file types with specific criteria within their own app and potentially make their implementation available to other apps and Windows.

A contract implemented in an app indicates that it is prepared to interact with other apps without the need to know how they work. The contract is an agreement between multiple apps that defines the requirements they must implement to participate in the interaction. The Settings contract provides users with a clean, intuitive way to manage application settings. The Search contract enables users to search content within an app as well as content from other apps. You can let users of your app share content with another app or service through the Share Target contract, or your app can act as a target for sharing content from other apps.

Objectives in this chapter:

- Objective 2.1: Access and display contacts
- Objective 2.2: Design for charms and contracts
- Objective 2.3. Implement search
- Objective 2.4: Implement Share in an app
- Objective 2.5: Manage app settings and preferences

Objective 2.1: Access and display contacts

Windows Store apps can use the contact picker to enable users to access their contacts to be able to share content from within the application. The *Windows.ApplicationModel. Contacts* namespace provides the options for selecting contacts through a Windows Store app. An app can pick contacts from one or more Windows Store apps by selecting the provider of contacts from a drop-down list.

Windows Store apps can act as contact providers by declaring the contact picker extension in the package manifest. These apps are available in the people picker drop-down menu when the user selects one or more contacts.

The *ContactPicker* class is used to set up the user interface (UI). The *ContactPickerUI* class, provided by the *Windows.ApplicationModel.Contacts.Provider* namespace, is used to display selected contacts. You can filter the contacts to be displayed in your application by specifying which fields from the contacts to use when selecting them. You can create new contacts and update their properties, such as their thumbnail, from within your app.

This objective covers how to:

- Call the *ContactPicker* class.
- Filter which contacts to display.
- Select specific contact data.
- Display a set number of contacts.
- Create and modify contact information.

Calling the *ContactPicker* class

In your Windows Store app, you can allow users to choose one or more contacts to share content or send a customized message. You can provide your users with the option of either selecting a single contact or multiple contacts at a time. Windows provides a standard UI through which users access their contacts, as shown in Figure 2-1.

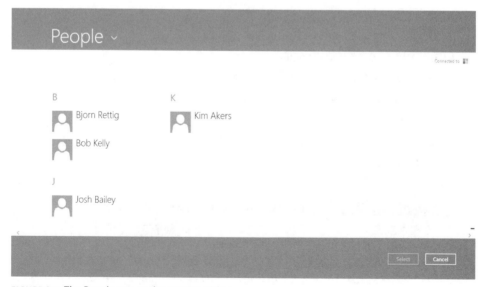

FIGURE 2-1 The People app as the contact picker

To incorporate the contact picker in a Windows Store app, create an instance of the *ContactPicker* class. Call the *PickSingleContactAsync* or *PickMultipleContactsAsync* method to select one or more contacts. *PickSingleContactAsync* returns a single contact; *PickMultipleContactsAsync* returns one or more contacts. After the user has selected the contact(s), process the information contained in the result. The information about a contact is stored in a *ContactInformation* object. Listing 2-1 shows how to use the *ContactPicker* class with the *PickSingleContactAsync*.

LISTING 2-1 Using the *ContactPicker* class with the *PickSingleContactAsync* method

```
private async void PickContacts_Click(object sender, RoutedEventArgs e)
{
    var contactPicker = new Windows.ApplicationModel.Contacts.ContactPicker();
    contactPicker.CommitButtonText = "Select a contact";

    ContactInformation contact = await contactPicker.PickSingleContactAsync();

    // You can allow the user to pick multiple contacts with the
    // PickMultipleContactsAsync method. Each member of the returned list
    // is a ContactInformation object. Example:
    // IReadOnlyList<ContactInformation> contacts =
    //      await contactPicker.PickMultipleContactsAsync();

    if (contact != null)
    {
        // Display the name of the contact
        ContactNameTextBox.Text = contact.Name;

        // Display the emails
        if (contact.Emails.Count > 0)
        {
            StringBuilder sb = new StringBuilder();
            foreach (IContactField field in contact.Emails)
            {
                sb.AppendFormat("{0} ({1}) \n", field.Value, field.Category);
            }
            EmailsTextBox.Text = sb.ToString();
        }

        // Display the contact's thumbnail
        Windows.Storage.Streams.IRandomAccessStreamWithContentType stream =
            await contact.GetThumbnailAsync();

        if (stream != null && stream.Size > 0)
        {
            BitmapImage image = new BitmapImage();
            image.SetSource(stream);
            ContactThumbnailImage.Source = image;
        }
        else
        {
            ContactThumbnailImage.Source = null;
```

```
        }
    }
}
```

The code in Listing 2-1 works when your application occupies the entire screen. When the app is in the snapped state, it throws an exception. Before you invoke *PickSingleContactAsync* or *PickMultipleContactsAsync*, you must ensure that your app can show the picker by checking whether the app is unsnapped; if it is in a snapped state, it can be unsnapped to open the picker. Listing 2-2 shows how to check the state of the app before invoking the method on the *ContactPicker* class.

LISTING 2-2 Checking whether the app is unsnapped

```
using Windows.UI.VIewManagement;
public sealed partial class AddUsersPage : Page
{
    // This method ensures that the Contact Picker user interface is presented
    // only when your application is not in snapped state.
    private bool EnsureUnsnapped()
    {
        bool unsnapped = ((ApplicationView.Value != ApplicationViewState.Snapped) ||
                        ApplicationView.TryUnsnap());
        return unsnapped;
    }

    private async void PickContacts_Click(object sender, RoutedEventArgs e)
    {
        // Before you call the PickSingleContactAsync or PickMultipleContactsAsync,
        // use the above method like so:
        if (this.EnsureUnsnapped())
        {
            // Run the ContactPicker code.
        }
    }
}
```

The *ContactInformation* class provides the *QueryCustomFields* method, with which you can obtain the value of a custom field stored in a contact. The *ContactInformation* class has the following properties that can be used in your app after retrieving the contact(s):

- **CustomFields** A read-only list of custom fields stored in the contact, in which each member in the list is an object of type *ContactField*.

- **Emails** A read-only list of emails stored in the contact, in which each member in the list is an object of type *ContactField*.

- **InstantMessages** A read-only list of instant messaging accounts stored in the contact, in which each member in the list is an object of type *ContactInstantMessageField*.

- **Locations** A read-only list of *ContactLocationField* objects stored in the contact. A *ContactLocationField* object contains information about the user's location and address.

- **Name** The name of the contact (a string).

- **PhoneNumbers**   A read-only list of phone numbers associated with the contact, in which each member in the list is an object of type *ContactField*.

The *ContactField* class used to represent members in a *ContactInformation* object consists of the following properties:

- **Category**   The category specified by the *ContactFieldCategory* enumeration that the contact belongs to
- **Name**   The name of the field
- **Type**   The type of contact data specified by the *ContactFieldType* enumeration
- **Value**   The value of the field

A *ContactField* object must contain a string value and a value for the *Type* property from the enumeration *ContactFieldType*, at a minimum. The *Type* property specifies whether the data in the *ContactField* object is a phone number, email address, location, or something else. Optionally, a *ContactField* object can contain a value in the *Category* property to distinguish between home, work, mobile, or other data.

Filtering which contacts to display

In your Windows Store app, you might need the email addresses of the contacts your users select for a feature. When you invoke either the *PickSingleContactAsync* or the *PickMultiple-ContactsAsync* method of the *ContactPicker* class, the default behavior is to show the contact as a complete entity. You can set the *SelectionMode* property of the *ContactPicker* class to one of the values of the *ContactSelectionMode* enumeration. Table 2-1 describes the *ContactSelection-Mode* enumeration members.

TABLE 2-1 *ContactSelectionMode* enumeration members

MEMBER	VALUE	DESCRIPTION
Contacts	0	Specifies that the user wants to select the entire contact. This is the default behavior.
Fields	1	Specifies that the user wants to select only certain fields.

To filter the contacts your app wants to display, you need to set the *SelectionMode* property to *ContactSelectionMode.Fields* and populate the *DesiredFields* array (property of the *ContactPicker* class) to members of the *KnownContactField* class. If you add only one field to the *DesiredFields* array, a contact will be considered a match if it has that field. If you add multiple fields to the *DesiredFields* array, a contact is considered a match if it has any of the fields. The *KnownContactField* class has the following properties:

- **Email**   Contains the name of the field used for email addresses
- **InstantMessage**   Contains the name of the field used for instant messaging accounts
- **Location**   Contains the name of the field used for the contact's location
- **PhoneNumber**   Contains the name of the field used for phone numbers

If your application requires the fields of a contact to be selected in order of preference, you should add them to the *DesiredFields* property in that order of preference. For example, if you want both the email addresses and phone numbers of the selected contacts, but prefer the phone numbers, put the *PhoneNumber* field before the *Email* field in the *DesiredFields* array, as shown in Listing 2-3.

LISTING 2-3 Using the *DesiredFields* property for order of preference

```
private async void PickContacts_Click(object sender, RoutedEventArgs e)
{
    if (this.EnsureUnsnapped())
    {
        var ContactPicker = new Windows.ApplicationModel.Contacts.ContactPicker();
        contactPicker.CommitButtonText = "Select a contact";

        // Filter the contacts which have their email and phone numbers, with
        // Email as the preference
        contactPicker.SelectionMode = ContactSelectionMode.Fields;
        contactPicker.DesiredFields.Add(KnownContactField.Email);
        contactPicker.DesiredFields.Add(KnownContactField.PhoneNumber);

        ContactInformation contact = await ContactPicker.PickSingleContactAsync();


        If (contact != null)
        {
            // Display the name of the contact
            ContactNameTextBox.Text = contact.Name;

            // Display the emails
            if (contact.Emails.Count > 0)
            {
                StringBuilder sb = new StringBuilder();
                foreach (IContactField field in contact.Emails)
                {
                    sb.AppendFormat({0} ({1}) \n", field.Value, field.Category);
                }
                emailsTextBlock.Text = sb.ToString();
            }
        }
    }
}
```

Selecting specific contact data

The *ContactInformation* class contains information about a contact obtained from a call to the *ContactPicker* class. Properties of the *ContactInformation* class such as *Emails* and *PhoneNumbers* can contain more than one value in the collection.

In your app, you might be required to display the contact's work phone number and email, specifically avoiding their home phone number and email for privacy reasons. To implement such a requirement, you should check the *Type* and *Category* properties of the *ContactField* object you need to evaluate.

The *ContactFieldCategory* enumeration defines the categories of data the *ContactField* class can belong to. You can use the value of this enumeration to show, hide, or highlight a particular category of data (for example, you can bold all work-related contact information). Table 2-2 describes the *ContactFieldCategory* enumeration members.

TABLE 2-2 *ContactFieldCategory* enumeration members

MEMBER	VALUE	DESCRIPTION
None	0	Data doesn't belong to any category.
Home	1	Data belongs to the Home category.
Work	2	Data belongs to the Work category.
Mobile	3	Data belongs to the Mobile category.
Other	4	Data belongs to the Other category.

The *ContactFieldType* enumeration defines the type of contact data in the *ContactField* class. Your application can select to display only specific type(s) of contact data by checking the value of this field in the *ContactField* class. Table 2-3 describes the *ContactFieldType* enumeration members.

TABLE 2-3 *ContactFieldType* enumeration members

MEMBER	VALUE	DESCRIPTION
Email	0	The contact's email address
PhoneNumber	1	The contact's phone number
Location	2	The contact's location
InstantMessage	3	The contact's instant message user name
Custom	4	A custom value for the contact

Listing 2-4 shows how to use the *Type* and *Category* properties of the *ContactField* object to select specific contact data.

```
private void DisplayContactInformation(TextBlock emailTextBlock,
                                       TextBlock phoneTextBlock,
                                       IReadOnlyCollection<ContactField> fields)
{
    if (fields.Count > 0)
    {
        foreach (IContactField field in fields)
        {
            // Display the work email
            if (field.Type == ContactFieldType.Email &&
                field.Category == ContactFieldCategory.Work)
            {
                emailTextBlock.Text = field.Value;
            }

            // Display the work phone number
            if (field.Type == ContactFieldType.PhoneNumber &&
                field.Category == ContactFieldCategory.Work)
            {
                phoneTextBlock.Text = field.Value;
            }
        }
    }
}
```

Displaying a set number of contacts

Your Windows Store app can act as a contact picker provider when it declares the contact picker extension in the list of declarations in the package manifest file, shown in Figure 2-2. An application that declares this extension is expected to provide a UI through which the user can select one or more contacts.

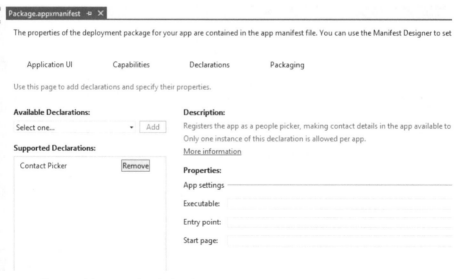

FIGURE 2-2 Contact picker extension declaration

When a Windows Store app provides the user with an option to select one or more contacts, an app that is registered with Windows as a contact information provider is launched as an app embedded within the Windows Store app. The user has the option to choose either your app or the People app in Windows as the contact picker source, as shown in Figure 2-3.

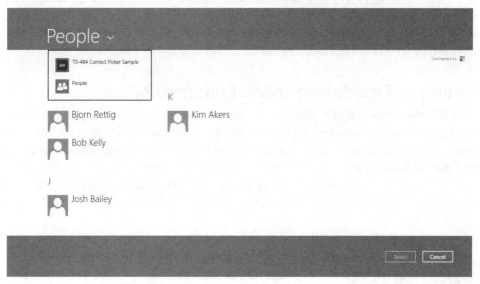

FIGURE 2-3 Contact picker selection option

A Windows Store app that has declared the contact picker extension receives an *OnActivated* event with the activation kind set to *ActivationKind.ContactPicker* in the event arguments of the type *Windows.ApplicationModel.Activation.IActivatedEventArgs*. In the event handler, you can create an instance of the page that implements the UI of the contact picker, as shown in Listing 2-5.

LISTING 2-5 Using the *OnActivated* event handler

```
using Windows.ApplicationModel.Activation;

public partial class App : Application
{
    protected override void OnActivated(IActivatedEventArgs args)
    {
        // Check if we have been activated to acts as contact picker source
        if (args.Kind == ActivationKind.ContactPicker)
        {
            // The ContactPickerPage has an Activate method. In this method, the
            // the content of the current window is set to the page and the window
            // is activated.
            var page = new ContactPickerPage();
            page.Activate((ContactPickerActivatedEventArgs)args);
        }
        else
        {
```

```
            base.OnActivated(args);
        }
    }
}
```

A Windows Store app that implements the contact picker extension has the capability to restrict the number of contacts that will be displayed and made available to the user for selection. The app can query remote web services or a local database for the list of contacts, and can filter the list of contacts even before the list is displayed.

Creating and modifying contact information

When a Windows Store app that declares the contact picker extension is activated by another Windows Store app, an instance of the *ContactPickerUI* class is available through the *Contact-PickerActivatedEventArgs* event argument as a property. The *ContactPickerUI* object represents the section that lists the contacts when the user wants to select contacts. (See App 2 in Figure 2-4.) When the user selects one or more contacts from the list, the selected contacts are then passed back to the calling application as a list of *ContactInformation* objects.

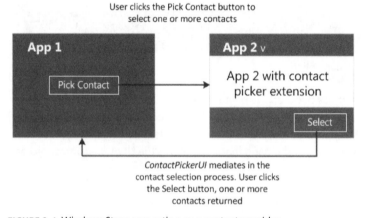

FIGURE 2-4 Windows Store app acting as a contact provider

A Windows Store app that is a provider of contacts should display a list of contacts to the user upon request. The user then selects one or more contacts from this list. The selected contacts are added to the *ContactPickerUI* object, as shown in Listing 2-6.

LISTING 2-6 Using the *ContactPickerUI* object

```
using Windows.ApplicationModel.Activation;

public void AddContact(TwitterContact twContact)
{
    Windows.ApplicationModel.Contacts.Contact contact =
        new Windows.ApplicationModel.Contacts.Contact();

    contact.Name = twContact.Name;

    // Add the email
    if (string.IsNullOrEmpty(twContact.Email))
        contact.Fields.Add(new ContactField(twContact.Email,
            ContactFieldType.Email, ContactFieldCategory.Work));

    // Add the phone number
    if (string.IsNullOrEmpty(twContact.Phone))
        contact.Fields.Add(new ContactField(twContact.Phone,
            ContactFieldType.PhoneNumber, ContactFieldCategory.Work));

    switch (contactPickerUI.AddContact(twContact.Id, contact))
    {
        case AddContactResult.Added:

            Status.Text = twContact.Name + " was already added to the basket";
            break;

        case AddContactResult.AlreadyAdded:
            Status.Text = twContact.Name + " is already added to the basket";
            break;

        case AddContactResult.Unavailable:
        default:
            Status.Text = twContact.Name + " could not be added to the basket";
            break;
    }
}
```

When the user clicks the Select button, one or more *ContactInformation* objects are returned to the app that invoked the contact picker. The user might decide to cancel the selection, in which case *PickSingleContactAsync* or *PickMultipleContactsAsync* returns null.

The *ContactPickerUI* class provides a highly flexible way to incorporate contact sources in Windows Store apps. Users have the option to change or edit the contact information before adding to the basket of choices they have made before finalizing their selection.

Thought experiment

Building a Windows Store app contacts manager

In this thought experiment, apply what you've learned about this objective. You can find answers to these questions in the "Answers" section at the end of this chapter.

Your manager has asked you to develop a Windows Store app that enables users to import contacts into the app from their preferred email provider as well from files that contain archived contact data.

One of the requirements of your app is to provide users with the ability to filter and select contacts during the import. In addition, your app is required to provide contacts to other Windows Store apps whenever required. The app should also provide the ability to filter contacts with specific fields.

Answer the following questions for your manager:

1. Will your application be capable of importing contacts from remote web sources and files exported by devices while acting as a contact provider at the same time?

2. How will you ensure the app works in all view states?

3. Will users be able to select as many contacts as they want from the imported list?

Objective summary

- The *ContactPicker* class provides Windows Store apps with the capability to select one or more contacts.

- You can set up the *ContactPicker* class to select contacts with values in specific fields, such as those with email addresses and phone numbers.

- The type and category of data in a contact can be used to select the information to be displayed in the app.

- A Windows Store app can implement the contact picker extension and act as a provider of contacts for other apps.

Objective review

Answer the following questions to test your knowledge of the information in this objective. You can find the answers to these questions and explanations of why each answer choice is correct or incorrect in the "Answers" section at the end of this chapter.

1. You have been asked to design a contact picker app. Which contact fields are available in the *ContactInformation* class? (Choose all that apply.)

    A. Name

    B. Designation

    C. Organization Name

    D. Work Address

    E. Work Phone Number

2. You have been asked to implement an application in which the user can select one or more contacts. What code should you use to provide this option to the user?

    A. *while (true) { ContactPicker.PickSingleContactAsync(); }*

    B. *IReadOnlyList<Contact> contacts = await ContactPicker.PickMultipleContactsAsync();*

    C. *IReadOnlyList<ContactInformation> contacts = await contactPicker.PickMultiple-ContactsAsync();*

    D. *IReadOnlyList<ContactInformation> contacts = contactPicker.PickMultipleContact-sAsync();*

3. You are asked to design an app that acts as a provider of contacts. The app must function on tablets, touch laptops, and PCs. Which requirement is valid?

    A. There is no need to consider the form factor or application's view state.

    B. The app should see whether the app is unsnapped; if not, it should attempt to unsnap it.

    C. The app will function only when it is in the snapped state.

    D. The system checks for the application's view state and carries layout changes accordingly.

Objective 2.2: Design for charms and contracts

Microsoft design style emphasizes the "content over chrome" principle, which minimizes distractions for the user. A well-designed app should provide the user with an easy way to perform actions to interact with the app. Actions that are less frequently used, such as search and share or changing the settings of the app, are placed in the charms bar.

Windows Store apps can integrate actions provided by the charms bar such as search, share, connect to devices for printing or streaming media, or display application settings. The UI presented through the charms bar is placed on top of the app, so any UI elements below it will be hidden.

The Search, Share Target, and Play To contracts are exposed in a Windows Store app through a declaration in the app's manifest file and an implementation in the app. Each contract implemented in an app is available to the user through the respective charm, for example, if an app implements the Search contract, it is invoked in the app through the Search charm. Windows provides the Settings charm as a universally accessible entry point in context to your app for the user to update settings that affect the app as well as settings exposed by the system. A Windows Store app can implement the Settings contract and include settings the user can update while using the app.

> **This objective covers how to:**
> - Choose the appropriate charm based on app requirements.
> - Design your app in a charm- and contract-aware manner.
> - Configure the app manifest for correct permissions.

Choosing the appropriate charm based on app requirements

The charms bar appears when users swipe from the right side of the screen, when they hover the mouse on the top-right side of their monitor, or when they press the Windows+C keyboard shortcut. The charms bar with various charms is shown in Figure 2-5.

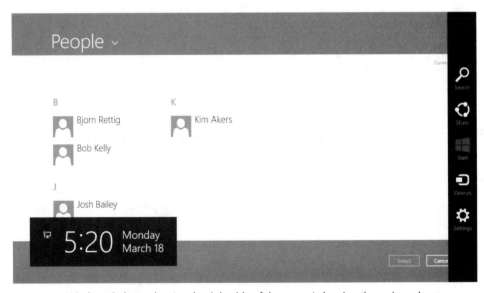

FIGURE 2-5 Windows 8 charms bar (on the right side of the screen) showing the various charms

The contracts available through the charms bar enable your app to interact with others. Some charms, such as Search, drive users into your app from other apps or the system, while others provide entry points for common requirements such as application settings. The contracts you can integrate in your app through the charms bar are the following:

- **Search**   The Search contract enables the user to search for anything within your app, search another app, or even search the entire PC. Your app can be activated if it participates in the Search contract and has results to show for the search term.

- **Share Target**   The Share Target contract provides users with the content to share from within your app with another app to perform an action such as sending an email without leaving your app.

- **Devices**   Wired and wireless devices connected to the PC can be accessed via the Devices contract. You can print content from your app to a printer, sync content with another device such a Windows Phone, or stream media to your TV.

- **Settings**   The Settings charm is used to change common settings of the PC and for your app. While app settings differ with apps, PC settings are the same in every app. You can implement the Settings contract to manage your application's settings through the Settings charm.

EXAM TIP

You should be familiar with the contracts and extensions available for Windows Store apps. You can read more about contracts and extensions at *http://msdn.microsoft.com/en-gb/library/windows/apps/hh464906.aspx.*

The Search contract enables users to search your app's content through the Search charm from anywhere in the system. Users can search for content in your app through the Search charm if your app is running, as shown on the left in Figure 2-6. Otherwise, users can enter the search term and select your app from the list of apps in the Search pane, as shown on the right in Figure 2-6.

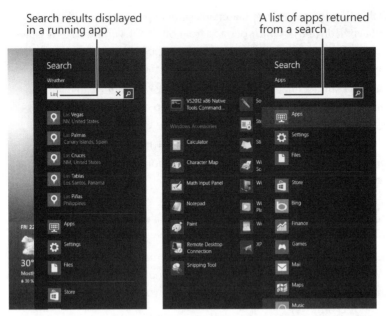

FIGURE 2-6 The Search charm can be used to search within an app when it is running, such as the Weather app on the left. It can also be used to search for apps in the system, shown on the right.

When a Windows Store app implements the Share Target contract, it can receive content from other apps through the Share charm. An app with content to share is the *share source*, whereas an app that can receive content is a *share target*. The user does not have to leave the app when they want to share content from the app. Your app prepares the data it shares in a specific format and provides it to the target app. Figure 2-7 shows content from the Weather app being shared with the Mail app.

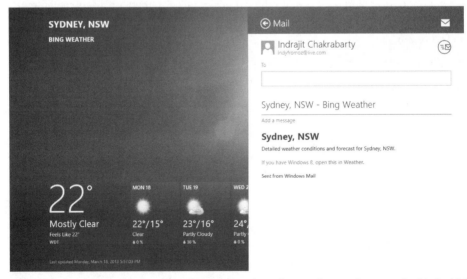

FIGURE 2-7 Share charm being used to share content from the Weather app in an email with the Mail app

Users should be able to send content to devices they use every day and are connected to their Windows 8 PCs and tablets. These devices include printers in the network, external monitors or televisions and smartphones, and other devices that support the tap and send experience. For example, you might want to print search results from Bing using a printer connected to the PC or share with a smartphone using tap and send. Figure 2-8 shows such a scenario.

FIGURE 2-8 Devices charm being used to send content from a page in Internet Explorer to other devices

The Settings contract provides users with an easy, in-context access to your app's settings as well as settings exposed by the system. The items that appear in the Settings charm for an app should affect the app only and should be used by the user only occasionally. For example, if the user needs to turn off or turn on automatic synchronization of feeds in an RSS reading, it should be included as a setting through the Settings charm. Figure 2-9 shows the Settings charms for some Windows 8 apps.

FIGURE 2-9 Settings charms of some Windows 8 applications

The commands in the Settings charm of the app link to secondary flyouts that provide users with a way to change their preferences in the app, update their credentials, and so on. A flyout is similar to a dialog box, except that a flyout can be dismissed by clicking or tapping outside its surface. In some apps, commands in the Settings charm link to external web pages that outline the privacy statement for the application. The command launches the external web page in the default browser configured by the user. The bottom of the Settings charm contains options to configure and change PC settings. These options are present in the Settings charm whenever it is open.

Designing your app in a charm-aware and contract-aware manner

It is important to design your Windows Store app with consideration for the various charms and contracts available. A great app should appeal with a unique design and user experience.

Windows Store apps fall into a variety of categories, for example, news and general information, productivity, media, and so on. Some types of apps, such as productivity, require a deeper level of interaction with their users and provide more commands than other types of apps. In a productivity app, users create tasks and reminders, add and delete notes, import content, and so on. You can implement the Search contract so that users can easily locate items they have created with your app with the Search charm.

As mentioned previously, several types of apps share their content with other apps and sometimes act as share targets. Productivity apps are great examples of share targets. Users want to import content from other apps or websites into a productivity app without switching context between multiple apps. The Share Target contract and its implementation through the Share charm provide a good user experience in this regard. If your app shares data with other apps, it is important to support as many types of data as will be meaningful for users to share. This ensures your app is capable of sharing content with a broad set of Windows Store apps.

Today's PCs and other Windows 8 devices have the ability to connect to printers, monitors, televisions, and smartphones, either wirelessly or with wires. Implementing the Devices charm in your app means it will be able to share content with a variety of devices seamlessly.

If your Windows Store app has a number of options and user preferences that are global to the app, implementing the Settings contract via the Settings charm provides an in-context entry point across multiple pages. You can implement one or more settings flyouts in your app and even deep-link a specific flyout from an app page.

Design guidelines for the Search charm

When you implement the Search contract in your app, users can search the content in your app from anywhere in the system using the Search charm. If your app is frequently used to carry out search, it makes your app more visible among the list of apps that support search through the Search charm. Therefore, you should rely on the Search charm instead of creating your own UI to search your app's content.

If your app enables users to explore content through search, you should consider adding a search icon to your app's UI. The Search charm can be programmatically opened by clicking the search icon, thereby keeping your app's search experience consistent with that of Windows 8 and other apps.

If search is the primary way users interact with your app, consider adding a search box to your app's canvas. This is useful if your app requires a custom layout and more details in the search result than those provided through the Search charm. Users will still use the Search charm to carry out search. Therefore, the user can have two separate search histories for your app—one that is attached to the search box in the app and the other attached to the Search charm. Adding a search box in your app means that the searches carried out using your in-app search box will not increase your app's rank and visibility in the Search charm.

If you add a search box to your app's UI, use the *TrySetQueryText* method of the *SearchPane* class to keep the search query string added through the search box in sync with the Search charm. If the user clears the text in the search box, the Search charm should also be cleared. If the user prefers to use the Search charm to enter their query while the search box is visible in the app, the search box should be disabled, as shown in the Bing example in Figure 2-10.

Search box is enabled when
the Search charm is not visible

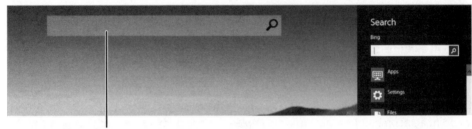

Search box is disabled when
the Search charm is visible

FIGURE 2-10 The Bing app uses a search box that is disabled when the Search charm is visible

If you decide to add a search box in your app, remember to place it in the UI so it is not hidden by the charms bar or a flyout. You should not place the search box in the app bar.

In Windows Store apps that are text-heavy, such as document viewers, consider incorporating a feature to enable users to search in the text. Such a feature usually provides a full-screen experience and helps users move through large bodies of text. You should not implement this feature through the Search charm. Instead, add it to the app bar, paired with other commands such as Replace, at a page level. You should add the Ctrl+F keyboard shortcut, which is the default Find feature for Windows.

When the user starts typing into the search box in the Search charm, search suggestions appear below the search box. These suggestions are supplied by the app that's visible on the screen if it has implemented the Search contract. Search suggestions do not appear if the app has not implemented the Search contract. There are two types of search suggestions an app can provide:

- **Query suggestions** These are auto-completions of the user's query text and suggest queries the user might want to search for. If the user clicks a query suggestion, the app displays the search results page for that query. Query suggestions are strings provided by the application.

- **Result recommendations** These are strong or exact matches to the user's query that the user might want to view immediately. If the user clicks a result recommendation, the app displays the page with the results. Result suggestions are strings provided by the application.

Your app should provide result recommendations to direct the user to the details of a particular result without the requirement to navigate through a search results page. A result recommendation consists of a thumbnail image, a title or label, and a brief description. Separate multiple result recommendations using labeled separators to help users distinguish the results. A Windows Store app can provide a maximum of five suggestions, and each separator counts toward this limit. Figure 2-11 shows the search suggestions and result recommendations from the Store app.

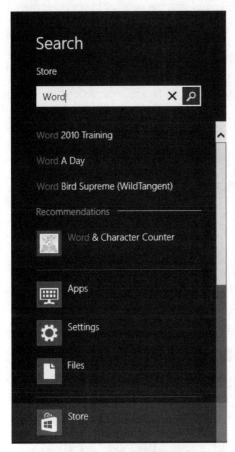

FIGURE 2-11 Query suggestions and result recommendation from the Store app in Windows 8

In a Windows Store app that supports the Search contract, search results should be presented in a separate page after the user has selected a query suggestion or a result recommendation or used their own search query. The search results should be presented such that each result has an image or thumbnail (if the data model provides one), title, and brief description of the item. In the search results, the query string should be displayed prominently.

> ***IMPORTANT*** **VISIBILITY OF SEARCH RESULTS**
>
> **Because the charms bar will be open until the user clicks your app or touches a result item, you should ensure that important search results are not hidden by the charms bar.**

If the query string for a search produces a large number of results, you can provide a set of filters and arrange results with their scope set to the various filters. When the user clicks or taps a filter, the Search charm closes. It is recommended that the number of results for each filter be indicated clearly in the respective view, and there should be a way to view all the search results in one page. You can highlight the user's query string in each search result, which is called *hit highlighting*. Figure 2-12 shows the search results for file names that contain the word *screenshot*, with various filters applied. The results include the total number of results for each filter, the query string highlighted, and hit highlighting of the query string.

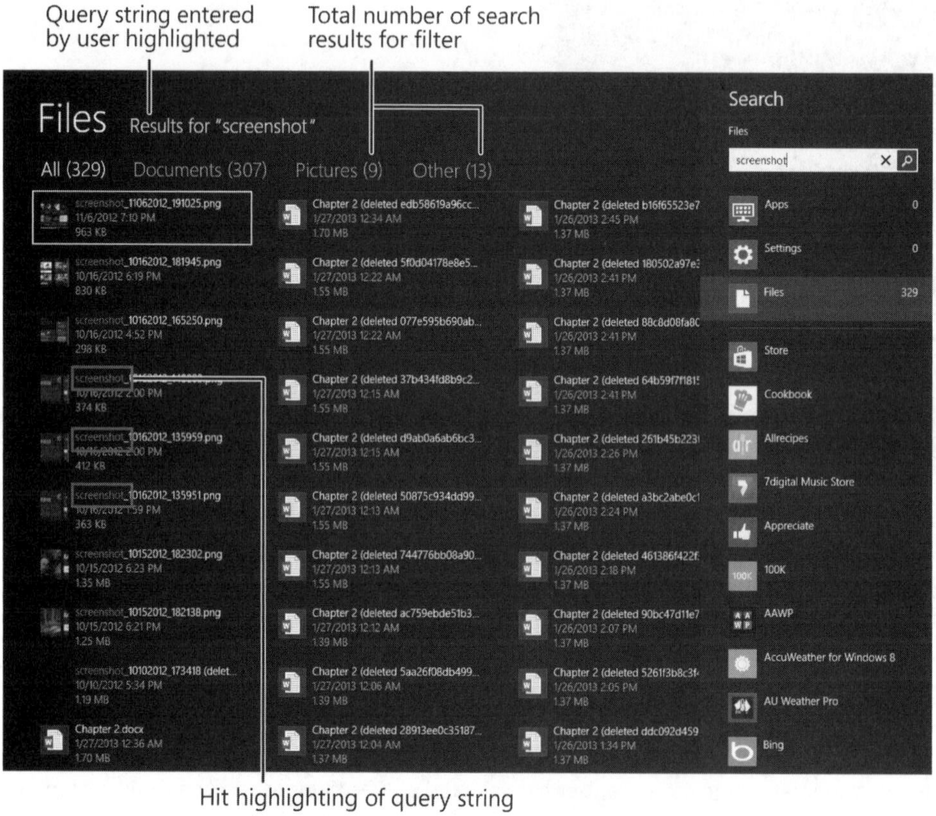

FIGURE 2-12 Search results obtained with the Files app in Windows 8

A Windows Store app can be activated when the user carries out a search query through the Search charm because the user chooses an app to search with when entering the query string. When the app activates, the *QueryText* property of the *SearchActivatedEventArgs* (in the *OnSearchActivated* method) provides the string entered by the user. The string can be used to carry out the search in the app.

It is possible for an app to activate with an empty *QueryText* string. In such a case, show the app's last-viewed page if the app is running or suspended. If the app isn't running or suspended, and is activated with an empty *QueryText* string, display the landing page for search results. In order to support scenarios in which your app is activated with an empty *QueryText* string, save the state of your app before the app is suspended or closed by the user.

If the app is in the snapped state when it is activated by the user carrying our search using the Search charm, the app automatically unsnaps. Therefore, the app should adjust itself to be the main app on the screen. You can use the *SizeChanged* event to adjust the layout of the app's search result page. Save the search results currently displayed in the app as well as the query string, in case the app is activated to search for that query again. If the search results are prone to change over time, you should refresh the search results after displaying the saved search results.

Design guidelines for the Share charm

In a Windows Store app that acts as a source of content to be shared, the typical user action is to swipe the side of the screen (or use the Windows+H keyboard shortcut); display the charm; press the Share charm; and, using the Share window, share content from within the app. The app provides the content, and the metadata is presented in the content preview. The app that is used to share content implements the Share Target contract.

One or more QuickLinks are shown under the Share heading in the Share charm. A *QuickLink* is a deep link that invokes the respective share target. An app displays QuickLinks and the applications linked through them if they are relevant to the content provided by the source application. When the target app reports the sharing operation has completed, it can return a QuickLink to be displayed in the share window. Figure 2-13 shows content being shared from an app with a list of QuickLinks in the Share charm as well as a list of apps that support the Share Target contract.

QuickLinks available
in the Share charm

Apps that support the
Share Target contract

FIGURE 2-13 Share charm with QuickLinks

In some cases, a sharing operation can take a long time to complete. In such cases, the user can switch to another app and reopen the share window to check the progress of the sharing operation. Windows will display a message in a dialog box from the target app if the sharing operation fails.

If your app acts like a share source, you should consider including links to content available online instead of the content that has been downloaded and saved locally. Your app should not modify the selection made by the user; for example, it shouldn't include a link to a web page if the user wants to share only a portion of the text from the web page. You should consider providing metadata to the shared content (such as a title and description) that conveys what the user is trying to share. Whenever possible, include a thumbnail of an image being shared or a link to a web page to provide a reference to the user.

The Share charm should always be invoked using the charms bar. Windows adds a default message indicating that sharing is not supported from an app. Users might want to share the same content with multiple apps; therefore, it is a good practice to preserve the content selected by the user for sharing.

When your app is selected as a share target, the UI shown to the user is a minimal version of the interface when your app is the only app that is visible on the screen. It is important for the app to present the essential features for sharing content similar to that of the app when it occupies the full screen. Your app should not dismiss the UI after the sharing operation is completed.

You should avoid complex interactions and application logic when implementing the share target UI. The target app should not wait for additional content to be downloaded while the Share UI is open; the download should be completed before the UI is displayed. If your app must download data or process content to be shared before the Share UI is displayed, a message informing the user that the sharing operation is underway is helpful. Place buttons that the user is likely to use through the Share UI on the right side of the Share charm, so they can be reached by the right thumb. Figure 2-14 shows the UI for a share target, the Mail app.

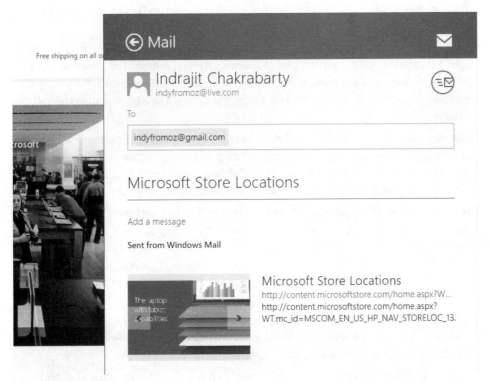

FIGURE 2-14 UI of the Mail app when used as the share target. Note that buttons should be placed on the right edge of the Share charm.

By acting as a source of content, your application has the capability to share content with devices in its close proximity as enabled by tap and send. Many Windows 8 devices have Near Field Communication (NFC) support and are capable of using tap and send with other Windows 8 devices and Windows Phone devices.

Design guidelines for the Settings charm

The Settings charm provides a simple, universally accessible entry point to your application with a single swipe from the right edge of a touch device or through the Windows+I keyboard shortcut. Windows automatically adds a set of commands to the Settings pane. These are the app name and publisher, a Rate and Review command that opens the app's page in the Windows Store, and a Permissions command if the app has any capabilities declared in the manifest. Your app can provide up to eight additional commands. Ideally, the maximum number of commands added in an app's Settings charm should be limited to four. If your app attempts to add more than eight commands to the Settings charm, an exception occurs.

The commands your app adds in the Settings charm are available throughout the app; that is, the commands are available through the Settings charm in all pages of the app. If a page requires commands specific to the page, implement these commands as menu items in the app bar.

A command in the Settings charm of a Windows Store app can either link to a web page or invoke a secondary flyout panel with more specific settings controls. The Windows Store app certification requirements make it mandatory for apps that collect any kind of personal information to provide a privacy policy. This is typically included as a command in the Settings charm.

Secondary settings flyout panels are limited to two sizes: narrow (346 pixels) or wide (646 pixels). In your Windows Store app, all the secondary panes should be the same size. The permissions flyout is provided by Windows, and the items listed in the flyout are configured according to the capabilities declared in your applications' manifest file.

It is recommended that your app should include account/profile management through the Settings charm because the user might want to update these settings from within any page in the app. When designing the settings flyout for a command, you should minimize the number of controls. Use simple controls such as toggle switches for on/off values, radio buttons for mutually exclusive items, list box controls for single/multiple value selection, and text input boxes wherever dynamic text input is required.

You should minimize vertical scrolling in a secondary flyout and avoid any hierarchy of settings. Place the controls in a secondary flyout in a single column and configure them so that any changes in the settings are committed instantaneously.

The Settings charm is a great location for engaging the user with your app and providing them with the option to communicate with you by providing feedback about your app, bug reports and submit feature requests. Figure 2-15 shows a feedback form included in the Weather app in Windows 8 through the settings flyout.

FIGURE 2-15 A feedback form included in the Weather app in Windows 8

A vertical scrollbar is automatically added by the Settings charm to the settings flyout if the content does not fit the space available vertically.

Configuring the app manifest for correct permissions

In your Windows Store app, you can consider implementing the Search contract and even add share target support. In both cases, you will need to declare these contracts in the app manifest so that the permissions required in your app are set up correctly. Note that you are not required to add the Share Target contract if your app acts as a share source only.

Visual Studio provides developers with the templates for implementing the Search contract and Share contract. When an app is created with one of these templates, Visual Studio adds the appropriate declaration to the app manifest. When you right-click your Windows Store project in Visual Studio and then click Add New Item, you are presented with the dialog box shown in Figure 2-16.

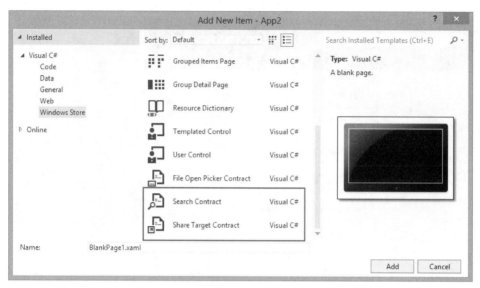

FIGURE 2-16 Visual Studio templates to add Share and Search contracts

Visual Studio adds a page that is shown when your app is chosen as the share target and code to override the *OnShareTargetActivated* method in the App.xaml.cs file. When your app acts as a share target, you are provided with the option to support multiple data formats such as text, uniform resource identifiers (URIs), bitmaps, Hypertext Markup Language (HTML), and/or file types such as .jpg and .docx. Your app is expected to support at least one data format or file type. The app manifest is where you configure the data formats and file types your app will support.

Visual Studio adds a search results page and code to override the *OnSearchActivated* method in the App.xaml.cs file. The method provides the text entered by the user through the *QueryText* property of the *SearchActivatedEventArgs* argument. You can show the search results page to the user using this method. Note that Windows Store apps can have only one instance of the declaration for Share and Search contracts.

In the Settings charm of your app, the system adds a command to display the permissions required by your app. Windows provides the Permissions flyout based on the capabilities declared in your application's manifest. Some capabilities such as location can be controlled by the user through the Permissions flyout.

Thought experiment

Porting a legacy app to a Windows Store app

In this thought experiment, apply what you've learned about this objective. You can find answers to these questions in the "Answers" section at the end of this chapter.

You have been asked to port a legacy desktop application to a Windows Store app. You are expected to focus on the UI and use key features available for Windows Store developers.

You determine that the ported app will appeal to users if you incorporate features such as searching the app for data and formatting, sending content via email, and connecting to printers.

Briefly explain the three steps you must take to incorporate search, share, and the capability to print content from your ported app.

Objective summary

- In your app's design, consider using the Search, Share, Devices, and Settings charms to help users interact with your app.
- You should provide query suggestions and result recommendation when you implement the Search contract and integrate it in your app through the Search charm.
- The UI provided by your app while implementing the Share Target contract should be minimal and simple for the user to use. You should integrate the Share Target contract in your app through the Share charm.
- The Settings charm provides an entry point for your application's settings, permissions, privacy statement, user session management, and a command to rate and review your app in the Windows Store.
- Contracts implemented in Windows Store apps must be declared in the app manifest; otherwise, exceptions will occur if the user tries to access the features implemented through the contract.

Objective review

Answer the following questions to test your knowledge of the information in this objective. You can find the answers to these questions and explanations of why each answer choice is correct or incorrect in the "Answers" section at the end of this chapter.

1. You are developing a Windows Store app and you have been asked to investigate the feasibility of supporting contracts in the app via the charms bar. Which Windows 8 contract features are applicable to your app? (Choose all that apply.)

    A. The charms bar is available only in touch-based devices.

    B. A Search contract can be used to search within a page that is currently visible.

    C. The app will be available as a share target if the Share Target contract is implemented.

    D. The Settings charm is available for all Windows Store apps to provide settings commands.

    E. Query suggestions and result recommendations improve the usability of the application.

2. In a Windows Store app, you can use the Settings charm to provide a number of commands with their respective settings flyouts. Which commands should you implement in the Settings charm for your app? (Choose all that apply.)

    A. Account/session management

    B. Theme preferences

    C. A shortcut to close the app

    D. An option for the user to provide feedback on the app

    E. An option to share content from within your app

3. You need to support app activation via search. Which event is invoked by the system in your app when it is activated?

    A. *OnWindowCreated*

    B. *OnLaunched*

    C. *OnSearchActivated*

    D. *OnActivated*

Objective 2.3: Implement search

While designing your Windows Store app, if you have planned to implement the Search contract, you should expose this feature via the Search charm. Adding the Search contract to your app through the Search charm enables the user to search within your app from anywhere within the system. Your app can provide search query suggestions and result suggestions while the user is searching through the Search charm.

When the user enters a search query string and selects your app from a list of apps that implement the Search contract, your app is activated by Windows if it is not running. The query string entered by the user is available through the *OnSearchActivated* method. You can implement a page in your app to display search results with a preview of each item. This page is shown whenever the *OnSearchActivated* method is invoked.

> **This objective covers how to:**
> - Provide and constrain search within an app.
> - Provide search result previews.
> - Provide search suggestions using the *SearchPane* class.
> - Implement activation from within search.
> - Search for and launch other apps.

Providing and constraining search within an app

Visual Studio makes it easy for developers to add the Search contract in their Windows Store apps. When you select the Search Contract template in Visual Studio, code is added to override the *OnSearchActivated* virtual method in the *Application* class in your Windows Store app, and the app manifest is updated with the correct permission, as shown in Figure 2-17.

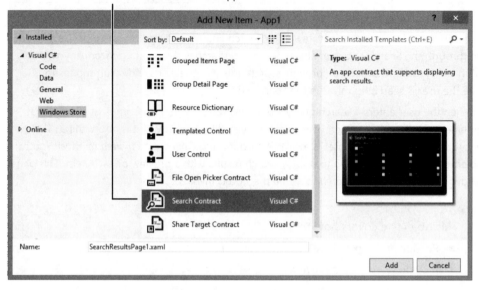

Visual Studio is used to add Search contract in a Windows Store app

Visual Studio updates the app manifest with correct permission

FIGURE 2-17 The Search Contract template available in Visual Studio can be used to implement Search Contract in a Windows Store app, which adds the correct permission in the package manifest

In order to speed up the search process when the app is visible on screen, the *Query-Submitted* event can be used instead of waiting for the *OnSearchActivated* method to be invoked by Windows. When the *QuerySubmitted* event is invoked, your app should respond by displaying the search results page and populating it with results using the query string available in the *QueryText* property of the *SearchPaneQuerySubmittedEventArgs* parameter for the event.

You should register an event handler for this event in the *Application* class, as shown in Listing 2-7.

LISTING 2-7 Registering an event handler in the *Application* class

```
using Windows.Foundation;
using Windows.ApplicationModel;
using Windows.ApplicationModel.Activation;
using Windows.ApplicationModel.Search;
// Other namespaces removed for brevity

sealed partial class App : Application
{
    protected override void OnWindowCreated(WindowCreatedEventArgs args)
    {
        SearchPane.GetForCurrentView().QuerySubmitted +=
            OnQuerySubmitted;
    }

    // Event handler for the QuerySubmitted event
    private void OnQuerySubmitted(object sender,
        SearchPaneQuerySubmittedEventArgs args)
    {
        // Use the query string in args.QueryText to initiate the search and navigate
        // to the Search results page
        var previousContent = Window.Current.Content;
        var frame = previousContent as Frame;

        if (frame != null)
        {
            frame.Navigate(typeof(SearchResultsPage), args.QueryText);

            Window.Current.Content = frame;
            Window.Current.Activate();
        }
    }
}
```

The search results page added by Visual Studio contains a *GridView* control and a *ListView* control to display the results in various view states; these controls are arranged in a *Grid* control. You can modify the *DataTemplate* of these controls to lay out the results from the search query.

> **MORE INFO**   **VIEW STATES AND CONTROLS**
>
> You will learn about view states, grids, the *Grid* and *GridView* controls, and the *ListView* control in Chapter 3.

The query string typed by the user is available in the app through the *OnSearchActivated* method or the *QuerySubmitted* event and is passed to the search results with the *Navigate* method. You must implement the search mechanism and create a list of user-selectable result categories. The search results page contains a Back button to let users navigate back to the page where they were before carrying out the search. Without writing any code in the *SearchResultsPage* class, the UI of the search results page is shown in Figure 2-18.

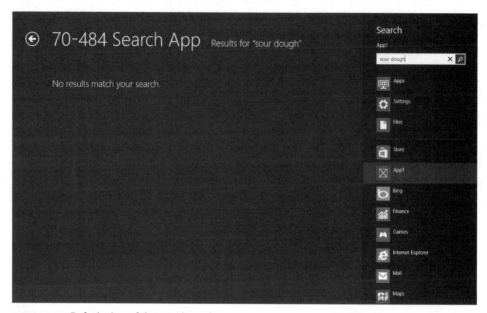

FIGURE 2-18 Default view of the search results page

When your app does not return any results in the search, the user can clear the query string, type a new string, and carry out the search again. The system raises a *QueryChanged* event whenever the user changes the search query, with the *SearchQueryChangedEventArgs* providing the query string in your app. To speed up the search process, you can register for this event and carry out the search whenever this event is raised. Listing 2-8 registers your app for the *QueryChanged* event and responds to the event.

LISTING 2-8 Registering *an app for the QueryChanged event*

```
using Windows.Foundation;
using Windows.ApplicationModel;
using Windows.ApplicationModel.Activation;
using Windows.ApplicationModel.Search;
// Other namespaces removed for brevity

sealed partial class App : Application
{
    protected override void OnWindowCreated(WindowCreatedEventArgs args)
    {
        SearchPane.GetForCurrentView().QuerySubmitted +=
            OnQuerySubmitted;
```

```
        SearchPane.GetForCurrentView().QueryChanged +=
            OnQueryChanged;
    }


    // Event handler for the QuerySubmitted event
    private void OnQuerySubmitted(object sender,
        SearchPaneQuerySubmittedEventArgs args)
    {
        // Use the query string in args.QueryText to initiate the search and navigate
        // to the Search results page
        var previousContent = Window.Current.Content;
        var frame = previousContent as Frame;

        if (frame != null)
        {
            frame.Navigate(typeof(SearchResultsPage), args.QueryText);

            Window.Current.Content = frame;
            Window.Current.Activate();
        }
    }

    // Event handler for the QueryChanged event
    private void OnQueryChanged(object sender,
        SearchPaneQueryChangedEventArgs args)
    {
        // Use the query string in args.QueryText to clear the search results page and
        // carry out a new search
    }
}
```

The Search charm, if visible, is dismissed whenever the user swipes or taps the search results screen or clicks an item. You might want users to be able to carry out search by opening
the Search charm when they start typing on the keyboard. You can add the ability to access
the Search charm from the keyboard in your app's main page and the search results page. To
implement this feature, turn on type to search in the *OnNavigatedTo* event in the page and
turn it off in the *OnNavigatedFrom* event, as shown in the following code:

```
using Windows.UI.Xaml.Navigation;
using Windows.ApplicationModel.Search;

public sealed partial class SearchResultsPage : Page
{
    // Turn on type to search.
    protected override void OnNavigatedTo(NavigationEventArgs args)
    {
        SearchPane.GetForCurrentView().ShowOnKeyboardInput = true;
        base.OnNavigatedTo(args);
    }

    // Turn off type to search
    protected override void OnNavigatedFrom(NavigationEventArgs args)
```

```
        {
            SearchPane.GetForCurrentView().ShowOnKeyboardInput = false;
            base.OnNavigatedFrom(args);
        }
    }
```

Providing search result previews

When you add support for the Search contract in your Windows Store app, Visual Studio adds the XAML for the controls that display the search results in the autogenerated search results page. The default data template of each item in the search results page is shown in Listing 2-9 (defined in StandardStyles.xaml).

LISTING 2-9 Default data template of items in the search results page

```xml
<!-- Grid-appropriate 300 by 70 pixel item template as seen in the SearchResultsPage -->
<DataTemplate x:Key="StandardSmallIcon300x70ItemTemplate">
    <Grid Width="294" Margin="6">
        <Grid.ColumnDefinitions>
            <ColumnDefinition Width="Auto"/>
            <ColumnDefinition Width="*"/>
        </Grid.ColumnDefinitions>
        <Border Background="{StaticResource
                ListViewItemPlaceholderBackgroundThemeBrush}"
                Margin="0,0,0,10" Width="40" Height="40">
            <Image Source="{Binding Image}" Stretch="UniformToFill"/>
        </Border>
        <StackPanel Grid.Column="1" Margin="10,-10,0,0">
            <TextBlock Text="{Binding Title}" Style="{StaticResource BodyTextStyle}"
                    TextWrapping="NoWrap"/>
            <TextBlock Text="{Binding Subtitle}" Style="{StaticResource BodyTextStyle}"
                    Foreground="{StaticResource
                        ApplicationSecondaryForegroundThemeBrush}"
                    TextWrapping="NoWrap"/>
            <TextBlock Text="{Binding Description}" Style="{StaticResource
                        BodyTextStyle}"
                    Foreground="{StaticResource
                        ApplicationSecondaryForegroundThemeBrush}"
                    TextWrapping="NoWrap"/>
        </StackPanel>
    </Grid>
</DataTemplate>
```

The search results page is designed for a specific data model. It expects you to define a class and represent each item of the user's search result with this class. Such a class is shown in the following example:

```
sealed class SearchResultItem
{
    public Uri Image { get; set; }
    public string Title { get; set; }
    public string Subtitle { get; set; }
    public string Description { get; set; }
}
```

The *LoadState* method for your search results page is invoked with the search query string passed through navigation arguments in the *OnSearchActivated* method or the *QuerySubmitted* event. You should initialize the search, and query your web service or local data source within this event.

After you have the search results, cache them until the user carries out the search again. At that point, process the results to set up the filters and the data collection that binds with the data control in the page, as shown in Listing 2-10.

LISTING 2-10 Setting up filters and the data collection for search results

```
// Populates the page with content passed during navigation.
protected override void LoadState(object navigationParameter,
                    Dictionary<string, object> pageState)
{
    var queryString = navigationParameter as string;
    List<SearchResultItem> SearchResultCollection = new List<SearchResultItem>();

    // Carry out the search using your web service or local data source and populate
    // the SearchResultCollection.


    // Prepare filters based on the categories in the search result.
    var filters = new List<Filter>();
    filters.Add(new Filter("All", this.SearchResultCollection.Count, true)); // Default
    filters.Add(new Filter("Recipes", this.SearchResultCollection. Count(item =>
            item.Category = "Recipes"), false));
    filters.Add(new Filter("Items", this.SearchResultCollection. Count(item =>
            item.Category = "Items"), false));

    this.DefaultViewModel["QueryText"] = '\u201c' + queryString + '\u201c';
    this.DefaultViewModel["Filters"] = filters;
    this.DefaultViewModel["ShowFilters"] = filters.Count > 1;

    // Prepare the results for the "All" filter
    this.DefaultViewModel["Results"] = this.SearchResultCollection.Select(item =>
                        new SearchResultItem {
                            Image = item.ImageUri,
                            Title = item.Title,
                            Subtitle = item.Subtitle,
                            Description = item.Description
                        }).ToList();
}
```

The result of a search carried out with a Windows Store app is shown in Figure 2-19.

FIGURE 2-19 Search results in a Windows Store app with previews of search result items

When you provide a preview for each search result item along with a filter that the user can choose to view a subset of all the items displayed, it is easier for the user to browse through the search results.

Providing search suggestions using the *SearchPane* class

When your app is used to search for content, Windows automatically provides a history of the user's recent searches. You can enhance the user experience by providing query suggestions and result suggestions in your app. You might decide to support only one of them based on your app's requirements and design decisions. Your app can obtain search suggestions from a variety of sources, such as:

- From a remote web service, a local database, or a static list in the app
- From a uniform resource locator (URL) that supports suggestions in the OpenSearch format
- From a URL that supports suggestions in the XML search suggestions format

> *MORE INFO*   **OPENSEARCH FORMAT AND XML SEARCH SUGGESTIONS**
>
> You can learn about the OpenSearch format specification at *http://www.opensearch.org/ Specifications/OpenSearch/Extensions/Suggestions*. The XML search suggestions specification is available at *http://msdn.microsoft.com/library/cc891508.aspx*.

Your app can provide search suggestions as the user types in the search box in an event handler of the *SuggestionsRequested* event provided by the *SearchPane* class. This event is fired multiple times as the user types the search query string. A maximum of five search suggestions are shown in the Search charm even if your app adds more suggestions to the list. In the event handler, you should check for a match of the query string with data in your app, as shown in Listing 2-11.

LISTING 2-11 Checking for a match between the query string and app data

```
using Windows.Foundation;
using Windows.ApplicationModel;
using Windows.ApplicationModel.Activation;
using Windows.ApplicationModel.Search;
// Other namespaces removed for brevity

sealed partial class App : Application
{
    // Override the OnWindowCreated event to register the QuerySubmitted and
    // QueryChanged event handlers at window creation time. This registration
    // happens only once so that the app can receive user queries at any time.
    protected override void OnWindowCreated(WindowCreatedEventArgs args)
    {
        SearchPane.GetForCurrentView().QuerySubmitted +=
            OnQuerySubmitted;

        SearchPane.GetForCurrentView().QueryChanged +=
            OnQueryChanged;

        // Subscribe to SuggestionsRequested event to provide suggestions
SearchPane.GetForCurrentView().SuggestionsRequested +=
            OnSuggestionsRequested;
    }

    // Event handler for the SuggestionsRequested event
    private void OnSuggestionsRequested(object sender,
        SearchPaneSuggestionsRequestedEventArgs args)
    {
        // Use the query string in args.QueryText to look up a remote web service
        // or a database.
        if (!string.IsNullOrEmpty(args.QueryText))
        {
            List<string> suggestions = QueryDatabaseForSuggestions(args.QueryText);
            foreach (string suggestion in suggestions)
            {

                // Note: Only a maximum of five items are shown.
                args.Request.SearchSuggestionCollection.AppendQuerySuggestion(
                    suggestion);
            }
        }
    }
}
```

Figure 2-20 shows the search suggestions from a Windows Store app as the user starts typing a search query.

FIGURE 2-20 Search pane with search suggestions from a Windows Store app

In a Windows Store app that provides search suggestions, by default the Search pane will add the user's previous searches and include them in the suggestions as well. The *SuggestionsRequested* event places search queries from previous searches in the Search pane at a higher priority than the suggestions provided by your app. You can turn off this behavior by setting *SearchPane*'s *SearchHistoryEnabled* property to *False* when you set up the event handler for the *SuggestionsRequested* event (within the *OnWindowCreated* method override in the *Application* class).

You can add one or more recommendations in the search suggestions based on the query string entered by the user. You might want to add a separator with a headline indicating this. Note that the maximum of five items in the list of search suggestions rule still applies. Therefore, a separator counts as one item in the list.

To provide result recommendations within your search suggestions, you should use the *AppendSearchSeparator* and *AppendResultSuggestion* methods of the *SearchSuggestionCollection* member in the *SearchPaneSuggestionsRequestedEventArgs* argument of the *SuggestionsRequested* event. You can add a thumbnail for the recommendation (an image sized 40 × 40) as an *IRandomAccessStreamReference*. The *AppendResultSuggestion* method accepts a tag in the third parameter for the result recommendation. The tag is useful for identifying the recommendation when the recommendation is selected by the user in the Search charm. Listing 2-12 shows how a result recommendation is added to the list of results.

LISTING 2-12 Adding a recommendation to a list of results

```
// Event handler for the SuggestionsRequested event
private void OnSuggestionsRequested(object sender,
        SearchPaneSuggestionsRequestedEventArgs args)
```

```
{
    // Use the query string in args.QueryText to look up a remote web service
    // or a database.
    if (!string.IsNullOrEmpty(args.QueryText))
    {
        List<string> suggestions = QueryDatabaseForSuggestions(args.QueryText);
        foreach (string suggestion in suggestions)
        {
            args.Request.SearchSuggestionCollection.AppendQuerySuggestion(
                suggestion);
        }

        if (args.QueryText.ToLower().Contains("sugar"))
        {
            IRandomAccessStreamReference thumbnail =
                RandomAccessStreamReference.CreateFromUri(new
                    Uri("http://contoso.com/sberries.jpg"));
            args.Request.SearchSuggestionCollection.AppendSearchSeparator(
                "Recommended for you");
            // "sugar-berry" is the tag
            args.Request.SearchSuggestionCollection.AppendResultSuggestion("Sugar coated
                strawberries", "Sugar coated strawberries are great for afternoon tea",
                "sugar-berry",
                        thumbnail, "Sugar coated strawberries");
        }
    }
}
```

Figure 2-21 shows the Search pane for a Windows Store app with a result recommendation for the user.

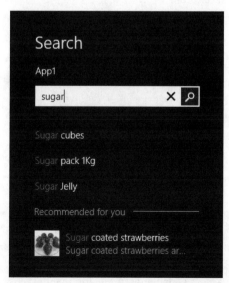

FIGURE 2-21 Search pane with search suggestions and a recommendation for the user from a Windows Store app

When the user selects one of the suggested results provided by your app and displayed in the Search pane, the system raises the *ResultSuggestionChosen* event. The result suggestion's tag is provided with this event and it can be used to highlight the search query string in the result. You should set up your Windows Store app with an event handler for the *ResultSuggestionChosen* event, as shown in Listing 2-13.

LISTING 2-13 Creating an event handler for the *ResultSuggestionChosen* event

```
using Windows.Foundation;
using Windows.ApplicationModel;
using Windows.ApplicationModel.Activation;
using Windows.ApplicationModel.Search;
// Other namespaces removed for brevity

sealed partial class App : Application
{
    // Override the OnWindowCreated event to register the QuerySubmitted &
    // QueryChanged event handlers at window creation time. This registration
    // happens only once so that the app can receive user queries at any time.
    protected override void OnWindowCreated(WindowCreatedEventArgs args)
    {
        SearchPane.GetForCurrentView().QuerySubmitted +=
            OnQuerySubmitted;

        SearchPane.GetForCurrentView().QueryChanged +=
            OnQueryChanged;

        // Subscribe to SuggestionsRequested event to provide suggestions from
        // your app.
        SearchPane.GetForCurrentView().SuggestionsRequested +=
            OnSuggestionsRequested;

        // Subscribe to ResultSuggestionChosen event to highlight the selected item.
        SearchPane.GetForCurrentView().ResultSuggestionChosen +=
            OnResultSuggestionChosen;
    }

    // Event handler for the ResultSuggestionChosen event
    private void OnResultSuggestionChosen(object sender,
        SearchPaneResultSuggestionChosenEventArgs args)
    {
        // Use the tag in the event argument to highlight a result.
    }
}
```

In some Windows Store apps, you might decide to provide suggestions based on local files present in the system. You can invoke the *SetLocalContentSuggestionSettings* method of the *SearchPane* class with an instance of the *LocalContentSuggestionSettings* class to specify the locations of files that are used to provide suggestions and a list of file properties to use. Note that your app must declare the relevant folder access capabilities in the app manifest to access those files. You can use the *PropertiesToMatch* property of the *LocalContentSuggestionSettings* class to specify a list of file properties used to provide the suggestions. If the list is empty, all the file properties that are available are used for suggestions. The *AqsFilter* property can be used to specify an Advanced Query Syntax (AQS) string to limit the types and kinds of files that are included in the suggestions. The following code shows how to set up the *LocalContentSuggestionSettings* class to provide photo suggestions from the Pictures library:

```
using Windows.ApplicationModel.Search;
using Windows.Storage;
using Windows.UI.Xaml.Navigation;

sealed partial class App : Application
{

    protected override void OnWindowCreated(WindowCreatedEventArgs args)
    {
        var settings = new LocalContentSuggestionSettings();
        settings.Enabled = true; // You have to set this explicitly
        settings.Locations.Add(KnownFolders.PicturesLibrary);
        settings.AqsFilter = "kind:pics";
        SearchPane.GetForCurrentView().SetLocalContentSuggestionSettings(settings);
    }
}
```

Implementing activation from within search

When a user opens the Search charm, a list of apps appears that can be selected to perform the search. If your app is not visible in the screen and is selected by the user in the Search charm to carry out the search, it is activated and is visible in the screen. The *OnSearchActivated* method or the *QuerySubmitted* event is invoked in your app with the search query provided in the *QueryText* property of the event argument. Visual Studio adds the *OnSearchActivated* method when you use the Search contract template, as shown in Listing 2-14.

LISTING 2-14 Overriding the *OnSearchActivated* method

```
protected async override void OnSearchActivated(SearchActivatedEventArgs args)
{
    var previousContent = Window.Current.Content;
    var frame = previousContent as Frame;

    if (frame == null)
    {
        frame = new Frame();
        SuspensionManager.RegisterFrame(frame, "AppFrame");

        if (args.PreviousExecutionState == ApplicationExecutionState.Terminated)
        {
            try
            {
                await SuspensionManager.RestoreAsync();
            }
            catch (SuspensionManagerException)
            {
```

```
                // Error restoring state, continue.
            }
        }
    }

    frame.Navigate(typeof(SearchResultsPage), args.QueryText);
    Window.Current.Content = frame;
    Window.Current.Activate();
}
```

If your app is restored from a suspended state or if it is started anew, you might want to check the *PreviousExecutionState* and perform initialization before proceeding with the search. In some cases, simply showing an extended splash screen provides a good user experience.

EXAM TIP

You are not expected to remember all the events and methods required to implement the Search contract for the exam. However, it is important for you to know the way search works in a Windows Store app.

Searching for and launching other apps

In a Windows Store app, you can provide the user with the option to search for content within the app and include local content such as files of specific types in the search results. Your app might be capable of opening these files for the user or it might launch another app that supports the file type or a URI scheme association.

A Windows Store app can launch another app with the *Launcher* class (in the *Windows. System* namespace) using either of two methods:

- **LaunchFileAsync** Starts the default app associated with the specified file, optionally including the specified *LauncherOptions*.
- **LaunchUriAsync** Starts the default app associated with the URI scheme name for the specified URI, optionally including the specified *LauncherOptions*.

The *LauncherOptions* class specifies the options used to launch the default app for the file or URI. It has the following properties:

- **ContentType** Gets or sets the content type associated with the URI of a file on the network.
- **DisplayApplicationPicker** Gets or sets a value for a flag that indicates whether the Open With dialog box should be shown.
- **FallbackUri** Gets or sets a value of a URI that the browser should open if there is no app to handle the file type or URI.
- **PreferredApplicationDisplayName** Gets or sets a value of the display name of the app in the Windows Store that the user should install if there is no app to handle the file type or URI.

- **PreferredApplicationPackageFamilyName**   Gets or sets a value of the package family name of the app in the Windows Store that the user should install if there is no app to handle the file type or URI.

> **NOTE USING APPROPRIATE PROPERTIES**
>
> The PreferredApplicationDisplayName and PreferredApplicationPackageFamilyName properties should be used together.

- **TreatAsUntrusted**   Get or sets a value for a flag that indicates if the system should display a warning that the file or URI is potentially unsafe when starting the app with the file or URI.
- **UI**   Gets the UI options when starting a default app. The value of this property is a *LauncherUIOptions* object. The object contains details such as the position of the UI element associated with the app that was launched.

Thought experiment
Building a search-friendly Windows Store app

In this thought experiment, apply what you've learned about this objective. You can find answers to these questions in the "Answers" section at the end of this chapter.

Your Windows Store app has received feedback from users asking you to include the capability to search content in your app. You have investigated the feasibilty of supporting search in your app.

What are the four steps you should take to support search in your app?

Objective summary

- You should use the *QuerySubmitted* and *QueryChanged* events to implement search in your Windows Store app when it is visible on the screen.
- You should provide a preview of the items listed in your app's search result page. Users can browse the details of a result by looking at the preview of the item.
- Search suggestions and result recommendations enhance the user experience of a Windows Store app. Whenever required, you can turn off the search history of the user for your app.
- You should ensure that your app is activated when the user selects it after entering a search string.
- If your app includes local files in the search results, you should ensure your app can launch Windows Store apps that can open these files.

Objective review

Answer the following questions to test your knowledge of the information in this objective. You can find the answers to these questions and explanations of why each answer choice is correct or incorrect in the "Answers" section at the end of this chapter.

1. You are preparing to implement the Search contract in your app. Which event handlers should you consider implementing in your app to provide a rich user experience? (Choose all that apply.)

   A. The *QuerySubmitted* event, which fires when the user submits a search query

   B. The *QueryChanged* event, which fires when the user changes a search query

   C. The *Loaded event of the Page class.* which fires when the search results page is loaded

   D. The *OnSearchActivated* event, which fires when the app is activated through search

   E. The *Unloaded* event of the You can use the *SearchPane* class to provide search suggestions to your app's users. Which event should you handle to provide search suggestions?

   F. *QueryChanged*

   G. *SuggestionsRequested*

   H. *ResultSuggestionChosen*

   I. *QuerySubmitted*

2. When your app provides result suggestions to the user performing a search, which event is fired to indicate that a suggested result has been selected by the user?

   A. *ResultSuggestionChosen*

   B. *QuerySubmitted*

   C. *QueryChanged*

   D. *SuggestionsRequested*

Objective 2.4: Implement Share in an app

Windows Store apps can share data with other apps in a variety of ways. Applications with a lot of text can use the Clipboard for copying and pasting content. Other apps can share content by saving it in a file and providing a save location and real-time file updates to other apps through the File Open Picker contract, File Save Picker contract, and Cached File Updater contract. The Share Target contract in Windows Store apps provides a simple, in-context, and universal experience to users interested in sharing content.

A Windows Store app can share data with other apps with the *DataTransferManager* class. A *DataTransferManager* object is available in every page that provides content to be shared with others apps. The content shared by an app can be limited by using the *DataPackage* object. An app can implement the Share Target contract and be activated through the *OnShareTargetActivated* event when another app selects it for sharing content.

> **This objective covers how to:**
> - Use the *DataTransferManager* class to share data with other apps.
> - Limit the scope of sharing using the *DataPackage* object.
> - Accept sharing requests by implementing activation from within Share.
> - Implement in-app share outside of the Share charm.

Using the *DataTransferManager* class to share data with other apps

If your Windows Store app contains data that can be shared with other apps, your app can be a share source without implementing a contract or configuring anything in the app manifest. By acting as a share source, your app can share rich, meaningful content such as thumbnails and images, rich text, files, and custom data. It also enables your app to decide the content that should be shared, unlike the use of the Clipboard, in which the user explicitly selects and copies data.

The *Windows.ApplicationModel.DataTransfer* namespace provides a number of classes for a Windows Store app to exchange data between a source app and a target app. These classes are used in share and Clipboard copy/paste operations.

To act as a share source, your app needs to implement an event handler for the *DataRequested* event, usually in the *OnNavigatedTo* event in a page, as shown in Listing 2-15.

LISTING 2-15 Implementing an event handler for the *DataRequested* event

```
// Register the current page as a share source
protected override void OnNavigatedTo(NavigationEventArgs args)
{
    DataTransferManager dtManager = DataTransferManager.GetForCurrentView();
    dtManager.DataRequested += OnDataRequested;
}

// Unregister the current page as a share source
protected override void OnNavigatedFromNavigationEventArgs args)
{
    DataTransferManager dtManager = DataTransferManager.GetForCurrentView();
    dtManager.DataRequested -= OnDataRequested;
}

// Event handler for the DataRequested event
private void OnDataRequested(DataTransferManager sender, DataRequestedEventArgs args)
{
```

```
        DataRequest request = args.Request;
        request.Data.Properties.Title = "70-484 Share text example";
        request.Data.Properties.Description = "A demo of how a Windows Store app can
                    act as share source";
        request.Data.SetText("Hello Exam 70-484!");
}
```

Figure 2-22 shows the Share pane when a Windows Store app shares content from within a page.

Once the mail app is selected for sharing content, the Share pane is populated with content from the app

The Share charm shows a list of applications available for sharing content

FIGURE 2-22 Share charm with a list of apps available for sharing content and the Share pane with content shared by a Windows Store app

It is the responsibility of the target app to use the data shared by your Windows Store app. The target app might not be able to read all the data in the *Properties* object set by the source app. When the Share charm is invoked, two properties you set through the *DataRequest* object are shown in the Share pane: *Title* and *Description*. You should ensure that, in the source app, the actual data to be shared is specified in all the formats supported by the app, such as plain text, HTML, URI, RTF, *IStorageItem* (when sharing a binary file), image, or custom. (Figure 2-25, later in this chapter, shows the formats.) If your app provides data in multiple formats, there is a greater chance of the shared data to work with more Windows Store apps. The target app might prefer to use a specific type of content in the *DataRequest* object. For example, if HTML content and plain text content are both available in the *DataRequest* object, the Mail app will use the HTML content instead of the text content.

You should note that the target app cannot process arbitrary HTML content from your Windows Store app. You should use the *CreateHtmlFormat* method in the *HtmlFormatHelper* class (in the *Windows.ApplicationModel.DataTransfer* namespace) to prepare HTML content, as shown in the following code:

```
// Event handler for the DataRequested event
private void OnDataRequested(DataTransferManager sender, DataRequestedEventArgs args)
{
    DataRequest request = args.Request;
    request.Data.Properties.Title = "70-484 Share text example";
    request.Data.Properties.Description = "A demo of how a Windows Store app can
                act as share source";
    request.Data.SetText("Hello Exam 70-484!");
    request.Data.SetHtmlFormat(HtmlFormatHelper.CreateHtmlFormat("
                <i>Exam 70-484 </i><b>rocks!</b>"));
}
```

A Windows Store app can contain a number of pages from which the user will share content. To facilitate sharing, you need to subscribe/unsubscribe for the *DataRequested* event and implement the event handler that packages the data in the *DataRequest* object. It is a good practice to implement the subscribe/unsubscribe code in an abstract base class and provide the implementation of the event handler in the pages from which the user will share content. Such an abstract class is shown in Listing 2-16.

LISTING 2-16 Using an abstract base class for sharing tasks

```
// Namespace usings removed for brevity. LayoutAwarePage is a class that derives from
// the Page class. It adds a number of features to the Page class, you will learn about
// these features in the next objective.
public abstract class SharePageBase : LayoutAwarePage
{

    private DataTransferManager dataTransferManager;

    protected override void OnNavigatedTo(NavigationEventArgs args)
    {
        this.dataTransferManager = DataTransferManager.GetForCurrentView();
        this.dataTransferManager.DataRequested += OnDataRequested;
    }

    protected override void OnNavigatedFrom(NavigationEventArgs args)
    {
        this.dataTransferManager = DataTransferManager.GetForCurrentView();
        this.dataTransferManager.DataRequested -= OnDataRequested;
    }

    private void OnDataRequested(DataTransferManager sender,
                            DataRequestedEventArgs args)
    {
        SetupShareContent(args.Request);
    }

    // This method is implemented by each page that acts as a share source.
    public abstract void SetupShareContent(DataRequest request);
}
```

When the user chooses a target for sharing the data from a source app, the system fires a *TargetApplicationChosen* event in the *DataTransferManager* class. You can use this event in your Windows Store app to record information about the target app used for sharing the content from your app. You can use this event to log and record the apps used by the user to share the content, thereby improving the user experience in future releases of your app.

In some cases, a Windows Store app can fail to share data with a target app. You can handle such situations using the *FailWithDisplayText* method available in the *DataRequest* object in the *OnDataRequested* event handler to display a text message to the user if anything goes wrong when your app is sharing content.

Accepting sharing requests by implementing activation within the Share charm

A Windows Store app can act both as a share source and share target. In the latter case, it must implement the Share Target contract. This contract sets up your Windows Store app to be presented as an option when the user invokes the Share charm, and the data shared from the source app is supported by your app. Your app has the option to support a definite number of formats, and you should register for only the formats your app can handle.

If you want your app to receive content shared by other apps, you should configure your app's manifest file to indicate that it supports the Share Target contract. This step ensures that Windows includes your app as an option when the user invokes the Share charm when data formats supported by your app are shared. Windows shows only those target apps that support the data format used for sharing the content.

In a Windows Store app that acts as a share target, most of the work during a share operation is handled by the *ShareOperation* class in the *Windows.ApplicationModel.DataTransfer. ShareTarget* namespace. In addition, the *QuickLink* class is used to represent shortcuts that help users share content with apps they use most. Your app can optionally return a QuickLink created after the sharing operation is completed. The QuickLink then appears in a list whenever the Share charm is opened for sharing content. QuickLinks make it easier and simpler for users to frequently share content with the same person or group.

Visual Studio provides developers with a template for adding the Share Target contract in a Windows Store app. When you click the Add|New Item menu option in your Visual Studio Windows Store project, you have an option to add Share Target Contract to your app (see Figure 2-23). This step adds the appropriate declaration to the package manifest and adds a new page, which is used by other apps to share content with your app.

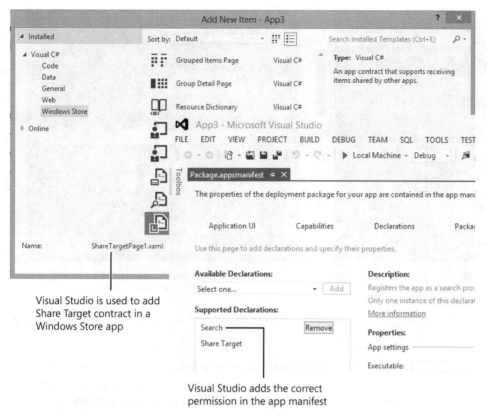

Visual Studio is used to add Share Target contract in a Windows Store app

Visual Studio adds the correct permission in the app manifest

FIGURE 2-23 Adding the Share Target contract in a Windows Store app

Visual Studio adds the following code when your app is activated for sharing by another Windows Store app when content is ready to be shared:

```
// Invoked when the application is activated as the target of a sharing operation.
protected override void OnShareTargetActivated(ShareTargetActivatedEventArgs args)
{
    var shareTargetPage = new ShareTargetSample.ShareTargetPage();
    shareTargetPage.Activate(args);
}
```

If your app includes the Share Target contract, the app will appear in the list of available apps for sharing user content. If you select your app, a basic UI for the Share Target page appears, as shown in Figure 2-24.

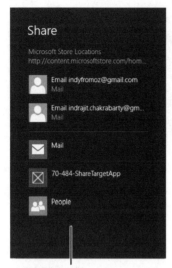

The Share charm shows a
list of applications available
for sharing content

The default page provided by Visual Studio
for sharing content from other apps

FIGURE 2-24 Share pane with your app (left) and the default Share Target page hosted in the Share pane (right)

The data that is shared with your app is contained in the *ShareOperation* object in the *ShareTargetActivatedEventArgs* event argument. The *OnShareTargetActivated* method override added by Visual Studio in the *Application* class can be used to navigate to the Share Target page in the app. In the *OnNavigatedTo* method of the Share Target page, you can retrieve the shared data by examining the *DataPackageView* object, as shown in Listing 2-17.

LISTING 2-17 Navigating to the Share Target page

```
// This method defined in the Application class is invoked when the application
// is activated as the target of a sharing operation. It is used to navigate to the
// Share Target page.
protected override void OnShareTargetActivated(ShareTargetActivatedEventArgs args)
{
    var rootFrame = new Frame();
    rootFrame.Navigate(typeof(ShareTargetPage), args.ShareOperation);
    Window.Current.Content = rootFrame;
    Window.Current.Activate();
}

// This method defined in the Share Target page is invoked when the page is shown
// to the user.
```

```
protected override async void OnNavigatedTo(NavigationEventArgs args)
{
    ShareOperation shareOperation = (ShareOperation)args.Parameter;
    this._shareOperation = ShareOperation; // Save a copy for use in other events

    this.sharedDataTitle = shareOperation.Data.Properties.Title;
    this.sharedDataDescription = shareOperation.Data.Properties.Description;

    // Check the DataPackageView for the data formats and use them accordingly
    if (shareOperation.Data.Contains(StandardDataFormats.Uri))
    {
        try
        {
            this.sharedUri = await ShareOperation.Data.GetUriAsync();
        }
        catch (Exception)
        {
            // Notify user of the exception.
        }
    }
    if (shareOperation.Data.Contains(StandardDataFormats.Text))
    {
        try
        {
            this.sharedText = await ShareOperation.Text.GetUriAsync();
        }
        catch (Exception)
        {
            // Notify user of the exception.
        }
    }
}
```

Visual Studio adds the Text and URI data formats in the package manifest when the Share Target template is used. You can add more data formats in the package manifest of your app; these formats are mapped to the members of the *StandardDataFormat* enumeration. The system extracts information about your app's supported data formats and file types from the package manifest. It is therefore important to update the manifest with the data formats and file types your app supports, as shown in Figure 2-25.

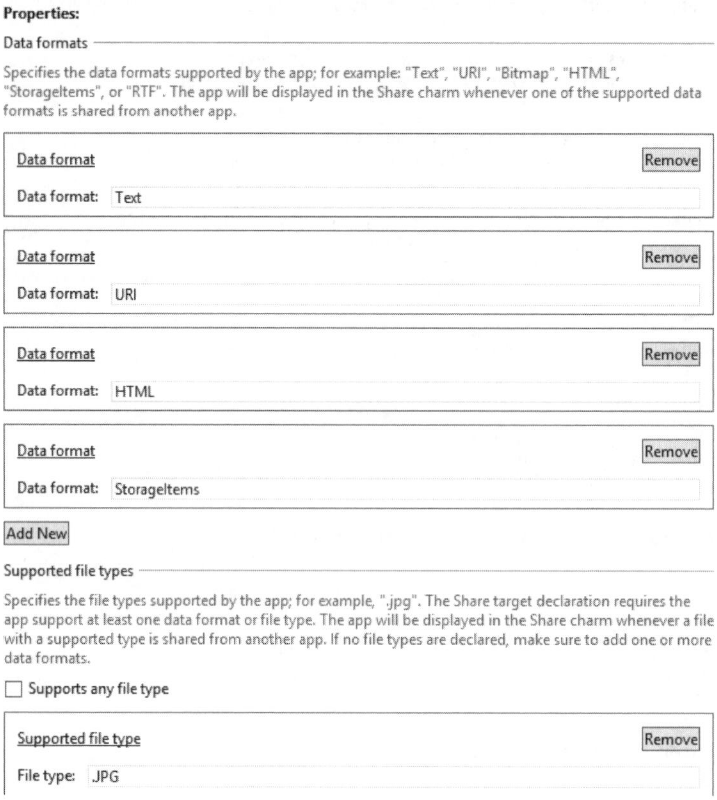

Properties:

Data formats ───

Specifies the data formats supported by the app; for example: "Text", "URI", "Bitmap", "HTML", "StorageItems", or "RTF". The app will be displayed in the Share charm whenever one of the supported data formats is shared from another app.

Data format	Remove
Data format: Text	

Data format	Remove
Data format: URI	

Data format	Remove
Data format: HTML	

Data format	Remove
Data format: StorageItems	

Add New

Supported file types ───

Specifies the file types supported by the app; for example, ".jpg". The Share target declaration requires the app support at least one data format or file type. The app will be displayed in the Share charm whenever a file with a supported type is shared from another app. If no file types are declared, make sure to add one or more data formats.

☐ Supports any file type

Supported file type	Remove
File type: .JPG	

FIGURE 2-25 Data formats and file types supported in a Windows Store app specified in the package manifest

When a user has selected your app to share content, you should not force the user to remain with the share UI if your app takes time to parse the data to be shared. You should instead use the *ReportStarted* method of the *ShareOperation* object to inform the system that your app is processing the request to share content. This ensures the share operation continues to run in your app even after the user dismisses the share UI and returns to the source app.

The user can dismiss the source app before your app has finished acquiring data from the *DataPackage* object. Therefore, you should notify the system with the *ReportDataRetrieved* method of the *ShareOperation* object when your app has all the data it expects from the source app. The system can then suspend or terminate the source app.

In some apps, the share operation can include instructions to retrieve the content to be shared from a remote location. For example, the URI of a resource is shared instead of the resource itself. The target application downloads the resource from the URI as part of the share operation. The target application typically uses background transfer to download the resource and notify the system that a background transfer is under way with the *ReportSubmittedBackgroundTask* method of the *ShareOperation* object.

If there is an error during the share operation, your app can report it with the *ReportError* method of the *ShareOperation* object. At such a point, the target app shuts down and the share operation ends. The user will have to start the share operation again.

When your app successfully processes the shared content, you should call the *ReportCompleted* method of the *ShareOperation* object to notify the system that the share operation has completed. The Share charm that displays the Share Target page from your app is dismissed after the share operation is complete.

Methods provided by the *ShareOperation* class are invoked only once in the order described previously when the user chooses your app to share content. However, a target app can call *ReportDataRetrieved* before calling the *ReportStarted* method. An example is when the app retrieves the data as part of a task in the activation handler but doesn't call the *ReportStarted* method until the user clicks the Share button. Unhandled exceptions in a target app terminate it immediately. Therefore, a Windows Store app should handle exceptions arising from invalid data and report them to the user. Perform long-running operations in the background; otherwise, the system assumes your app is not responding and displays an error. You should store the *ShareOperation* object and process data asynchronously in your app.

Implementing the Share Target contract is a great way to make your app stand out among other Windows Store apps. Windows 8 lists apps used previously for sharing content in a list when the user opens the Share charm. This is supported via QuickLinks, which are shortcuts preconfigured with information required for sharing content. For example, you frequently share content with a friend using email. Your app can create a QuickLink that creates a new email message preconfigured with your friend's email address.

A QuickLink created by your app is returned to the system by calling the *ReportCompleted* method of the *ShareOperation* object. A QuickLink consists of a title, an icon, and an ID. The title and icon appear when the user opens the Share charm. Listing 2-18 shows how to create a QuickLink for a share operation and report it using the *ReportCompleted* method of the *ShareOperation* class.

LISTING 2-18 Creating a QuickLink for a share operation and reporting it

```
QuickLink quickLinkInfo = new QuickLink
{
    Id = QuickLinkId.Text,
    Title = QuickLinkTitle.Text,
    // For QuickLinks, the supported FileTypes and DataFormats
    // are set independently from the manifest.
    SupportedFileTypes = { "*" },
    SupportedDataFormats =
    {
        StandardDataFormats.Text,
        StandardDataFormats.Uri,
        StandardDataFormats.Bitmap,
        StandardDataFormats.StorageItems,
        StandardDataFormats.Html

    }
};
```

```
try
{
    StorageFile iconFile = await
            Package.Current.InstalledLocation.CreateFileAsync("assets\\user.png",
                    CreationCollisionOption.OpenIfExists);
    quickLinkInfo.Thumbnail = RandomAccessStreamReference.CreateFromFile(iconFile);
    this._shareOperation.ReportCompleted(quickLinkInfo);
}
catch (Exception ex)
{
    // Even if the QuickLink cannot be created it is important
    // to call ReportCompleted. Otherwise, if this is a long-running share,
    // the app will stick around in the long-running share progress list.
    this._shareOperation.ReportError("Error during share operation (" + ex.ToString()
            + ")");
    this._shareOperation.ReportCompleted();
    throw;
}
```

Limiting the scope of sharing using the *DataPackage* object

Whether your Windows Store app acts as a share source or share target, you should consider the data formats and file types your app will support. If your app acts as a share source, it cannot obtain the data formats supported by the target app chosen by the user for sharing the content from your app. If your app is sharing formatted text from a web page, it is a good practice to include plain text versions of the content and perhaps the URL from where the content originated.

Windows provides a number of built-in data formats that can be used with the *DataPackage* class. These formats are represented as static properties of the *StandardDataFormats* class that return the string values used to declare the data formats supported by an app in its package manifest. The formats are as follows:

- **Bitmap** Bitmap format, used for sharing images
- **Html** HTML format, used for sharing HTML content
- **Rtf** Rich Text Format, used for sharing RTF content
- **StorageItems** *StorageItem* format, used for sharing files
- **Text** Text format, used for sharing plain text
- **Uri** Uniform resource identifier (URI) format, used for sharing URIs

The *DataPackage* class provides methods to share data in the formats represented by the *StandardDataFormats* class. These methods are the following:

- **SetBitmap** Sets the bitmap image present in the *DataPackage* object (as a *RandomAccessStreamReference*).
- **SetHtmlFormat** Sets the HTML content.

- **SetRtf**   Sets the RTF content contained in a document.
- **SetStorageItems**   Sets the files and folders contained in a *DataPackage* object. You can specify if the files are read-only by using a Boolean flag.
- **SetText**   Sets the text.
- **SetUri**   Sets the URI.

You have the option to support all the formats represented by the *StandardDataFormats* class in your app that is a share target. If all the formats are present in the content being shared, it is recommended you process the format most relevant for the sharing operation. For example, if your app shares images and it receives content that contains the image and URI of the location of the images, your app should process the image.

In some cases, you can choose to define a custom format and use it to share content from your app. For example, if your app is a movie titles browser, users can choose to share the title, rating, director, and cast of a movie. Because the data to be shared is more specific than the standard formats supported, you should consider supporting one of the many schemas at *http://www.schema.org* and prepare the data package accordingly. If you cannot find a schema at Schema.org, consider using a format ID such as *Windows8-Preview-<schema>*. In your app, you can collect information about the content to be shared, package the content in the JavaScript Object Notation (JSON) format, and use *SetData* to add the content to the *DataPackage*. In the *SetData* method, the schema name is used as the key for the JSON data being shared. The share target application uses the schema name to extract the JSON data.

If your app is a share target and supports one or more custom formats, you should add a data format that identifies the schema supported by your app in your app's manifest. In the package manifest, use *Windows-8-Preview-<schema>* as the data format, where *<schema>* is the name of the schema your app supports. If you cannot find a schema at Schema.org that fulfills the requirements of your app, you can create your own custom format. In this case, you should choose a name and use it in both the source and target app as well as considering publishing the format so that other developers can benefit from it.

In some Windows Store apps, preparing data when sharing content with other apps can take significant time. For example, if your app resizes images before sharing them with the target app, the resizing operation can take a significant amount of time before the data is ready for sharing. You should use the *SetDataProvider* method of the *DataPackage* class with a format from the *StandardDataFormats* class and a *DataProviderHandler* method that puts data using the *SetData* method when invoked.

When your app receives data as a share target, a read-only version of the *DataPackage* class called *DataPackageView* is used. The *DataPackageView* object has a property called *AvailableFormats* that is a read-only list of all the formats that the *DataPackageView* contains. Alternatively, you can see whether a specific format is present in the *DataPackageView* object by using the *Contains* method with the format ID from the *StandardDataFormats* class. The *Contains* method returns *True* if the format is present in the shared content; otherwise, it returns *False*.

Implementing in-app share outside the Share charm

Windows Store apps that act as a share source integrate the sharing experience through the Share charm. These apps use the *DataRequested* event handler with the *DataPackage* class to share content with other apps. In some apps, sharing content through the Share charm can result in a poor user experience, for example, when a game is active, and the user wants to share their score with other players. You should not expect the user to open the Share charm by swiping the right edge of the screen or through the Windows+C keyboard shortcut. In such cases, you should use the *ShowShareUI* method of the *DataTransferManager* class to launch the Share charm, as shown in the following code:

```
// Namespace usings removed for brevity
protected void ShowUIButton_Click(object sender, RoutedEventArgs args)
{
    DataTransferManager.ShowShareUI();
}
```

 Thought experiment

Adding share support in your Windows Store app

In this thought experiment, apply what you've learned about this objective. You can find answers to these questions in the "Answers" section at the end of this chapter.

One of the updates you planned after releasing your Windows Store app was to incorporate sharing of content via the Share Target contract. You have implemented the Share Target contract and are ready to submit the update to the Windows Store.

While reading reviews of other Windows Store apps, you realize your app connects to popular social networking sites and your app should be a share target.

Answer the following questions to help determine the feasibility of supporting the Share Target contract:

1. Can a Windows Store app act as a share source and share target at the same time? If yes, are there any limitations on these features if both are included in the same app?

2. What should you consider so that most Windows Store apps can use the data you have shared with your app as a share source?

3. You want most Windows Store apps to be able to use your app to share data. What should you do to ensure your app can act as a share target with most Windows Store apps?

Objective summary

- Windows Store apps should share data with other apps through the Share charm to provide a simple, in-context and rich user experience.

- You should use the *DataTransferManager* class along with the *DataPackage* class to implement sharing from your app as a source. The data formats and file types supported by your app should be declared in the package manifest.

- If processing data shared from an app takes a fair amount of time to complete, consider using background tasks to avoid your app from being unresponsive.

- Your app should implement the Share Target contract to promote itself among other apps. Users might find your app convenient to use for sharing content and use it regularly, which in turn will make it appear in the list of apps available for sharing content if it implements the Share Target contract.

- Windows provides standard formats to share data. You can use a custom data format, such as those defined at Schema.org, or create your own. You can publish your custom format, if you create one, for other apps to use.

Objective review

Answer the following questions to test your knowledge of the information in this objective. You can find the answers to these questions and explanations of why each answer choice is correct or incorrect in the "Answers" section at the end of this chapter.

1. You are about to implement shared content via your app. Which event should you handle to provide the data you plan to share from an app page?

    A. *OnNavigatedTo*

    B. *OnNavigatedFrom*

    C. *DataRequested*

    D. *Loaded*

2. After you finish processing the data shared by another app, which method should you invoke to inform the system of completion?

    A. *ReportCompleted*

    B. *ReportDataRetrieved*

    C. *ReportStarted*

    D. *ReportError*

3. You are developing a game from which you will allow users to share their achievements with other users. You cannot exit the UI nor can you use the charms bar to open the Share charm. What is the best solution for such a requirement?

   A. Save the data in local storage and share it later when the app resumes.

   B. Save the data in local storage and upload it to a server using background tasks.

   C. Use *DataTransferManager.ShowShareUI()* to programmatically open the Share charm.

   D. Use *DataTransferManager.GetForCurrentView()* to programmatically open the Share charm.

Objective 2.5: Manage app settings and preferences

Windows Store apps can integrate with the Settings charm and provide their own links that invoke commands, open their settings page, and so on. The Settings pane is populated with commands from your app and displays various system functions at the bottom. Windows adds a Rate & Review command if the app was downloaded and installed from the Windows Store and a Permissions command if the app has capabilities declared in the manifest.

The Settings charm is available from within any page in a Windows Store app and provides a simple way to update its global settings. You can construct a Settings pane using the *Popup* control, and provide standard Windows 8 controls such as toggle buttons to configure app settings. The application settings can be saved in the roaming data store so users can access them after closing and restarting the app.

This objective covers how to:

- Choose which app features are accessed in *AppSettings*.
- Add entry points for *AppSettings* in the Settings window.
- Create settings flyouts using the *Popup* control.
- Add settings to *Popup*.
- Store and retrieve settings from the roaming app data store.

Choosing which app features are accessed in *AppSettings*

Windows Store apps can provide users with a consistent way to access app settings. You should use the Settings charm as the primary entry point of your app's settings and put all your settings in the Settings pane. If your app has more than one category of settings, consider using settings flyouts for each category. Use as few settings as possible in your app and provide defaults for all of them. Your app should immediately implement a settings change, such as changing the default font size, because a settings flyout can close immediately if the user touches or clicks anywhere outside the flyout.

It is important to carefully consider the settings you want to make available through the Settings charm. Here are some guidelines for adding settings to your app:

- Add settings that are occasionally changed by the user, for example, the font size of text in an RSS reader app or the temperature units in a weather app.
- If your app logs in to a remote service, provide a command to the user to log out and an option to remember your credentials in the PC.
- Add user preference options, such as color themes or data refresh intervals.
- Add information about your app that is occasionally used, such as the privacy policy, help, copyright, and app version.

It is recommended that you use up to four entry points (from a maximum of eight) for grouping similar or related options together. These entry points should be visible wherever the user is in your app. You can disable some settings in a certain context. Each entry point in the Settings pane should use a single word as a label. If a command opens a web page instead of a flyout, you should inform your users with a visual clue.

Adding entry points for *AppSettings* in the Settings window

Unlike the Search Target contract or the Share Target contract, a Windows Store app that provides access to its settings through the Settings charm does not require a capability or a declaration in the package manifest. Entry points for *AppSettings* are added in the *CommandsRequested* event of the *SettingsPane* object, as shown in Listing 2-19.

LISTING 2-19 Adding entry points for *AppSettings* in the *CommandsRequested* event

```
using Windows.UI.ApplicationSettings;
// Other namespace usings removed for brevity
public sealed partial class App : Application
{
    public OnWindowCreated()
    {
        SettingsPane.GetForCurrentView().CommandsRequested += OnCommandsRequested;
    }

    void OnCommandsRequested(SettingsPane sender,
                             SettingsPaneCommandsRequestedEventArgs e)
    {
        e.Request.ApplicationCommands.Add(
                new SettingsCommand(1, "Account", OnAccountCommand));

        e.Request.ApplicationCommands.Add(
                new SettingsCommand(2, "General", OnGeneralCommand));

        e.Request.ApplicationCommands.Add(
                new SettingsCommand(3, "Theme", OnThemeCommand));

        e.Request.ApplicationCommands.Add(
                new SettingsCommand(4, "Credits", OnCreditsCommand));
```

```
            e.Request.ApplicationCommands.Add(
                    new SettingsCommand(4, "Feedback", OnFeedbackCommand));
    }

    void OnAccountCommand(IUICommand command)
    {
        // Show the account settings pane
    }

    void OnGeneralCommand(IUICommand command)
    {
        // Show the general settings pane
    }

    void OnThemeCommand(IUICommand command)
    {
        // Show the theme settings pane
    }

    void OnCreditsCommand(IUICommand command)
    {
        // Show the credits pane
    }

    void OnFeedbackCommand(IUICommand command)
    {
        // Show the feedback pane
    }
}
```

The commands are integrated and shown in the Settings pane when the application is run, as shown in Figure 2-26.

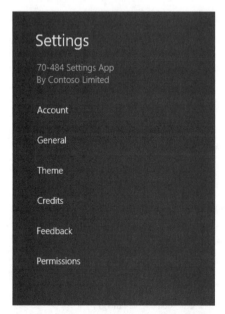

FIGURE 2-26 Entry points for the Windows Store app available in the Settings charm

The content of the settings flyout for the Permissions command is prepared from the capabilities declared in the package manifest, as shown in Figure 2-27.

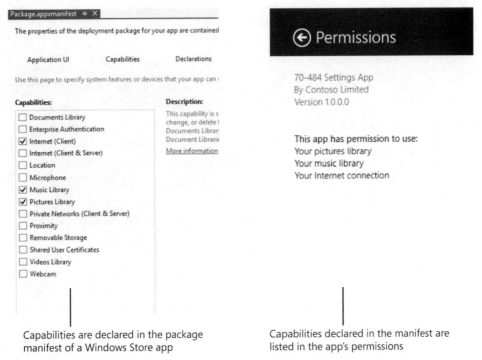

Capabilities are declared in the package manifest of a Windows Store app

Capabilities declared in the manifest are listed in the app's permissions

FIGURE 2-27 Capabilities declared in the package manifest and listed in the app's permissions, available as a command in the Settings charm

Creating settings flyouts using the *Popup* control

When a command is clicked in the Settings charm, your app should display a UI similar to the Settings pane. You are not allowed to add controls into the Settings pane itself; instead, you should provide your own control that is loaded into the UI provided by the Settings pane.

One way to implement your own Settings pane is to create a XAML user control that can be reused across your app. A simple way to display content inside the *SettingsPane* class is to use the *Popup* control, as shown in the XAML in Listing 2-20.

LISTING 2-20 Using the *Popup* control to display content in the *SettingsPane* class

```
<UserControl x:Class="70-484SettingsApp.ThemeSettingsPane"
  xmlns="http://schemas.microsoft.com/winfx/2006/xaml/presentation"
  xmlns:x="http://schemas.microsoft.com/winfx/2006/xaml">
    <Popup x:Name="settingsPopup" IsLightDismissEnabled="True"
           Closed="SettingsPopup_Closed"
           HorizontalAlignment="Right" Width="345">
        <Popup.Transitions>
            <TransitionCollection>
```

```
                <PaneThemeTransition/>
            </TransitionCollection>
        </Popup.Transitions>
        <Grid x:Name="popupGrid" Width="345">
            <StackPanel VerticalAlignment="Top" Margin="21,30,0,0">
                <!-- The header, with a back button and title -->
                <StackPanel Orientation="Horizontal">
                    <Button Style="{StaticResource SnappedBackButtonStyle}"
                            Click="BackButton_Click"/>
                    <TextBlock Text="Application Settings" FontWeight="Normal"
                               Style="{StaticResource SubheaderTextStyle}"
                               Margin="-2,-2,0,0"/>
                </StackPanel>
                <!-- Controls for specific flyout go here -->
            </StackPanel>
        </Grid>
    </Popup>
</UserControl>
```

The user control created for the settings flyout uses the same transitions as the Settings pane, ensuring the user experience is maintained. The *PaneThemeTransition* is invoked when an element initially enters the view. Therefore, the *Popup* must be detached from the layout and reattached every time it is displayed. In addition, the height of the *Popup* is set to the screen's height.

The Back button of the user control shows the Settings pane programmatically. The code-behind of the control is shown in Listing 2-21.

LISTING 2-21 Creating a user control for the Settings pane

```
using Windows.UI.ApplicationSettings;
// Other namespace usings removed for brevity
public sealed partial class ThemeSettingsPane: UserControl
{
    public ThemeSettingsPane()
    {
        this.InitializeComponent();

        // This will invoke the PaneThemeTransition when the control is
        // displayed again.
        this.Content = null;

        // Set the pane's height to the height of the screen
        this.LayoutUpdated += (sender, e) =>
            {
                this.popupGrid.Height = this.ActualHeight;
            };
    }

    // Display the popup
    public void Show(IUICommand command)
    {
        this.Content = this.settingsPopup;
        this.settingsPopup.IsOpen = true;
    }
```

```
    // Detach the popup from the content, this will invoke the PaneThemeTransition
    private void SettingsPopup_Closed(object sender, object e)
    {
        this.Content = null;
    }

    private void BackButton_Click(object sender, RoutedEventArgs args)
    {
        SettingsPane.Show();
    }
}
```

Adding settings to *Popup*

With the settings flyout created using the *Popup* control, you can add settings for a Windows
Store app in the XAML. Use data binding to read and set values for these settings added as
controls in the XAML. Listing 2-22 shows how a *ToggleSwitch* control can be used to toggle
between a dark theme and a light theme of an app.

LISTING 2-22 Using a *ToggleSwitch* control to switch between a dark theme and a light theme

```
<UserControl x:Class="70-484SettingsApp.ThemeSettingsPane"
  xmlns=http://schemas.microsoft.com/winfx/2006/xaml/presentation
  xmlns:x="http://schemas.microsoft.com/winfx/2006/xaml">
    <Popup x:Name="settingsPopup" IsLightDismissEnabled="True"
           Closed="SettingsPopup_Closed"
           HorizontalAlignment="Right" Width="345">
        <Popup.Transitions>
            <TransitionCollection>
                <PaneThemeTransition/>
            </TransitionCollection>
        </Popup.Transitions>
        <Grid x:Name="popupGrid" Width="345">
            <StackPanel VerticalAlignment="Top" Margin="21,30,0,0">
                <!-- The header, with a back button and title -->
                <StackPanel Orientation="Horizontal">
                    <Button Style="{StaticResource SnappedBackButtonStyle}"
                            Click="BackButton_Click"/>
                    <TextBlock Text="{Binding PaneTitle}" FontWeight="Normal"
                               Style="{StaticResource SubheaderTextStyle}"
                               Margin="-2,-2,0,0"/>
                </StackPanel>
                <!-- Controls for specific flyout go here -->
                <StackPanel Margin="13,0,0,0">
                    <!-- The LightThemeOn variable is data-bound to a property
                         that is used to set the theme of the application. In the
                         simplest form, it is used to change the background color -->
                    <ToggleSwitch Header="Use Light Theme"
                                  IsOn="{Binding LightThemeOn}" />
                </StackPanel>
            </StackPanel>
        </Grid>
    </Popup>
</UserControl>
```

The flyout with the Settings pane for a Windows Store app is shown in Figure 2-28.

FIGURE 2-28 Settings flyout implemented using a *Popup* control for a Windows Store app

Storing and retrieving settings from the roaming app data store

Windows 8 provides three application data stores: local, roaming, and temporary. When designing your app's data layer, you should consider one of these stores for a particular kind of application data.

You can save an application's settings and user preferences to a roaming app data store, which retains the information and makes it available across multiple devices. If a user has your app installed on one device and then downloads and installs it on another device, the data saved in the roaming data store in the first device will be available on the second device, and vice versa. Therefore, using the roaming app data store to save app settings will provide a uniform experience to the user across multiple devices.

You should consider application data such as view preferences, background color or theme customization, and similar settings in your app to be saved in the roaming app data store. In addition, you can also save the last position in the app's context, such as a news item being read, game level and score data, and navigation history.

> **IMPORTANT   USAGE OF THE ROAMING DATA STORE**
>
> You should not use the roaming app data store to save data relevant to a device, such as the path to a local file resource on a PC. Note that roaming data is not synchronized instantaneously and therefore should not be used to store frequently changing information such as up to the second position in a movie or a song.

In a Windows Store app, you must use the roaming app data store via the *RoamingSettings* property of the *ApplicationData* object. A new *ApplicationDataContainer* is created to store your application's settings. You must subscribe to the *DataChanged* event to receive changes in the data stored in the roaming data store and raise a data changed event by calling *Signal-DataChanged* to notify a change in the data stored in the roaming data store. This process is shown in the C# code in Listing 2-23.

LISTING 2-23 Subscribing to the *DataChanged* event to receive changes in the data stored

```csharp
using Windows.UI.Storage;
// Other namespace usings removed for brevity
public sealed partial class MainPage : Page
{
    ApplicationData applicationData = null;
    ApplicationDataContainer roamingSettings = null;

    public MainPage()
    {
        this.InitializeComponent();

        applicationData = ApplicationData.Current;
        roamingSettings = applicationData.RoamingSettings;
        applicationData.DataChanged += DataChangedHandler;

    }

    // Update the theme and store the modified settings
    public void UpdateSettings(bool useLightTheme)
    {
        roamingSettings.Values["Theme"] = useLightTheme;

        // Update the theme based on the user's choice

        // Signal a change in settings
        applicationData.SignalDataChanged();
    }


    // Event handler that is invoked whenever the data in the roaming store changes
    private async void DataChangedHandler(ApplicationData appData, object e)
    {
        // Data has changed, update settings
        if (roamingSettings.Values.ContainsKey("Theme"))
        {
            bool theme = (bool) roamingSettings.Values["Theme"];

            // Update the theme if it is has changed
        }
    }
}
```

Composite values can be used to store a number of settings as key/value pairs in the roaming data store. If you are required to store and retrieve composite values, you can do so using the following C# code:

```
using Windows.Storage;

//
//
ApplicationDataCompositeValue compositeVal = new ApplicationDataCompositeValue();
compositeVal["Theme"] = false;
compositeVal["FontSize"] = 18;
roamingSettings.Values["themeSettings"] = compositeVal;
```

Each app has a quota for roaming application data. You should check the *ApplicationData.RoamingStorageQuota* property to obtain the total size of roaming data allowed.

Thought experiment

Using the Settings charm and application settings

In this thought experiment, apply what you've learned about this objective. You can find answers to these questions in the "Answers" section at the end of this chapter.

You have been engaged as a consultant to review the current set of features of a Windows Store app, interview existing customers, and suggest recommendations. The Windows Store app is used by a number of fleet sales agents who are on the road most of the day as well as employees in the headquarters.

During the interview process, you have discovered a number of shortcomings in the app, particularly around application settings and how the Settings charm is used in the app.

You have found that the primary form of communication is by email created through a page in the app itself. There is a page specifically for application settings, and most of the configuration is static. You have also found that data for the app is tied to the user and the device.

What are the top three recommendations you incorporate in a report to the managing director of the company?

Objective summary

- A Windows Store app should integrate with the Settings charm and provide one or more Settings panes with commands to invoke the panes. The panes can contain a group of application settings, grouped by their type.
- You should include properties, such as background color and font size used in an app in the Settings, to allow the user to configure their preferences.

- You should create and use settings flyouts using the *Popup* control, providing a flyout for each Settings command.

- You should use as few controls as possible in the settings flyouts, providing default values for the controls wherever possible.

- You should use the roaming app data store to save user settings. This will ensure that the settings are persisted across multiple devices, providing a great user experience.

Objective review

Answer the following questions to test your knowledge of the information in this objective. You can find the answers to these questions and explanations of why each answer choice is correct or incorrect in the "Answers" section at the end of this chapter.

1. You are developing a Windows Store game and want to save user settings when the app is suspended. Which data storage strategy should you use?

   A. Save the settings in local storage and retrieve when needed.

   B. Save in the local registry and read from it when needed.

   C. Save in the roaming app data store and read from it when needed.

   D. Save in the local directory and read from the file when needed.

2. You are required to provide a list of permissions used in your app. This list is displayed via the Settings charm. How should you implement this requirement?

   A. Create a command in the Settings charm. When it is fired, a pop-up dialog box opens with a list of all the permissions used by the app.

   B. The package manifest is used to declare all the capabilities used by the app. The Permissions command automatically populates the Settings pane with this list.

   C. Create a command in the Settings charm. When it is fired, a settings flyout opens with a list of all the permissions used by the app.

   D. Create a command in the Settings charm. When it is fired, navigate the user to a new page that displays a list of all the permissions used by the app.

3. You are using roaming app data storage to store the settings of your app. Your app should update the stored settings whenever the user changes them. What should you do to implement this requirement?

   A. Nothing; data is automatically updated in the data store by the Settings contract.

   B. Call the *SignalDataChanged* method after saving the data in the *ApplicationData-Container*.

   C. Subscribe to the *DataChanged* event; when this event is raised, save the updated data in the roaming store.

   D. When the app is being suspended, save a copy of the data in the roaming app data store.

Chapter summary

- Windows Store apps can use the *ContactPicker* and *ContactPickerUI* classes to provide contacts to other apps. The *ContactPicker* class supports the selection of a single contact or multiple contacts at a time.

- Contacts can be filtered and selected by specifying the fields used in the selection using the *KnownContactField* class. Selected fields of a contact can be displayed using the *ContactFieldCategory* and *ContactFieldType* classes.

- Whenever possible, you should integrate your app with the charms bar and the Search, Share Target, Settings, and Devices contracts. This helps your app to be popular among your users as they find it easier to use your app for searching and sharing content.

- You should configure your app's manifest with the right permissions. This is important when you support various contracts in your app.

- You should provide search result previews in your app. This helps users to easily select an item from the search result.

- Query suggestions and result recommendations enrich the search experience for the user; you should consider implementing them in your app whenever possible.

- Your app is discovered and used more often if you support activation by search. Users can pick your app to carry out their search even if your app is not running.

- If your application has content to share, consider implementing the code to set up your app as a share source. You should consider supporting as many formats as possible so that the user has multiple choices of apps to use for sharing content from your app.

- While accepting share requests from other apps, you should support as many formats as possible. This enables your app to be used in most scenarios. Add a QuickLink for a sharing action; this helps your app to be found in the list of suggested apps available for sharing content.

- Use the *DataPackage* and *DataPackageView* objects to share data and view shared data, respectively. If you require a custom format to share data, check the custom formats already available.

- Your app should provide the user to customize settings per their preference. You should have about four commands that open the settings flyout with a set of controls.

- You should use a roaming app data store to save the applicable settings of your app. This helps with having the user's settings available across multiple devices.

Answers

This section contains the solutions to the thought experiments and answers to the lesson review questions in this chapter.

Objective 2.1: Thought experiment

1. Yes. A Windows Store app can act as a contact provider while including other features such as importing data from local and remote sources.

2. One of the requirements of the *ContactPickerUI* class is that the application should not be in the snapped state. You should check the app's view state and try to unsnap it if it is in the snapped state.

3. Yes. If the calling application uses *PickMultipleContactsAsync*, users will be able to select more than one contact at any time. Users will be able to select one contact at a time if *PickSingleContactAsync* is used.

Objective 2.1: Review

1. **Correct answers:** A, D, E

    A. **Correct:** *Name* is a property of the *ContactInformation* class.

    B. **Incorrect:** Designation is not a property of the *ContactInformation* class.

    C. **Incorrect:** Organization Name is not a property of the *ContactInformation* class.

    D. **Correct:** The *Locations* property of the *ContactInformation* class contains the work address.

    E. **Correct:** The *PhoneNumbers* property of the *ContactInformation* class contains the work phone number.

2. **Correct answer:** C

    A. **Incorrect:** Because *PickSingleContactAsync* is called within a while loop that never exits; therefore, the user will not be able to select a contact.

    B. **Incorrect:** The *PickMultipleContactsAsync* method does not return a list of *Contact* objects.

    C. **Correct:** The *PickMultipleContactsAsync* method returns a read-only list of *ContactInformation* objects.

    D. **Incorrect:** The *PickMultipleContactsAsync* method must be invoked asynchronously.

3. **Correct answer:** B

    A. **Incorrect:** The app should always check for the application's view state.

    B. **Correct:** The *ContactPickerUI* can be used when the app is in the filled state.

    C. **Incorrect:** The *ContactPickerUI* does not function in the snapped state of an app.

    D. **Incorrect:** The view state of the application should be checked by the app itself.

Objective 2.2: Thought experiment

1. You should implement the Search contract in your app with the *OnSearchActivated* event implemented to make sure your app is activated if it is selected during the search. You should consider including search suggestions and recommendations.

2. You should implement content sharing in the pages of your app. Doing so ensures that third-party apps such as the Mail application can be used to share content from within your app.

3. You should use the Devices charm to discover printers in the network and allow the app to select a printer and print content.

Objective 2.2: Review

1. **Correct answers:** C, D, E

    A. **Incorrect:** The charms bar is available on all Windows 8 and WinRT devices.

    B. **Incorrect:** An app should use find-in-page to search within a page; the search contract is used to search within the whole app.

    C. **Correct:** A Windows Store app that implements a mechanism to share content from other apps must implement the Share Target contract.

    D. **Correct:** The Settings charm is available to all Windows Store apps. The Settings charm can be used to provide users with a way to customize the application's settings.

    E. **Correct:** Query suggestions and result recommendations enable users to quickly search for content and access content that they frequently view with the app.

2. **Correct answers:** A, B, D

   A. **Correct:** Account/session management is a user-specific requirement and hence should be included in the Settings charm.

   B. **Correct:** Theme preferences are specific to the user and should be included in the Settings charm.

   C. **Incorrect:** Windows Store apps are closed with a gesture (pressing down on the app at the top and dragging it down), and applications are not allowed to provide a way to close them.

   D. **Correct:** The Settings charm is the right location for a feedback form.

   E. **Incorrect:** An app should use find-in-page to search within an app.

3. **Correct answer:** C

   A. **Incorrect:** The *OnWindowCreated* method is invoked by the system when the application creates a window.

   B. **Incorrect:** The *OnLaunched* method is invoked by the system when the application is launched.

   C. **Correct:** The *OnSearchActivated* method is invoked when the application is opened through a search query.

   D. **Incorrect:** The *OnActivated* method is invoked when the application is opened by any means other than the user launching the app. Because the activation kind needs to be checked to determine the source that activated the app, it is better to use *OnSearchActivated* method to support app activation via search.

Objective 2.3: Thought experiment

1. Update the package manifest to declare your app implements the Search contract. Implement code to handle the *QuerySubmitted* and *QueryChanged* event. Check to see whether the query string is empty and show the default page to the user if it is empty.

2. Provide the user with query suggestions and result recommendations. If the user clicks a result recommendation and views the result in the app, prepare a QuickLink for the result recommendation so that your app appears in the list of apps available for search.

3. If a user is in your app and begins typing, open the Search charm and allow the user to carry out search.

4. Implement the *OnSearchActivated* event so that your app is activated whenever it is selected to carry out the search.

Objective 2.3: Review

1. **Correct answers:** A, B, D

   A. **Correct:** Use the *QuerySubmitted* event to carry out the search using the query text entered by the user.

   B. **Correct:** Use the *QueryChanged* event to obtain the text entered by the user in the Search charm and carry out the search.

   C. **Incorrect:** The *Loaded* event is fired when the page is loaded. It is likely that the search operation is underway while the page finishes loading; therefore, the *Loaded* event is not required to implement search.

   D. **Correct:** The *OnSearchActivated* method is invoked when the app is opened by the user carrying out a search with the app when it is not running and visible.

   E. **Incorrect:** The *Unloaded* event is fired after the page is unloaded; therefore, it is not useful for implementing search.

2. **Correct answer:** B

   A. **Incorrect:** The *QueryChanged* event is raised when the search query text entered by the user changes.

   B. **Correct:** The *SuggestionsRequested* event fires when the user's query text changes, and the app needs to provide suggestions.

   C. **Incorrect:** The *ResultSuggestionChosen* event fires when the user selects a result recommendation from the list provided in the Search charm.

   D. **Incorrect:** The *QuerySubmitted* event is raised when the user submits a query to commence search.

3. **Correct answer:** A

   A. **Correct:** The *ResultSuggestionChosen* event fires when the user selects one of the suggested results provided by the app and displayed in the Search charm.

   B. **Incorrect:** The *QuerySubmitted* event fires when the user submits text in the search box, and the app is expected to carry out the search.

   C. **Incorrect:** The *QueryChanged* event fires when the user changes the query text in the search box.

   D. **Incorrect:** The *SuggestionsRequested* event fires when the query text in the search box is changed by the user, and the app needs to provide new suggestions.

Objective 2.4: Thought experiment

1. Yes, a Windows Store app can act as both share source and target. There are no limitations on the features of share source and target if both are present in the same app.

2. Data should be packaged so that published formats are used in the data package. This ensures that a maximum numbers of Windows Store apps can read the data.

3. Your app should support data to be provided in a data package, and it should be able to parse the *DataPackage* for common formats.

Objective 2.4: Review

1. **Correct answer:** C

   A. **Incorrect:** The *OnNavigatedTo* method is invoked only once when the page is about to be navigated to. This method can be used to subscribe to the *DataRequested* event.

   B. **Incorrect:** The *OnNavigatedFrom* method is invoked when the page is navigated away from. This method can be used to unsubscribe from the *DataRequested* event.

   C. **Correct:** The *DataRequested* event is used to provide the data to be shared by an app.

   D. **Incorrect:** The *Loaded* event fires when the page is first loaded.

2. **Correct answer:** B

   A. **Incorrect:** The *ReportCompleted* method should be used to inform the system that the share operation has completed.

   B. **Correct:** The *ReportDataRetrieved* method should be used to report completion of processing of data shared by the source app.

   C. **Incorrect:** The *ReportStarted* method is used to inform the system that the app has started to retrieve the data shared by another app.

   D. **Incorrect:** The *ReportError* method is used to inform the system the sharing process encountered an error.

3. **Correct answer:** C

   A. **Incorrect:** The Share Target contract is used with data that is currently available within the app.

   B. **Incorrect:** Although you can use background tasks to synchronize data with remote servers, sharing a result should be done without any delays.

   C. **Correct:** The *ShowShareUI* method of the *DataTransferManager* class can be used to programmatically open the Share charm.

   D. **Incorrect:** The *GetForCurrentView* method of the *DataTransferManager* class is used to retrieve an instance of the search pane from which users can search within the app.

Objective 2.5: Thought experiment

1. Application settings that do not store values specific to a PC or a device, such as the path to a file, should be stored in the roaming app data store. This will ensure data is available on all the devices and PCs accessed by the user.

2. The settings flyout should be used to send custom data to other users. If required, the app should programmatically open the Share charm and provide the user the choice of selecting a Windows Store app to share their data.

3. The app should employ the Settings charm to incorporate the settings required for the app. The app should provide default values for the settings and it should minimize the amount of configurable parameters as much as possible.

Objective 2.5: Review

1. **Correct answer:** C

    A. **Incorrect:** Settings and preferences stored in local storage are not available on other devices.

    B. **Incorrect:** Settings and preferences stored in the registry of the device are not available on other devices.

    C. **Correct:** Settings and preferences stored in roaming storage are available on other devices.

    D. **Incorrect:** A file can be used to store and retrieve data, but it is not available on other devices.

2. **Correct answer:** B

    A. **Incorrect:** The app manifest contains a list of all the capabilities declared by the app. This list is displayed in the Permissions command in the Settings pane; there is no need to display the list in a pop-up window.

    B. **Correct:** The app manifest has a list of all the capabilities declared by the app. This list is displayed in the Permissions command in the Settings pane.

    C. **Incorrect:** The app manifest has a list of all the capabilities declared by the app. This list is displayed in the Permissions command in the Settings pane; there is no need to display the list in a settings flyout.

    D. **Incorrect:** The app manifest has a list of all the capabilities declared by the app. This list is displayed in the Permissions command in the Settings pane; there is no need for the user to navigate to a different page.

3. **Correct answer:** B

   A. **Incorrect:** Application data is not updated by the Settings contract.

   B. **Correct:** The *SignalDataChanged* method is provided by the system to notify that the data stored in the roaming store has changed.

   C. **Incorrect:** The *DataChanged* event informs Windows Store apps that data stored in the roaming store has changed.

   D. **Incorrect:** Although you can save a copy of the data in the roaming app data store when the app is being suspended, to propagate any changes in the data, you should call *SignalDataChanged* in your app

CHAPTER 3

Create the user interface

Windows RT (WinRT) and Windows 8 are operating systems installed on small handheld tablets to desktop PCs with large multi-touch displays. The resolution, pixel density, and aspect ratio of screens vary greatly among different hardware. Users expect a Windows Store app to adapt to various screen sizes and orientations without changing the app's usability.

The WinRT application programming interface (API) enables developers to build Windows Store apps with dynamic user interfaces (UIs). The *Canvas*, *StackPanel*, and *Grid* layout controls, for example, let an app adjust to changes in screen size and orientation. App bars provide users with easy access to commands without obstructing the UI.

A well-designed Windows Store app presents data to users so they can select, zoom, and perform other operations easily. The *GridView*, *ListView*, and *FlipView* controls display data in a Windows Store app and can be customized through data templates. Styles can be applied based on events and property changes so that the UI is updated accordingly.

Objectives in this chapter:

- Objective 3.1: Create layout aware apps to handle view states.
- Objective 3.2: Implement layout controls.
- Objective 3.3. Design and implement the app bar.
- Objective 3.4: Design and implement data presentation.
- Objective 3.5: Create and manage XAML styles and templates.

Objective 3.1: Create layout aware apps to handle view states

A well-designed Windows Store app provides a smooth and pleasant user experience across a variety of device form factors, screen sizes, and application view states by employing a predictive behavior in the UI. Your app should look great when users view it on a tablet, on a desktop PC, or on a large high-definition screen; when they change the orientation of their device; and when they change the view state of the app.

Microsoft design guidelines specify Windows Store app layouts that help you arrange controls in the UI. The UI responds to changes in the size and orientation of the screen by raising events. You can support multiple view states in your app by applying styles to specific view states in these events. The content in your app is presented through controls embedded in views. A view responds to changes in size and orientation of the screen; application view states; user actions such as panning, zooming, scaling, and resizing; and manipulation of specific UI elements by the user.

A Windows Store app can support one or more view states in the UI. Your app receives notifications whenever the view state changes and, it can query for the current view state to help with the arrangement of controls in views for a certain layout. To support multiple view states, you should use styles for each view state, which are applied to the view whenever the view state changes.

The users of your app can change the orientation of their device to suit their convenience. For example, if your app is a news or blog reader, the user might find it convenient to hold their tablet in the portrait orientation. Therefore, it is important to consider various orientations of a device and support them in your app.

This objective covers how to:

- Handle view state events from *ViewStateManager*.
- Choose between style patterns for different view states.
- Set up app orientation in the manifest.

Handling view state events from *ViewStateManager*

In traditional desktop applications, a developer must incorporate tools for a user to change the app's orientation and screen size. However, Windows Store apps can occupy the entire screen, so developers must also consider an app's view state. View states, shown in Figure 3-1, represent the various modes in which a user can use an app.

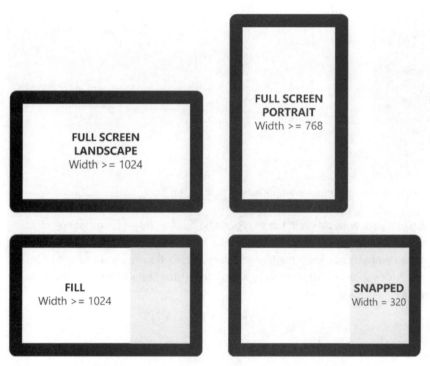

FIGURE 3-1 Some view states and orientations of a Windows Store app

The minimum width of a Windows Store app in full screen landscape and full screen portrait modes is related to the minimum resolution of 1024 × 768, which all apps must support. Microsoft recommends 1366 × 768 as the optimum resolution that designers and developers should target.

Windows 8 enables users to use two apps simultaneously in the screen when their device is in landscape orientation. An app can be in the snapped view state if the horizontal resolution of the screen is at least 1366 pixels. The minimum horizontal resolution of an app is 1024 pixels, the width of a snapped app is 320 pixels, and the width of the splitter separating the two apps is 22 pixels. If the horizontal resolution of the screen is less than 1366 pixels, only one app can be displayed at a time.

Width specifications for various view states are in logical pixels. Therefore, an app in the snapped state will look different on screens with the same display resolution but different physical sizes. You can test your application in the Windows Simulator for various screen sizes and resolutions, which are shown in Figure 3-2.

FIGURE 3-2 Screen sizes and resolutions available in the Windows Simulator

You can also test your application in the snapped and fill view states for different screen sizes and resolutions using the Microsoft Visual Studio XAML designer. Click Device in the left tab bar, open the Display drop-down menu, and select a resolution you want to test your app with. You can test for various visual states by opening the Visual State drop-down menu and selecting an option, as shown in Figure 3-3.

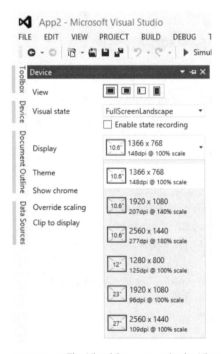

FIGURE 3-3 The Visual State menu in the Visual Studio XAML designer

To update your app's UI when the user changes the view state, you should subscribe to the *SizeChanged* or *LayoutUpdated* event. The *SizeChanged* event is fired whenever the size of the UI element to which you attached the event handler changes. The *LayoutUpdated* event is fired when the layout updates. Within the event handler, you should check for the static *Value* property of the *Windows.UI.ViewManagement.ApplicationView* class to obtain the current view state of the app. The value of this property is one of the members of the *Application-ViewState* enumeration, described in Table 3-1.

TABLE 3-1 *ApplicationViewState* enumeration members

MEMBER	VALUE	DESCRIPTION
FullScreenLandscape	0	The app is in full screen mode, in landscape orientation, with no snapped app next to it.
Filled	1	The app is in the fill state, occupying part of the screen with another app in the snapped state.
Snapped	2	The app is in the snapped state, occupying part of the screen with another app in the fill state.
FullScreenPortrait	3	The app is in full screen mode, in portrait orientation, with no snapped app next to it.

If a Windows Store app supports all the view states, it should respond to changes in the view state by updating the layout of the UI. Windows provides the Visual State Manager (VSM) (*VisualStateManager* class in the *Windows.UI.Xaml* namespace) to help manage layouts for various view states. The VSM handles the logic of the view states and transitions for controls among these states. The VSM can be used to manage the state of pages, custom and user controls, and control templates.

You can use the VSM with any UI element that derives from the *Control* class, for example, the *Page* element. The VSM should be present at the root of the control's template. The XAML code of a page with the VSM is as follows:

```
<Page>
    <Grid x:Name="LayoutRoot">
        <VisualStateManager.VisualStateGroups>
            <VisualStateGroup x:Name="OrientationStates">
                <VisualState x:Name="FullScreen" />
                <VisualState x:Name="Filled" />
                <VisualState x:Name="Snapped" />
                <VisualState x:Name="Portrait" />
            </VisualStateGroup>
        </VisualStateManager.VisualStateGroups>
    </Grid>
</Page>
```

A visual state (represented by the *VisualState* class) consists of XAML for the UI elements in the page for that state. For example, you can display your app's content in a grid when it is in the fill view state in the landscape orientation, and in a list when it is in the snapped view state and portrait orientation.

In the code-behind of the page that defines the visual state groups (represented by the *VisualStateGroup* class and containing a group of visual states), you should implement the logic to transition between the visual states in the *SizeChanged* event. See Listing 3-1.

LISTING 3-1 Transitioning between visual states in the *SizeChanged* event

```
using Windows.UI.ViewManagement;

public sealed partial class VSMSamplePage: Page
{
    public VSMSamplePage
    {
        this.InitializeComponent();
        Window.Current.SizeChanged += OnSizeChanged;
    }

    // Handle the SizeChanged event
    public void OnSizeChanged(object sender,
                             Windows.UI.Core.WindowSizeChangedEventArgs args)
    {
        switch (ApplicationView.Value)
        {
            case ApplicationViewState.Filled:
                VisualStateManager.GoToState(this, "Filled", false);
                break;
            case ApplicationViewState.FullScreenLandscape:
                VisualStateManager.GoToState(this, "FullScreen", false);
                break;
            case ApplicationViewState.Snapped:
                VisualStateManager.GoToState(this, "Snapped", false);
                break;
            case ApplicationViewState.FullScreenPortrait:
                VisualStateManager.GoToState(this, "Portrait", false);
                break;
            default:
                break;
        }
    }
}
```

The *GoToState* method accepts a Boolean parameter that indicates whether visual transitions should be used when transitioning between states. Transitions are animations controlled by a *StoryBoard* object that occurs between each visual state when the state changes. A *StoryBoard* can contain one or more animations, which are associated with UI elements. Transitions are not used in most control templates, and the transition between various states occurs instantaneously.

If you decide to use transitions between visual states, you can define them as a combination of the start state and end state in your control's set of visual states. Transitions are defined by the *Transitions* property of *VisualStateGroup* in XAML. The *VisualTransition* class represents the visual behavior when a control transitions from one visual state to another. A *VisualTransition* initiates a *StoryBoard*, which outlines the duration that animations between two visual states will run.

A *VisualTransition* can reference a *From* state only, a *To* state only, or both a *From* state and a *To* state. The *To* value references the name of a state that is the new state requested by the *GoToState* method. The *From* value references the name of the previous state. The *VisualStateManager* class uses the following logic to decide which transition to apply:

- If a *VisualTransition* exists that uses a *From* state as the old state and the new state as *To*, use that transition.
- If a *VisualTransition* exists that uses *To* state as the new state but does not specify *From*, use that state.
- If a *VisualTransition* exists that uses the *From* state as the old state but does not specify *To*, use that state.
- If none of the above applies, the *VisualStateManager* does not apply any transitions.

The *GeneratedDuration* property of the *VisualTransition* class sets the time for the transition to occur. A *VisualTransition* can have a *StoryBoard* value, a *GeneratedDuration* value, or both. If a *VisualTransition* has neither a *StoryBoard* value nor a *GeneratedDuration* value, that *VisualTransition* does nothing for animations, even if the *From* and *To* values refer to states defined in the *VisualStateGroup*.

An implicit transition is one that does not target a specific dependency property, although it can include a *GeneratedDuration* value to set the duration of the animation. Implicit transitions apply to properties with a *Double*, *Color*, or *Point* value; that is, the property must be possible to implicitly animate with an animation of type *DoubleAnimation*, *PointAnimation*, or *ColorAnimation*. If you need to create a transition animation on any other value, you should put that animation in the *StoryBoard* and give the animation a *Duration* that you want it to run.

Another category of animations is transition animations. A transition animation represents a change in the relationship between a UI element and the UI. For example, with a change in the view state, you might want to move a UI element in the layout container of the page. A transition animation applies to various *Transition* properties of a *UIElement* class and its derived classes, not to a *VisualStateGroup*. Transition animations are usually built into the default behavior of a control. The XAML in Listing 3-2 shows the *Transitions* property of *VisualStateGroup* used to define the transition for a control. The first three transitions are examples of implicit transitions, and the fourth is an explicit transition that targets a specific property.

LISTING 3-2 Defining the transition for a control

```
<VisualStateGroup x:Name="OrientationStates">
    <VisualStateGroup.Transitions>
        <!-- The following three visual transitions are implicit transitions -->
        <VisualTransition To="Snapped" GeneratedDuration="0:0:0.1" />
        <VisualTransition To="Filled" GeneratedDuration="0:0:0.5" />
        <VisualTransition From="Portrait" To="FullScreen" GeneratedDuration="0:0:0.1" />
        <!-- The following visual transition is an explicit transition -->
        <VisualTransition From="FullScreen" To="Portrait" GeneratedDuration="0:0:1.5">
            <Storyboard>
                <DoubleAnimationUsingKeyFrames
                    Storyboard.TargetProperty="X"
                    Storyboard.TargetName="TopRect"
                    FillBehavior="HoldEnd" >
                    <LinearDoubleKeyFrame Value="80" KeyTime="0:0:1" />
                </DoubleAnimationUsingKeyFrames>
            </Storyboard>
        </VisualTransition>
    </VisualStateGroup.Transitions>

    <VisualState x:Name="Snapped" />
    <VisualState x:Name="FullScreen" />
    <VisualState x:Name="Filled">
        <Storyboard>
            <ColorAnimation Storyboard.TargetName="BorderBrush"
                Storyboard.TargetProperty="Color" To="Green" />
        </Storyboard>
    </VisualState>
    <VisualState x:Name="Portrait">
        <Storyboard >
            <ColorAnimation Storyboard.TargetName="BorderBrush"
                Storyboard.TargetProperty="Color" To="Transparent"/>
        </Storyboard>
    </VisualState>
</VisualStateGroup>
```

Although you might decide to not define the snapped view state in your Windows Store app, the user can still snap your app. This can result in the addition of scrollbars in the controls of the page that is currently visible, or the UI might be partially visible. If your app requires a lot of space for the user to effectively utilize the features in your app, you can include a button that unsnaps your app. In the event handler, call the *TryUnsnap* method of the *ApplicationView* class, as follows:

Sample of C# code

```
using Windows.UI.ViewManagement;

// Try to unsnap the app
private void UnsnapButton_Click(object sender, RoutedEventArgs args)
{
    bool unsnapped = ApplicationView.TryUnsnap();

    // Check the value of unsnapped to see if the application unsnapped.
    // Respond with a message if the app must unsnap.
}
```

Choosing between style patterns for different view states

The usability of a well-designed Windows Store app does not vary between view states although the layout can change between the various view states. You can implement your app's UI layout based on view states, window dimensions (that is, the size of your app), a combination of view states and window dimensions, or none of them. The presentation of content in your app depends on the type of content as well as your app's usage pattern. For example, for an app that displays news articles, tablet users might want to use portrait and landscape modes, whereas laptop or desktop PC users will use only landscape orientation.

When a device is in landscape orientation, the available area in the vertical direction is limited. The layout of UI elements is therefore constrained in the vertical direction and the elements should be laid out in the horizontal direction. When the device is in portrait orientation, the available area in the horizontal direction is limited and the layout of UI elements is horizontally constrained.

The design of the UI of your app in the snapped and fill views requires special attention. In well-designed applications, the UI in the snapped state adapts to a vertical layout with attention to vertical arrangement of content. Although the fill view state provides a fair amount of window size, important content should appear on the left side of the window to ensure that it is visible.

A Windows Store app with well-designed snapped and fill views as well as for the portrait orientation is likely to be used along with other apps. For example, a tourist planning a visit to a distant city might open the Maps app and the Weather app and use them together. Supporting all the view states in such apps allows users to regularly use them, thereby increasing the visibility of these apps.

You can use the VSM, along with the various application view states, styles, and control templates, to build Windows Store apps with adaptive layouts. The VSM defines groups that consist of mutually exclusive states and, optionally, transitions between those states. The states are mutually exclusive because the VSM allows only one state to be visible at a time. The *GoToState* method of the *VisualStateManager* initiates the transition between states. The VSM or the system does not expect you to write code that updates the layout and controls of the UI. This helps decouple the details of the UI and controls in a state and the state itself.

Visual Studio provides developers with Windows Store app templates that include support for using the VSM with an adaptive layout. An example of an app built with the Grid App template showing various view states, as shown in Figure 3-4.

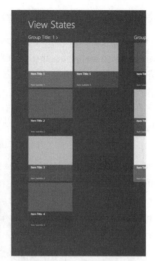

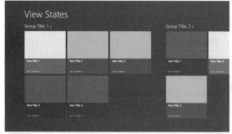

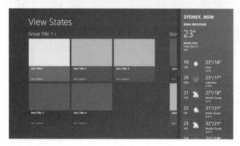

FIGURE 3-4 Windows Store app in various view states; the app was built with the Grid App template provided in Visual Studio

When a Windows Store app transitions between states, styles and control templates can be applied based on the content displayed on the screen. A layout with whitespace to create a visual separation between groups of data might work in a full screen landscape or fill state; however, in the snapped state, the app needs to minimize whitespace and update the layout to use the vertical dimension. A closer view of the app prepared using the Grid App template is shown in Figure 3-5.

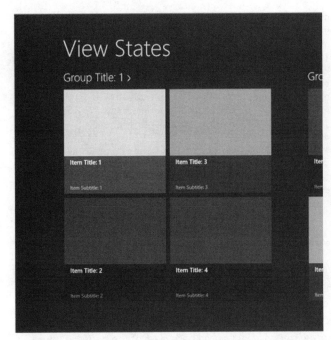

FIGURE 3-5 A Windows Store app built with the Grid App template in the full screen landscape view state (left) and snapped state (right)

You can implement controls that render content in specific view states and hide the content in all other view states. Similarly, you can group the use of buttons, images, and font properties in styles that are applied for a specific visual state. In Figure 3-5, the app uses a *GridView* control in the full screen landscape and fill states to lay out content, and uses a *ListView* control to lay out the same content in the snapped view state. In this case, the visual state transitions control the visibility of these controls as well as various other properties of other controls such as font size of text blocks and size of images in an individual item of the list. The XAML of the *VisualStateGroup* of the page in Figure 3-5 is shown in Listing 3-3.

LISTING 3-3 Defining the XAML of the VisualStateGroup

```
<VisualStateManager.VisualStateGroups>
    <VisualStateGroup x:Name="ApplicationViewStates">
        <VisualState x:Name="FullScreenLandscape"/>
        <VisualState x:Name="Filled"/>
        <!-- The back button and title have different styles when snapped,
             and the list representation is substituted for the grid
             displayed in all other view states
        -->
        <VisualState x:Name="Snapped">
            <Storyboard>
                <ObjectAnimationUsingKeyFrames Storyboard.TargetName="backButton"
                                    Storyboard.TargetProperty="Style">
                    <DiscreteObjectKeyFrame KeyTime="0"
                            Value="{StaticResource SnappedBackButtonStyle}"/>
```

```
            </ObjectAnimationUsingKeyFrames>
            <ObjectAnimationUsingKeyFrames Storyboard.TargetName="pageTitle"
                                           Storyboard.TargetProperty="Style">
                <DiscreteObjectKeyFrame KeyTime="0"
                        Value="{StaticResource SnappedPageHeaderTextStyle}"/>
            </ObjectAnimationUsingKeyFrames>
            <ObjectAnimationUsingKeyFrames Storyboard.TargetName="itemListView"
                                           Storyboard.TargetProperty="Visibility">
                <DiscreteObjectKeyFrame KeyTime="0" Value="Visible"/>
            </ObjectAnimationUsingKeyFrames>
            <ObjectAnimationUsingKeyFrames Storyboard.TargetName="itemGridView"
                                           Storyboard.TargetProperty="Visibility">
                <DiscreteObjectKeyFrame KeyTime="0" Value="Collapsed"/>
            </ObjectAnimationUsingKeyFrames>
        </Storyboard>
    </VisualState>
  </VisualStateGroup>
</VisualStateManager.VisualStateGroups>
```

The VSM makes it easy for developers to support multiple view states in the layout of pages without having to implement pages specifically for a view state. The project template provided by Visual Studio adds a class called *LayoutAwarePage* that includes code to support the *VisualStateManager* class along with the *SizeChanged* event to cater for view state changes. You should use the *LayoutAwarePage* class as the base class of the pages in your Windows Store apps to include support for view state changes.

Setting up app orientation in the manifest

For some Windows Store apps, it is important to restrict their visual experience to specific view states. They start in a specific orientation and are not expected to respond to any changes in the orientation. A movie player is a good example. The user can hold their device in portrait orientation, thereby making the video appear in a letter box if the movie player supports both portrait and landscape orientations.

Visual Studio provides you with the option to select the supported orientations of your app through the package manifest, shown in Figure 3-6.

Package.appxmanifest ⊕ ✕

The properties of the deployment package for your app are contained in the app manifest file. You can use the Manifes:

Application UI   Capabilities   Declarations   Packaging

Use this page to set the properties that identify and describe your app.

Display name: SplashSample

Entry point: SplashSample.App

Default language: en-US   More information

Description: Splash Sample

Supported rotations: An optional setting that indicates the app's orientation preferences.

☑ Landscape   ☐ Portrait   ☐ Landscape-flipped   ☐ Portrait-flipped

FIGURE 3-6 Package manifest options for setting the preferred orientation

A Windows Store app that does not support portrait orientation must support the fill, snapped, and full screen view states in landscape orientation. The choice of orientations supported by the app determines the layout of the pages in the app as well as the splash screen. If an application supports the portrait orientation only, the splash screen is always shown in the portrait mode.

Thought experiment
Designing an app to support multiple screen sizes

In this thought experiment, apply what you've learned about this objective. You can find answers to these questions in the "Answers" section at the end of this chapter.

You have been asked to participate in a project to port a popular and successful iOS app used in the healthcare industry to Windows 8. Currently, organizations can use a companion desktop app as well as a web application to manage various parts of the business workflow. You are expected to merge all applications into a single Windows Store app that will run on tablets, laptops, and desktop PCs. The devices support multiple screen sizes and resolutions, and the Windows Store app must support them as well as all view states. Some devices use a touch interface; others provide input through a keyboard and mouse.

You have been asked to lead the app's development and provide guidance on design principles. What are three recommendations you are likely to present to your development team?

Objective summary

- While designing and implementing your Windows Store app, you should consider various screen sizes and resolutions of devices and PCs as well as the view states your app can be in.

- You should use the *VisualStateManager* class with the *VisualState* class for the view states you support in your app.

- Styles and control templates enable reuse of visual elements. They should be used with the *VisualStateManager* class to lay out UI elements.

- You can provide the preferred orientations of your app through its package manifest. Note that the user can still put your app in the snapped view state even if you do not support portrait orientation. The snapped and fill view states are available only in landscape orientation.

Objective review

Answer the following questions to test your knowledge of the information in this objective. You can find the answers to these questions and explanations of why each answer choice is correct or incorrect in the "Answers" section at the end of this chapter.

1. You are developing a Windows Store app that will be used in all possible orientations and view states. You have updated the package manifest in Visual Studio to configure the supported orientations. Which view states do you need to support? (Choose all that apply.)

   A. Full screen view state in the landscape orientation

   B. Fill view state in the landscape orientation

   C. Snapped view state in the landscape orientation

   D. Snapped view state in the portrait orientation

   E. Fill view state in the portrait orientation

2. You are implementing support for the snapped and fill view states in your news reader app. You want the user to be able to read a summary of each news item with its title and, if available, a thumbnail. What is the recommended way of implementing this requirement?

   A. Create a *VisualState* for each view state. Use implicit transitions to move and resize UI elements in the layout.

   B. Create a *VisualState* for each view state. Use explicit transitions on the properties of the UI element to arrange them in the layout.

   C. Create styles and control templates for the view states. Use the *VisualStateManager* to switch between the view states.

   D. Allow Windows to automatically add vertical and horizontal scrollbars; there is no need to add anything to support multiple view states.

3. You are porting a desktop application to a Windows Store app. Users want to use your app in any orientation they like, and they want the content to be readable in all view states. What steps should you follow to implement these requirements? (Choose all that apply.)

   A. Declare the orientations your app will support in the package manifest.

   B. Define visual states in the XAML of various pages in the application.

   C. In the *OnLaunched* event of the app, examine the current value of the *Application-ViewState* and use the *VisualStateManager* to change the layout for the view state.

   D. In the *OnSizeChanged* event of a page, examine the current value of the *ApplicationViewState* and use the *VisualStateManager* to change the layout for the view state.

   E. In the constructor of a page, examine the current value of the *ApplicationViewState* and use the *VisualStateManager* to change the layout for the view state.

Objective 3.2: Implement layout controls

The layout of a Windows Store app is an important feature that designers and developers should pay attention to. Unlike other platforms, Windows 8 screens can range from small handheld tablets to large high-definition wall-mounted displays. Users expect Windows Store apps to smoothly handle multiple screen sizes and orientations and use the available area on the screen. Microsoft provides developers with layout controls that help with the arrangement of content in a scale-free way as well as adapting to multiple view states and orientations.

A Windows Store app consists of a root UI element (called *Frame*) that represents the area occupied by the application on a Windows 8 PC or device. The *Frame* acts as a container of the content in the app and supports navigation in an app with multiple pages. (Each page is represented by the *Page* UI element.) A *Page* consists of a set of controls that provide the look and feel you decide to implement. Layout controls such as *Canvas*, *Grid*, *WrapGrid*, *Variable-SizedWrapGrid*, and *StackPanel* make it very easy for developers to position content within their apps.

The *Grid* control provides a flexible yet powerful way of arranging UI elements in a page of a Windows Store app. It helps with the layout of controls in multiple rows and multiple columns, and provides a number of ways to control their height and width. Using a grid in a page is similar to using *<table>* elements in a HTML page to arrange items in rows and columns. You can even use a mix of fixed and proportional dimensions for rows and columns in a grid, allowing your app to adjust to variations in the screen size, resolution, and view states.

Implementing the Grid control to structure the app layout

The layout of Windows Store apps differs from the layout of traditional desktop apps. You have a number of options in which to place controls, such as the app window, flyouts, pop-ups, dialog boxes, and app bars. The app page forms the base surface of your app's UI. Ideally, you should use this surface to integrate the UI elements. An error message, for example, can appear as highlighted inline text with an animation and hidden after the user has viewed it, instead of using the traditional pop-up dialog box. A Windows Store app can have as many app pages as necessary to meet business requirements and user scenarios.

In an app page, use a layout control to build its structure along with the set of controls provided by Visual Studio. The *Grid* control is the most commonly used control for creating layouts in Windows Store apps. Similar to a HTML table, the *Grid* allows you to specify a number of rows and columns and their dimensions. The size of cells in a grid are specified in pixels, as a ratio relative to the size of other cells, or to automatically resize based on the size of the cell's contents.

Using a grid-based layout in a Windows Store app offers several benefits. A well-designed Windows Store app applies the basic Microsoft design style principles of being fast and fluid with an emphasis on content rather than UI elements such as whitespace, gradient, and color. This means your app follows a consistent pattern of page headers, margins, padding, gutter widths, and so on. A prominent feature of the grid-based layout is the silhouette, which consists of a wide margin on the top, bottom, and left edges. This provides users with a visual guide to scroll or pan the content horizontally.

Visual Studio provides a set of templates that use a grid layout to arrange controls with support for multiple view states. Figure 3-7 shows the layout of two Windows Store apps using the templates provided by Visual Studio.

Silhouette

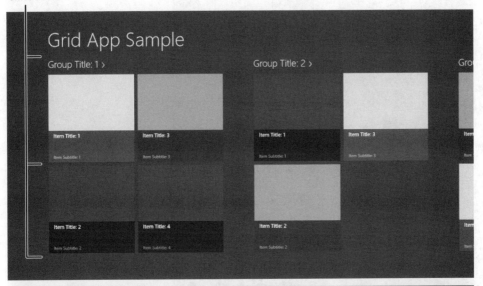

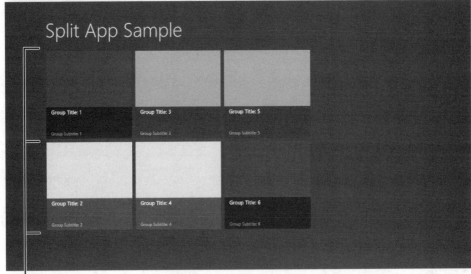

Silhouette

FIGURE 3-7 Layout of the Visual Studio Grid App and Split App templates

To support multiple view states, you can define visual states and styles associated with them. Visual Studio templates include support for orientation and view state changes. Figure 3-8 shows a few templates in the snapped view state.

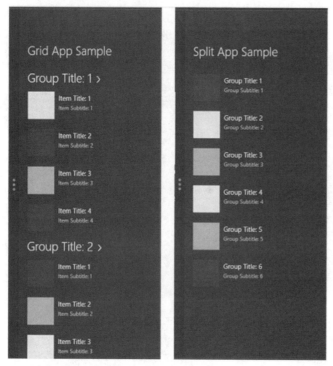

FIGURE 3-8 Layouts of the Visual Studio Grid App and Split App templates in the snapped view state

The apps created using the Grid App and Split App templates in Visual Studio have some unique visual features:

- The apps have their silhouettes clearly defined. The silhouette is visible in the snapped view state.
- The padding between groups of data is consistent across the app, in all view states.
- The padding between items in a group is consistent across the app, in all view states.

The consistency in the appearance of Windows Store apps using a grid to lay out pages is an incentive for users to use your app. Microsoft prepared some guidelines while designing the controls and the grid-based templates. These guidelines should be followed by Windows Store app developers whenever possible; they are summarized here:

- The grid layout system is made up of units and subunits, the unit being the basic unit of measurement. A unit is 20 × 20 pixels square. It is divided into subunits of 5 × 5 pixels; therefore, there are 16 subunits per unit. It is a good practice to compose your UI in multiples of units and subunits.
- The baseline of the app page header is 5 units, or 100 pixels from the top. The left margin for the page header is 6 units, or 120 pixels. The recommended font for the page header is SegoeUI Stylistic Set 20, light weight.

- The content region has a top margin of 7 units, or 140 pixels. The left margin is 6 units, or 120 pixels. Therefore, there is a 2-unit, or 40-pixel, separation between the top of the content area and the baseline of the page header.

- Horizontal padding between content items varies with the type of item. Items with hard edges such as images and user tiles are separated from accompanying text by 2 subunits, or 10 pixels of padding. Hard-edged items are separated by 2 units, or 40 pixels of padding. Lists in columns are separated by 2 units, or 40 pixels of padding.

- The horizontal padding between groups of items is 4 units, or 80 pixels. Whitespace helps users distinguish between groups while panning or scrolling across many groups horizontally.

- Vertical padding between content items varies with the type of item. Tile and text lists have 1 unit, or 20 pixels, of vertical padding between items in a row. Hard-edged items placed in rows have 2 subunits, or 10 pixels, of padding between items in a row.

MORE INFO **PAGE LAYOUT AND TYPOGRAPHY GUIDELINES**

Microsoft provides designers of Windows Store apps with page layout and typography guidelines. Page layout guidelines are available at *http://msdn.microsoft.com/en-au/library/windows/apps/hh872191.aspx*, and typography guidelines are available at *http://msdn.microsoft.com/en-au/library/windows/apps/hh700394.aspx*.

Using a grid layout for app pages enables automatic scaling at different screen sizes and resolutions. Larger screen sizes support a higher resolution, which can be a challenge for developers to rearrange UI elements in response to events that are raised when screen resolution is updated. The application created with the Grid App template shown in Figure 3-7 is running in a 10.6" screen at 1366 × 768 resolution. The same application is also shown in Figure 3-9, running in a 23" screen at 1920 × 1080 resolution. You will notice that the layout of the UI elements changes automatically with the screen resolution. The extra space is used to lay out more groups in the visible area of the screen.

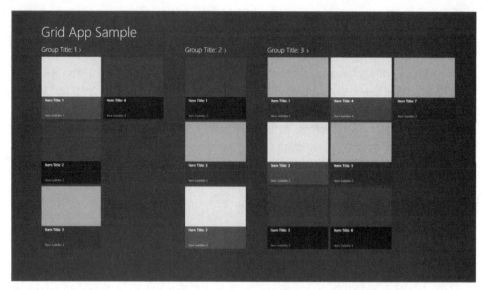

FIGURE 3-9 Change in the arrangement of controls in an app using a grid layout in a 23" screen running at 1920 × 1080 resolution

Microsoft recommends you design Windows Store apps for a minimum resolution of 1024 × 768 and an optimum resolution of 1366 × 768. Recall that in the former case, the screen size is not adequate for your app to be snapped. For large screens, the general recommendation is to fill up the available area while maintaining the guidance for the silhouette of your app.

If your app will cater to larger screens, you can implement a fixed layout in which there is a fixed amount of content, or a scale-to-fit layout to have your fixed layout fill the screens of various sizes. The scale-to-fit approach is built into the Windows 8 platform. You can place fixed content in a *ViewBox* control, which scales a fixed layout to fit the whole screen. The *ViewBox* control should be sized to 100% width and height, and its fixed size properties should be sized to the fixed pixel sizes of the layout (for example, 1366 × 768). If your app will support an adaptive layout, you should determine how your app will use the extra space available on a larger screen.

> ***MORE INFO*** **WINDOWS 8 USER EXPERIENCE GUIDELINES**
>
> Microsoft provides designers and developers of Windows Store apps with a handbook of user experience guidelines that can be downloaded from *http://www.microsoft.com/en-au/download/details.aspx?id=30704.*

Setting the number of rows/columns and size

The *Grid* control has a collection of rows and columns that can create various control arrangements that compose the UI. Some of the properties that are commonly specified for a *Grid* control are the following:

- **ColumnDefinitions**   This property contains a collection of one or more *ColumnDefinition* objects. A *ColumnDefinition* object defines column-specific properties that apply to *Grid* elements. The *Width* property of *ColumnDefinition* specifies the width of a column in a grid.

- **RowDefinitions**   This property contains a collection of one or more *RowDefinition* objects. A *RowDefinition* object defines row-specific properties that apply to *Grid* elements. The *Height* property of *RowDefinition* specifies the height of a row in a grid.

- **Background**   This property is used to specify the *Brush* used as the background of the control. A brush can be a solid color or an image.

- **Height** and **Width**   These properties control the size of the *Grid* control. In most design scenarios, the height and width of the *Grid* control is not specified and is allowed to occupy all available space in the frame.

The following XAML code shows how you can use the *RowDefinitions* and *ColumnDefinitions* properties to define a grid layout with three rows and two columns:

```
<Grid x:Name="PageLayoutRoot">
    <Grid.ColumnDefinitions>
        <ColumnDefinition />
        <ColumnDefinition />
    </Grid.ColumnDefinitions>
    <Grid.RowDefinitions>
        <RowDefinition />
        <RowDefinition />
        <RowDefinition />
    </Grid.RowDefinitions>
</Grid>
```

You can place and position controls within the grid by specifying their *Grid.Row* and *Grid.Column* properties to the respective row and column of the grid. You should note that the rows and columns follow a zero-based index. For example, if you want to place a colored rectangle in the first column, second row of the control, use the following XAML code:

```
<Grid x:Name="PageLayoutRoot">
    <Grid.ColumnDefinitions>
        <ColumnDefinition />
        <ColumnDefinition />
    </Grid.ColumnDefinitions>
    <Grid.RowDefinitions>
        <RowDefinition />
        <RowDefinition />
        <RowDefinition />
    </Grid.RowDefinitions>
    <Rectangle Grid.Row="1" Grid.Column="0" Fill="Wheat" />
</Grid>
```

In some Windows Store apps, you might need to position a control so it occupies multiple rows or columns. You can use a combination of the *RowSpan* and *ColumnSpan* properties in the *RowDefinitions* and *ColumnDefinitions* properties for arranging controls in a grid, as follows:

```
<Grid x:Name="PageLayoutRoot">
    <Grid.ColumnDefinitions>
        <ColumnDefinition />
        <ColumnDefinition />
        <ColumnDefinition />
        <ColumnDefinition />
        <ColumnDefinition />
    </Grid.ColumnDefinitions>
    <Grid.RowDefinitions>
        <RowDefinition />
        <RowDefinition />
        <RowDefinition />
        <RowDefinition />
        <RowDefinition />
    </Grid.RowDefinitions>
    <Rectangle Grid.Row="1" Grid.Column="1" Fill="LightBlue" />
    <Rectangle Grid.Row="2" Grid.Column="0" Fill="DarkBlue" Grid.ColumnSpan="2" />
    <Rectangle Grid.Row="3" Grid.Column="1" Fill="Tomato" Grid.RowSpan="2" />
</Grid>
```

Figure 3-10 illustrates how the controls are arranged in the grid layout when viewed in the Visual Studio XAML designer.

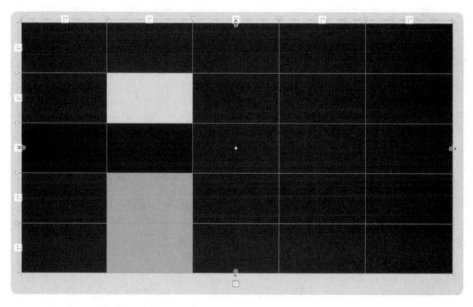

FIGURE 3-10 Controls in the grid layout of a page

If you look at Figure 3-10 closely, you will notice that the Visual Studio designer has placed *1** against the rows and columns of the grid. This results from the associated XAML—the members of the *RowDefinitions* and *ColumnDefinitions* of the grid do not specify their dimensions. Therefore, the available screen area is distributed equally among all rows and columns. Although this might be adequate for arranging controls in a grid layout in many scenarios, you will sometimes require more control over the dimensions of grid rows and columns.

The *Grid* control supports three ways of specifying the dimensions of *RowDefinition* and *ColumnDefinition*:

- **Auto** Setting the *Height* or *Width* to *Auto* results in the child elements in the cells defined by the rows and columns occupying as much space as required to render. The height of a row is the height of the tallest UI element in that row, and the width of a column is the width of the widest UI element in that column.

- **Fixed Size** You can specify the width or height in logical pixels, which results in fixed sizes of the rows and columns.

- **Star Sizing** You can set the height of a row or the width of column to *. This results in the available space being distributed equally among elements or based on ratios. Note that you can use either 1* and * for star sizing a column or row in a layout.

The option of using star sizing to control column width and row height in a grid is a powerful technique for arranging elements that use available space in various screen sizes and resolutions. There are some rules you need to follow to use star sizing:

- When you set a row's height or column's width to *, the row or column occupies all remaining space if the heights of other rows and widths of other columns are fixed.

- When you set the height of multiple rows or width of multiple columns to *, the remaining space is equally divided among the rows or columns.

- You can apply a weight to rows and columns by placing a coefficient in front of the *. The rows and columns with the applied weight occupy more space than other rows and columns. For example, a row with its height set to *3** occupies three times the height of a row with height set to *.

In your app, you might need to arrange controls so that the row or column they are placed in is a proportion of the other rows or columns. The following XAML shows the second row is twice as wide as other rows, and the fourth column is half as wide as other columns:

```
<Grid x:Name="PageLayoutRoot">
    <Grid.ColumnDefinitions>
        <ColumnDefinition />
        <ColumnDefinition />
        <ColumnDefinition />
        <ColumnDefinition Width="0.5*"/>
        <ColumnDefinition />
    </Grid.ColumnDefinitions>
    <Grid.RowDefinitions>
        <RowDefinition />
        <RowDefinition Height="2*" />
        <RowDefinition />
```

```
            <RowDefinition />
            <RowDefinition />
        </Grid.RowDefinitions>
        <Rectangle Grid.Row="1" Grid.Column="1" Fill="LightBlue" />
        <Rectangle Grid.Row="2" Grid.Column="0" Fill="DarkBlue" Grid.ColumnSpan="2" />
        <Rectangle Grid.Row="3" Grid.Column="1" Fill="Tomato" Grid.RowSpan="2" />
        <Rectangle Grid.Row="4" Grid.Column="2" Fill="ForestGreen" Grid.ColumnSpan="3" />
</Grid>
```

Figure 3-11 shows the XAML rendered in the Visual Studio XAML designer.

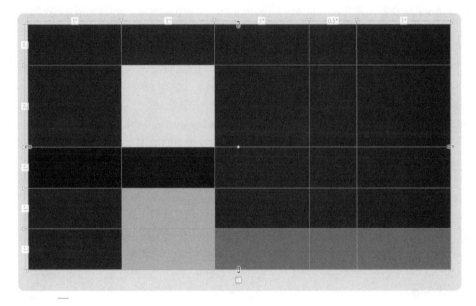

FIGURE 3-11 The rows and columns in a grid configured with proportional height and width

EXAM TIP

You will not be required to write XAML in the exam. However, you might be asked questions where XAML will be shown for creating layouts per the requirements of a Windows Store app. Therefore, you must understand how the *Grid* control is used with layout controls in an app.

Enabling scroll and zoom capabilities in layout controls

In some Windows Store apps, the amount of data to display on the screen might not be known until the user starts using the app. Data might overflow the visible area on the screen, and the user might not be able to view a lot of the data. For example, the data returned from a remote web service consists of groups of data displayed horizontally, with the items in each group displayed vertically in columns. In such a scenario, the data in the columns might not fit in the screen and will not be visible to the user.

The *ScrollViewer* control is available for developers to lay out UI elements so they are visible within the available screen area. It provides a virtual surface adequate for rendering all UI elements placed within it. The *ScrollViewer* can handle horizontal and vertical scrolling, which depend on the preferences you set when you configure it. Content placed within the *ScrollViewer* is displayed within the visible area of the control, called the viewport.

The following are commonly used properties of *ScrollViewer*:

- **Height and Width**   These properties are used to specify the height and width of the viewport. If the content placed within the *ScrollViewer* occupies more area than that specified by the *Height* and *Width*, it will be clipped or scrollbars will be added based on their visibility settings.

- **HorizontalScrollBarVisibility**   This property controls whether the *ScrollViewer* should display a horizontal scrollbar. The values allowed for this property are *Disabled*, *Auto*, *Hidden* and *Visible*. The default value is *Disabled*.

- **VerticalScrollBarVisibility**   This property controls whether the *ScrollViewer* should display a vertical scrollbar. The values allowed for this property are *Disabled*, *Auto*, *Hidden* and *Visible*. The default value is *Visible*.

- **Content**   This property can be used to set the content of the *ScrollViewer* control. The child element specified through the *Content* property is then scrolled using the *ScrollViewer*.

The *HorizontalScrollBarVisibility* and *VerticalScrollBarVisibility* properties of the *ScrollViewer* can be specified in the XAML of a page or its code-behind. Their values belong to the *ScrollBarVisibility* enumeration, as described in Table 3-2.

TABLE 3-2 *ScrollBarVisibility* enumeration members

MEMBER	VALUE	DESCRIPTION
Disabled	0	The scrollbar is not visible, and scrolling is not available for the content even when the viewport cannot display it. The content is allowed to occupy the visible area in the parent UI element.
Auto	1	The scrollbar appears when the content is large enough to require scrolling; that is, it does not fit within the viewport.
Hidden	2	The scrollbar does not appear even though the content can be scrolled and the viewport cannot display all the content. This value should be avoided in Windows Store apps because the user might not realize that the content in the ScrollViewer needs scrolling.
Visible	3	The scrollbar always appears whenever there is focus on the ScrollViewer. If the content fits within the viewport, the scrollbar will be disabled and will appear grayed-out.

The *Height* and *Width* properties can be used to explicitly specify the height and width of a *ScrollViewer* control. When placed in a layout within a grid, the *ScrollViewer* occupies the available area by default. Whenever required, you can use a *ScrollViewer* with scrollable content placed in a child UI element, such as a *Grid* or *StackPanel*. See the XAML code in Listing 3-4.

LISTING 3-4 Using a *ScrollViewer* with scrollable content

```xaml
<Page>
    <Grid x:Name="PageLayoutRoot">
        <Grid.RowDefitions>
            <RowDefinition Height="140" />
            <RowDefinition Height="*" />
        </Grid.RowDefinitions>
        <Grid Grid.Row="0">
            <!-- Content for title-->
        </Grid>
        <Grid Grid.Row="1">
            <Grid.RowDefinitions>
                <RowDefinition Height="*" />
            </Grid.RowDefinitions>
            <Grid.ColumnDefinitions>
                <ColumnDefinition Width="*" />
                <ColumnDefinition Width="*" />
                <ColumnDefinition Width="*" />
            </Grid.ColumnDefinitions>
            <ScrollViewer Grid.Column="0">
                <StackPanel Orientation="Vertical"> <!-- Child of ScrollViewer -->
                <!-- TextBlocks for the column are placed here -->
                </StackPanel>
            </ScrollViewer>
            <ScrollViewer Grid.Column="1">
                <StackPanel Orientation="Vertical"> <!-- Child of ScrollViewer -->
                <!-- TextBlocks for the column are placed here -->
                </StackPanel>
            </ScrollViewer>
            <ScrollViewer Grid.Column="2">
                <StackPanel Orientation="Vertical"> <!-- Child of ScrollViewer -->
                <!-- TextBlocks for the column are placed here -->
                </StackPanel>
            </ScrollViewer>
        </Grid>
    </Grid>
</Page>
```

Figure 3-12 shows the page of the Windows Store app for the XAML. Whenever the mouse hovers over the app or the user touches the surface, scrollbars appear for each column. In this example, the user can scroll vertically to view the content of each column.

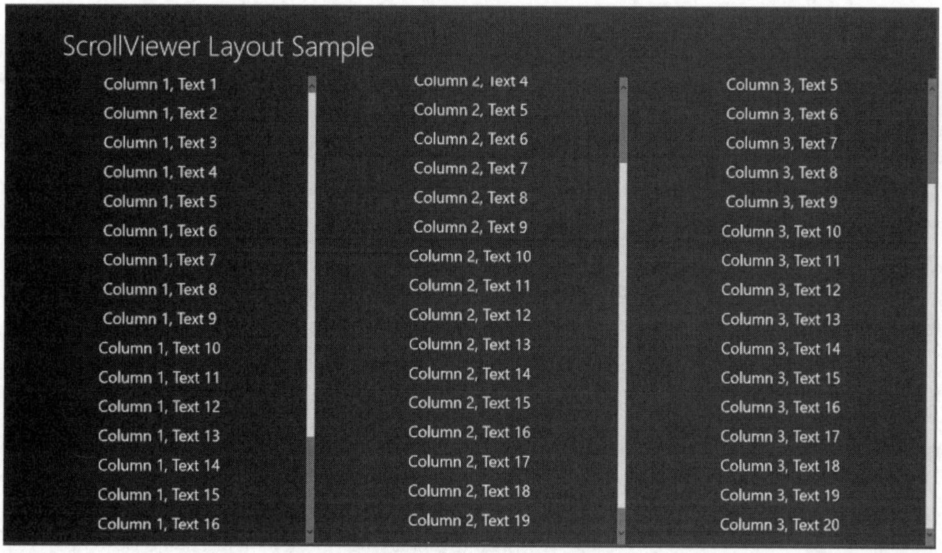

FIGURE 3-12 An app with multiple columns, each with a *ScrollViewer* in which the content is embedded

In addition to providing support for a dynamic layout in pages, the *ScrollViewer* control has built-in support for touch and zoom. By default, it enables the pinch-to-zoom touch gestures on the content. The properties of the *ScrollViewer* relevant for zooming are the following:

- **ZoomMode** This is a Boolean that indicates whether zooming is available in the *ScrollViewer*. The values allowed for this property are *Enabled* and *Disabled*.

- **ZoomFactor** This property sets the current value for scaling content. The default value of this property is *1.0*, which indicates no scaling. Use the *ZoomToFactor* method to change the value of this property at runtime.

- **MinZoomFactor** and **MaxZoomFactor** These properties specify the minimum and maximum runtime values for *ZoomFactor*. The default value of *MinZoomFactor* is 0.1, and the default value of *MaxZoomFactor* is 10.0.

- **IsZoomChainingEnabled** This property specifies whether zoom chaining is enabled from this child to its parent. Zoom chaining controls whether the zooming action carried out by the user on a child element should be available on the parent *ScrollViewer* control.

- **IsZoomInertiaEnabled** This property specifies whether the zoom actions should include inertia in their behavior and value. Inertia in zooming action slows down the effect of zooming in or out of a UI element.

You can provide snap points in a Windows Store app to control zooming behavior. Snap points are logical points at which manipulation of content is stopped, and a subset of the content is visible in the page. It is recommended you provide snap points at common zoom resolutions, such as 100%, 75%, 50%, and 25%. You can provide mandatory snap points in your app for the user to continue panning the content until a snap point is reached, or you can provide proximity snap points to continue panning only when the current location is close to a snap point. You can specify a list of zoom snap points through the *ZoomSnapPoints* property and the zoom behavior through the *ZoomSnapPointsType* property. The value of the *ZoomSnapPointsType* property is set by using the *SnapPointsType* enumeration, as described in Table 3-3.

TABLE 3-3 *SnapPointsType* enumeration members

MEMBER	VALUE	DESCRIPTION
None	0	No value is set.
Optional	1	Viewer will snap to points when the current location is close to a snap point.
Mandatory	2	Viewer will always snap to a snap point on interaction.
OptionalSingle	3	Snap points are optional and cannot be jumped over.
MandatorySingle	4	Snap points are mandatory and cannot be jumped over.

Managing text flow and presentation

Windows Store apps that display textual content use either the *TextBlock* or the *RichText-Block* controls. Both these controls have different use cases. The *TextBlock* control is used in the most basic cases where some text needs to be displayed. When your app needs to embed text with advanced formatting such as including UI elements, such as a hyperlink to a webpage or needs to display text in multiple columns for better readability, the *RichTextBlock* class can be used in such scenarios.

The *TextBlock* class can be used with a *ScrollViewer* control in the layout of a page. This ensures the text that overflows the visible screen area can be viewed by the user with the scrollbars or panning using touch. In its simplest form, you can use the *TextBlock* control within a *ScrollViewer* control, as shown in the XAML code in Listing 3-5.

LISTING 3-5 Using a *TextBlock* control in a *ScrollViewer* control

```
<Page>
    <Grid x:Name="PageLayoutRoot">
        <Grid.RowDefitions>
            <RowDefinition Height="140" />
            <RowDefinition Height="*" />
        </Grid.RowDefinitions>
        <Grid Grid.Row="0">
```

```
            <TextBlock Text="TextBlockSample"
                       Style="{StaticResource PageHeaderTextStyle}" />
        </Grid>
        <Grid Grid.Row="1">
            <Grid.ColumnDefinitions>
                <ColumnDefinition Width="*" />
            </Grid.ColumnDefinitions>
            <!-- The ScrollViewer is set up with a left margin of 120 pixels or 6 units -->
            <ScrollViewer Margin="120,0,0,40" Grid.Column="0">
                <TextBlock TextWrapping="Wrap" Margin="0,0,20,0">
                    <Run FontSize="28">
                        <!-- Text removed for brevity -->
                        Lorem ipsum dolor sit....
                    </Run>
                    <LineBreak />
                    <Run FontSize="28" FontStyle="Italic">
                        <!-- Text removed for brevity -->
                        Aenean orci ante,...
                    </Run>
                </TextBlock>
            </ScrollViewer>
        </Grid>
    </Grid>
</Page>
```

Figure 3-13 shows the Windows Store app with the text displayed.

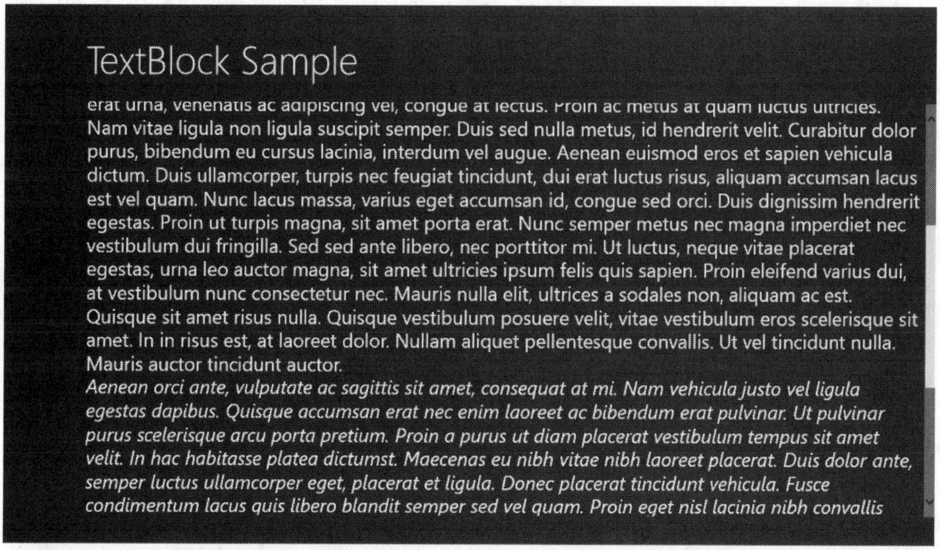

FIGURE 3-13 A Windows Store app with a *TextBlock* placed within a *ScrollViewer* control

You can use the *Text* property of the *TextBlock* control to set the text; however, you can also place a block text within *<Run>* tags to format it. You can use multiple *Run*s in the same *TextBlock* to apply finer control on formatting the text. Note that a *LineBreak* element is not allowed within a *Run* element. Similar to the *Run* element, Windows provides the *Underline* element to embed text for underlining because there is no property on the *TextBlock* to achieve this. The following are properties of the *TextBlock* class:

- **CharacterSpacing**   This property sets the spacing between characters in units of a thousandth of an em. Note that an em is equal to the font size of the element. You can use a negative value to reduce spacing between letters.

- **FlowDirection**   This property sets the direction of text flow and other UI elements within the *TextBlock*. The property can be set to either *LeftToRight* (the default) or *RightToLeft*.

- **Font properties**   The *FontFamily*, *FontSize*, *FontStretch*, *FontStyle*, and *FontWeight* properties customize the look and feel of the font used in the *TextBlock*.

- **IsTextSelectionEnabled**   This property specifies whether text selection is enabled in the *TextBlock*. It can be either *False* (the default value) or *True*.

- **LineHeight**   This property sets the height of each line in the *TextBlock*, specified in device-independent pixels. A value of zero (the default value) indicates the line height is determined automatically from the characteristics of the font used in the text block. A nonzero value sets the height specified in pixels.

- **LineStackingStrategy**   This property specifies how a line box will be determined for each line. The default value is *MaxHeight*, which is the smallest value that contains all the inline elements on that line when those elements are properly aligned. It can be set to *BlockLineHeight* and used in conjunction with the *LineHeight* property to set the line height. Finally, it can be set to *BaselineToBaseline*, which sets the value to the distance between text baselines.

- **TextAlignment**   This property specifies the horizontal alignment of the text content. It can have one of four values: *Center*, *Left*, *Right*, or *Justify*. The default value is *Left*.

- **TextTrimming**   This property sets the behavior of the text in case it doesn't fit within the available content area. You can set it to either *None* (the default value) so that text is clipped when it overflows, or *WordEllipsis*, which places an ellipsis in the end.

- **TextWrapping**   This property specifies whether text can wrap into additional lines. You can set it *NoWrap* (the default value) or *Wrap*.

A Windows Store app such as a news or periodical reader can display figures inline and use multi-column layouts to arrange text in the available surface area. The *RichTextBlock* class provides more advanced formatting capabilities than the *TextBlock* control. The content in a *RichTextBlock* is set using the *Paragraph* element. In addition to applying bold, italic, or underline formatting to text in a *Paragraph* element with *<Bold>*, *<Italic>*, and *<Underline>* tags, respectively, you can embed one or more UI elements derived from the *UIElement* class; for example, images by using the *InlineUIContainer* class. The XAML of the *TextBlock* sample in Listing 3-5 can be modified to use a *RichTextBlock* and include an *InlineUIContainer* to display an image inline. See the XAML code in Listing 3-6.

```
<Page>
    <Grid x:Name="PageLayoutRoot">
        <Grid.RowDefitions>
            <RowDefinition Height="140" />
            <RowDefinition Height="*" />
        </Grid.RowDefinitions>
        <Grid Grid.Row="0">
            <!-- Content for title, etc -->
        </Grid>
        <Grid Grid.Row="1">
            <Grid.ColumnDefinitions>
                <ColumnDefinition Width="*" />
            </Grid.ColumnDefinitions>
            <ScrollViewer Margin="120,0,0,40" Grid.Column="0">
                <RichTextBlock TextWrapping="Wrap" Margin="0,0,20,0">
                    <Paragraph FontSize="28">
                        <!-- Text removed for brevity -->
                        Lorem ipsum dolor sit....
                    </Paragraph>
                    <Paragraph FontSize="28" FontStyle="Italic">
                        <InlineUIContainer>
                            <Image Source="Assets/MediumGray.png" Stretch="None" />
                        </InlineUIContainer>
                        <Bold>Aenean orci ante</Bold>,...
                        <!-- Text removed for brevity -->
                    </Paragraph>
                </RichTextBlock>
            </ScrollViewer>
        </Grid>
    </Grid>
</Page>
```

Figure 3-14 shows the Windows Store app with the text displayed using a *RichTextBlock* and *InlineUIContainer* to display an image.

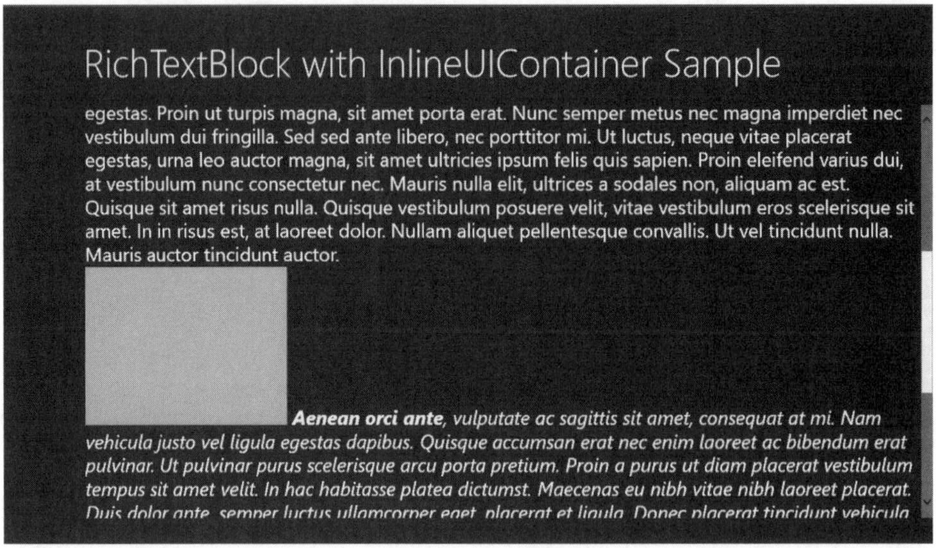

FIGURE 3-14 A Windows Store app with a *RichTextBlock* control with *InlineUIContainer* for an image; they are placed within a *ScrollViewer* control

In the examples so far, we have used a *ScrollViewer* to make the text readable in a *TextBlock* or a *RichTextBlock* control when it does not fit in the available surface area. You can use an element called *RichTextBlockOverflow* to display text that spills over from a *RichTextBlock*. If the content doesn't fit in one *RichTextBlockOverflow*, it can spill into another *RichTextBlockOverflow,* and so on.

To use *RichTextBlockOverflow*, set the *RichTextBlock OverflowContentTarget* property to an instance of *RichTextBlockOverflow*. *RichTextBlockOverflow* has its own *OverflowContentTarget* property; therefore, you can keep adding *OverflowContentTarget* in a sequence. In Listing 3-7, two *RichTextBlockOverflow* elements are chained with a single *RichTextBlock*, and the text font size varies with the slider.

LISTING 3-7 Chaining *RichTextBlockOverflow* elements with a *RichTextBlock*

```
<StackPanel Margin="20,0,0,50">
    <TextBlock TextWrapping="Wrap" Text="FontSize:" Margin="0, 0, 20, 0"/>
    <Slider x:Name="fontSizeSlider" Width="200" Value="16" Minimum="8" Maximum="24"
            TickFrequency="4" Orientation="Horizontal" HorizontalAlignment="Left" />
</StackPanel>
<Grid x:Name="columnGrid" Width="900" Height="300">
    <Grid.ColumnDefinitions>
        <ColumnDefinition/>
        <ColumnDefinition/>
        <ColumnDefinition/>
    </Grid.ColumnDefinitions>
    <RichTextBlock Grid.Column="0"
                FontSize="{Binding Value, ElementName=fontSizeSlider}"
                OverflowContentTarget="{Binding ElementName=firstOverflowContainer}"
                TextAlignment="Justify" Margin="20,0" FontFamily="Segoe UI">
```

```
        <Paragraph>
            <!-- Text Content -->
        </Paragraph>
    </RichTextBlock>
    <RichTextBlockOverflow x:Name="firstOverflowContainer" Grid.Column="1"
            OverflowContentTarget="{Binding ElementName=secondOverflowContainer}"
            Margin="20,0"/>
    <RichTextBlockOverflow x:Name="secondOverflowContainer" Grid.Column="2"
            Margin="20,0"/>
</Grid>
```

Figure 3-15 shows how *RichTextBlockOverflow* arranges the text in two columns with the default font size.

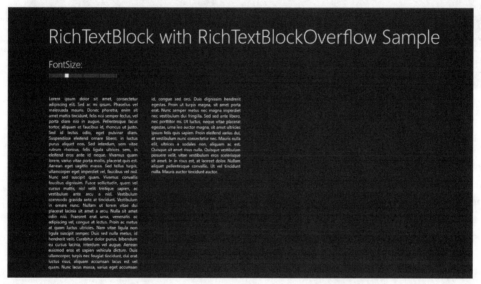

FIGURE 3-15 Screenshot of a Windows Store app showing a *RichTextBlock* control with two *RichTextBlock-Overflow* controls for displaying text that does not fit in the *RichTextBlock*

At the default font size, the text shown in Figure 3-15 is almost impossible to read. When the user selects a larger font size with the slider, the text spills over to the second *RichText-BlockOverflow* control and is displayed legibly, as shown in Figure 3-16.

RichTextBlock with RichTextBlockOverflow Sample

FontSize:

Lorem ipsum dolor sit amet, consectetur adipiscing elit. Sed ac mi ipsum. Phasellus vel malesuada mauris. Donec pharetra, enim sit amet mattis tincidunt, felis nisi semper lectus, vel porta diam nisi in augue. Pellentesque lacus tortor, aliquam et faucibus id, rhoncus ut justo. Sed id lectus odio, eget pulvinar diam. Suspendisse eleifend ornare libero, in luctus purus aliquet non. Sed interdum, sem vitae rutrum rhoncus, felis ligula ultrices sem, in eleifend eros ante id neque. Vivamus quam lorem, varius vitae porta mollis, placerat quis est. Aenean eget sagittis massa. Sed tellus turpis, ullamcorper eget imperdiet vel, faucibus vel nisl. Nunc sed suscipit quam. Vivamus convallis faucibus dignissim. Fusce sollicitudin, quam vel cursus mattis, nisl velit tristique sapien, ac vestibulum ante arcu a nisl. Vestibulum commodo gravida ante at tincidunt. Vestibulum in ornare nunc. Nullam ut lorem vitae dui placerat lacinia sit amet a arcu. Nulla sit amet odio nisi. Praesent erat urna, venenatis ac adipiscing vel, congue ac lectus. Proin ac metus at quam luctus ultricies. Nam vitae ligula non ligula suscipit semper. Duis sed nulla metus, id hendrerit velit. Curabitur dolor purus, bibendum eu cursus lacinia, interdum vel augue. Aenean euismod eros et sapien vehicula dictum. Duis ullamcorper, turpis nec feugiat tincidunt, dui erat luctus risus, aliquam accumsan lacus est vel quam. Nunc lacus massa, varius eget accumsan id, congue sed orci. Duis dignissim hendrerit egestas. Proin ut turpis magna, sit amet porta erat. Nunc semper metus nec magna imperdiet nec vestibulum dui fringilla. Sed sed ante libero, nec porttitor mi. Ut luctus, neque vitae placerat egestas, urna leo auctor magna, sit amet ultricies ipsum felis quis sapien. Proin eleifend varius dui, at vestibulum nunc consectetur nec. Mauris nulla elit, ultrices a sodales non, aliquam ac est. Quisque sit amet risus nulla. Quisque vestibulum posuere velit, vitae vestibulum eros scelerisque sit amet. In in risus est, at laoreet dolor. Nullam aliquet pellentesque convallis. Ut vel tincidunt nulla. Mauris auctor tincidunt auctor.

FIGURE 3-16 The Windows Store app shown in Figure 3-15 with an increased font size; the text uses the additional *RichTextBlockOverflow* control to render the text

To make it easier to display text using the *RichTextBlock* and *RichTextBlockOverflow* controls, Visual Studio provides a control called *RichTextColumns* with the Grid App and Split App Windows Store application templates. This control is located in the *Common* folder in your application's project directory. To use the control, set the *Width* and *Margin* properties of the *RichTextBlockOverflow* control. Depending on the style of the text, the *RichTextColumns* control creates one or more *RichTextBlockOverflow* controls to display the text.

Thought experiment

Understanding advantages of Windows Store apps over desktop applications

In this thought experiment, apply what you've learned about this objective. You can find answers to these questions in the "Answers" section at the end of this chapter.

Your organization has been invited to present a proposal to build a Windows Store app for a designer and manufacturer of engineering equipment. The manufacturer currently uses a desktop app with no touch support to create, view, and edit 3D models of heavy engineering machinery and visualize graphs of various manufacturing processes.

Your responsibility is to select three important advantages of Windows Store apps over traditional desktop applications and present them to the customer. Select the three features you will present from what you have learned in this chapter.

Objective summary

- You should design a Windows Store app to adapt to changes in screen size, resolution, and orientation.

- Use the *Grid* control to create flexible layouts in Windows Store apps. A *Grid* control has rows and columns with adjustable dimensions for creating fixed and fluid layouts.

- The *ScrollViewer* control can be used to lay out content that overflows a visible area in the screen. The control has built-in support for touch and zoom.

- The *TextBlock* control can be used with the *ScrollViewer* control to display text in a Windows Store app. Text is wrapped within the *TextBlock*, and the *ScrollViewer* provides the virtual surface area to render the text.

- Use the *RichTextBlock* control to display text embedded with photos or hyperlinks, for example. You can use the companion control, *RichTextBlockOverflow,* to display text that does not fit in the *RichTextBlock* control.

Objective review

Answer the following questions to test your knowledge of the information in this objective. You can find the answers to these questions and explanations of why each answer choice is correct or incorrect in the "Answers" section at the end of this chapter.

1. You have developed a Windows Store app with a grid layout using fixed row heights and column widths. Your testers have reported that controls overlap each other in the portrait orientation. However, the UI appears properly in other orientations. What is the best solution for this problem?

   A. Create and apply styles and control templates for the portrait orientation.

   B. Use proportional ratios and star sizing for the dimensions of rows and columns. Wherever necessary, adjust the size of controls using styles and templates for various view states.

   C. Remove the *Grid* control and create your own layout for the portrait orientation.

   D. Place the controls in a *ScrollViewer* and let the user scroll or pan through the content.

2. While testing your news reader application, you find that in some news articles, pictures cause the text to overflow and often get clipped. The main UI element is a *RichTextBlock* control within a *ScrollViewer* to allow content to be scrolled vertically. You want to enhance the user experience in all view states. Which implementation choices should you make? (Choose all that apply.)

   A. Develop a custom control and use it as the root UI element to lay out controls in the page.

   B. Use a *RichTextBlock* embedded in the root UI element.

   C. For the various view states, use star sizing to lay out *RichTextBlock* controls in columns. Consider using grid layouts for specific view states with styles and templates.

   D. Use *RichTextBlockOverflow* controls with the parent *RichTextBlock* control display overflow content.

   E. Use the *VisualStateManager* class to switch between styles and templates for various view states.

3. How do you justify using the *Grid* control along with the *ScrollViewer* control to lay out content in your Windows Store app? (Choose all that apply.)

   A. The *Grid* control can be used with star sizing to create a fluid layout that adapts easily to changes in screen size, resolution and orientation.

   B. The *Grid* control is the only control available for layout of content in Windows Store apps.

   C. The *ScrollViewer* control is capable of supporting only horizontal scrolling, so it is suitable for building apps that have content placed in the horizontal direction.

   D. The *ScrollViewer* control has built-in touch and zoom capabilities, handy for devices that support multi-touch.

   E. The *ScrollViewer* control presents a virtual surface area where content can overflow but be visible though scrolling or panning.

Objective 3.3: Design and implement the app bar

App bars in Windows Store apps provide users with a consistent way to access commands whenever they need them in the context of the current page (and even for the app) to navigate through various sections in an app. App bars (a bottom app bar and, optionally, a top app bar) are hidden by default and are accessible with a swipe gesture from the bottom of the screen, with a right-click of the mouse, or with the Windows+Z keyboard shortcut. They are dismissed when the user makes an edge swipe or when the user interacts with the user. App bars can also be shown and hidden programmatically.

Windows Store app developers should consider using the app bars to place commands in the context of the page as well as navigation shortcuts. Commands that are relevant to a page might not be required in other pages of your app. To provide consistent user experience, you should ensure that commands likely to be used most often are placed at the two edges of the app bar because these edges can be reached easily by the user's fingers. The fundamental rule for creating commands that are placed in the bottom app bar is that they should directly interact with the content presented in the page. The top app bar should be used for global commands and navigation within the app. This design helps the user to focus on the content in your app and prevents distraction from commands that are not frequently used.

> **This objective covers how to:**
> - Determine what to put on the app bar based on app requirements.
> - Design the placement of controls in the app bar.
> - Style and position app bar items.
> - Handle *AppBar* events.

Determining what to put on the app bar based on app requirements

Designing the UI of your Windows Store with a consideration for the commands you will require to implement in every page is quite important. In your design, if you display the content in a page without including any distractions, such as buttons or drop-downs, the user will most likely find it easy to use your app. However, a dynamic, interactive app needs commands available for common operations throughout the app.

You have the option to use the charms bar for implementing common app commands such as search, share, and configuring settings. However, having page-specific commands in the charms bar is not a good UI design and actually violates Microsoft design principles. Therefore, you should consider the app bars as placeholders for commands that help the user interact with your app.

We can draw some conclusions about the design pattern followed in app bars by examining the Weather app shown in Figure 3-17:

- Commands are placed in the app bar starting from the right edge.
- The top app bar is used for navigation between various sections of an app.
- The bottom app bar contains commands that invoke actions specific to the page.
- Commands that are available in multiple pages of an app are placed separate from commands specific to a page.

Command specific to the page

Commands available in other pages of the app

FIGURE 3-17 The Weather app showing content and the two app bars

The app bar in a Windows Store app can contain commands that are used to help the user find the right content to explore or share, such as by providing filters that can be selected one at a time. The Bing app, which you saw in Chapter 2, provides this functionality. The app bar can contain commands that help the user select a specific view of the page while remaining in the page; for example, the day, week, and month views in a calendar app. Common guidelines for app bars are summarized as follows:

- Use command groups to group distinct sets of commands and place them at opposite sides of the app bar. For example, if you have two set of commands in a page, one for creating new content and the other for operating on existing content such as applying filters, place them on opposite sides of the app bar. If you have more than two sets of commands in a page, use a separator to separate them.

- If you need to implement app bars in multiple pages, make sure the commands in the app bars are in the same location or as close to the same location as possible.

- Separate critical commands from other commands to avoid accidental execution.

- Show the app bars automatically whenever an item in the content is selected. Because most users are right-handed, contextual commands for the item should be placed in the left side of the app bar. This will prevent their arms or hands from blocking their view of the commands.

- When there are too many commands to fit in the app bar, consider using context menus and flyouts.

- Microsoft provides default styles for commands, menus, and flyouts. Use these default styles in your application to arrange commands in the app bar. The default layout is designed to support touch and to fit up to 10 commands on all supported screen widths. You can change the color of the background, icons, and labels, but avoid changing the size or padding of the buttons.

- Design your app bar for snap and portrait views. The horizontal dimensions of the app in these views are different, and special attention is required to lay out the commands in the app bar in these views. If you have up to 10 commands, Windows automatically hides labels and adjusts padding in the app bar when the user snaps your app or rotates to the portrait orientation.

- You should provide tooltips for the commands in the app bar. This is helpful in view states when the system hides the labels in the buttons.

- Use the top app bar for navigation and the bottom app bar for commands.

- Whenever there are contextual commands in the app bar, make the app bar sticky so it is not dismissed when the user touches in the main area of the screen. For example, in a photo-editing program, the app bar should be visible as long as the user is editing the photo displayed on the screen.

- If your app requires horizontal scrolling, reduce the height of the scrollable area when the app bar appears in sticky mode to avoid content from being hidden beneath the app bar. You can set the *Background* property of the app bar to *{x:Null}* to prevent the app bar from blocking taps and clicks on content beneath the app bar.

- Whenever possible, use the built-in icons for commands to have a consistent appearance with other apps.

- Avoid putting critical commands in your app bar. For example, in a camera application, the button to take a photo should be placed in the main surface, not in the app bar.

- Do not put Clipboard commands such as cut, copy, and paste in the app bar; put them in a context menu in the app page instead.

- Do not put settings commands, search, and commands for sharing content in the app bar. Use the charms available for these operations.

- The background of the app bar can match your app's main color.

You should also consider cases when the user is likely to use the right mouse button to interact with your app. In most applications, right-clicking the app displays the app bar. However, if your app depends on critical commands to be carried out with right-click, it should ignore the events that show the app bar. To provide a consistent user experience, consider using the app bar for other commands. Here are some guidelines for implementing the UI with the right mouse button in mind:

- If your app depends on a right mouse click for a critical function, use it for that function only. Ignore the events that are raised for the app bar and do not activate any contextual UI.

- Open the app bar when right-clicking regions of the app that do not require app-specific actions, such as the borders.

- If your app needs right mouse click support in the whole canvas, consider showing the app bar when the user right-clicks the topmost horizontal row of pixels, the bottommost horizontal row of pixels, or both.

- Do not provide an alternative behavior for the Windows+Z keyboard combination in your app.

The top app bar can be used in conjunction with the traditional navigation mechanism of using the Back button in a Windows Store app. The top app bar is convenient for switching between various contexts within an app; for example, multiple tabs in a browser, various categories of news items in a news reader, and so on. You should consider using a simple thumbnail for each item in the top app bar.

Designing the placement of controls on the app bar

When you choose to use the app bar to include commands for the page currently in view, button placement in the app bar is important. You should group the commands that act on existing content in the page in view on the right edge of the app bar, grouping similar commands in a section with a separator between them, and commands that create new content or are not specific to the page on the left edge of the app bar. This placement provides ease of use to right-handed users because they are likely to use the buttons on the right edge of the app bar.

In a Windows Store app, such as for an MP3 player, you declare the bottom app bar and arrange the buttons for the various commands such as play, pause, and stop as shown in Listing 3-8.

LISTING 3-8 Declaring a bottom app bar and arranging command buttons

```
<Page.BottomAppBar>
    <AppBar x:Name="bottomAppBar" IsSticky="True">
        <Grid>
            <Grid.RowDefinitions>
                <RowDefinition Height="Auto"/>
            </Grid.RowDefinitions>

            <StackPanel x:Name="leftAppBarPanel" Orientation="Horizontal">
                <Button Style="{StaticResource FolderppBarButtonStyle}"/>
                <Button Style="{StaticResource OpenFileAppBarButtonStyle}"/>
            </StackPanel>
```

```
            <StackPanel x:Name="rightAppBarPanel"
                        Orientation="Horizontal" HorizontalAlignment="Right">
                <Button Style="{StaticResource SkipBackAppBarButtonStyle}"/>
                <Button Style="{StaticResource SkipAheadAppBarButtonStyle}"/>
                <Line X1="0" Y1="60"  Margin="0,10,0,0"
                      StrokeThickness="1" Stroke="White"></Line>
                <Button Style="{StaticResource PlayAppBarButtonStyle}"/>
                <Button Style="{StaticResource PauseAppBarButtonStyle}"/>
                <Button Style="{StaticResource StopAppBarButtonStyle}"/>
            </StackPanel>
        </Grid>
    </AppBar>
</Page.BottomAppBar>
```

In Listing 3-8, notice how a vertical line separates groups of app bar controls for specific features. Figure 3-18 shows the app bar with the separator.

FIGURE 3-18 An app bar for a Windows Store MP3 player app

A Windows Store MP3 player app is likely to be used along with other applications by the user, with the MP3 player snapped to one side of the screen, as shown in Figure 3-19.

FIGURE 3-19 App bar of a MP3 player Windows Store app in the snapped view state

In the snapped and full screen portrait view states, you can use the *Styles* and *VisualStates* of the app bar buttons to hide each button's label and reduce its width. The various *Visual-States* of app bar buttons are defined in StandardStyles.xaml (which you learn about shortly); however, controls are not aware of changes in their view state. If your application uses one of the standard Windows Store app templates provided by Visual Studio, you can use the *Start-LayoutUpdate* method provided by the *LayoutAwarePage* base class to register and receive visual state changes that correspond to app view state changes. Therefore, an app bar button can go to the snapped view state when your application is snapped. The app bar of the MP3 player application you have seen previously is shown in Figure 3-20, in the snapped state.

FIGURE 3-20 App bar of a Windows Store MP3 player app in the snapped view state with *VisualStates* used for the buttons

Figure 3-21 shows the app bar after the app's orientation changes to portrait, and the buttons are resized.

FIGURE 3-21 App bar of a Windows Store MP3 player app in the full screen portrait view state with *VisualStates* used for the buttons

Styling and positioning app bar items

Visual Studio provides the StandardStyles.xaml file, which contains styles and resources that enable you to match the design of other Windows Store apps. The file includes 192 styles for app bar buttons. These styles are based on the *AppBarButtonStyle* resource, which provides the templates and visual states for the app bar buttons. *AppBarButtonStyle* uses a glyph from the Segoe UI Symbol font as the icon visible in the button. By default, the app bar button styles are commented out in the StandardStyles.xaml file, and you should uncomment the styles you use in your app. Listing 3-9 shows the XAML for *EditAppBarButtonStyle*.

LISTING 3-9 Providing the style for an app bar button

```
<Style x:Key="EditAppBarButtonStyle" TargetType="Button"
       BasedOn="{StaticResource AppBarButtonStyle}">
  <Setter Property="AutomationProperties.AutomationId" Value="EditAppBarButton"/>
  <Setter Property="AutomationProperties.Name" Value="Edit"/>
  <Setter Property="Content" Value="&#xE104;"/>
</Style>
```

The style of an app bar button is designed to look for the value of *AutomationProperties. Name*, typically used in UI automation scenarios. It uses the value of the *String* property as the text for a *TextBlock* below each circle. It is a good practice to specify the value of *AutomationProperties.AutomationId* because it is useful in creating test scripts for testing the UI. You can use this principle to create your own app bar button style; for example, Listing 3-10 shows the XAML for an Edit app bar button with an icon.

LISTING 3-10 Creating a button style for an Edit app bar button

```
<Button Style="{StaticResource EditAppBarButtonStyle}"
        AutomationProperties.Name ="Edit"
        AutomationProperties.AutomationId="EditAppBarButton">
  <Image Source="Assets/Icons/AppBar/Edit.png"/>
</Button>
```

Although the XAML in Listing 3-10 provides you the flexibility to use your own icons, it can be tedious to provide assets for every icon and create styles for them. Whenever possible, use the styles provided by Visual Studio. If you need to look up a certain symbol to use in an app bar button style, use the Character Map tool, shown in Figure 3-22.

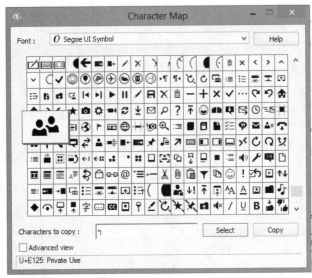

FIGURE 3-22 Character Map tool showing the various icons in the Segoe UI Symbol font family; the groups symbol is selected

You can copy and paste characters directly into your app or use the XML escape sequence *&#xHexValue*, where *HexValue* is the hexadecimal value shown in the bottom of the Character Map tool after you select a symbol. The following XAML is for an app bar button for the groups symbol:

```
<Style x:Key="GroupsAppBarButtonStyle" TargetType="Button"
        BasedOn="{StaticResource AppBarButtonStyle}">
    <Setter Property="AutomationProperties.AutomationId" Value="GroupsAppBarButton"/>
    <Setter Property="AutomationProperties.Name" Value="Groups"/>
    <Setter Property="Content" Value="&#xE125;"/>
</Style>
```

The button created with the XAML is shown in Figure 3-23.

FIGURE 3-23 App bar button with a custom style defined in XAML

In the previous example, you saw how to use the Character Map tool and a style definition to create an app bar button. You can also choose a font family in the Character Map tool, select a character, copy its hex value, and use it with the *Content* property of a button. You can also use your own images from the assets available in the app as icons for buttons in the app bar. If you require an icon that is not available as a font glyph or as an image, you can use a XAML *Path* element to specify an icon. When you create an icon using *Path*, it does not respond to state changes such as pointer over, pressed, and disabled (unlike a font glyph).

This is because a *Path* element does not have a *Foreground* property, so you must change its *Stroke* and *Fill* properties instead.

Handling *AppBar* events

You can set up the app bar in your Windows Store app using XAML with button styles. Each button you include has a *Click* event for which you provide an event handler. The app bar raises a number of events; some common events are described as follows:

- **Loaded**   Raised when the app bar has been constructed and is available to the user.
- **Unloaded**   Raised when the app bar is no longer available as a visual element.
- **Opened**   Raised when the app bar is visible.
- **Closed**   Raised when the app bar is no longer visible.
- **Tapped**   Raised when the user taps on the app bar. When the user clicks on a button in the app bar, the button's *Clicked* event is raised.

You can use the *Loaded* and *Unloaded* events that are fired when the page is created or destroyed with the *VisualStateManager* class to change the styles of the app bar buttons when the view state changes, as shown in the XAML code in Listing 3-11.

LISTING 3-11 Changing app bar button styles when the view state changes

```
<Page.BottomAppBar>
    <AppBar x:Name="bottomAppBar" IsSticky="True"
            Loaded="AppBar_Loaded" Unloaded="AppBar_Unloaded">
        <Grid>
            <Grid.RowDefinitions>
                <RowDefinition Height="Auto"/>
            </Grid.RowDefinitions>

            <StackPanel x:Name="leftAppBarPanel" Orientation="Horizontal">
                <Button Style="{StaticResource FolderppBarButtonStyle}"/>
                <Button Style="{StaticResource OpenFileAppBarButtonStyle}"/>
            </StackPanel>
            <StackPanel x:Name="rightAppBarPanel"
                        Orientation="Horizontal" HorizontalAlignment="Right">
                <Button Style="{StaticResource SkipBackAppBarButtonStyle}"/>
                <Button Style="{StaticResource SkipAheadAppBarButtonStyle}"/>
                <Line X1="0" Y1="60"  Margin="0,10,0,0"
                        StrokeThickness="1" Stroke="White"></Line>
                <Button Style="{StaticResource PlayAppBarButtonStyle}"/>
                <Button Style="{StaticResource PauseAppBarButtonStyle}"/>
                <Button Style="{StaticResource StopAppBarButtonStyle}"/>
            </StackPanel>
        </Grid>
    </AppBar>
</Page.BottomAppBar>
```

The event handler code assumes that the app bar uses a layout with a *Grid* control as the root UI element that contains additional panels that host the buttons. Each *Button* is registered to receive state changes when the app bar is loaded and is unregistered when the app bar is unloaded. See the C# code in Listing 3-12.

LISTING 3-12 Receiving state changes when the app bar is loaded and unloaded

```csharp
private void AppBar_Loaded(object sender, RoutedEventArgs e)
{
    // Get the App bar's root Grid.
    Grid root = ((AppBar)sender).Content as Grid;
    if (root != null)
    {
        // Get the Panels that hold the controls.
        foreach (Panel panel in root.Children)
        {
            // Get each control and register for layout updates.
            foreach (UIElement child in panel.Children)
            {
                base.StartLayoutUpdates(child, new RoutedEventArgs());
            }
        }
    }
}

private void AppBar_Unloaded(object sender, RoutedEventArgs e)
{
    // Get the app bar's root Grid.
    Grid root = ((AppBar)sender).Content as Grid;
    if (root != null)
    {
        // Get the Panels that hold the controls.
        foreach (Panel panel in root.Children)
        {
            // Get each control and unregister layout updates.
            foreach (UIElement child in panel.Children)
            {
                base.StopLayoutUpdates(child, new RoutedEventArgs());
            }
        }
    }
}
```

You can update the UI using the *Opened* and *Closed* event, for example, to change the margin of a layout so buttons critical for user interaction are not hidden underneath the app bar. Setting the *IsSticky* property to *True* will make the app bar visible when the user interacts with the page. Close the app bar by setting its *IsOpen* property to *False*.

Thought experiment
Building a Windows Store app with app bar

In this thought experiment, apply what you've learned about this objective. You can find answers to these questions in the "Answers" section at the end of this chapter.

You are building a Windows Store app that will be used in handheld devices and desktop PCs. In your design, you have considered using the app bar to provide commands to users.

Answer the following questions regarding app design:

1. Will you use the app bar to implement search and share in your app? Why or why not?

2. You have decided to use the top app bar to provide navigation shortcuts. What is the advantage of this decision?

3. How will you support changes in the layout of the app bar in multiple view states in your app?

Objective summary

- The app bars in a Windows Store app provide a simple and intuitive surface for placing navigation and in-context commands. Use the app bar to add commands in your app for the design to be consistent with other apps.

- Follow the design guidelines for app bars while designing them.

- Actions such as search, share, and settings should be performed using the charms bar; these commands should not be implemented in the app.

- Group similar commands on the app bar. Separate commands that are critical to the app's execution from other commands to prevent the critical commands from being accidentally invoked.

- You should use the app bar button styles defined in the StandardStyles.xaml file whenever possible. You can use standard font families, your own images, or XAML paths to customize the appearance of the app bar buttons.

- Consider various view states your app can be in while designing the app bars. The *Opened* and *Closed* events can be used to set up the app bar in different view states.

Objective review

Answer the following questions to test your knowledge of the information in this objective. You can find the answers to these questions and explanations of why each answer choice is correct or incorrect in the "Answers" section at the end of this chapter.

1. You are developing a Windows Store text editor app. You have implemented a number of commands using buttons; however, during a usability review, you have been asked to remove some of the commands from the surface and move them into the app bar. Which functionality should you move to the app bar? (Choose all that apply.)

   A. Searching within text

   B. Cutting, copying, and pasting

   C. Increasing and decreasing the font size

   D. Creating, editing, and deleting a new file

   E. Sending a file as an email attachment

2. What can you use as icons in app bar buttons, in addition to the styles provided in application templates? (Choose all that apply.)

   A. Hexadecimal code for a font symbol from a font family

   B. An image asset available within your app

   C. None; the system automatically sets the images for the buttons, so there is no need to provide images

   D. A XAML *Path*

   E. An image located somewhere on the Internet

3. You are building a Windows Store app with commands in the app bar. The app supports all view states for a better user experience. Which events and/or properties of the *AppBar* class should you use? (Choose all that apply.)

   A. *Loaded* event to subscribe to layout update events

   B. *Unloaded* event to unsubscribe from layout update events

   C. *IsSticky* set to *True* to make the app bar persistent in pages where the interaction requires commands from the app bar

   D. *Opened* event to create the app programmatically

   E. *Closed* event to destroy the app bar programmatically

Objective 3.4: Design and implement data presentation

Windows Store apps that follow the Microsoft design style and use the basic set of controls provide a consistent user experience. Similarities among apps are seen in the layout of controls, presentation of content, and patterns of interaction through gestures and commands. This helps users to rapidly adopt the user experience of these applications. Whenever there is a list of data that needs to be displayed along with navigation to the details of each item, data controls play an important role.

Windows provides developers with a number of data controls for use in applications in which data plays a central role. The *GridView* and *ListView* controls are typically used in scenarios in which an individual item in the list has some details and needs to be viewed in a separate page. The *FlipView* control is useful in scenarios in which photos in an album or pages of text need to be displayed in sequence.

This objective covers how to:

- Choose and implement data controls to meet app requirements.
- Create data templates to meet app requirements.

Choosing and implementing data controls to meet app requirements

The *ListView* and *GridView* controls are useful in applications that display data in a list or grid, respectively. Typically, users tap an item in a list and view the details of the item, pan or scroll through the items, and use zooming to view the data as categories or groups. Both these controls are derived from the *ListViewBase* base class, which provides all the methods, properties, and events available in these controls. Thus, a *GridView* is a grid of items, and a *ListView* is a list of items. The *FlipView* control displays a list of items as a sequence with a "flip" behavior to traverse through the collection of items.

The *GridView* control

The *GridView* control enables you to display a list of data that can be scrolled or panned horizontally. It can also handle grouped data. This means you can arrange categories of data in groups and add subheaders to mark categories present in the data. It provides you with a control template that can be used to customize the way individual items are arranged and a data template for individual items.

You can customize the *GridView* control to make individual items of variable height and width. In your Windows Store app, you might want to highlight a particular data item by making the size of an item larger than the others in the same category. In applications in which a large dataset is displayed using a *GridView*, navigation among categories can pose a serious challenge to the user. The *GridView* supports Semantic Zoom, which provides an easy way to navigate categories or groups of data in the *GridView*. *Semantic Zoom* alters the visual appearance of content when the user zooms in or out of the content displayed in the *GridView*. For example, the zoomed-out view can be represented by thumbnails of categories or groups of data, and the zoomed-in view can contain a fixed number of data items.

The *GridView* control provides a layout to display data so that the user can drill down to the details of an item, browse through large sections of data, and respond to changes in the view state. The Windows Store Grid App template provided by Visual Studio helps you build apps with the *GridView* control. In its default form, the main application page with a *GridView* control is shown in Figure 3-24.

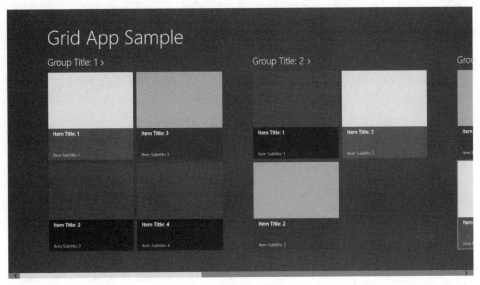

FIGURE 3-24 The *GridView* control used in the Windows Store Grid App template provided by Visual Studio

The XAML used for laying out the *GridView* in the page is shown in Listing 3-13.

LISTING 3-13 Laying out the *GridView*

```xaml
<GridView
    x:Name="itemGridView"
    AutomationProperties.AutomationId="ItemGridView"
    AutomationProperties.Name="Grouped Items"
    Grid.RowSpan="2"
    Padding="116,137,40,46"
    ItemsSource="{Binding Source={StaticResource groupedItemsViewSource}}"
    ItemTemplate="{StaticResource Standard250x250ItemTemplate}"
    SelectionMode="None"
    IsSwipeEnabled="false"
    IsItemClickEnabled="True"
    ItemClick="ItemView_ItemClick">

    <GridView.ItemsPanel>
        <ItemsPanelTemplate>
            <VirtualizingStackPanel Orientation="Horizontal"/>
        </ItemsPanelTemplate>
    </GridView.ItemsPanel>
    <GridView.GroupStyle>
        <GroupStyle>
            <GroupStyle.HeaderTemplate>
                <DataTemplate>
                    <Grid Margin="1,0,0,6">
```

```
                <Button
                        AutomationProperties.Name="Group Title"
                        Click="Header_Click"
                        Style="{StaticResource TextPrimaryButtonStyle}" >
                        <StackPanel Orientation="Horizontal">
                            <TextBlock Text="{Binding Title}" Margin="3,-7,10,10"
                                        Style="{StaticResource GroupHeaderTextStyle}" />
                            <TextBlock Text="{StaticResource ChevronGlyph}"
                                        FontFamily="Segoe UI Symbol"
                                        Margin="0,-7,0,10"
                                        Style="{StaticResource GroupHeaderTextStyle}"/>
                        </StackPanel>
                </Button>
            </Grid>
        </DataTemplate>
    </GroupStyle.HeaderTemplate>
    <GroupStyle.Panel>
        <ItemsPanelTemplate>
            <VariableSizedWrapGrid Orientation="Vertical" Margin="0,0,80,0"/>
        </ItemsPanelTemplate>
    </GroupStyle.Panel>
    </GroupStyle>
    </GridView.GroupStyle>
</GridView>
```

In the declaration of the *GridView* control, a number of properties define the style and data binding. The properties of the *GridView* control you will use most often are these:

- **ItemContainerStyle**   This property specifies the style that is used when rendering the item containers. Item containers are used for laying out individual items in the *Grid-View* control.

- **ItemsSource**   This property is the source of data for the *GridView*, typically a *CollectionViewSource* that consists of data organized in groups. This property is defined in the *Page.Resources* section in the XAML of a page.

- **ItemTemplate**   This property sets the *DataTemplate* used to display each item in the *GridView*. A number of data templates are defined in the StandardStyles.xaml file added by Visual Studio when you create apps with a Windows Store project template. When used with a grouped data source, multiple child UI elements that make up the *DataTemplate* are used to visually represent the data.

- **ItemsPanel**   This property sets the *ItemsPanelTemplate* that defines the panel used to lay out items in the *GridView*. If the value of this property is not set, a *StackPanel* is used as the default *ItemsPanelTemplate*. In Listing 3-13, a *VirtualizingStackPanel* optimizes the display of items in a grid by creating only those UI elements that are currently visible on the screen.

- **SelectionMode**   This property specifies the selection mode of items in the *GridView*. It can have one of these values: *None*, *Single*, *Multiple*, or *Extended*. In the *Extended* selection mode, the user can select multiple items from the *GridView* by entering into a special mode. When the Control key is pressed, the user can select multiple items using the space bar, a mouse click, or a touch tap on the screen. When the Shift key is pressed, the user can select multiple contiguous items by clicking or tapping on the first item and then the last item in the selection.

- **IsSwipeEnabled**   This property indicates whether the *GridView* control will allow selection of items with the swipe gesture.

- **IsItemClickEnabled**   This property indicates whether the items in the *GridView* can raise an *ItemClick* event when an item is clicked. The default value is set to *False*. When set to *True*, a click event is raised instead of triggering an item selection.

- **GroupStyle**   This property specifies the style of each group of data in the *GridView*. The *GroupStyle* property is discussed in more detail later in this section.

- **CanDragItems, CanReorderItems** and **AllowDrop**   These properties, when set to *True*, enable users to reorder items in a *GridView*. These properties can be individually set to *True* to allow a specific action to occur. For example, if *CanDragItems* is set to *True* and the rest are set to False, the user can drag items in a *GridView*; however, the items cannot be reordered or dropped elsewhere.

The *GroupStyle* property defines the style of each group of data. It has three important properties:

- **ContainerStyle**   This property sets the style of the *GroupItem* generated for each item. A *GroupItem* is used to display of collection of items in a group in a *GridView*.

- **HeaderTemplate**   This property sets the template used to display the header of each group of data.

- **Panel**   This property specifies the *ItemsPanelTemplate* used to lay out individual *ItemTemplate* instances. An *ItemsPanelTemplate* contains a UI element derived from the *Panel* class; for example, the *StackPanel* or *VirtualizingStackPanel* class.

- **HidesIfEmpty**   This property specifies whether items in empty groups should be displayed or not.

The *CollectionViewSource* is declared in the XAML as a resource in the *Page.Resources* section in the page. For grouped data, the data source consists of an *IList* or an *IEnumerable* collection of groups of items. For such a *CollectionViewSource* object, the *IsSourceGrouped* property is set to *True*, and the *ItemsPath* property is set to the collection of items present in the data source specified through the *Source* property. The following XAML code shows the configuration of a *CollectionViewSource* for the *GridView* described earlier:

```
<!-- This is declared within the Page.Resources section. The source of data for the
    CollectionViewSource is set in the code-behind -->
<CollectionViewSource x:Name="groupedItemsViewSource"
                Source="{Binding Groups}"
                IsSourceGrouped="true"
                ItemsPath="TopItems" />
```

The *ItemClick* event can be used with an event handler to show the details of an item in the *GridView*. This event is raised only when the *IsItemClickEnabled* property is set to *True*.

The *ListView* control

The *ListView* control is often used to display a list of data that can be scrolled or panned vertically. This control shares the same base class as the *GridView* control: *ListViewBase*. Other than their own constructors, the *GridView* and *ListView* controls do not extend the features of the *ListViewBase* class. Items in a *ListView* control are arranged similar to the *GridView* control except that the default direction of scrolling or panning is vertical.

A good example of the *ListView* control used in app layouts is seen in the full screen portrait and snapped view states of a Window Store app. Visual Studio's Grid App template uses a *GridView* control for fill and full screen landscape view states, and a *ListView* control for the other view states. Figure 3-25 shows an app in snapped and full screen portrait view states.

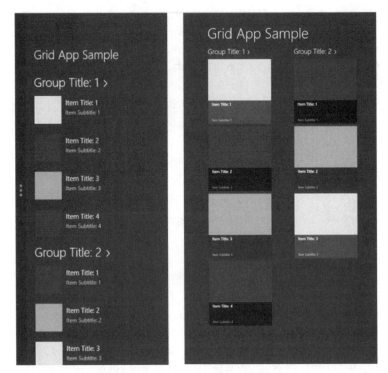

FIGURE 3-25 *ListView* control used in the Grid App Windows Store app template provided by Visual Studio when the app is in the snapped and full screen portrait view states

The XAML used to configure a *ListView* control in the Grid App template in Visual Studio is shown in Listing 3-14.

LISTING 3-14 Configuring a *ListView control*

```
<ListView x:Name="itemListView"
    AutomationProperties.AutomationId="ItemListView"
    AutomationProperties.Name="Grouped Items"
    Grid.Row="1"
    Visibility="Collapsed"
    Margin="0,-10,0,0"
    Padding="10,0,0,60"
    ItemsSource="{Binding Source={StaticResource groupedItemsViewSource}}"
    ItemTemplate="{StaticResource Standard80ItemTemplate}"
    SelectionMode="None"
    IsSwipeEnabled="false"
    IsItemClickEnabled="True"
    ItemClick="ItemView_ItemClick">

    <ListView.GroupStyle>
        <GroupStyle>
            <GroupStyle.HeaderTemplate>
                <DataTemplate>
                    <Grid Margin="7,7,0,0">
                        <Button AutomationProperties.Name="Group Title"
                            Click="Header_Click"
                            Style="{StaticResource TextPrimaryButtonStyle}">
                            <StackPanel Orientation="Horizontal">
                                <TextBlock Text="{Binding Title}" Margin="3,-7,10,10"
                                    Style="{StaticResource GroupHeaderTextStyle}" />
                                <TextBlock Text="{StaticResource ChevronGlyph}"
                                    FontFamily="Segoe UI Symbol"
                                    Margin="0,-7,0,10"
                                    Style="{StaticResource GroupHeaderTextStyle}"/>
                            </StackPanel>
                        </Button>
                    </Grid>
                </DataTemplate>
            </GroupStyle.HeaderTemplate>
        </GroupStyle>
    </ListView.GroupStyle>
</ListView>
```

You might notice that the XAML for the *ListView* control is set up similar to the *GridView* control. You should use *ListView* for displaying content when limited space is available and in the snapped and full screen portrait view states.

The *FlipView* control

The *FlipView* control displays a list of items in a container with navigation controls that indicate the current position of the displayed data element within a collection. You can use this control when you expect users to be fully immersed in the content displayed, such as an image viewer app or a book reader app. In a touch-enabled device, the *FlipView* control provides a smooth transition between items when the user swipes in the left or right direction. Alternatively, you can click the forward and back buttons to navigate through the content and with a keyboard, the left and right arrow keys. Figure 3-26 shows the *FlipView* control used in the item details page in a Windows Store app created with the Grid App template in Visual Studio.

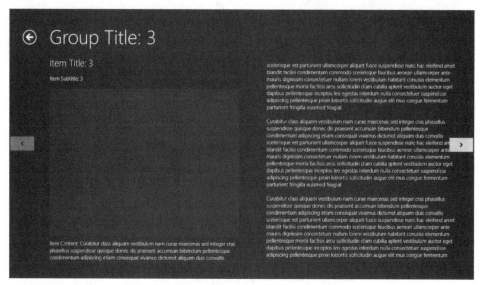

FIGURE 3-26 The item details page in a Windows Store app created with the Grid App template in Visual Studio uses the *FlipView* control

The XAML sample code in Listing 3-15 shows how the *FlipView* control is declared and used in the item details page.

LISTING 3-15 Declaring and using the *FlipView* control

```
<FlipView x:Name="flipView"
    AutomationProperties.AutomationId="ItemsFlipView"
    AutomationProperties.Name="Item Details"
    TabIndex="1"
    Grid.RowSpan="2"
    ItemsSource="{Binding Source={StaticResource itemsViewSource}}">

    <FlipView.ItemContainerStyle>
        <Style TargetType="FlipViewItem">
            <Setter Property="Margin" Value="0,137,0,0"/>
        </Style>
    </FlipView.ItemContainerStyle>

    <FlipView.ItemTemplate>
        <DataTemplate>
            <!-- UserControl chosen as the templated item because
                 it supports visual state management. Loaded/unloaded
                 events explicitly subscribe to view state updates from the page -->
            <UserControl Loaded="StartLayoutUpdates" Unloaded="StopLayoutUpdates">
```

```
        <ScrollViewer x:Name="scrollViewer"
                       Style="{StaticResource HorizontalScrollViewerStyle}"
                       Grid.Row="1">
            <!-- Content is allowed to flow across as many columns as needed -->
            <!-- The RichTextColumns control provided by Visual Studio is used -->
            <!-- VisualStateGroups for various view states -->
        </ScrollViewer>
      </UserControl>
    </DataTemplate>
  </FlipView.ItemTemplate>
</FlipView>
```

The XAML used to define a *FlipView* control uses a number of properties:

- **ItemsSource**   This property specifies the *CollectionViewSource* used to data-bind the control.

- **DisplayMemberPath**   This property specifies the name or path of the property that is displayed for each data item; this property is used with data binding.

- **ItemContainerStyle**   This property specifies the style that is used when rendering the item containers.

- **ItemTemplate**   This property sets the *DataTemplate* used to display each item.

Creating data templates to meet app requirements

Data controls such as *GridView*, *ListView*, and *FlipView* use data binding to display data in a collection. These controls require a "template" to specify the UI of each element in the collection when rendered on the screen. A *DataTemplate* is a section of the UI that is specified independent of the control it is used in. You can use one or more data templates with a data control if elements in your data collection cannot be represented with a single *DataTemplate*. Therefore, you can support complex layouts with a loose coupling between the data and the UI. It is a matter of updating the data template if the underlying data model changes for any reason.

In your Windows Store app, you might need to display the same data collection in multiple pages, perhaps in the same or different data control. Data templates are very helpful with reuse—you can define a *DataTemplate* within a *ResourceDictionary* available to the entire app. You could then use it in multiple pages. When you apply a data template to a data control, a data context is implicitly associated with it. This is through data binding. In many cases, raw data might not be adequate for displaying in the screen with data templates. In such cases, a viewmodel that acts as the data source can be used to customize the data. Because a data template is unaware of the underlying data context, whether it is a raw data source or a viewmodel, this technique helps with separation of concerns and reusing data templates, exactly what they are meant for.

In perhaps the simplest form, data templates are defined inline within the data control, such as in the *ListView* shown in the XAML in Listing 3-16.

LISTING 3-16 Defining data templates inline

```
<ListView ItemsSource="{Binding Source={StaticResource officeMembers}}">
    <ListView.ItemTemplate>
        <DataTemplate>
            <Grid Height="120" Margin="10">
                <Grid.ColumnDefinitions>
                    <ColumnDefinition Width="Auto"/>
                    <ColumnDefinition Width="*"/>
                </Grid.ColumnDefinitions>
                <Border Width="120" Height="120">
                    <Image Source="{Binding MemberPhoto}" Stretch="None"/>
                </Border>
                <StackPanel Grid.Column="1" VerticalAlignment="Top" Margin="8,2,2,2">
                    <TextBlock Text="{Binding Name}"/>
                    <TextBlock Text="{Binding Designation}"/>
                    <TextBlock Text="{Binding Phone}"/>
                </StackPanel>
            </Grid>
        </DataTemplate>
    </ListView.ItemTemplate>
</ListView>
```

In some Windows Store apps, you might need to display data based on the value of a property. For example, in Listing 3-16, the data template cannot be used to differentiate between various kinds of team members in an organization. Your app might need to set a property of a UI element to highlight a certain category of team members—developers, for example. Windows provides the *DataTemplateSelector* class for implementing a template selection mechanism based on the data being bound to a data control. You need to implement your own template selector class, as shown in the C# code in Listing 3-17.

LISTING 3-17 Implementing a template selector class

```
// Namespaces omitted for brevity
public class HighlightItemTemplateSelector : DataTemplateSelector
{
    public DataTemplate DefaultTemplate { get; set; }
    public DataTemplate HighlightTemplate { get; set; }

    protected override DataTemplate SelectTemplateCore(object item,
                        DependencyObject container)
    {
        if (item != null &&
            item is Person)
        {
            Person person = (Person)item;

            if (person.Designation.ToLower().Contains("developer") ||
                person.Designation.ToLower().Contains("engineer"))
            {
                return HighlightItemTemplate;
            }
        }
```

```
            return DefaultTemplate;
    }
}
```

The *HighlightItemTemplateSelector* class checks the item's *Designation* property and returns the appropriate template. In the XAML, the two data templates are declared along with the template selector. To reuse data templates, consider putting them in the application's resources in the App.xaml file. The *ListView*'s *ItemTemplateSelector* property is set to the template selector, as shown in Listing 3-18.

LISTING 3-18 Providing a template selector for a *ListView* control

```xaml
<DataTemplate x:Key="ListView_DefaultItemTemplate">
    <Grid Height="120" Margin="10">
        <Grid.ColumnDefinitions>
            <ColumnDefinition Width="Auto"/>
            <ColumnDefinition Width="*"/>
        </Grid.ColumnDefinitions>
        <Border Width="120" Height="120">
            <Image Source="{Binding MemberPhoto}" Stretch="None"/>
        </Border>
        <StackPanel Grid.Column="1" VerticalAlignment="Top" Margin="8,2,2,2">
            <TextBlock Text="{Binding Name}"/>
            <TextBlock Text="{Binding Designation}"/>
            <TextBlock Text="{Binding Phone}"/>
        </StackPanel>
    </Grid>
</DataTemplate>

<DataTemplate x:Key="ListView_HighlightItemTemplate">
    <Grid Height="120" Margin="10">
        <Grid.ColumnDefinitions>
            <ColumnDefinition Width="Auto"/>
            <ColumnDefinition Width="*"/>
        </Grid.ColumnDefinitions>
        <Border Width="120" Height="120">
            <Image Source="{Binding MemberPhoto}" Stretch="None"/>
        </Border>
        <StackPanel Grid.Column="1" Background="Green"
                    VerticalAlignment="Top" Margin="8,2,2,2">
            <TextBlock Text="{Binding Name}"/>
            <TextBlock Text="{Binding Designation}"/>
            <TextBlock Text="{Binding Phone}"/>
        </StackPanel>
    </Grid>
</DataTemplate>

<local:HighlightItemTemplateSelector x:Key="listViewHighlightItemTemplateSelector"
        DefaultTemplate="{StaticResource ListView_DefaultItemTemplate}"
        HighlightTemplate="{StaticResource ListView_HighlightItemTemplate }" />

<ListView ItemsSource="{Binding Source={StaticResource officeMembers}}"
        ItemTemplateSelector="listViewHighlightItemTemplateSelector" />
```

For an item in the collection that has "developer" or "engineer" in its *Designation* property, the *HighlightTemplate* will be used as the *DataTemplate*, and *DefaultTemplate* will be used in all other cases.

Thought experiment
Making design choices for a movie browser application

In this thought experiment, apply what you've learned about this objective. You can find answers to these questions in the "Answers" section at the end of this chapter.

A popular movie database and search engine website is about to provide access to their data through its public API. It expects developers to build applications on all major platforms, including Windows 8.

Armed with your experience in implementing Windows Store apps, you start the process of drawing up the requirements and wireframes of your app. With your knowledge of working with common data controls in Windows 8, list the five features you will implement in your app that will enable it to have an edge over the competition.

Objective summary

- *GridView*, *ListView*, and *FlipView* are data controls with built-in support for interaction through touch and zoom. Visual Studio provides developers with application templates that are setup with these controls for displaying data.
- The *GridView* control is used in UIs in which data is laid out horizontally. It can be scrolled and panned in the horizontal direction, so it is the ideal choice for supporting the fill and full screen landscape view states.
- The *ListView* control is used in UIs with horizontal space constraints. It can be scrolled and panned in the vertical direction, so it is the ideal choice for supporting the snapped and full screen portrait view states.
- The *FlipView* control should be used in distraction-free UIs such as photo albums and news readers. It has built-in support for the swipe gesture and supports accessibility through the keyboard and mouse.
- Data templates provide the flexibility in the usage of data controls. They are used to compose the UI independent of the underlying data model. Data binding is used to connect the UI with view models with the data templates acting as the glue between the two.
- The *DataTemplateSelector* class provides the capability to switch between multiple data templates in data controls. Templates are applied based on one or more conditions that are applicable on an item in the dataset.

Objective review

Answer the following questions to test your knowledge of the information in this objective. You can find the answers to these questions and explanations of why each answer choice is correct or incorrect in the "Answers" section at the end of this chapter.

1. You are building a page in an app that displays graphs of the user's physical performance training program. A page can contain one or more graphs; the app does not expect the user to interact with the page other than browsing through the graphs using swipe gestures or the keyboard or mouse. The pages you build in the app will not be reused in the other apps. Which controls will you choose to create such a page? (Choose all that apply.)

   A. A *GridView* control with variable sized items, one of them being the graph

   B. A *FlipView* control that binds to the source data

   C. *RichTextBlock* and *RichTextBlockOverflow* controls for displaying text

   D. A grid to lay out the text and the graph in the *DataTemplate* of each item

   E. A custom control that implements swipe gestures and embeds the graph and text

2. The local library has asked you to build a Windows Store app for its catalog. For the first release, it expects the app to display titles available in the library in a page with basic search functionality. The library also expects the app to be used by members of the library who use touch-enabled tablets, desktop PCs, and touch-enabled screen terminals on the library premises. Which controls will you use to meet the app's requirements? (Choose all that apply.)

   A. The *FlipView* control to swipe between pages of data

   B. The *GridView* control to lay out data for the fill and full screen landscape view states

   C. The *ListView* control to lay out data for the snapped and full screen portrait view states

   D. The *Grid* control to lay out the data controls

   E. The *ListView* control with a data template that uses the *ScrollViewer* control to scroll content horizontally

3. You have developed a Windows Store app that tracks the music albums a user has listened to, enabling the user to mark an album as a favorite. As an enhancement, you plan to implement a feature that highlights an album in the *GridView* when it is a favorite of the user. The pages you build in the app are specific to the requirements of the app and will not be reused in other apps. What is the best way to implement this feature?

   A. Create a user control using the *GridView*. Implement template selection logic in the code-behind based on the data item.

   B. Create your own *DataTemplateSelector* class along with two data templates: one for albums that are favorites and the other for albums that aren't favorites. Based on the item, apply one template or the other with your *DataTemplateSelector* class.

   C. Create a custom control with the *ContentControl* class as the base class. Implement your own logic to apply a template per the requirement.

   D. Set the XAML to be displayed for a favorite item from within the code-behind.

Objective 3.5: Create and manage XAML styles and templates

In a Windows Store app, the UI is built with standard controls, and a set of custom and user controls is also used whenever necessary. XAML is used to declare various controls and define their properties in a page. To customize the look and feel of the controls in a page, the properties of various controls are set to meet the app's requirements. This approach of composing a UI is powerful because it separates the UI from the underlying data model.

In a complex UI with a large number of controls, customizing the look and feel of each control using XAML becomes very tedious. In such scenarios, you want to define a set of styles that enable you to separate the values of properties of an element from the element itself. This approach is similar to using Cascading Style Sheets (CSS) to customize HTML elements in webpages. In Windows, the visual representation of a control is completely decoupled from its code. A control's template defines the look and feel of the control, so the template can be modified while keeping the functionality of the control intact. In a Windows Store app, styles and templates are used to customize the appearance of controls.

This objective covers how to:

- Implement and extend styles and templates.
- Implement gradients.
- Modify styles based on event and property triggers.
- Create shared resources and themes.

Implementing and extending styles and templates

The appearance of controls in a Windows Store app can be modified and customized to provide the look and feel of the UI per the app's requirements. The *Style* property, represented by the *Windows.UI.Xaml.Style* class, is defined on *FrameworkElement*. The *Style* property can be used on UI elements that derive from the *Control* class, such as *TextBlock* and *Button*; as well as elements that don't, such as *Rectangle* and *Ellipse*. You can create a style and apply it to a particular UI element in the XAML, or you can create it so it can be applied to all instances of the control.

Consider the example of a registration form that a Windows Store app uses to register a user for a service. The registration process requires some mandatory fields and includes some optional fields. The XAML in Listing 3-19 declares a few controls with their properties set to meet these requirements.

LISTING 3-19 Declaring controls with mandatory and optional fields

```
<Grid Grid.Row="1" Margin="120,0,0,0">
    <Grid.RowDefinitions>
        <RowDefinition Height="Auto"/>
        <RowDefinition Height="Auto" />
        <RowDefinition Height="Auto"/>
        <RowDefinition Height="Auto"/>
        <RowDefinition Height="Auto"/>
        <RowDefinition Height="Auto"/>
    </Grid.RowDefinitions>
    <StackPanel Orientation="Horizontal" Grid.Row="0" >
        <TextBlock Foreground="Red"  FontSize="24" Width="150"
                Text="First Name" VerticalAlignment="Center" />
        <TextBox FontSize="24" VerticalAlignment="Center" Width="200"
                Margin="0,10,10,10"/>
    </StackPanel>
    <StackPanel Orientation="Horizontal" Grid.Row="1">
        <TextBlock Foreground="Red" FontSize="24" Text="Last Name" Width="150"
                VerticalAlignment="Center"/>
        <TextBox FontSize="24" VerticalAlignment="Center" Width="200"
                Margin="20,10,10,10"/>
    </StackPanel>
    <StackPanel Orientation="Horizontal" Grid.Row="2">
        <TextBlock FontSize="24" Text="Gender" VerticalAlignment="Center" Width="150" />
        <TextBox FontSize="24" Height="28" Margin="0,10,10,10" Width="200"
                VerticalAlignment="Center" />
    </StackPanel>
    <StackPanel Orientation="Horizontal" Grid.Row="3">
        <TextBlock Foreground="Red" FontSize="24" Text="Username" Width="150"
                VerticalAlignment="Center"/>
        <TextBox FontSize="24" VerticalAlignment="Center" Width="200"
                Margin="0,10,10,10"/>
    </StackPanel>
    <StackPanel Orientation="Horizontal" Grid.Row="4">
        <TextBlock Foreground="Red" FontSize="24" Text="Password"
                VerticalAlignment="Center"/>
```

```
        <TextBox FontSize="24" VerticalAlignment="Center" Width="200" Width="150"
                Margin="0,10,10,10"/>
    </StackPanel>
</Grid>
```

Figure 3-27 shows the controls rendered in the page.

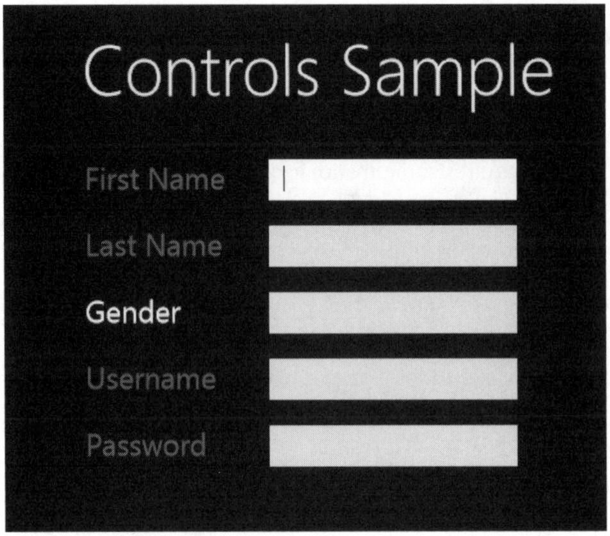

FIGURE 3-27 An app with a set of *TextBlock* and *TextBox* controls with their properties set in XAML

In Listing 3-19, some properties of the UI elements—such as *Margin*, *Width*, *FontSize*, and *VerticalAlignment*—are set at the same value across multiple times. You can create a style for the text blocks and another for the text boxes, and apply them as shown in the XAML in Listing 3-20.

LISTING 3-20 Applying styles for text blocks and text boxes

```
<Grid Grid.Row="1" Margin="120,0,0,0">
    <Grid.RowDefinitions>
        <RowDefinition Height="Auto"/>
        <RowDefinition Height="Auto" />
        <RowDefinition Height="Auto"/>
        <RowDefinition Height="Auto"/
        <RowDefinition Height="Auto"/>
        <RowDefinition Height="Auto"/>
    </Grid.RowDefinitions>
    <Grid.Resources>
        <Style x:Key="MandatoryTextBlockStyle" TargetType="TextBlock">
            <Setter Property="Foreground" Value="Red" />
            <Setter Property="FontSize" Value="24" />
            <Setter Property="Width" Value="150" />
            <Setter Property="VerticalAlignment" Value="Center" />
        </Style>
        <Style x:Key="RegistrationTextBoxStyle" TargetType="TextBox">
            <Setter Property="FontSize" Value="24" />
```

```xml
                    <Setter Property="Margin" Value="0,10,10,10" />
                    <Setter Property="Width" Value="200" />
                    <Setter Property="VerticalAlignment" Value="Center" />
                </Style>
            </Grid.Resources>
            <StackPanel Orientation="Horizontal" Grid.Row="0" >
                <TextBlock Style="{StaticResource MandatoryTextBlockStyle}" Text="First Name" />
                <TextBox Style="{StaticResource RegistrationTextBoxStyle}"/>
            </StackPanel>
            <StackPanel Orientation="Horizontal" Grid.Row="1">
                <TextBlock  Style="{StaticResource MandatoryTextBlockStyle}" Text="Last Name"/>
                <TextBox Style="{StaticResource RegistrationTextBoxStyle}"/>
            </StackPanel>
            <StackPanel Orientation="Horizontal" Grid.Row="2">
                <!-- You can create a new style for this TextBlock based on the
                     MandatoryTextBlockStyle and override the Foreground property in the
                     definition of the new style. However, since style will be required
                     in only one TextBlock, it is better to override the Foreground
                     property here. -->
                <TextBlock  Style="{StaticResource MandatoryTextBlockStyle}" Foreground="White"
                            Text="Gender" />
                <TextBox Style="{StaticResource RegistrationTextBoxStyle}" />
            </StackPanel>
            <StackPanel Orientation="Horizontal" Grid.Row="3">
                <TextBlock Style="{StaticResource MandatoryTextBlockStyle}" Text="Username" />
                <TextBox Style="{StaticResource RegistrationTextBoxStyle}"/>
            </StackPanel>
            <StackPanel Orientation="Horizontal" Grid.Row="4">
                <TextBlock  Style="{StaticResource MandatoryTextBlockStyle}" Text="Password" />
                <TextBox Style="{StaticResource RegistrationTextBoxStyle}"/>
            </StackPanel>
        </Grid>
```

In the XAML of a page, styles are declared with a unique key that is then used by UI elements. Windows looks for the *Style* definition in the parent element, then in the *Page.Resources* section of the *Page* that contains the XAML, and then in App.xaml, which can contain embedded *ResourceDictionaries*. In the *TextBlock* that is used as the label for the gender field, the *Foreground* property is set inline, overriding the value set through the *Style*. Therefore, you can override any property for a UI element set in the *Style* definition by specifying it inline.

Visual Studio provides styles for some UI elements such as the *TextBlock*. You can edit the built-in style of any control placed on an app's design surface, create an empty style declaration and choose the properties of the control you plan to customize, or start with the default style of the control by selecting the Edit a Copy option. The last option creates a copy of the style in the page on which the control is placed, in App.xaml or in StandardStyles.xaml, which holds the app's resource dictionary. These options are shown in Figure 3-28.

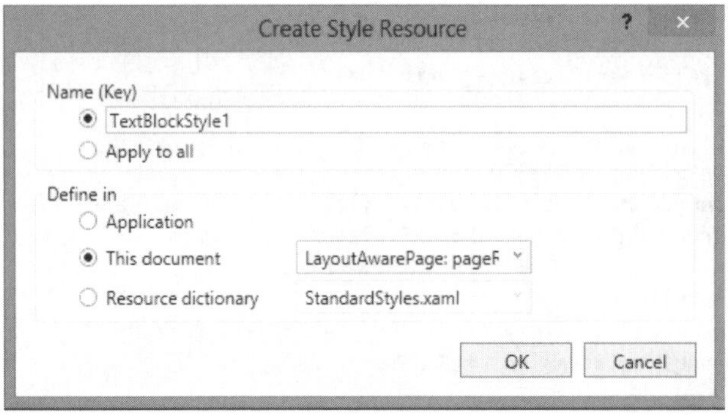

FIGURE 3-28 Visual Studio provides you with multiple options to place the Style resource in your application

If you plan to use the style in multiple pages of your app, you should create it in App.xaml or StandardStyles.xaml. If you plan to use the style within a single page, Visual Studio places the newly created *Style* resource within the *Page.Resources* section.

You can share the styles used for the *TextBlock* and *TextBox* controls in Figure 3-27 with other controls if their *TargetType* is set to *Control*. These styles can be defined without the *Key*, which causes the style to be applied for all controls of that *TargetType*. This is called an *implicit style*, in contrast with the styles discussed earlier that are *explicit styles*. For example, if you wanted all the *TextBlock* controls in a page to have some properties set to the same value, you can apply the following style in XAML:

```
<Style TargetType="TextBlock">
    <Setter Property="FontSize" Value="24" />
    <Setter Property="Width " Value="200" />
</Style>
```

The implicit style will be applied to all *TextBlock*s in a page if the style is declared in the *Page.Resources* section or it will be applied to all *TextBlock*s in your app if it is added with the *ResourceDictionary* section in App.xaml. Any *TextBlock* in the app can override the appearance set by the implicit style by explicitly setting individual properties of the *Style*. You can also apply the default style to a *TextBlock* in the app by setting its *Style* to *null*. An important property of the *Style* class is *BasedOn*. This property allows you create new styles based on existing styles referred using the *StaticResource* XAML extension. For example, the following code defines a style for the *TextBlock* control:

```
<Style x:Key="OptionalTextBlockStyle" TargetType="TextBlock"
        BasedOn="{StaticResource MandatoryTextBlockStyle}">
    <Setter Property="Foreground" Value="White" />
</Style>
```

The *Style* property of any control is useful in customizing its built-in appearance. You can change the built-in appearance of a control by using the *ControlTemplate* class to create a new style for the control. A *ControlTemplate* consists of a tree of elements that composes the control's visual appearance. If you need to modify the appearance of a control, you can edit a copy of the control's *ControlTemplate* (which is a part of its style) using Visual Studio. For some controls, such as *ListView*, you can edit and customize the *ItemTemplate* used to render an individual item.

After you have created a template for a control, you can reference it within the *Style* element in XAML and then apply the style on the control. For example, you might need to create a template for a button in your app. The button needs an icon added next to the text content. You can create a copy of the control template using Visual Studio, as shown in the XAML in Listing 3-21.

LISTING 3-21 Creating a copy of the control template

```
<Page.Resources>
    <Style x:Key="UmbrellaButtonStyle" TargetType="Button">
        <Setter Property="Background"
                Value="{StaticResource ButtonBackgroundThemeBrush}"/>
        <!-- Other Setters removed for brevity -->
        <Setter Property="Template">
            <Setter.Value>
                <ControlTemplate TargetType="Button">
                    <Grid>
                        <VisualStateManager.VisualStateGroups>
                            <!-- Visual States for the Pressed, Disabled, Normal, etc -->
                        </VisualStateManager.VisualStateGroups>
                        <Border x:Name="Border" BorderBrush="{TemplateBinding BorderBrush}"
                                BorderThickness="{TemplateBinding BorderThickness}"
                                Background="{TemplateBinding Background}" Margin="3">
                            <ContentPresenter x:Name="ContentPresenter"
                                    ContentTemplate="{TemplateBinding ContentTemplate}"
                                    ContentTransitions="{TemplateBinding ContentTransitions}"
                                    Content="{TemplateBinding Content}"
                                    HorizontalAlignment="{TemplateBinding
                                        HorizontalContentAlignment}"
                                    Margin="{TemplateBinding Padding}"
                                    VerticalAlignment="{TemplateBinding
                                        VerticalContentAlignment}"/>
                        </Border>
                        <!-- Rectangles for the border drawn in some visual states -->
                    </Grid>
                </ControlTemplate>
            </Setter.Value>
        </Setter>
    </Style>
</Page.Resources>
```

Assuming you will not use this button elsewhere in your app, remove the border and use a *StackPanel* to lay out an *Image* and the *ContentPresenter*. The modified XAML is shown in Listing 3-22.

LISTING 3-22 Modifying the control template

```xml
<Page.Resources>
    <Style x:Key="UmbrellaButtonStyle" TargetType="Button">
        <Setter Property="Background"
                Value="{StaticResource ButtonBackgroundThemeBrush}"/>
        <!-- Other Setters removed for brevity -->
        <Setter Property="Template">
            <Setter.Value>
                <ControlTemplate TargetType="Button">
                    <Grid>
                        <VisualStateManager.VisualStateGroups>
                            <!-- Visual States for the Pressed, Disabled, Normal, etc -->
                        </VisualStateManager.VisualStateGroups>
                        <StackPanel x:Name="Border" Orientation="Horizontal"
                                    Background="{TemplateBinding Background}" Margin="3">
                            <Image Source="Assets/umbrella.png" Height="30" Width="30"
                                   Stretch="Uniform" Margin="10,0,0,0" />
                            <ContentPresenter x:Name="ContentPresenter"
                                    ContentTemplate="{TemplateBinding ContentTemplate}"
                                    ContentTransitions="{TemplateBinding ContentTransitions}"
                                    Content="{TemplateBinding Content}"
                                    HorizontalAlignment="{TemplateBinding
                                        HorizontalContentAlignment}"
                                    Margin="{TemplateBinding Padding}"
                                    VerticalAlignment="{TemplateBinding
                                    VerticalContentAlignment}"/>
                        </StackPanel>
                        <!-- Rectangles for the border drawn in some visual states -->
                    </Grid>
                </ControlTemplate>
            </Setter.Value>
        </Setter>
    </Style>
</Page.Resources>
```

Figure 3-29 shows two buttons, first with its default style, and second with its style set to *UmbrellaButtonStyle*.

FIGURE 3-29 The first button uses the default style; the second button uses a customized control template set in its style

If you plan to use the button's style elsewhere in your app with other icons, you can reuse the *ControlTemplate* for the *Button* by specifying a binding for the *Source* property of the image. When you define the button in the XAML of the page, the *Source* property of the *Image* can be set through the *Binding*.

You can use the *ControlTemplate* to define the visual structure of a button. The default template of a control also specifies the visual behavior of the control, that is, the appearance of the control in various states. For example, a button can be in the *PointerOver*, *Pressed*, *Disabled*, *Focused*, *Unfocused*, and *PointerFocused* states. A visual state is represented by the *VisualState* class; thus, a *ControlTemplate* contains a number of *VisualState* objects, each representing a visual state. A *VisualState* contains a *StoryBoard* animation that changes the appearance of elements in the *ControlTemplate*. The *StoryBoard* of a *VisualState* begins when the control enters the state specified by the *Name* property of the *VisualState* object. One or more *VisualState* objects belong to a *VisualStateGroup*, and one or more *VisualStateGroup* objects are added to the *VisualStateManager.VisualStateGroups* element, which is set at the root element of the *ControlTemplate*.

Implementing gradients

The controls provided by Windows and used in Windows Store apps have a *Background* or *Fill* property to create a solid color. This gives the UI a flat look. In some cases, you might want to add a soft gradient in the controls to improve the user experience of your app. For example, you want to add a three-dimensional look to some or all the buttons in a page. It is possible to use bitmap images to achieve this; however, there are advantages of using gradients:

- Animations are supported by gradients. Therefore, you can change a gradient's colors for a certain user action; for example, when they press a button with a gradient as the background.

- A gradient is not prone to loss of quality with scale because it is used on vector graphics, unlike an image.

- Gradients use hardware acceleration when it is available.

- The size of your application is less because you do not have to embed bitmap images for the background.

Thus, gradients provide better performance than images. However, carefully consider the use of gradients in app controls. Gradients can be distracting when used too often on a page. It's better to use a gradient to highlight a particular control, which draws the attention of the user.

You can define gradients in the XAML for a control and use them for setting the value of the *Background* or *Fill* property of the control. The XAML in Listing 3-23 shows a *LinearGradientBrush* defined as a resource for the page and later used in a *Rectangle* control.

```
<Page>
    <Page.Resources>
        <LinearGradientBrush x:Key="BlueGradientBackground"
                             StartPoint="0.5,0" EndPoint="0.5,1">
            <GradientStop Color="#FFEBF9FF" Offset="0"/>
            <GradientStop Color="#FF008BC7" Offset="1"/>
            <GradientStop Color="#FF00B8FF" Offset="0.20"/>
            <GradientStop Color="#FF00B3FF" Offset="0.90"/>
        </LinearGradientBrush>
    </Page.Resources>

<Grid>
    <Grid.RowDefinitions>
        <RowDefinition Height="Auto" />
        <RowDefinition Height="*" />
    </Grid.RowDefinitions>
    <StackPanel Grid.Row="6" Orientation="Horizontal">
        <Rectangle Width="170" Height="65" Margin="10"
                   HorizontalAlignment="Left" Fill="#FF00B8FF" />
        <Rectangle Width="170" Height="65" Margin="10"
                   HorizontalAlignment="Left"
                   Fill="{StaticResource BlueGradientBackground}" />
    </StackPanel>
</Grid>
</Page>
```

Figure 3-30 shows the two rendered rectangle controls.

FIGURE 3-30 Using a gradient as the *Background* or *Fill* property of a control achieves a three-dimensional appearance in the rectangle on the right

Modifying styles based on event and property triggers

The values of various properties of a control set through a style or a control template you created might require updates when certain conditions are met. For example, when a button is pressed, you want the color of the foreground to change.

Unlike technologies such as Windows Presentation Foundation (WPF) and Silverlight, in which triggers can be used to modify styles and control templates, Windows 8 provides the *VisualStateManager* to manage these changes. The *VisualStateManager* is responsible for managing visual states and the transitions between these states for controls. The *VisualStateGroups* element is used to define the visual states of a control in XAML. Alternatively, the *GoToState* method of the *VisualStateManager* class is used to transition between the various states of a control in the code-behind of the page that contains the control.

Listing 3-24 shows the XAML for *VisualStateGroups* and the *VisualState*s of a button defined in its *ControlTemplate*.

LISTING 3-24 Visual state groups and visual states defined in a control template

```xml
<VisualStateManager.VisualStateGroups>
    <VisualStateGroup x:Name="CommonStates">
        <VisualState x:Name="Normal"/>
        <VisualState x:Name="PointerOver">
            <Storyboard>
                <ObjectAnimationUsingKeyFrames Storyboard.TargetProperty="Background"
                                    Storyboard.TargetName="Border">
                    <DiscreteObjectKeyFrame KeyTime="0" Value="{StaticResource
                                        ButtonPointerOverBackgroundThemeBrush}"/>
                </ObjectAnimationUsingKeyFrames>
                <ObjectAnimationUsingKeyFrames Storyboard.TargetProperty="Foreground"
                                        Storyboard.TargetName="ContentPresenter">
                    <DiscreteObjectKeyFrame KeyTime="0" Value="{StaticResource
                                        ButtonPointerOverForegroundThemeBrush}"/>
                </ObjectAnimationUsingKeyFrames>
            </Storyboard>
        </VisualState>
        <VisualState x:Name="Pressed">
            <Storyboard>
                <ObjectAnimationUsingKeyFrames Storyboard.TargetProperty="Background"
                                        Storyboard.TargetName="Border">
                    <DiscreteObjectKeyFrame KeyTime="0" Value="{StaticResource
                                        ButtonPressedBackgroundThemeBrush}"/>
                </ObjectAnimationUsingKeyFrames>
                <ObjectAnimationUsingKeyFrames Storyboard.TargetProperty="Foreground"
                                        Storyboard.TargetName="ContentPresenter">
                    <DiscreteObjectKeyFrame KeyTime="0" Value="{StaticResource
                                        ButtonPressedForegroundThemeBrush}"/>
                </ObjectAnimationUsingKeyFrames>
            </Storyboard>
        </VisualState>
        <VisualState x:Name="Disabled">
            <Storyboard>
                <ObjectAnimationUsingKeyFrames Storyboard.TargetProperty="Background"
                                        Storyboard.TargetName="Border">
                    <DiscreteObjectKeyFrame KeyTime="0" Value="{StaticResource
                                        ButtonDisabledBackgroundThemeBrush}"/>
                </ObjectAnimationUsingKeyFrames>
                <ObjectAnimationUsingKeyFrames Storyboard.TargetProperty="BorderBrush"
                                        Storyboard.TargetName="Border">
                    <DiscreteObjectKeyFrame KeyTime="0" Value="{StaticResource
                                        ButtonDisabledBorderThemeBrush}"/>
                </ObjectAnimationUsingKeyFrames>
                <ObjectAnimationUsingKeyFrames Storyboard.TargetProperty="Foreground"
                                        Storyboard.TargetName="ContentPresenter">
                    <DiscreteObjectKeyFrame KeyTime="0" Value="{StaticResource
                                        ButtonDisabledForegroundThemeBrush}"/>
                </ObjectAnimationUsingKeyFrames>
            </Storyboard>
        </VisualState>
    </VisualStateGroup>
    <VisualStateGroup x:Name="FocusStates">
        <VisualState x:Name="Focused">
            <Storyboard>
```

```
            <DoubleAnimation Duration="0" To="1" Storyboard.TargetProperty="Opacity"
                            Storyboard.TargetName="FocusVisualWhite"/>
            <DoubleAnimation Duration="0" To="1" Storyboard.TargetProperty="Opacity"
                            Storyboard.TargetName="FocusVisualBlack"/>
        </Storyboard>
    </VisualState>
    <VisualState x:Name="Unfocused"/>
    <VisualState x:Name="PointerFocused"/>
  </VisualStateGroup>
</VisualStateManager.VisualStateGroups>
```

In the code-behind of a page, an event handler can be defined for an event such as when the mouse hovers over a button or when it is clicked. To prevent the user from continuously clicking the button after it has been clicked once, you should provide a disabled look to the button and prevent further click events until an action is complete. The *GoToState* method of the *VisualStateManager* class can be used to transition between states configured in the *ControlTemplate* of the button. In the code-behind of the page, use the *Clicked* event handler of the button to change its visual appearance by applying a style that resembles a disabled button.

Creating shared resources and themes

While building a Windows Store app, you can reuse the styles and control templates you create to customize the visual appearance of controls. Collections of styles and control templates can be defined for the application in resource dictionary. You can create a resource dictionary using Visual Studio with the Add New Item option for your project, as shown in Figure 3-31.

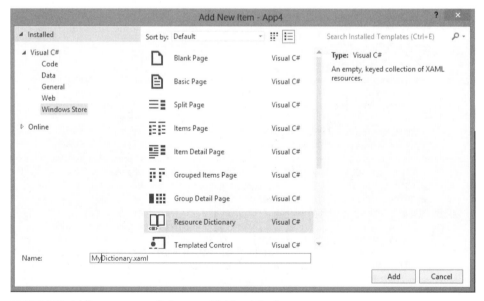

FIGURE 3-31 Adding a resource dictionary with Visual Studio

You add the newly created resource dictionary to your app by specifying it in the list of application resources in App.xaml, as follows:

```xml
<Application.Resources>
   <ResourceDictionary>
      <ResourceDictionary.MergedDictionaries>
         <ResourceDictionary Source="Common/StandardStyles.xaml"/>
         <ResourceDictionary Source="MyDictionary.xaml" />
      </ResourceDictionary.MergedDictionaries>
      <x:String x:Key="AppName">Grid App Sample</x:String>
   </ResourceDictionary>
</Application.Resources>
```

Windows Store project templates provided by Visual Studio specify the default styles of controls within a resource dictionary defined in the StandardStyles.xaml file. The *ResourceDictionary* class defines a dictionary of objects that are shareable across your app. *ResourceDictionary* supports styles and templates, brushes and colors, animations including *StoryBoard*, transforms, and other objects Resources from the *ResourceDictionary* are accessed with the *StaticResource* XAML extension.

You can merge multiple resource dictionaries into a single resource dictionary and use it in your app. A theme dictionary can define a dictionary of objects depending on the theme currently selected by the user. Each object in this dictionary is a *ResourceDictionary* with a unique key. The following XAML shows two themes defined with *ResourceDictionary* objects and included within the *ThemedDictionaries* collection:

```xml
<Application.Resources>
   <ResourceDictionary>
      <ResourceDictionary.ThemeDictionaries>
         <ResourceDictionary x:Key="Default">
            <SolidColorBrush
               x:Key="ButtonBackground">#FF000000</SolidColorBrush>
         </ResourceDictionary>
         <ResourceDictionary x:Key="Light">
            <SolidColorBrush
               x:Key="ButtonBackground">#FFCCDDCC</SolidColorBrush>
         </ResourceDictionary>
      </ResourceDictionary.ThemeDictionaries>
      <ResourceDictionary.MergedDictionaries>
         <ResourceDictionary Source="Common/StandardStyles.xaml"/>
         <ResourceDictionary Source="MyDictionary.xaml" />
      </ResourceDictionary.MergedDictionaries>
      <x:String x:Key="AppName">Grid App Sample</x:String>
   </ResourceDictionary>
</Application.Resources>
```

A theme defined as a *ResourceDictionary* can be applied in an application using the *RequestedTheme* property of the *Application* class, as shown in the following XAML:

```xml
<Application x:Class="GridAppSample.App" RequestedTheme="Light">
</Application>
```

Thought experiment

Supporting themes in a Windows Store app

In this thought experiment, apply what you've learned about this objective. You can find answers to these questions in the "Answers" section at the end of this chapter.

You have developed an app used for educating children in primary school. The app has received good feedback as well as feature requests.

One feature request is to enable users to choose a theme based on a movie, fable, or fairy tale. You decide to enhance your app and implement support for themes. Which three Windows 8 features will you use to implement the feature request?

Objective summary

- Windows provides styles and templates for customizing the visual appearance and behavior of controls. They can be reused across multiple pages in an application. Visual Studio can be used to edit a copy of the style or template of a control.

- In some applications, a gradient applied to a control can draw the attention of the user for a particular task. Gradients have a number of advantages over images, mainly in performance and scaling to multiple screen resolutions.

- The visual states of a control are managed with the *VisualStateManager* class. *VisualStateGroups* is used to define the various states in which a control can exist. The *GoToState* method of the *VisualStateManager* can be used to change between various states of a control based on events of the control.

- Resource dictionaries can be used to specify sets of styles and templates. These dictionaries can then be included in the application. *ThemedDictionaries* are used to define themes that can be selected based on user preferences.

Objective review

Answer the following questions to test your knowledge of the information in this objective. You can find the answers to these questions and explanations of why each answer choice is correct or incorrect in the "Answers" section at the end of this chapter.

1. Due to a change in requirements, a Windows Store app you developed requires an update. The UI displays a list of items from a remote web service from which the user can select one or more items and carry out some operations. After the update, the app is expected to highlight the buttons that the user clicks to perform the operations. You are not likely to use this feature in other Windows Store apps you will build. How will you implement this requirement?

A. Create a user control based on the *Button* class. Replace the buttons with this new user control.

B. Create a custom control and package it in an assembly. Use this control to implement the requirement.

C. Create a new style for the buttons with the *Background* property set to a *LinearGradientBrush* that makes the appearance of the button more prominent.

D. Replace the buttons with the *ToggleSwitch* control. An operation is performed if the user sets the *ToggleSwitch* to *On*.

2. While building a Windows Store app, you realize you are specifying the properties of some controls in every page. You want to have clean and simple XAML with maximum reuse of the XAML within the app you have written. What steps should you take? (Choose all that apply.)

A. Create styles for these controls and place them in the page where they are required.

B. Create implicit styles wherever possible and include properties set with the same value across multiple pages.

C. Create styles for the controls and set the properties that are common across multiple declarations of the control.

D. Create a resource dictionary and include it in the application level. Use the resource dictionary to define new styles so they are available throughout the app.

E. Create custom controls and set the properties in the code-behind.

3. Users have reported that some UI elements in your app are barely visible in bright light conditions. You decide to update your app to address the problem. What is the best way to address this problem and implement a solution without updating the entire app?

A. Create a set of styles and control templates that help the user view the app's controls in bright light. Update each page of your app to apply these newly created styles and templates.

B. Create a set of themes optimized for various light conditions, such as bright light and dark interiors, and include them in the *ThemedDictionaries* section in the App.xaml file. Allow the user to select a theme through the Settings charm.

C. Create sets of styles and templates for various light conditions. Detect the ambient light using the proximity sensor and apply these resources throughout the app.

D. Build a version of your app specifically for bright light conditions and make it available through the Windows Store.

Chapter summary

- Any Windows Store app can be used in a variety of devices with different screen sizes and resolutions. You should develop your app such that it renders well on all screens. Based on your app's core features, you can restrict the orientations supported in the app by selecting a specific orientation in the package manifest.

- The *Grid* control can create a flexible and fluid layout. In situations where content is likely to overflow the visible area, use the *ScrollViewer* control.

- For displaying content with pictures or hyperlinks, for example, consider using the *RichTextBlock* control with the *RichTextBlockOverflow* companion control.

- The top app bar provides navigation among various sections of an app.

- The bottom app provides access to commands that are in-context with the page currently being viewed by the user.

- Avoid too many commands in the app bar and consider using a context menu instead. Place commands you expect to be used frequently toward the edges of the app bar.

- To display lists of data, use the *GridView*, *ListView*, and *FlipView* controls. These controls have built-in touch support and should be used based on the type of data to be displayed.

- Data templates provide flexibility with data controls in displaying data without the detailed knowledge of the underlying data model. The *DataTemplateSelector* class applies data templates selectively.

- Styles and control templates can be used to customize the visual appearance of controls. Gradients are helpful in drawing the attention of users towards certain actions.

- The *VisualStateManager* class can be used with *VisualStateGroups* element in XAML to define various states a control can exist. The *GoToState* method can be used to change between various states.

- You can create resource dictionaries and use them in your app to customize the appearance of various controls. Themes with one or more resource dictionaries can be used to provide a consistent look and feel in your app.

Answers

This section contains the solutions to the thought experiments and the answers to the lesson review questions in this chapter.

Objective 3.1: Thought experiment

1. **Use layout controls**   The layout controls provided by Microsoft, such as Grid, help build a fluid layout, which helps provide a consistent user experience across various devices and screens.

2. **Design for touch, support keyboard and mouse**   The app must support users with touch-enabled devices as well as input from a keyboard and mouse.

3. **Support multiple orientation and screen sizes**   To improve the user experience, your app should support multiple orientations and various screen sizes.

Objective 3.1: Review

1. **Correct answers:** A, B, C

    A. **Correct:** Windows supports the full screen view state in landscape orientation.

    B. **Correct:** Windows supports the fill view state in landscape orientation.

    C. **Correct:** Windows supports the snapped view state in landscape orientation.

    D. **Incorrect:** Windows supports the snapped view state in the landscape orientation only; the snapped view state is not supported in the portrait orientation.

    E. **Incorrect:** Windows supports the fill view state in the landscape orientation only; the fill view state is not supported in the portrait orientation.

2. **Correct answer:** C

    A. **Incorrect:** Implicit transitions update properties that are a *Double*, *Color*, or *Point* value, with animations. Using implicit transitions is not enough to meet the requirement.

    B. **Incorrect:** Explicit transitions are applied on properties such as *Length* and *Width*, usually with animations.

    C. **Correct:** The *VisualStateManager* with *VisualState*s for the supported view states is the preferred way to implement this requirement. Properties of individual UI elements are not altered; instead, they are invisible after the transition to a different orientation.

    D. **Incorrect:** The constructor is invoked when the page is created, so the app will not respond to changes in its orientation after it is visible. The *VisualStateManager* should be used in the *OnSizeChanged* event of the page to update its layout.

3. **Correct answers:** A, B, D

    A. **Correct:** Your app might not support all the orientations that the device can be in. You should declare the supported orientations in the package manifest.

    B. **Correct:** The *VisualStateManager* can be used to swap visual states defined in the XAML of a page. Each visual state usually represents the layout for a certain view state.

    C. **Incorrect:** The *OnLaunched* event is fired only once when the application is launched by the user. To update the view state of a page, the visual state should change after the page is visible and when the user changes the orientation.

    D. **Correct:** The *OnSizeChanged* event is fired whenever the height and width of a page changes; for example, when the user changes the device's orientation. The *VisualStateManager* can be used to update the layout of the page.

    E. **Incorrect:** The constructor of a page runs only once, when the page is created. However, users can change the orientation of their device while using your application. The *OnSizeChanged* event should be used to update the visual state.

Objective 3.2: Thought experiment

1. **Built-in support for touch** It is easier to manipulate 3D models on a multi-touch monitor. The organization will benefit from built-in touch support in the controls provided by Windows.

2. **Built-in support for zoom** In many uses, zooming into a 3D model is necessary. Windows 8 controls have built-in support for zoom.

3. **Same user experience across multiple screen sizes** The app is likely to be used in the manufacturing division on tablets. Therefore, users might find it convenient to use the app with zoom through touch interactions.

Objective 3.2: Review

1. **Correct answer:** B

    A. **Incorrect:** Creating styles and templates for each orientation makes it difficult to use them.

    B. **Correct:** Star sizing of rows and columns in a grid uses the available dimensions of the page and distributes the available area proportionally among the rows and columns. Styles and templates should be used for various view states to adjust the size of the controls.

    C. **Incorrect:** A layout you create needs to support various orientations, view states, a mechanism to arrange controls, and so on. The *Grid* control implements this functionality and provides additional features.

    D. **Incorrect:** A user might not know more content exists and that they need to swipe through all items in that page.

2. **Correct answers:** B, C, D

    A. **Incorrect:** A custom control needs to implement support for various orientations and view states, layout of controls in the page, and so on. The *Grid* control provides this functionality and is recommended for laying out a page.

    B. **Correct:** A *RichTextBlock* control should be placed in the root layout element and used along with *RichTextBlockOverflow* controls to allow text to overflow.

    C. **Correct:** You can use columns with star sizing to lay out a *RichTextBlock* control along with one or more *RichTextBlockOverflow* controls to render overflowing text.

    D. **Correct:** The *RichTextBlockOverflow* control and the *RichTextBlock* control display overflow text.

    E. **Incorrect:** The fundamental problem is choosing the right layout method across multiple view states and therefore, using styles and templates only will not solve the problem.

3. **Correct answers:** A, D, E

    A. **Correct:** The *Grid* control supports fluid layouts and easily adapts to orientation changes. Start sizing distributes available area proportionally among rows and columns.

    B. **Incorrect:** Although the *Grid* control is a popular control for creating layouts, you can also use the *Canvas* and *StackPanel* controls as layout controls.

    C. **Incorrect:** *ScrollViewer* supports horizontal and vertical scrolling.

    D. **Correct:** The *ScrollViewer* control has built-in support for touch-enabled devices. Therefore, users can interact with content rendered within a *ScrollViewer* through touch gestures.

    E. **Correct:** The *ScrollViewer* control automatically adds vertical and/or horizontal scrollbars whenever content overflows the visible area of the screen.

Objective 3.3: Thought experiment

1. Search and share are implemented in a Windows Store app using their respective charms. The app bar provides commands relevant for a page in the app.

2. The user can use the top app bar to navigate to a section instead of returning to the hub page and navigating from there.

3. You can use *Styles* and *VisualState*s to customize the buttons in the app bar and (optionally) their layout.

Objective 3.3: Review

1. **Correct answers:** A, C, D

   A. **Correct:** Search within the page can be implemented as a button in the app bar that, when pressed, opens a search box for searching the text.

   B. **Incorrect:** Cut, copy, and paste should be implemented in a context menu visible when the user has selected some text.

   C. **Correct:** The user is likely to change the font size occasionally, so these commands should be placed in the app bar.

   D. **Correct:** The user is likely to create, edit, and delete files when an existing file is open in the app. Therefore, these commands should be placed toward the left edge of the app bar.

   E. **Incorrect:** The recommended way to share a file from within an app is to use the Share charm.

2. **Correct answers:** A, B, D

   A. **Correct:** You can create a button for the app bar using the hexadecimal character of a font symbol obtained with the Character Map tool.

   B. **Correct:** You can use an image as the content of a button in the app bar.

   C. **Incorrect:** If you do not set the content of a button in the app bar, it will not help the user identify it.

   D. **Correct:** You can convert an image or icon into an XAML path and use it in a button for the app bar.

   E. **Incorrect:** The device might not be connected to the Internet, in which case a button in the app bar that uses an Internet resource will not provide visual guidance to the user.

3. **Correct answers:** A, B, C

   A. **Correct:** The *Loaded* event is fired after the app bar is available for interaction in the app. Therefore, the app should subscribe for layout update events in the event handler of the *Loaded* event.

   B. **Correct:** The *UnLoaded* event is fired after the app bar is dismissed. The app should unsubscribe for layout update events in the event handler of the *UnLoaded* event.

   C. **Correct:** Setting *IsSticky* for the app bar to *True* ensures it is visible even when the actions such as tap on the surface to hide the app bar are carried out.

   D. **Incorrect:** The *Opened* event is fired after the app bar is created and is visible in the page.

   E. **Incorrect:** The *Closed* event is fired when the app bar is no longer visible in the page.

Objective 3.4: Thought experiment

1. **Smooth, fluid layout**   You can use the *Grid* control to create a smooth and fluid layout that adapts to various view states.

2. **Sophisticated data controls**   *GridView* and *ListView* provide users with an easy-to-use interface to browse through lists.

3. **Distraction-free experience**   A *FlipView* control enables users to browse through the catalog in which they're viewing an item.

4. **Frequently used controls in one location**   The app bar provides in-context access to controls, letting the user focus on content.

5. **Multiple view state support**   Your app is likely to be used more often if it supports the snapped view state and even the full screen portrait view state. Users might often snap your app and use it with other apps or they might decide to read movie reviews in portrait mode.

Objective 3.4: Review

1. **Correct answers:** B, C, D

   A. **Incorrect:** Each page has a limited amount of data that can be displayed using layout controls such as *Grid*.

   B. **Correct:** The *FlipView* control displays a list of items without showing other items in the list. Users can view various graphs in this control while flipping through the list.

   C. **Correct:** The *RichTextBlock* and *RichTextBlockOverflow* controls are useful for rendering text whose length is unknown. They can be used in various orientations while laid out in a *Grid* control.

   D. **Correct:** A grid is suitable for laying out a graph and associated text using the *RichTextBlock* and *RichTextBlockOverflow* controls.

   E. **Incorrect:** You should develop a custom control only when you expect to use it in other Windows Store apps as well.

2. **Correct answers:** B, C, D

   A. **Incorrect:** The *FlipView* control displays item details for a list of items.

   B. **Correct:** The *GridView* control is suitable for laying out items horizontally in the screen.

   C. **Correct:** The *ListView* control is suitable for laying out items vertically in the screen.

   D. **Correct:** The *Grid* control can be set up with star sizing to lay out data controls.

   E. **Incorrect:** The *ListView* control is recommended for layouts that take advantage of vertically scrolling through a list of items, such as the snapped and full screen portrait view states.

3. **Correct answer:** B

   A. **Incorrect:** A user control will require modifications whenever there is a change in the requirements, such as addition of a new template for the items in the *GridView*.

   B. **Correct:** The *DataTemplateSelector* class can be used with the *GridView* control to apply a specific data template to an item based on the item's value.

   C. **Incorrect:** You should use a custom control when you plan to implement the same feature in multiple Windows Store apps.

   D. **Incorrect:** A code-behind approach means strong coupling between the UI and the business logic, which can cause maintenance problems in the future.

Objective 3.5: Thought experiment

1. Use styles, control templates, and visual states to customize controls as much as possible, with a view to reuse them across a page and within the app.

2. Use the *VisualStateManager* class to implement updates in the properties of controls whenever necessary.

3. Use multiple resource dictionaries to implement themes and make them all available to the user.

Objective 3.5: Review

1. **Correct answer:** C

   A. **Incorrect:** A user control created to implement the requirement might need modification if requirements change.

   B. **Incorrect:** A custom control is typically used to implement a fundamental requirement across a number of apps and share the XAML and code across multiple pages in more than one app. In this case, the requirement is specific to the app and does not justify creation of a custom control.

   C. **Correct:** Styles defined in XAML allow for decoupling of the UI from the business logic. Therefore, any future updates can be carried out with ease.

   D. **Incorrect:** The *ToggleSwitch* control is used to apply any one of two values for a property. Therefore, it might confuse the user if it is used to highlight an action.

2. **Correct answers:** B, C, D

   A. **Incorrect:** Styles in a page are available for controls within the page only. This minimizes their use across multiple pages in an app.

   B. **Correct:** Implicit styles created for a specific control are applied on all instances of the control in an app.

   C. **Correct:** When a property of a control is set to the same value multiple times in an app, it can be set through a style that is applied on all instances of that control. Implicit styles are suitable in such cases.

   D. **Correct:** Styles defined in a resource dictionary are available throughout the application.

   E. **Incorrect:** Custom controls are created to implement a set of requirements that are applicable to a number of apps. For example, they are useful for branding a set of apps. Therefore, custom controls are not suitable when the XAML is reused within a Windows Store app.

3. **Correct answer:** B

   A. **Incorrect:** If you update the styles and templates in your app to improve the user experience in bright light conditions, you might have problems in other lighting conditions.

   B. **Correct:** Themes consist of a group of styles and templates suitable for a set of requirements, such as bright light, low light, and dark light. The user will find it convenient to select a theme based on lighting conditions.

   C. **Incorrect:** Not all user devices contain the proximity sensor.

   D. **Incorrect:** Creating a separate version of your app that supports bright light means you have to support multiple versions of your app, and you might need to create versions for other lighting conditions.

Program the user interaction

The Windows 8 Start screen is a collection of tiles. Some tiles are updated regularly with new text or images, and they can contain a badge that informs the user of the status of an action or update. A tile on the Start screen launches an app. Your app's tile is a way to communicate with the user when it is not running. Therefore, you should use your app's tile to show fresh content and the latest status with badges. Users often like to bookmark items. Secondary tiles in Windows 8 are used to pin a shortcut to an item or a page in your app on the Start screen.

Your app might need to draw the user's attention to perform a critical task by launching it when it is not running. Live tiles are not adequate for this purpose when the user is inside another app. In such cases, your app can send a toast notification that pops up on the top right of the screen. Tapping the toast launches your application. Toast notifications can be initiated from within your app or by a remote service. You can schedule notifications to be shown in the future, for example, to show a reminder for a task. A toast typically consists of text and an image, and you can optionally play a sound when it is displayed.

A well-designed Windows Store app should work properly irrespective of the device on which it is running. Your app might be used with a touchscreen, a hardware or software keyboard, or a pen/stylus device (generally referred to as a "stylus" throughout the chapter). The behavior of your app when used with different input devices should not change. You can implement custom gestures in your app to manipulate content and interact in a variety of ways. Windows 8 apps support stylus device input, along with inking support for drawing, capturing, rending, selecting, and deleting ink strokes.

Most Windows Store apps consist of multiple pages. Windows provides a navigation framework that is helpful for implementing navigation in an app. Microsoft Visual Studio provides developers with application templates that contain support for caching data for a page and integration between navigation and session state. Designing and implementing navigation is an important phase in the development of your app. Microsoft provides a set of guidelines to help developers implement navigation. In applications with grouped data, Semantic Zoom can be implemented to navigate among groups in a simple yet powerful way.

Objectives in this chapter:

- Objective 4.1: Create and manage tiles.
- Objective 4.2: Notify users by using toast.
- Objective 4.3. Manage input devices.
- Objective 4.4: Design and implement navigation in an app.

Objective 4.1: Create and manage tiles

When a Windows Store app is installed on a Windows 8 PC or device, a tile is created on the Start screen. An app's tile is like an icon in a list of programs, but it is lot more powerful than a simple icon. A tile is useful for communicating with the user even when the associated app is not visible on the screen. A tile can display the latest content from a news website, weather updates, or the latest stock prices. In addition, badges convey status information from apps (for example, whether a remote service is available or the number of unread news articles in a newsreader application). Notifications can be delivered through an app's tile by the app itself, or the app can add the notification to be delivered according to a schedule or even periodically with an expiry date. Remote services can send push notifications to apps for communicating status and other data.

> **This objective covers how to:**
> - Create and update tiles and tile contents.
> - Create and update badges using the *TileUpdateManager* class.
> - Respond to notification requests.
> - Choose an appropriate tile update schedule based on app requirements.

Creating and updating tiles and tile contents

Every Windows Store app displays on the Start screen as a tile. This tile, which is a shortcut for launching the app, is known as the primary tile. The tile appears on the Start screen as soon as an app finishes installing. A sample of Windows Store apps and their tiles are shown in Figure 4-1.

FIGURE 4-1 Primary tiles of some Windows Store apps in the Windows 8 Start screen

Some of the tiles shown in Figure 4-1 are static; others display updates such as the Weather app. Some of the tiles are rectangular and others are square. The default static tile in Visual Studio is a 150 × 150 pixel logo. In addition, you can create a 310 × 150 pixel logo for the wide static tile. A wider tile provides more area to display content. Users can select between the square tile and the wide tile of your application to be displayed on the Start screen if you specify a logo for the wide tile.

Working with primary tiles

You set logos in the package manifest file of the app. Using Visual Studio, you specify the 150 × 150 pixel logo in the "Logo" section on the Application UI tab, and the 310 × 150 pixel logo in the "Wide logo" section. See Figure 4-2.

FIGURE 4-2 Visual Studio configuration for the logos of a Windows Store app

The primary tile for your application defined in the package manifest is visible until it is updated through a tile notification. It changes back to its default specification when there is no notification to display. A notification expires after a period of time, after which it is no longer visible on the tile.

Windows Store apps can update their tiles with dynamic content using tile notifications. A tile notification can be delivered in several ways:

- Delivered when the app is running
- Scheduled for delivery at a future date
- Retrieved periodically from a remote web service
- Sent by a cloud-based service through the Windows Push Notification Services (WNS)

A tile with dynamically updating content is commonly known as a *live tile.* By default, tile notifications delivered by the app do not expire, so an expiry date should be set before they are delivered. Tile notifications delivered by one of the other methods, as listed in the previous bulleted list, expire after three days. With this feature, old and outdated content is removed from your app's live tile.

A tile notification is prepared using an XML template. Windows provides a large number of XML templates that contain a mix of images and text for both square and wide tiles. Note that any image you select for your tile notification should not be larger than 1024 × 1204 pixels in dimensions and should not be larger than 200 kilobytes (KB) in size. If you use an image larger than these specifications, the notification is not delivered to the tile. The *TileUpdateManager* (in the *Windows.UI.Notifications* namespace) can be used to deliver a local notification. To prepare a tile notification, select an XML template and update it with your own content.

> **MORE INFO** **THE TILE TEMPLATE CATALOG**
>
> Microsoft provides a catalog of XML templates for use with tile notifications. This catalog is available at *http://msdn.microsoft.com/en-US/library/windows/apps/xaml/hh761491.* You can select a tile template in code with one of the values of the *TileTemplateType* enumeration listed at *http://msdn.microsoft.com/en-us/library/windows/apps/xaml/windows. ui.notifications.tiletemplatetype.aspx.*

If your application is configured with a wide tile, you should include both a square tile and a wide tile in the notification. This is achieved by inserting the XML template for the square tile into the root XML element, as shown in the C# code in Listing 4-1.

LISTING 4-1 Including both a square tile and a wide tile in the tile notification

```
public void SendLocalTileNotification()
{
    // Create and populate the wide tile
    XmlDocument wideImageAndTextTileXml =
        TileUpdateManager.GetTemplateContent(TileTemplateType.TileWideImageAndText01);
    XmlNodeList wideTileTextAttributes =
            wideImageAndTextTileXml.GetElementsByTagName("text");
    wideTileTextAttributes[0].InnerText = "Awesome cats make Windows 8 awesomer!!";

    XmlElement tileImage = wideImageAndTextTileXml.GetElementsByTagName("image")[0]
        as XmlElement;
    tileImage.SetAttribute("src", "ms-appx:///Assets/Cat-1.JPG");
```

```
    tileImage.SetAttribute("alt", "Awesome Cats");

    // Create and populate the square tile
    XmlDocument squareTileXml =
              TileUpdateManager.GetTemplateContent(TileTemplateType.TileSquareText04);
    XmlNodeList squareTileTextAttributes = squareTileXml.GetElementsByTagName("text");
    squareTileTextAttributes[0].AppendChild(squareTileXml.CreateTextNode(
                    "Awesome cats make Windows 8 awesomer!"));

    // Import the XML template for the square tile into the wide tile
    IXmlNode node = wideImageAndTextTileXml.ImportNode(
          squareTileXml.GetElementsByTagName("binding").Item(0), true);
    wideImageAndTextTileXml.GetElementsByTagName("visual").Item(0).AppendChild(node);
    TileNotification tileNotification = new TileNotification(wideImageAndTextTileXml);

    // Add an expiration time of 30 minutes
    tileNotification.ExpirationTime = DateTimeOffset.UtcNow.AddSeconds(1800);


    // Send the local tile notification
    TileUpdateManager.CreateTileUpdaterForApplication().Update(tileNotification);
}
```

The XAML configured for the wide and square tile is shown as follows:

```
<tile>
  <visual>
    <binding template="TileWideImageAndText01">
      <image id="1" src=" ms-appx:///Assets/Cat-1.JPG" alt="Awesome Cats"/>
      <text id="1">Awesome cats make Windows 8 awesomer!!</text>
    </binding>
    <binding template="TileSquareText04">
      <text id="1">Awesome cats make Windows 8 awesomer!! #cats</text>
    </binding>
  </visual>
</tile>
```

An example of a tile notification delivered to the wide tile of an application using the XAML code is shown in Figure 4-3.

FIGURE 4-3 A local tile notification with an image and text (photo courtesy of Microsoft Office Imagery)

It can often be challenging to load the XML template and prepare it for use with the *TileUpdater* of your app. The *NotificationExtensions* library provides strongly typed objects for preparing tile notifications.

> **MORE INFO**   **NOTIFICATIONEXTENSIONS LIBRARY**
>
> More information about the *NotificationExtensions* library is available at *http://msdn.micro-soft.com/en-us/library/windows/apps/hh969156.aspx*.

To clear the notifications in your application's tile, use the following C# code:

```
public void ClearTileNotifications()
{
    // Clear all notification and set the tile to display default content
    TileUpdateManager.CreateTileUpdaterForApplication().Clear();
}
```

Users can choose to turn off the live tile of your application or they can choose the square tile instead of the wide tile. The system provides this option when your application's tile is selected by the user, as shown in Figure 4-4.

FIGURE 4-4 Users can choose to turn live tiles on or off for an application and select the square tile instead of the wide tile (Photo courtesy of Microsoft Office Imagery)

 EXAM TIP

You are not expected to know the names of common tile templates for the exam. You should be familiar with setting up a tile notification, delivering it through the *TileUpdater*, and clearing tile notifications.

If you choose to use live tiles in a Windows Store app, the content of tile notifications should encourage users to launch your app. In addition, selecting the right method of delivering tile notifications and regularly updating the contents creates a good user experience.

Freshly delivered content such as the latest news headlines, traffic updates based on the user's current location, or new movie releases matching the user's tastes make a live tile compelling.

> **MORE INFO** **GUIDELINES FOR TILES AND BADGES**
>
> Microsoft provides a set of guidelines for developers to use live tiles and badges in their applications at *http://msdn.microsoft.com/en-us/library/windows/apps/hh465403.aspx*.

Working with secondary tiles

In a Windows Store app, users might open a certain item more frequently, such as a page showing a preferred category of movies or a page showing the weather forecast of a city they will visit soon. In such cases, instead of letting the user navigate to the page in the traditional way, you can provide secondary tiles that are pinned on the Start screen and act as shortcuts to these pages. A secondary tile enables direct access to a specific page or experience within an app. When the user taps or clicks the secondary tile, the app is launched with the pinned content visible on the screen. You can create a secondary tile with the *SecondaryTile* class (in the *Windows.UI.StartScreen* namespace).

Although the content that can be pinned to a secondary tile is controlled by an app, the action of pinning content is controlled by the user. Your app cannot pin content on behalf of the user. The action to pin a page to the Start screen is usually presented as a Pin to Start context menu when the button in the app bar is clicked or tapped by the user. A secondary tile can be removed either through the Start screen or while the user is in the parent app.

Secondary tiles are similar to primary and live tiles. They must include a 150 × 150 pixel logo and, optionally, a wide 310 × 150 pixel logo. Tile notifications can be delivered using tile templates and they can be rearranged on the Start screen. They are removed from the Start screen when the app is uninstalled. There are some differences between primary tiles and secondary tiles. Secondary tiles can be deleted at any time without deleting the parent app. They can be created at runtime, unlike primary tiles, which can be created only once during installation.

To create a secondary tile for a page in your Windows Store app, start by adding the styles for the app bar buttons and declaring the bottom app bar, as shown in Listing 4-2.

LISTING 4-2 Creating a secondary tile—XAML

```
<Page.Resources>
    <Style x:Key="PinAppBarButtonStyle" TargetType="Button"
           BasedOn="{StaticResource AppBarButtonStyle}">
        <Setter Property="AutomationProperties.AutomationId" Value="PinAppBarButton"/>
        <Setter Property="AutomationProperties.Name" Value="Pin to Start"/>
        <Setter Property="Content" Value="&#xE141;"/>
    </Style>
    <Style x:Key="UnpinAppBarButtonStyle" TargetType="Button"
           BasedOn="{StaticResource AppBarButtonStyle}">
        <Setter Property="AutomationProperties.AutomationId" Value="UnpinAppBarButton"/>
        <Setter Property="AutomationProperties.Name" Value="Unpin from Start"/>
```

```
                <Setter Property="Content" Value="&#xE196;"/>
            </Style>
        </Page.Resources>

        <Page.BottomAppBar>
            <AppBar x:Name="SecondaryTileAppBar" Padding="10,0,10,0" >
                <Grid>
                    <Grid.ColumnDefinitions>
                        <ColumnDefinition Width="30*"/>
                    </Grid.ColumnDefinitions>
                    <StackPanel x:Name="RightPanel" Orientation="Horizontal"
                                Grid.Column="1" HorizontalAlignment="Right">
                    </StackPanel>
                </Grid>
            </AppBar>
        </Page.BottomAppBar>
```

In the code-behind of the page, the app bar button is added based on whether the page is not pinned or already pinned on the Start screen, and the button click event handler is set up as shown in Listing 4-3.

LISTING 4-3 Creating a secondary tile—the code-behind

```
using Windows.UI.StartScreen;
using Windows.UI.Xaml.Controls;

public sealed partial class AwesomeCatPage : LayoutAwarePage
{
    // Unique Id for the page
    public const string appbarTileId = "SecondaryTile.AwesomeCatPage";

    public AwesomeCatPage()
    {
        this.InitializeComponent();
        InitializeAppBar();
    }

    // Initialize the app bar by checking whether the page is already
    // pinned on the Start page. Set up the event handler for the app
    // bar button click event.
    private void InitializeAppBar()
    {
        this.BottomAppBar.IsOpen = true;
        StackPanel rightPanel = this.FindName("RightPanel") as StackPanel;
        this.BottomAppBar.IsOpen = false;

        if (rightPanel != null)
        {
            Button pinToAppBar = new Button();
            ToggleAppBarButton(!SecondaryTile.Exists(appbarTileId));
            pinToAppBar.Click += PinToAppBar_Click;
            this.BottomAppBar.Opened += BottomAppBar_Opened;
            rightPanel.Children.Add(pinToAppBar);
        }
    }
```

```csharp
// Apply the correct style for the app bar button based on whether
// the page is pinned to the Start screen or not. The styles are defined in the
// Page.Resources section in the XAML of the page.
private void ToggleAppBarButton(bool showPinButton)
{
    if (pinToAppBar != null)
    {
        pinToAppBar.Style = (showPinButton) ?
                        (this.Resources["PinAppBarButtonStyle"] as Style) :
                        (this.Resources["UnpinAppBarButtonStyle"] as Style);
    }
}


// Once the button is pinned, update the style of the app bar button.
private void BottomAppBar_Opened(object sender, object e)
{
    ToggleAppBarButton(!SecondaryTile.Exists(appbarTileId));
}
// Event handler for the app bar button.
private async void PinToAppBar_Click(object sender, RoutedEventArgs e)
{
    this.BottomAppBar.IsSticky = true;

    if (SecondaryTile.Exists(appbarTileId))
    {
        SecondaryTile secondaryTile = new SecondaryTile(appbarTileId);
        bool isUnpinned = await
                    secondaryTile.RequestDeleteForSelectionAsync(
                        GetElementRect((FrameworkElement)sender),
                            Windows.UI.Popups.Placement.Above);
        ToggleAppBarButton(isUnpinned);
    }
    else
    {
        Uri logo = new Uri("ms-appx:///Assets/Cat-Sec-1.JPG");
        string tileActivationArguments = appbarTileId + " was pinned at " +
                        DateTime.Now.ToLocalTime().ToString();
        SecondaryTile secondaryTile = new SecondaryTile(appbarTileId,
                        "Awesome Cats",
                        "Awesome cats make Windows 8 awesomer!!",
                        tileActivationArguments,
                        TileOptions.ShowNameOnLogo | TileOptions.ShowNameOnWideLogo,
                        logo);

        secondaryTile.ForegroundText = ForegroundText.Dark;
        secondaryTile.SmallLogo =
                            new Uri("ms-appx:///Assets/Cat-Sec-2.JPG");
        secondaryTile.WideLogo = new Uri("ms-appx:///Assets/Cat-Sec-1.JPG");
        bool isPinned = await secondaryTile.RequestCreateForSelectionAsync(
                            GetElementRect((FrameworkElement)sender),
                                Windows.UI.Popups.Placement.Above);
        ToggleAppBarButton(!isPinned);
    }
    this.BottomAppBar.IsSticky = false;
}
```

```
// Gets the rectangle of the element
public static Rect GetElementRect(FrameworkElement element)
{
    GeneralTransform buttonTransform = element.TransformToVisual(null);
    Point point = buttonTransform.TransformPoint(new Point());
    return new Rect(point, new Size(element.ActualWidth, element.ActualHeight));
}
}
```

When users are in the page that they want to pin to the Start screen, they do so by opening the app bar and clicking the Pin to Start button in the context menu, as shown in Figure 4-5.

FIGURE 4-5 A page in a Windows Store app that can be pinned to the Start screen (photo courtesy of Microsoft Office Imagery)

After the page is pinned on the Start screen, the user can change the size of the secondary tile or unpin the tile by selecting it, as shown in Figure 4-6.

FIGURE 4-6 A secondary tile can be unpinned from the Start screen or its size can be changed by the user (photo courtesy of Microsoft Office Imagery)

Windows expects some properties of a secondary tile to be set before it is pinned. Each secondary tile is assigned a unique ID to distinguish it from other tiles. If you provide the unique ID of an existing secondary tile, that tile will be overwritten. If you provide a wide logo in addition to the mandatory small logo, you can set the name of the logo to be visible when the wide tile is shown. This is set through the tile options, as shown in Listing 4-3 (*TileOptions.ShowNameOnLogo* for the name to be displayed on the square tile, and *TileOptions.ShowNameOnWideLogo* for the name to display on the wide tile). You can also include *CopyOnDeployment* in the tile options, which ensures that the tile is pinned to the Start screen on any other computer with the same Microsoft account when the parent app is installed.

The code in Listing 4-4 changes the logo of a secondary tile after it is available on the Start screen. In addition, tile notifications can be delivered to secondary tiles similar to that of primary tiles.

LISTING 4-4 Changing the logo of a secondary tile

```
private void UpdateSecondaryTileLogo()
{
    SecondaryTile tileToUpdate = new SecondaryTile(appbarTileId);
    tileToUpdate.Logo =
        new Uri("ms-appx:///Assets/NewSecondaryTileDefaultImage.jpg");
    tileToUpdate.WideLogo =
        new Uri("ms-appx:///Assets/NewSecondaryTileDefaultWideImage.jpg");
    tileToUpdate.UpdateAsync();
}


private void SendNotificationToSecondaryTile()
{
    // Define the notification content.
    XmlDocument tileXml =
        TileUpdateManager.GetTemplateContent(TileTemplateType.TileWideText04);
    XmlNodeList tileTextAttributes = tileXml.GetElementsByTagName("text");
    tileTextAttributes[0].AppendChild(tileXml.CreateTextNode("Hello from awesome cat"));

    // Provide a square version of the notification.
    XmlDocument squareTileXml =
        TileUpdateManager.GetTemplateContent(TileTemplateType.TileSquareText04);
    XmlNodeList squareTileTextAttributes = squareTileXml.GetElementsByTagName("text");
    squareTileTextAttributes[0].AppendChild(squareTileXml.CreateTextNode("Hello
    from awesome cat"));

    // Add the square tile to the notification.
    IXmlNode node =
    tileXml.ImportNode(squareTileXml.GetElementsByTagName("binding").Item(0), true);
    tileXml.GetElementsByTagName("visual").Item(0).AppendChild(node);

    // Update the secondary tile.
    TileNotification tileNotification = new TileNotification(tileXml);
    TileUpdater secondaryTileUpdater =
        TileUpdateManager.CreateTileUpdaterForSecondaryTile(appbarTileId);
    secondaryTileUpdater.Update(tileNotification);
}
```

Creating and updating badges using the *TileUpdateManager* class

The live tile of a Windows Store app is commonly used to deliver new content to the user. In some cases, you might want to notify the user with a status or summary of new items that are ready for viewing. Badges display the status at the bottom-right corner in the tile of the application (on the bottom-left corner on a computer set to right-to-left language). A badge is either a glyph, which indicates status such as an alert or attention (available as a fixed set of glyphs) or a number between 1 and 99. Badges can display on both square and wide tiles.

To send a badge update to the tile of your app, you need to select the type of badge the tile should display. This is one of the two values of the *BadgeTemplateType* enumeration, which has the following members:

- **BadgeGlyph**   A glyph image provided by the system.
- **BadgeNumber**   A numerical value between 1 and 99. Values greater than 99 are displayed as 99+.

You can update the value of the *badge* element in the XML template of a badge and use the *Update* method of the *BadgeUpdater* class to update the badge in the tile. An instance of the *BadgeUpdater* class is obtained from the *BadgeUpdateManager* static class with the *CreateBadgeUpdaterForApplication* method for the live tile of the app and *CreateBadgeUpdaterForSecondaryTile* method for the secondary tile. The code in Listing 4-5 shows how to send a badge update for the primary tile as a number or a glyph and to clear all badge updates.

LISTING 4-5 Sending badge updates for the primary tile and clearing badge updates

```
private void SendBadgeUpdateAsNumber()
{
    XmlDocument badgeXml =
            BadgeUpdateManager.GetTemplateContent(BadgeTemplateType.BadgeNumber);
    XmlElement badgeElement = (XmlElement)badgeXml.SelectSingleNode("/badge");
    badgeElement.SetAttribute("value", "23");
    BadgeNotification badge = new BadgeNotification(badgeXml);
    BadgeUpdateManager.CreateBadgeUpdaterForApplication().Update(badge);
}

private void SendBadgeUpdateAsGlyph()
{
    XmlDocument badgeXml =
            BadgeUpdateManager.GetTemplateContent(BadgeTemplateType.BadgeGlyph);
    XmlElement badgeElement = (XmlElement)badgeXml.SelectSingleNode("/badge");
    badgeElement.SetAttribute("value", "attention");
    BadgeNotification badge = new BadgeNotification(badgeXml);
    BadgeUpdateManager.CreateBadgeUpdaterForApplication().Update(badge);
}

private void ClearBadgeUpdates()
{
    BadgeUpdateManager.CreateBadgeUpdaterForApplication().Clear();
}
```

Figure 4-7 shows a badge update containing a number (set to 23) delivered to a Windows Store app using the code in Listing 4-5.

FIGURE 4-7 Badge update in the live tile of a Windows Store app in the Start screen (photo courtesy of Microsoft Office Imagery)

Badges have many features in common with live tiles. You can periodically update badges, schedule a future update, and use push notifications to update the glyph or number displayed. You can set an *ExpirationTime* on a badge update when you create it, and your app can clear badges programmatically.

MORE INFO **BADGE CONTENT OPTIONS**

Microsoft provides a set of glyphs that can be used in a badge notification. For the full list of glyphs, refer to this page: *http://msdn.microsoft.com/en-us/library/windows/apps/xaml/hh779719.aspx.*

Responding to notification requests

Tile notification and badge updates in a Windows Store app are delivered in one of the following ways:

- **Local**   The app creates local updates to a live tile and delivers them using the *Update* method of the *TileUpdater* class. These updates do not expire if the expiration time is not set in the update.

- **Scheduled**   The app can schedule an update to be delivered at a later date and time. Scheduled updates expire three days after they are delivered or at a time set by your app. After a tile update is scheduled, your app does not have to be running.

- **Periodic**   Periodic updates poll a remote URL and fetch the XML for the tile at intervals from every half hour to every day. After it is configured, your app does not have to be running for the periodic updates to be delivered.

- **Push**   Push notifications, which are delivered through the WNS, can update tiles and badges.

Push notifications offer an ideal solution for Windows Store apps that provide regular updates to the user as they occur. For example, a weather app needs to show severe weather warnings through the live tile. Although scheduled or periodic updates fetch data at specific time intervals, to be effective, an app should use push notifications to update its tile and badges. Microsoft provides developers with the free WNS to help integrate push notifications in apps. The service handles the communication with your application and can handle millions of users. The following steps illustrate how to set up push notifications for tile and badge updates and other notifications:

1. The Windows Store app requests a push notification channel from WNS. The service returns a channel with a uniform resource identifier (URI) that is unique to the app and the device.

2. Your app sends this URI to a cloud service or a remote web service. It is important to ensure that this URI is not compromised by a third party, so you should encrypt the communication between your app and the cloud service.

3. When the remote service has an update for your app, the service notifies WNS using the channel URI obtained by your app. This is carried out by sending a HTTP POST operation with the notification payload, which typically consists of the XML for the tile or badge update.

4. WNS receives the request and routes the notification to the appropriate device.

The remote service uses one of the standard templates for a tile or badge, and sends a request to the WNS for the notification to be delivered. When the notification arrives in your app, the live tile is updated with the received tile or badge update. All classes for push notifications are defined in the *Windows.Networking.PushNotifications*. The code in Listing 4-6 shows how push notifications are typically set up in a Windows Store app.

LISTING 4-6 Setting up push notifications

```
using Windows.UI.Notifications;
using Windows.Networking.PushNotifications;
using Windows.Security.Cryptography;
using System.Net.Http;
using Windows.Networking.Connectivity;

private async void SetupPushNotifications()
{
    var profile = NetworkInformation.GetInternetConnectionProfile();

    // Check for internet connectivity and register for push notifications
    if (profile.GetNetworkConnectivityLevel() ==
            NetworkConnectivityLevel.InternetAccess)
    {
        PushNotificationChannel channel = null;

        try
        {
```

```
              // Obtain a PushNotificationChannel from WNS
              channel = await
PushNotificationChannelManager.CreatePushNotificationChannelForApplicationAsync();

              var buffer = CryptographicBuffer.ConvertStringToBinary(channel.Uri,
                                  BinaryStringEncoding.Utf8);
              var uri = CryptographicBuffer.EncodeToBase64String(buffer);
              var client = new HttpClient();

              // Update the cloud service with the PushNotificationChannel URI
              var response = await client.GetAsync(new
                      Uri("http://awesomecatsapp.cloudapp.net?uri" + uri + "&type=tile"));

              if (!response.IsSuccessStatusCode)
              {
                  // Record the problem in a log
              }
          }
          catch (Exception ex)
          {
              //
          }
      }
}
```

Your app can update a secondary tile using push notifications. Instead of using *Create-PushNotificationChannelForApplicationAsync*, you should use the *CreatePushNotificationChannelForSecondaryTileAsync* method of the *PushNotificationChannelManager* class with the secondary tile's unique ID.

You might want to intercept a push notification in your app and respond to it with some application logic before it updates a tile or a badge. For example, a specific value in a badge update can be used to trigger a background task. You can also suppress the display of the tile or badge update. You can set up an event handler for the *PushNotificationReceived* event provided by the *PushNotificationChannel* class. Within the event handler, you can check for the type of push notification and examine the contents of the notification. The code in Listing 4-7 shows how to subscribe to the *PushNotificationReceived* event and handle various types of push notifications.

LISTING 4-7 Subscribing to the *PushNotificationReceived* event and handling push notifications

```
private async void SetupPushNotifications()
{
    // Code removed for brevity

    // Obtain a PushNotificationChannel from WNS
    channel = await PushNotificationChannelManager.
CreatePushNotificationChannelForApplicationAsync();
    channel.PushNotificationReceived += OnPushNotification;
}
```

```csharp
// This event handler is used to intercept the push notification, examine its
// contents and suppress the display of the tile or badge update
private async void OnPushNotification(
        PushNotificationChannel sender, PushNotificationReceivedEventArgs e)
{
    string notificationContent = string.Empty;

    switch (e.NotificationType)
    {
        case PushNotificationType.Badge:
            notificationContent = e.BadgeNotification.Content.GetXml();
            break;

        case PushNotificationType.Tile:
            notificationContent = e.TileNotification.Content.GetXml();
            break;

        case PushNotificationType.Toast:
            notificationContent = e.ToastNotification.Content.GetXml();
            break;

        case PushNotificationType.Raw:
            notificationContent = e.RawNotification.Content;
            break;
    }

    if (!string.IsNullOrEmpty(notificationContent))
    {
        // Process the content and take action
    }

    // Cancel the delivery of the tile or badge update
    e.Cancel = true;
}
```

Configuring tile and badge updates for the lock screen

The lock screen is displayed when the user locks a device or when the device is switched on, rebooted, or wakes up from sleep. If your Windows Store app needs to keep the user up to date with the status of a task or deliver information in a text event when the screen is locked, tile and badge updates can be delivered on the lock screen. Up to seven Windows Store apps can be present on the lock screen, and one of these apps can show the text of the latest tile notification. A Windows Store has to request lock screen access from the user and then choose to display a badge update and, optionally, the text from their last tile notification. This process is configured in the package manifest, as shown in Figure 4-8.

More information

FIGURE 4-8 Configuring the package manifest for tile and badge updates to be delivered in the lock screen of an app

If you choose to display the tile text, you must provide a wide logo for your app, or else your manifest will be invalid. In addition, if your app displays a badge in the in the lock screen, you must provide a badge logo. An app with lock screen presence must declare a background task, which can be a Control Channel, a Timer, or Push Notification. If your app has secondary tiles, content from the tiles can be displayed on the lock screen. If you choose to display a logo for the secondary tile, you should set that with the *LockScreenBadgeLogo* property of the *SecondaryTile* class. You can also set the *LockScreenDisplayBadgeAndTileText* property to *True* to make the secondary tile eligible for display in the lock screen's detailed status slot.

Before your app has access to the lock screen, it must seek permission from the user. This step is available only once for your app. After your app has been granted access to the lock screen by the user, it can update the lock screen with badge updates and, optionally, tile text updates using the same code used for updating your app's tile. The *BackgroundExecution-Manager* class in the *Windows.ApplicationModel.Background* namespace provides ways for an app to be added and removed from the lock screen, and to query its current access to the background task and badge updates on the lock screen. The code in Listing 4-8 provides this functionality.

LISTING 4-8 Adding and removing an app from the lock screen

```
using Windows.UI.Notifications;
using Windows.ApplicationModel.Background;

// Event handler for button that requests access to the lock screen
private async void RequestLockScreenAccess_Click(object sender, RoutedEventArgs e)
{
    BackgroundAccessStatus status = await
                BackgroundExecutionManager.RequestAccessAsync();

    switch (status)
    {
```

```
        case BackgroundAccessStatus.AllowedWithAlwaysOnRealTimeConnectivity:
            // App is on the lock screen, has access to Always-On Real Time Connectivity
            break;
        case BackgroundAccessStatus.AllowedMayUseActiveRealTimeConnectivity:
            // App is on the lock screen, has access to Active Real Time Connectivity
            break;
        case BackgroundAccessStatus.Denied:
            // App is not on the lock screen
            break;
        case BackgroundAccessStatus.Unspecified:
            // User has not yet taken any action
            break;
        default:
            break;
    }
}

// Clear badge of all notifications
private void ClearBadge_Click(object sender, RoutedEventArgs e)
{
    BadgeUpdateManager.CreateBadgeUpdaterForApplication().Clear();
}

// Send a badge update to the lock screen
// Note: You can optionally check for the lock screen access status by calling
// BackgroundExecutionManager.GetAccessStatus() and evaluating the returned
// BackgroundAccessStatus value as seen in the event handler above.
private void SendBadgeUpdateOnLockScreen_Click(object sender, RoutedEventArgs e)
{
    string badgeXmlString = "<badge value='6'/>";
    Windows.Data.Xml.Dom.XmlDocument badgeDOM = new Windows.Data.Xml.Dom.XmlDocument();
    badgeDOM.LoadXml(badgeXmlString);
    BadgeNotification badge = new BadgeNotification(badgeDOM);
    BadgeUpdateManager.CreateBadgeUpdaterForApplication().Update(badge);
    rootPage.NotifyUser("Badge notification sent", NotifyType.StatusMessage);
}
```

When your app requests access to run in the background and use the lock screen to deliver badge and tile updates, the user is presented with the dialog box shown in Figure 4-9.

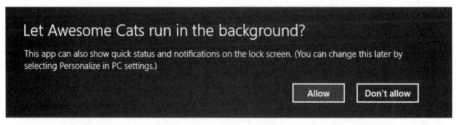

FIGURE 4-9 A Windows Store app requesting access to run in the background and access the lock screen

When a badge update arrives, it is delivered on the lock screen, as shown in Figure 4-10.

FIGURE 4-10 Badge updates seen in the lock screen of a device

Using PC Settings to remove an app from the lock screen

Users can remove your app from the lock screen and add it later through the lock screen section in the PC Settings, as shown in Figure 4-11.

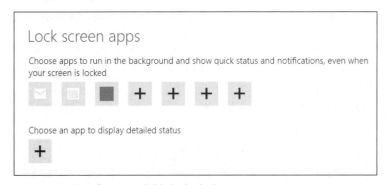

FIGURE 4-11 List of apps available in the lock screen

If your app has been removed from the lock screen, it is not allowed to request lock screen access again. If you use the *RequestAccessAsync* method of the *BackgroundExecutionManager* class after the user has removed your app from the lock screen, the request is ignored. However, if the seven slots available in the lock screen are all occupied by other apps, and the user does not replace an existing app in the lock screen with your app, a call to *RequestAccessAsync* from your app will display the dialog box shown in Figure 4-9. Your app can provide a command in the Settings charm for the user to remove it from the lock screen. The *RemoveAccess* method of the *BackgroundExecutionManager* class removes your app from the lock screen.

Choosing an appropriate tile update schedule based on app requirements

Windows Store apps can deliver local notifications through live tiles and badges when they are running. Push notifications enable remote servers to communicate with Windows Store apps and update their tiles and badges. Both options are powerful and are often adequate to meet your app's requirements. Sometimes, however, your app might need to update its tile at a specific time or regularly poll a remote URL for data that can be delivered to the user through a tile or badge update.

A Windows Store app can display up to five notifications in a cycle. The default behavior of a live tile on the Start screen is to display a single notification until the next notification arrives when the tile's contents are updated. Windows provides the option to enable a notification queue that can maintain up to five notifications, and the tile cycles through them until they expire. The notification queue can cycle tiles delivered locally from within the app via push notifications, via a schedule, or periodically.

The amount of time each notification in the queue is displayed and the order in which it appears on the tile is determined by the system. When the queue reaches its capacity of five notifications, the next new notification replaces the oldest notification in the queue. You can control this behavior by specifying a tag with the notification delivered. Windows examines the tag on a new notification, looks for a notification in the queue with a matching tag, and, if one is found, replaces that notification in the queue. If no notification with the tag is found, it uses the first-in, first-out (FIFO) rule to replace notifications with new ones. It is easy to enable the notification queue and use it in your app, as follows:

```
public void SendLocalTileNotification()
{
    // The following code is an addition to the code
    // shown previously for creating and updating tiles.

    TileNotification tileNotification = new TileNotification(wideImageAndTextTileXml);
    tileNotification.Tag = "FirstCatTile";

    // Enable notification queue
    TileUpdateManager.CreateTileUpdaterForApplication().EnableNotificationQueue(true);

    // Send the local tile notification
    TileUpdateManager.CreateTileUpdaterForApplication().Update(tileNotification);
}
```

Periodic notifications in Windows Store apps update tiles and badges at a fixed interval by downloading content from a remote server or a cloud service. You need the following to set up periodic notifications in an app:

- A URI of a cloud service that provides the content of a notification as correctly formatted XML of the tile to be shown.

- The frequency at which the URI should be polled and the tile or badge updated with new content.

- Optionally, you can specify the time at which the periodic updates will commence. If you do not specify this value, the updates will begin immediately.

Periodic updates can be used to deliver content among a large number of users without a significant investment in the infrastructure. The *StartPeriodicUpdate* method is provided with a URI and a time interval specified by the *PeriodicUpdateRecurrence* enumeration, which has the following members:

- **HalfHour**   Poll the URI every 30 minutes.
- **Hour**   Poll the URI every hour.
- **SixHours**   Poll the URI every 6 hours.
- **TwelveHours**   Poll the URI every 12 hours.
- **Daily**   Poll the URI once per day.

The *StartPeriodicUpdate* method is available for both the *TileUpdater* and *BadgeUpdater* classes, used to deliver updates for tiles and badges, respectively. The content returned from the URI should contain both wide and square versions of the tile. The following code shows how periodic updates are created for tiles (the same approach can be used for badges):

```
private void StartPeriodicUpdatesForUri(Uri uriToPoll)
{
    // Code removed for brevity

    // Poll every hour
    PeriodicUpdateRecurrence recurrence = PeriodicUpdateRecurrence.Hour;

    // Start the periodic updates
    TileUpdateManager.CreateTileUpdaterForApplication().StartPeriodicUpdate(
        uriToPoll, recurrence);
}
```

When used with the notification queue, you can provide an array of up to five unique URIs, one for each notification. The content from each URI should contain the expiration time for the notification and a unique tag value, which is a string of up to 16 characters. The *StartPeriodicUpdateBatch* method is available in the *TileUpdater* class for updating the tile of an app and is used as follows:

```
private void StartPeriodicUpdatesForUris(IEnumerable<Uri> urisToPoll)
{
    // Code removed for brevity

    // Poll every hour
    PeriodicUpdateRecurrence recurrence = PeriodicUpdateRecurrence.SixHours;

    // Enable notification queue
    TileUpdateManager.CreateTileUpdaterForApplication().EnableNotificationQueue(true);

    // Send the local tile notification
    TileUpdateManager.CreateTileUpdaterForApplication().StartPeriodicUpdateBatch(
        urisToPoll, recurrence);
}
```

When a Windows Store app needs to cancel the periodic updates for the tile or badge the updater is bound to, it should call the *StopPeriodicUpdate* method (available in both the *TileUpdater* and *BadgeUpdater* classes).

Windows Store apps that use live tiles can update users with information leading to a future event by scheduling tile notifications in advance. Scheduled tile notifications are similar to local notifications that are created by an app when it is running, except that they can be specified with a precise time when they should update the tile. The content for the future event is known when the scheduled notification is set up. Your app can schedule up to 4,096 notifications in advance. Scheduled notifications do not expire by default; however, it is a good practice to set their expiration time using the *ExpirationTime* property of the *ScheduledTile-Notification* class. The code in Listing 4-9 shows how to create a scheduled notification and cancel it.

LISTING 4-9 Creating and cancelling a scheduled notification

```
// Create a new scheduled notification
private void CreateScheduledNotificationForEvent(string eventName)
{
    // Prepare notification
    // Code removed for brevity

    // Schedule tile update three hours from now
    DateTime dueTime = DateTime.Now.AddHours(3);

    // Create a scheduled tile and assign a unique ID
    ScheduledTileNotification notification = new ScheduledTileNotification(
                tileXml, dueTime);
    notification.Id = eventName;

    // Schedule the notification
    TileUpdateManager.CreateTileUpdaterForApplication().AddToSchedule(notification);
}

// Remove a scheduled notification from the schedule
private void RemoveScheduledNotificationForEvent(string eventName)
{
    TileUpdater updater = TileUpdateManager.CreateTileUpdaterForApplication();
    var scheduledNotifications = updater.GetScheduledTileNotifications();
    for (int i = 0; i < scheduledNotifications.Length; i++)
    {
        if (scheduledNotifications[i].Id = eventName)
            updater.RemoveFromSchedule(scheduledNotifications[i]);
    }
}
```

Objective summary

- A Windows Store app can use tiles and badges to communicate with the user even when the app is not running. Live tiles encourage users to launch your app and interact with it.

- You can enable users to create shortcuts to specific pages within your app by using secondary tiles. Secondary tiles help users bookmark their favorite content or experience from your app on the Start screen.

- Live tiles can be updated locally by your app when it is running by periodically polling one or more remote URIs for tile content, via a scheduled update, or by push notifications. Updates deliver fresh content to the tiles.

- Badges provide a number or a glyph on the live tile when a status or a summary of items need to be displayed. When used with live tiles, badges provide the user with a concise picture of various events or updates your app is receiving.

- Badges and text of tiles can be shown in the lock screen of the user's device if the user allows your app to access the lock screen. Your app need to be configured with at least one background task declared in the manifest.

- Tiles and badges can be updated periodically by polling a remote server or a cloud service. Periodic updates are useful for delivering updates to a large number of users without a significant investment in the infrastructure.

- You can schedule an update to be delivered in the future when the content for the update is known. This helps when the user needs to be informed of an event at a specific date and time.

- A Windows Store app can display up to five notifications in a cycle if the notifications contain a unique tag. Notifications can use this feature to continuously deliver fresh content that is displayed in a cycle by Windows.

Objective review

Answer the following questions to test your knowledge of the information in this objective. You can find the answers to these questions and explanations of why each answer choice is correct or incorrect in the "Answers" section at the end of this chapter.

1. You are preparing to enhance a Windows Store music explorer app with live tiles. The app displays album categories, albums, popular artists, concerts, and the user's favorite items in the main page. What is the best approach for delivering a rich, live tile experience?

   A. Use push notifications to deliver new artists to inform users when a new album is released.

   B. Set up periodic notifications to poll for latest albums, popular artists, or concerts, for example. Update the live tile with this data.

   C. Schedule updates to be shown every hour with the favorite items of the user.

   D. Whenever a user runs the app, display pertinent information on the live tiles, such as artists or concerts.

2. You have developed a weather app for the Windows Store. You are working on an enhancement that will allow users to create shortcuts into your app for specific cities. What are the benefits of using secondary tiles in your app? (Choose all that apply.)

   A. Secondary tiles can be updated with the latest information for the city the user is interested in.

   B. Secondary tiles make it easier for the user to launch your app and browse to the page they are interested in.

   C. After you have created a secondary tile, you can delete the application's tile, thereby freeing up space on the Start screen.

   D. For the same Microsoft account, if your app is installed on a new device, the secondary tiles will be available on it. This helps the user to start using your app without re-creating the secondary tiles.

   E. Secondary tiles can be resized to any size the user prefers thereby saving screen area.

3. Your Windows Store app helps users manage and monitor their stock portfolio. What is the best way to implement live tiles in your app?

   A. Use push notifications to display the price of stocks in the user's portfolio every time their price changes.

   B. Use periodic updates to poll for the price of up to five stocks at regular intervals.

   C. Create scheduled updates that download and display the stock price at specific times during the day.

D. Create a Windows service that obtains the stock price and use your app to create local notifications to update the live tile.

E. Set up scheduled updates to remind the user to launch your app and view the current prices.

Objective 4.2: Notify users by using toast

Toast notifications are transient notifications sent by Windows Store apps to inform the user of an event such as new email or a friend request. A toast notification appears in the top-right corner of the primary monitor (top-left corner for right-to-left languages) for a specific period of time with an optional audio tone that can be customized. Toasts contain text with images in some cases and their duration can be controlled when they are configured for delivery. Toasts can be created locally when your application is running, they can be scheduled for delivery at a specific date and time in the future, or they can delivered via push notifications. Users can turn off notifications from apps from the PC Settings for a specific period of time or they can turn off toast notifications for all the apps.

This objective covers how to:

- Enable an app for toast notifications.
- Populate toast notifications with images and text using the *ToastUpdateManager* class.
- Control toast duration.
- Play sounds with toast notifications.
- Respond to toast events.

Enabling an app for toast notifications

Toast notifications are messages that appear for a short duration from a Windows Store app. They can appear even when the app is not running. They invite the user to access your app and carry out an action or view content. Users are provided with an opportunity to opt out of toast notifications if they do not want to be notified by your app. Toast notifications are expected to be used with other notification methods such as tile notifications and badge updates.

If you plan to implement toast notifications in your Windows Store app, you should configure your app's package manifest with the option to show toast notifications. You can configure your app for toast notifications using the manifest editor in Visual Studio, as shown in Figure 4-12.

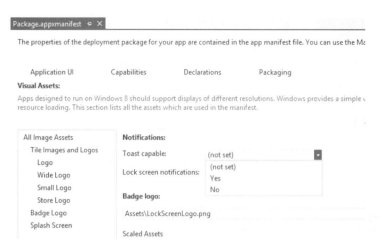

FIGURE 4-12 Configuring a Windows Store app for toast notifications using the package manifest editor in Visual Studio

After you have added support for toast notifications in your Windows Store app, the user can turn them off using the Settings charm of your app, as shown in Figure 4-13.

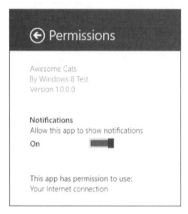

FIGURE 4-13 The Permissions section of the Settings charm of a Windows Store app can be used to turn off toast notifications

Windows provides users with the option to hide all notifications for a specific period of time from all apps that are capable of sending notifications. This option is available in the Settings charm, as shown in Figure 4-14.

FIGURE 4-14 The Settings charm in Windows can be used to hide notifications from all Windows Store apps for a specific period of time

Users can use their PC Settings to control notifications that can be shown by apps, choose whether they can appear on the lock screen, and choose whether apps are allowed to play notification sounds (see Figure 4-15).

FIGURE 4-15 PC Settings enables users to turn on or off notifications from apps, choose whether they appear on the lock screen, and choose whether sounds can be played with the notification

Populating toast notifications with images and text using the *ToastUpdateManager* class

After you have configured your app's package manifest file for toast notifications, you can set up toast notifications to be created and delivered when your app is running, schedule them for delivery at a future date and time, or use a remote cloud service and WNS to deliver toast notifications.

Microsoft provides developers with the option to add text, and optionally an image and sound, for a toast notification. You can choose from one of the eight standard templates listed in the toast template catalog. The template type can be specified with the *ToastTemplateType* enumeration (available in the *Windows.UI.Notifications* namespace).

> **MORE INFO   TOAST TEMPLATE CATALOG**
>
> The toast template catalog is available at *http://msdn.microsoft.com/en-us/library/windows/apps/xaml/hh761494.aspx*.

You should load the XML of the template you have chosen, set the values of the image and text elements, and use the *ToastNotificationManager* to display the toast. See Listing 4-10.

LISTING 4-10 Displaying a toast notification with text and an image

```
using Windows.UI.Notifications;
using Windows.Data.Xml.Dom;

private void ShowImageAndTextToastNotification()
{
    ToastTemplateType toastTemplate = ToastTemplateType.ToastImageAndText01;
    XmlDocument toastXml = ToastNotificationManager.GetTemplateContent(toastTemplate);

    XmlNodeList toastTextElements = toastXml.GetElementsByTagName("text");
    toastTextElements[0].AppendChild(toastXml.CreateTextNode(
        "Hello! I am an awesome cat... awesome cats make Windows 8 awesomer!!"));

    XmlElement tileImage = toastXml.GetElementsByTagName("image")[0] as XmlElement;
    tileImage.SetAttribute("src", "ms-appx:///Assets/Cat-2.JPG");
    tileImage.SetAttribute("alt", "awesome cat");

    ToastNotification toast = new ToastNotification(toastXml);
    ToastNotificationManager.CreateToastNotifier().Show(toast);
}
```

Figure 4-16 shows the toast notification created with the code in Listing 4-10.

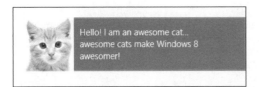

Hello! I am an awesome cat...
awesome cats make Windows 8
awesomer!

FIGURE 4-16 A toast notification with an image and some text (photo courtesy of Microsoft Office Imagery)

A Windows Store app might need to deliver a toast notification as a reminder for an event or to complete a task. In such cases, a toast notification can be scheduled for delivery at a future date and time. You can also create toast notifications that repeat at a specific interval; for example, a single toast notification can be shown four times, each five minutes apart, starting in one hour. It is recommended that a unique ID be added to toast notifications that are scheduled for delivery at a future time to cancel them if needed. The code in Listing 4-11 shows how to schedule a toast notification for delivery at a specific time and also schedule a number of toasts to be delivered in the future.

LISTING 4-11 Scheduling toast notifications

```csharp
using Windows.UI.Notifications;
using Windows.Data.Xml.Dom;

private void ScheduleTextToastNotification()
{
    ToastTemplateType toastTemplate = ToastTemplateType.ToastText01;
    XmlDocument toastXml = ToastNotificationManager.GetTemplateContent(toastTemplate);

    XmlNodeList toastTextElements = toastXml.GetElementsByTagName("text");
    toastTextElements[0].AppendChild(toastXml.CreateTextNode(
        "Message from a cat: Windows 8 is awesome"));

    DateTime dueTime = DateTime.Now.AddMinutes(2);

    ScheduledToastNotification toast = new ScheduledToastNotification(toastXml,
                                            dueTime);
    toast.Id = "scheduled-toast";
    ToastNotificationManager.CreateToastNotifier().AddToSchedule(toast);
}

private void ScheduleRecurringTextToastNotification()
{
    ToastTemplateType toastTemplate = ToastTemplateType.ToastImageAndText01;
    XmlDocument toastXml = ToastNotificationManager.GetTemplateContent(toastTemplate);

    XmlNodeList toastTextElements = toastXml.GetElementsByTagName("text");
    toastTextElements[0].AppendChild(toastXml.CreateTextNode(
        "Message from a cat: Feed me please..."));
    XmlElement tileImage = toastXml.GetElementsByTagName("image")[0] as XmlElement;
    tileImage.SetAttribute("src",
                "ms-appx:///images/awesome-cats-message.png");
    tileImage.SetAttribute("alt", "awesome cat");

    DateTime startTime = DateTime.Now.AddMinutes(2);

    // Create a scheduled toast notification that is shown five
    // times, each at an interval of two minutes
    ScheduledToastNotification toast = new ScheduledToastNotification(toastXml,
                                            startTime,
                                            new TimeSpan(0, 0, 2 * 60 * 1000), 5);
    toast.Id = " recur-toast-1";
    ToastNotificationManager.CreateToastNotifier().AddToSchedule(toast);
}
```

When you are scheduling a toast notification to be delivered at a future time and repeated a few times, note that the interval between each toast notification should not be less than 60 seconds or longer than 60 minutes, and the toast notification can displayed up to five times.

WNS can deliver toast notifications in a Windows Store app. After your app receives a push notification channel and notifies the cloud service, your app can send a push notification request to WNS, with XML prepared from a toast template and with the X-WNS-Type header in the HTTP POST message set to *wns/toast*. WNS parses the request and delivers a toast to your app.

Your app might need to cancel some or all scheduled notifications. The *GetScheduled-ToastNotifications* method in the *ToastNotifier* class provides a read-only list of *Scheduled-ToastNotification* objects. You should then use the *RemoveFromSchedule* method of the *ToastNotifier* class to remove toast notifications. You have the option to check the *Id* of the *ScheduledToastNotification* object before removing it. The code in Listing 4-12 shows how to remove a scheduled toast with a specific *Id* and clear all scheduled toast notifications.

LISTING 4-12 Removing scheduled toast notifications

```
using Windows.UI.Notifications;
using Windows.Data.Xml.Dom;

// Remove all scheduled notifications
private void ClearScheduledToastNotifications()
{
    var toastNotifier = ToastNotificationManager.CreateToastNotifier();
    foreach (var scheduledNotification in
                toastNotifier.GetScheduledToastNotifications())
    {
        toastNotifier.RemoveFromSchedule(scheduledNotification);
    }
}

// Remove a scheduled notification with a specified Id
private void ClearScheduledToastNotifiction(string id)
{
    var toastNotifier = ToastNotificationManager.CreateToastNotifier();
    foreach (var scheduledNotification in
                toastNotifier.GetScheduledToastNotifications())
    {
        if (scheduledNotification.Id == id)
        {
            toastNotifier.RemoveFromSchedule(scheduledNotification);
        }
    }
}
```

Controlling toast duration

Toast notifications are events that draw the attention of a user toward a message or reminder for an event. By default, these notifications remain on the screen for up to seven seconds set by the system. However, you can set the *toast* element's *duration* attribute in the XML template to *long*, which ensures that the toast is visible for at least 25 seconds. See Listing 4-13.

LISTING 4-13 Setting a toast notification's duration

```
using Windows.UI.Notifications;
using Windows.Data.Xml.Dom;

private void ShowLongDurationToastNotification()
{
    ToastTemplateType toastTemplate = ToastTemplateType.ToastImageAndText01;
    XmlDocument toastXml = ToastNotificationManager.GetTemplateContent(toastTemplate);

    XmlNodeList toastTextElements = toastXml.GetElementsByTagName("text");
    toastTextElements[0].AppendChild(toastXml.CreateTextNode(
        "Hello! I am an awesome cat... Awesome cats make Windows 8 awesomer!!"));

    XmlElement tileImage = toastXml.GetElementsByTagName("image")[0] as XmlElement;
    tileImage.SetAttribute("src",
            "http://placekitten.com/256/256");
    tileImage.SetAttribute("alt", "awesome cat");

    // Display the toast for 25 seconds. If you want the toast to be displayed for
    // 7 seconds, do not set the duration attribute to any value. The default value is
    // 'short' and the duration will be 7 seconds.
    XmlNode toastNode = toastXml.SelectSingleNode("/toast");
    ((XmlElement)toastNode).SetAttribute("duration", "long");

    ToastNotification toast = new ToastNotification(toastXml);
    ToastNotificationManager.CreateToastNotifier().Show(toast);
}
```

You should use a longer duration toast to notify users of an important message or event. However, keep in mind that allowing a toast to remain visible for too long might not provide a good user experience, even if the user dismisses the toast.

Playing sounds with toast notifications

Windows Store apps can play sounds when a toast notification is delivered. Windows plays the *Notification.Default* sound when an option to play audio is not specified in the toast's XML template. You can turn off audio playback for a toast by setting the *silent* attribute in the *audio* element of the toast's XML template to *True*.

> **MORE INFO   TOAST AUDIO OPTIONS CATALOG**
>
> You can add a sound to a toast notification from the toast audio options catalog available at *http://msdn.microsoft.com/en-us/library/windows/apps/xaml/hh761492.aspx.*

In case of long-duration toast notifications, you can set up the sound to loop until the notification expires or the user dismisses it. This is configured by setting the *loop* attribute of the *audio* element in the toast's XML template to *True*. The code in Listing 4-14 configures the XML template for a toast notification to play a sound and loop it as long as the toast notification is visible on the screen.

LISTING 4-14 Configuring sound for a toast notification

```
using Windows.UI.Notifications;
using Windows.Data.Xml.Dom;

private void ShowLongDurationToastNotificationWithLoopingSound()
{
    ToastTemplateType toastTemplate = ToastTemplateType.ToastImageAndText01;
    XmlDocument toastXml = ToastNotificationManager.GetTemplateContent(toastTemplate);

    XmlNodeList toastTextElements = toastXml.GetElementsByTagName("text");
    toastTextElements[0].AppendChild(toastXml.CreateTextNode(
        "Hello! I am an awesome cat... Awesome cats make Windows 8 awesomer!!"));

    XmlElement tileImage = toastXml.GetElementsByTagName("image")[0] as XmlElement;
    tileImage.SetAttribute("src",
            "http://placekitten.com/256/256");
    tileImage.SetAttribute("alt", "awesome cat");

    // Display the toast for 25 seconds
    XmlElement toastNode = (XmlElement)toastXml.SelectSingleNode("/toast");
    toastNode.SetAttribute("duration", "long");

    // Add a looping sound
    XmlElement audio = toastXml.CreateElement("audio");
    audio.SetAttribute("src", "ms-winsoundevent:Notification.Looping.Call");
    audio.SetAttribute("loop", "true");
    toastNode.AppendChild(audio);

    ToastNotification toast = new ToastNotification(toastXml);
    ToastNotificationManager.CreateToastNotifier().Show(toast);
}
```

Responding to toast events

Toast notifications draw the attention of the user when your app is running and when it is not visible on the screen. Windows provides developers with events to handle toast notifications and associated user actions. You can use these events to implement business logic in your Windows Store app.

When a toast notification is raised with your application running, you can respond to any or all of the following three events (provided by the *ToastNotification* class):

- **Activated** This event is raised if the user clicks or taps the toast notification when the app is running. If your app is not running when the user clicks or taps the notification, your app is launched, and the *OnLaunched* event is raised.

- **Dismissed** This event is raised when a toast notification is dismissed. You can determine the reason for dismissal by examining the *Reason* property of *ToastDismissedEventArgs* object received with the event. The value of the *Reason* property is specified by the *ToastDismissalReason* enumeration. A toast can be canceled by the user by clicking the X button (*UserCanceled*), the application can hide it (*ApplicationHidden*), or it can timeout after 7 or 25 seconds (*TimedOut*).

- **Failed** This event is raised when Windows fails to deliver the toast notification. One of the common reasons for this event to be raised is when notifications for the app are blocked in the settings by the user. You should check the *Setting* property of the *ToastNotifier* class to see whether toast notifications can be shown. The value of this property is specified by the *NotificationSetting* enumeration. Its members are *Enabled*, *DisabledByManifest*, *DisabledByGroupPolicy*, *DisabledForUser*, and *DisabledForApplication*. If toast notifications are disabled both by the user and by the Group Policy, this property returns *DisabledByGroupPolicy*.

The code in Listing 4-15 shows various event handlers being set up before a toast notification is displayed.

LISTING 4-15 Handling *Activated*, *Dismissed*, and *Failed* events associated with toast notifications

```
using Windows.UI.Notifications;
using Windows.Data.Xml.Dom;

private void ShowLongDurationToastNotificationWithLoopingSound()
{
    ToastTemplateType toastTemplate = ToastTemplateType.ToastImageAndText01;
    XmlDocument toastXml = ToastNotificationManager.GetTemplateContent(toastTemplate);

    XmlNodeList toastTextElements = toastXml.GetElementsByTagName("text");
    toastTextElements[0].AppendChild(toastXml.CreateTextNode(
        "Hello! I am an awesome cat... Awesome cats make Windows 8 awesomer!!"));

    XmlElement tileImage = toastXml.GetElementsByTagName("image")[0] as XmlElement;
    tileImage.SetAttribute("src",
            "http://placekitten.com/256/256");
    tileImage.SetAttribute("alt", "awesome cat");

    // Display the toast for 25 seconds
    XmlElement toastNode = (XmlElement)toastXml.SelectSingleNode("/toast");
    toastNode.SetAttribute("duration", "long");

    // Add a looping sound
    XmlElement audio = toastXml.CreateElement("audio");
    audio.SetAttribute("src", "ms-winsoundevent:Notification.Looping.Call");
    audio.SetAttribute("loop", "true");
    toastNode.AppendChild(audio);

    ToastNotification toast = new ToastNotification(toastXml);

    // ToastNotification events
    toast.Activated += ToastNotification_Activated;
    toast.Dismissed += ToastNotification_Dismissed;
    Toast.Failed += ToastNotification_Failed;

    ToastNotificationManager.CreateToastNotifier().Show(toast);
}
```

```
// This event is raised when the app is running. You should use the OnLaunched event
// if your app is activated when it is not running.
private void ToastNotification_Activated(ToastNotification sender, object args)
{
    // XML content
    var toastXml = sender.Content;

    // Take action based on content
}

private void ToastNotification_Dismissed(ToastNotification sender,
                        ToastDismissedEventArgs args)
{
    // Check the reason for dismissal
    switch (args.Reason)
    {
        case ToastDismissalReason.ApplicationHidden:
            // Application hid the toast with ToastNotifier.Hide
            break;
        case ToastDismissalReason.UserCanceled:
            // User dismissed the toast
            break;
        case ToastDismissalReason.TimedOut:
            // Toast has expired
            break;
    }
}

private void ToastNotification_Failed(ToastNotification sender,
                        ToastFailedEventArgs args)
{
    // Check the error code
    var errorCode = args.ErrorCode;
}
```

When an application is not running, and the user taps a toast notification delivered
through the application, the system launches the application. The application cannot distinguish how it is launched because the system does not provide an event when it launches the
app via toast notifications. You can add a context specific to your app in the toast notification
payload. This context information can be used by your app to decide the action to take when
it is launched. For example, if a toast delivered through push notification launches your app,
it can examine the payload and navigate to the appropriate page to display the news item.
The size of the payload must not exceed 5 KB. The code in Listing 4-16 adds a *launch* attribute to the XML template of a toast notification and handles the toast notification in an app's
OnLaunched event.

LISTING 4-16 Adding a *launch* attribute for a toast notification

```
using Windows.UI.Notifications;
using Windows.Data.Xml.Dom;

private void ShowLongDurationToastNotification()
{
    ToastTemplateType toastTemplate = ToastTemplateType.ToastImageAndText01;
    XmlDocument toastXml = ToastNotificationManager.GetTemplateContent(toastTemplate);

    XmlNodeList toastTextElements = toastXml.GetElementsByTagName("text");
    toastTextElements[0].AppendChild(toastXml.CreateTextNode(
        "Hello! I am an awesome cat... Awesome cats make Windows 8 awesomer!!"));

    XmlElement tileImage = toastXml.GetElementsByTagName("image")[0] as XmlElement;
    tileImage.SetAttribute("src",
            "http://placekitten.com/256/256");
    tileImage.SetAttribute("alt", "awesome cat");

    // Display the toast for 25 seconds
    XmlElement toastNode = (XmlElement)toastXml.SelectSingleNode("/toast");
    toastNode.SetAttribute("duration", "long");

    // Add a launch attribute. Note you must use "launch" as the attribute. The system
    // will ignore any other attribute name
    toastNode.SetAttribute("launch",
            "{\"type\":\"toast\",\"param1\":\"showNews\",\"itemId\":\"3898192\"}");


    ToastNotification toast = new ToastNotification(toastXml);
    ToastNotificationManager.CreateToastNotifier().Show(toast);
}

// Note: This method is defined in the Application class of the app
protected override void OnLaunched(LaunchActivatedEventArgs args)
{
    if (!string.IsNullOrEmpty(args.Arguments))
    {
        // Parse the launch attribute and navigate to appropriate page
    }
}
```

Thought experiment

Designing an app that uses toast notifications

In this thought experiment, apply what you've learned about this objective. You can find answers to these questions in the "Answers" section at the end of this chapter.

Your personal fitness trainer is impressed by your new Windows 8 devices. After you show her some apps and how you use them, she is interested in exploring the idea of building a Windows Store app that will be used by her customers.

Armed with your experience of developing Windows 8 apps, you start working on the requirements of such an app. To engage the customers in the best way possible, the app needs to communicate regularly with users. How can you use toast notifications in your app to provide users with a nice experience and encourage them to train at the fitness center?

Objective summary

- Windows 8 provides toast notifications for delivering transient messages to users. These messages are delivered even when the app is not running and can contain text and (optionally) images.

- Toast notifications can be scheduled for delivery at a future time. Up to five notifications can be shown, with a fixed interval between each toast notification ranging from 6 seconds to 60 minutes. Scheduled notifications can be canceled by your app.

- Toast notifications can be delivered through the WNS.

- Toast notifications can be configured to be visible for a longer duration (25 seconds instead of the default 7 seconds).

- You can configure the sound played with a toast notification by choosing one of the options from the toast template audio catalog. The sound can be set up to loop for a long-duration toast notification.

- When your app is running, it can respond to a toast notification's *Activated*, *Dismissed*, and *Failed* events. It can invoke an action based on the content of the toast notification in the *Activated* event. The *Dismissed* event arguments contain the reason for dismissal; the *Failed* event contains an *ErrorCode* that provides the reason for the error.

- Your app is launched when it is not running and a toast notification arrives. You can add a payload in the XML template of the toast notification and parse the information in the payload in the *OnLaunched* event of your app.

Objective review

Answer the following questions to test your knowledge of the information in this objective. You can find the answers to these questions and explanations of why each answer choice is correct or incorrect in the "Answers" section at the end of this chapter.

1. You have developed a calendar and reminder Windows Store app. It synchronizes with various online task- and calendar-management services. It also helps the user create new tasks, and edit and delete existing tasks. You are now ready to implement an important feature: showing reminders for tasks. What is the best way of delivering reminders to the user?

   A. Create a reminder event for each task and synchronize it with your own cloud service. Configure the cloud service to send push notifications when the reminder is due.

   B. Create scheduled toast notifications for the reminders. When they are delivered, and the user clicks the toast, open the item if the app is running, or launch the app and open the item otherwise.

   C. Create and send reminder events to the online services; let them send notifications to the user.

   D. The user is expected to keep the app running while it delivers toast notifications when the tasks are due.

2. A Windows Store app enables users to share voice messages of up to 30 seconds with their friends through the app. When a new message arrives at their friend's device, you want the app to inform the user that a new voice message has arrived. What is the best way to implement the feature?

   A. Deliver the voice message as an MP3 file in the toast notification payload. Configure the toast to be persistent for a duration longer than 30 seconds and use the MP3 file as the sound of the notification.

   B. Create a push notification with the details of the voice message. Deliver a toast notification with the default sound or that of a new email. Let the user tap the toast and launch the app if it is not running. Fire an action to download the voice message and play it as soon as it is downloaded.

   C. Create a push notification request with WNS; include the voice message as a payload. When the toast notification is delivered, play the voice message.

   D. Create a Windows service that checks the server for new messages. Whenever there is a new message, display a toast notification and let the Windows service play back the voice message.

3. You have been asked to present a proposal for developing a Windows Store app that enterprises will use for collaboration, messaging, tasks, and calendaring. You decide to

include support in the app for toast notifications to communicate and interact with the users. Which toast notification features can you use in the app? (Choose all that apply.)

A. Toast notifications can be configured to run other Windows Store apps when they arrive in a device.

B. Reminders for calendar events can be delivered through toast notifications for a user.

C. New messages from other users of the app can be delivered as toast notifications.

D. Voice messages can be delivered through toast notifications as a recorded MP3 file.

E. Toast notifications can be configured to launch your app and navigate the user to the page based on a type embedded in the toast notification payload.

Objective 4.3: Manage input devices

Windows Store apps are installed and used on a variety of devices. Windows 8 and Windows RT support a number of input modes such as touch, mouse, keyboard, and stylus. A large portion of the user experience in Windows 8 and Windows RT is delivered through Windows Store apps. Therefore, apps should interact with users consistently with all the available input modes.

Windows abstracts low-level events raised when users start their interaction with a Windows Store app via touch. The gesture recognizer raises additional events when it recognizes standard gestures and complex manipulation events. The default behavior of these events can be overridden, and you can add new events to the gesture recognizer based on the manipulations performed by the users.

Windows Store apps respond to a mouse attached to a PC with the same events used for touch and stylus input. Developers are not required to write separate code to handle mouse events and touch gestures, but they programmatically detect a mouse and use its special capabilities, such as the mouse wheel, to perform manipulations. In addition to supporting touch, mouse, and keyboard input, a Windows Store app can support stylus input. The input data that consists of pressure, angle, and velocity is used to represent geometric shapes on a device and saved to storage. The ink manager also supports handwriting recognition and various modes such as draw and erase.

This objective covers how to:

- Capture gesture library events.
- Create custom gesture recognizers.
- Listen to mouse events or touch gestures.
- Manage stylus input and inking.

Capturing gesture library events

Touch is a primary mode of interaction with Windows and Windows Store apps. Modern PCs and devices feature a touch screen, and users find it comfortable to use touch gestures for interactions. Therefore, supporting touch interactions in your app is likely to greatly enhance the user experience. Traditional input modes such as mouse, keyboard, and stylus are fully supported and are functionally consistent with the user experience.

The built-in controls provided by Windows are optimized for touch interactions while providing consistent interaction experience with other input modes. Touch gestures such as press and hold, tap, slide, swipe, pinch, stretch, and twist; and direct manipulations such as pan, zoom, rotate, and drag are supported by these built-in controls. Windows 8 provides the *Pointer* class in the *Windows.UI.Xaml.Input* namespace for representing low-level input devices such as mouse, stylus, and touch contact. Pointer events are the lowest-level events raised by these devices. Gestures are events representing actions such as press and hold, whereas manipulation events are higher-level events representing swipe, rotate, and pinch to zoom. These events are provided by the *UIElement* class, and the gesture events are managed by the gesture recognizer.

> **MORE INFO** **TOUCH INTERACTION DESIGN**
>
> You can read more about touch interaction design at *http://msdn.microsoft.com/en-US/library/windows/apps/xaml/hh465415*.

To effectively use events managed by the gesture recognizer of a *UIElement*, you should understand the role of the *Pointer* class and its associated classes:

- **Pointer**   The *Pointer* class represents a single, unique input contact from an input device such as a mouse, stylus, or single/multiple fingers; in other words, a coordinate on the screen. This class is defined in the *Windows.UI.Xaml.Input namespace*.

- **PointerDevice**   This class is used to obtain low-level properties of the hardware attached to a device. This class is defined in the *Windows.Devices.Input* namespace.

- **PointerPoint**   This class represents a single coordinate on the screen and provides its extended information. This class is defined in the *Windows.UI.Input* namespace.

- **PointerPointProperties**   This class represents extended properties of the *PointerPoint* class such as the bounding rectangle of the contact area from touch input, orientation of the pointer device, and the pressure exerted by a pointer device. This class is defined in the *Windows.UI.Input* namespace.

The *Pointer* class exposes four properties: *PointerId*, *PointerDeviceType*, *IsInRange*, and *IsInContact*. In most cases, you will use the *PointerId* (a *uint* data type) property to obtain the unique identifier for the input contact. It is useful when you need to detect and track multiple fingers on the screen, for example. The *PointerDeviceType* property with the same information is available in the *PointerDevice* class. The *PointerPoint* class provides basic properties for the input device; for example, it provides the *IsInContact* property, which is used to determine whether the input device is pressed down on the screen. The *PointerPointProperties* class provides extended properties for the input device; for example, it provides the *IsInRange* property, which indicates whether the input device is in close proximity to the screen or digitizer.

The *PointerDevice* class provides details of the hardware that are connected to the device and their low-level properties. You can get a list of all the *PointerDevices* connected to the system with the *GetPointerDevices* method. Alternatively, you can obtain information about a specific *PointerDevice* attached to the system with the *GetPointerDevice* method by provided the input pointer ID for the specific *Pointer*. The *MaxContacts* property is useful for determining the maximum number of simultaneous pointers supported by the input device (for example, *MaxContacts* is 1 for a mouse and 5 for many touch screens). The *PointerDeviceType* property has one of these three values: *Touch*, *Mouse*, or *Pen*.

The *PointerPoint* class provides the *GetCurrentPoint* static method that is useful for obtaining the current *PointerPoint* for a specific pointer ID. The *GetIntermediatePoints* method retrieves a collection of *PointerPoint* objects for a *Pointer* as the input device moves around the screen. This is used for high-resolution input devices such as touch screens and stylus digitizers. The *PointerPoint* class has the following properties:

- **Position** The location of the pointer input in client coordinates.
- **RawPosition** The raw location of the pointer input as reported by the input device in client coordinates. Input prediction can be used to compensate for hardware latency and set the value of the location of the pointer in the *Position* property correctly. For example, while reading a news article, you want to click a link, but your fingers do not hit the link precisely. In such cases, the system will set the correct value of the location of the pointer input in the *Position* property while providing the original value in the *RawPosition* property.
- **IsInContact** Boolean flag that indicates whether the input device is pressed down on the screen.
- **Properties** An instance of the *PointerPointProperties* class with extra information about the input pointer.
- **PointerDevice** An instance of the *PointerDevice* class containing information about the device associated with the input device.
- **PointerId** The unique identifier for the pointer.

The *PointerPointProperties* class, which is available through the *Properties* property of the *PointerPoint* class, provides detailed information about input devices. Some properties of this class are specific to a stylus, whereas others are relevant for the mouse, if attached to the device. Some of the important properties of this class are these:

- **IsInRange** Indicates whether the pointer device is within close proximity to a sensor in the device or a digitizer. Set to *True* if it is within the detection range.
- **IsPrimary** Indicates whether the input is from the primary pointer. This property is useful when multiple input devices are attached to the device; for example, a mouse attached to a touch-enabled PC.

- **IsCanceled**   Indicates whether the input was canceled by the pointer device. Input can be canceled for various reasons; for example, by the palm of the user or if the input device is removed.

- **ContactRect**   The bounding rectangle of the contact area in client window coordinates.

- **ContactRectRaw**   The bounding rectangle of the contact area as reported by the input device. In some cases, input prediction can be used to compensate for hardware latency, and the system can provide the correct value through the *ContactRect* property while providing the original value through the *ContactRectRaw* property.

Pointer events

The standard set of controls provided by Windows supports multiple input devices and raise events based on user interaction. These events should be used to handle pointer input in your Windows Store app. In some circumstances, you might need to obtain the pointer input in your application and apply your own logic in the event. Pointer events are eight low-level routed events raised by a *UIElement* control:

- **PointerEntered**   This event is raised when a pointer enters a *UIElement*'s bounding area. For example, this event is raised when the mouse cursor enters a rectangle.

- **PointerExited**   This event is raised when a pointer leaves a *UIElement*'s bounding area, but only if the pointer was initially in the *UIElement*'s bounding area. For example, this event is raised when the mouse cursor leaves a rectangle.

- **PointerMoved**   This event is raised when a pointer that has entered a *UIElement*'s bounding area moves within it. For example, this event is raised when the mouse cursor is moved within a rectangle.

- **PointerPressed**   This event is raised when the pointer makes its first contact within a *UIElement*'s bounding area. For example, this event is raised when the user clicks within a rectangle using a mouse.

- **PointerReleased**   This event is raised when the pointer that previously initiated a *PointerPressed* event is released while within the *UIElement*. You should note that other events such as *PointerCanceled* or *PointerCaptureLost* can fire instead of this event.

- **PointerCanceled**   This event is raised when the pointer that was previously in contact with the *UIElement* loses contact abnormally (for example, if a mouse is detached while the left key is pressed on a *Canvas*).

- **PointerCaptureLost**   This event is raised when the pointer is lost from the *UIElement* while the user is carrying out an action (for example, in a drag-and-drop operation, if users raise their finger when holding an element and moving it).

- **PointerWheelChanged**   This event is raised when a pointer wheel (for example, in a mouse) changes value.

The pointer events contain a *PointerRoutedEventArgs* object (defined in the *Windows.UI.Xaml.Input* namespace) that provides information about the pointer that raised the event (through the *Pointer* property). You can retrieve the *PointerPoint* object for the event by using the *GetCurrentPoint* method. The *GetIntermediatePoints* method provides a collection of *PointerPoint* objects that represent the history of pointer from the last pointer event up to the current pointer event. If you handle a pointer event for a *UIElement* and do not expect it to be passed to its parents, you should set the *Handled* property of the *PointerRoutedEventArgs* object to *True*.

Gesture events

The set of pointer events in *UIElement* can be used to implement actions in Windows Store apps using the pointer input. However, to detect gestures in a Windows Store app, you might need to implement complex logic in the pointer event handlers. In addition, there is a chance that your own implementation for detecting a gesture is inconsistent with other apps.

Windows has a gesture recognizer that abstracts low-level pointer events and raises high-level events when it recognizes standard gestures. These events are raised after users finish their interaction with the device. For example, when the user taps a *UIElement*, *PointerPressed* and *PointerReleased* are raised in quick succession. Windows provides a *Tapped* event when the user taps a *UIElement*; you should use this event instead of implementing your own logic through pointer events. The *GestureRecognizer* class provides the following gesture events:

- **Tapped**   This event is raised when the user taps the screen.
- **RightTapped**   This event is raised for when the user right-taps an item in the screen; this is the press and hold gesture for selecting an item.
- **Holding**   This event is raised when the user presses and holds an item in the screen while in the process of moving it or selecting it. Note that this event is fired twice: once when the holding starts, and once again when the holding ends.
- **CrossSliding**   This event is raised while the user swipes on a *UIElement* in a direction perpendicular to the scroll direction.
- **Dragging**   This event is raised when the user is sliding or swiping on a *UIElement*.

The events raised by the *GestureRecognizer* class contain an event argument which has a *PointerDeviceType* property that indicates if the input device is a touch device, stylus, or mouse. It also contains the current location of the pointer contact in the *Position* property of the argument.

> **MORE INFO   HANDLING *GESTURERECOGNIZER* EVENTS**
>
> To handle events raised by the gesture recognizer, you should set the *Settings* property of the *GestureRecognizer* object to one or a combination of values provided by the *Gesture-Settings* enumeration (the various members of this enumeration is listed here: *http://msdn.microsoft.com/en-us/library/windows/apps/windows.ui.input.gesturesettings.aspx*).

The code in Listing 4-17 shows a page in a Windows Store app configured to handle the *Tapped*, *RightTapped*, *Holding*, *CrossSliding*, and *Dragging* events of the *GestureRecognizer* class.

LISTING 4-17 Handling events raised by the *GestureRecognizer* class

```
using Windows.UI.Input;
using Windows.UI.Xaml.Controls;
using Windows.UI.Xaml.Input;

public sealed partial class GestureSamplePage : LayoutAwarePage
{
    public GestureSamplePage(Windows.UI.Xaml.Shapes.Rectangle target,
                Windows.UI.Xaml.UIElement parent)
    {
        this.InitializeComponent();

        // Configure gesture recognizer
        GestureRecognizer gestureRecognizer = new GestureRecognizer();
        gestureRecognizer.GestureSettings = GestureSettings.HoldWithMouse |
                            GestureSettings.RightTap |
                            GestureSettings.Tap  |
                            GestureSettings.CrossSlide | GestureSettings.Drag;
        // Register event handlers for gestures
        gestureRecognizer.Holding += OnHolding;
        gestureRecognizer.RightTapped += OnRightTapped;
        gestureRecognizer.Tapped += OnTapped;
        gestureRecognizer.CrossSliding += OnCrossSliding;
        gestureRecognizer.Dragging += OnDragging;
    }

    // In each of these event handlers, you can find out the input
    // device by checking the PointerDeviceType property of the event arguments.
    // This event is raised for the press and hold gesture.
    private void OnHolding(GestureRecognizer recognizer, HoldingEventArgs args)
    {
        // Application logic
    }

    // This event is raised for the right-tap gesture.
    private void OnRightTapped(GestureRecognizer recognizer, RightTappedEventArgs args)
    {
        // Application logic

    }

    // This event is raised for a tap gesture.
    private void OnTapped(GestureRecognizer recognizer, TappedEventArgs args)
    {
        // Application logic
    }
    // This event is raised for a slide or swipe gesture within a content area that
    // supports panning along the perpendicular direction of the gesture.
    private void OnCrossSliding(GestureRecognizer recognizer,
                                CrossSlidingEventArgs args)
```

```
    {
        // Application logic
    }
    // This event is raised for a slide or swipe
    // gesture
    private void OnDragging(GestureRecognizer recognizer,
                                        DraggingEventArgs args)
    {
        // Application logic
    }
}
```

In Listing 4-17, notice that the *HoldWithMouse* value from the *GestureSettings* enumeration is used in the *GestureSettings* property of the *GestureRecognizer,* along with other values from the GestureSettings enumeration. This is required to support the press-and-hold interaction with the mouse as well as with touch and stylus input. If you do not require the press-and-hold interaction with the mouse, you should use the *Hold* value of the *GestureSettings* enumeration. There is no event for a double-tap gesture, often used in applications for zooming an item on the screen. The *GestureSettings* enumeration has a member *DoubleTap* that you could add to the *GestureSettings* property of the *GestureRecognizer*. In the *Tapped* event, you can then use the *CanBeDoubleTap* method available in the *GestureRecognizer* class to determine whether the tap that raised this event can be interpreted as the second tap of a double-tap gesture.

Manipulation events

In addition to the gesture events provided by the system, some additional events are available for more-complex gestures. These gestures include panning, zooming, and turning elements in the user interface. These gestures raise their events when the interaction is still under way, unlike the events from standard gestures that are raised at the end of the interaction. The *UIElement* class provides the following events for manipulation gestures:

- **ManipulationStarting**   This event is raised when the pointer interacts with a *UIElement* and it enables manipulation of the *UIElement*. Gestures such as tap or hold cause this event to be raised.

- **ManipulationStarted**   This event is raised when the system has detected a movement in the pointer. It usually follows the *ManipulationStarting* event.

- **ManipulationCompleted**   This event is raised when the manipulation of a *UIElement* is complete.

- **ManipulationInertiaStarting**   The event is raised when the input device loses contact with the *UIElement* while manipulation is under way, and the velocity of manipulation is high enough to start inertia behavior. For example, translation of a *UIElement* can continue after the finger is lifted from a swipe gesture.

- **ManipulationDelta**   This event is raised when the input device changes its position while a manipulation is under way.

The *GestureRecognizer* class provides the *ManipulationStarted*, *ManipulationCompleted*, *ManipulationInertiaStarting*, and *ManipulationUpdated* events. The *ManipulationUpdated* event is raised when one or more input points have started a manipulation and the resulting motion (for example, translation) is under way. You can use the *ManipulationInertiaStarting* event handler to set the desired deceleration value of an element being manipulated.

In your Windows Store app, if you plan to use the manipulation events raised by the *UIElement* and handle them, you should set the value of the *ManipulationMode* property of the user interface element to *All*, to a single value, or to a combination of values of the *ManipulationModes* enumeration.

> **MORE INFO** **MANIPULATIONMODES ENUMERATION**
>
> The various members of the *ManipulationModes* enumeration are listed at *http://msdn.microsoft.com/en-US/library/windows/apps/xaml/windows.ui.xaml.input.manipulationmodes*.

The default value of the *ManipulationMode* property is *System*, which enables the control to use the built-in manipulation logic in the system to handle manipulation events. If your application chooses to handle manipulation events, you should set the *ManipulationMode* property of the *UIElement* object to a value other than *System* or *None*. See Listing 4-18.

LISTING 4-18 Handling manipulation gestures

```
using Windows.UI.Input;
using Windows.UI.Xaml.Controls;
using Windows.UI.Xaml.Input;

public sealed partial class ManipulationSamplePage : LayoutAwarePage
{
    public ManipulationSamplePage(Windows.UI.Xaml.Shapes.Rectangle target,
                Windows.UI.Xaml.UIElement parent)
    {
        // Configure gesture recognizer
        GestureRecognizer gestureRecognizer = new GestureRecognizer();
        gestureRecognizer.GestureSettings = GestureSettings.ManipulationRotate |
                                    GestureSettings.ManipulationScale |
                                    GestureSettings.ManipulationRotateInertia |
                                    GestureSettings.ManipulationScaleInertia;


        // Register event handlers for the manipulation gestures
        gestureRecognizer.ManipulationInertiaStarting += OnManipulationInertiaStarting;
        gestureRecognizer.ManipulationStarted += OnManipulationStarted;
        gestureRecognizer.ManipulationUpdated += OnManipulationUpdated;
        gestureRecognizer.ManipulationCompleted += OnManipulationCompleted;

    }

    // In each of these event handlers, you can find out the input
    // device by checking the PointerDeviceType property of the event arguments.
```

```
    // This event is raised for both the scale and rotate manipulation gestures
    // when inertia is involved.
    private void OnManipulationInertiaStarting (GestureRecognizer recognizer,
                        ManipulationInertiaStartingEventArgs args)
    {
        // Application logic
    }

    // This event is raised for the right-tap gesture.
    private void OnManipulationStarted(GestureRecognizer recognizer,
                        ManipulationStartedEventArgs args)
    {
        // Application logic

    }

    // This event is raised for a tap gesture.
    private void OnManipulationUpdated(GestureRecognizer recognizer,
                        ManipulationUpdatedEventArgs args)
    {
        // Application logic
    }

    // This event is raised for a slide or swipe geture within a content area that
    // supports panning along the perpendicular direction of the gesture.
    private void OnManipulationCompleted(GestureRecognizer recognizer,
                            ManipulationCompletedEventArgs args)
    {
        // Application logic
    }
}
```

One of the gestures not included in the *GestureSettings* enumeration is the edge gesture. This gesture is used to show or hide the bottom bar and the top app bar in a Windows Store app, whenever available. The edge gesture is managed by its own class: *EdgeGesture* (in the *Windows.UI.Input* namespace). It internally uses the *GestureRecognizer* to detect a vertical swipe from the top or bottom edge of the screen. (Note that the swipes from the left and right edges of the screen are reserved for app switching and the charms bar, respectively.)

If you need to use the edge gesture in your app, obtain an instance of the *EdgeGesture* class using the static *GetForCurrentView* method. You can then add event handlers for the following events of the *EdgeGesture* class:

- **Starting** This event is raised when the user initiates a gesture to show or hide the edge-based user interface.

- **Completed** This event is raised when the gesture has successfully completed (when the finger has lifted off the screen or the mouse key has been pressed).

- **Canceled** This event is raised when the edge gesture turns out to be some other gesture; for example, a swipe can start from the bottom edge and end at the top edge.

The code in Listing 4-19 shows a page in a Windows Store app configured to handle the *Starting*, *Completed*, and *Canceled* events of the *EdgeGesture* class.

LISTING 4-19 Handling events of the *EdgeGesture* class

```
using Windows.UI.Input;
using Windows.UI.Xaml.Controls;
using Windows.UI.Xaml.Input;

public sealed partial class EdgeGestureSamplePage : LayoutAwarePage
{
    public EdgeGestureSamplePage()
    {
        this.InitializeComponent();

        // Configure the EdgeGesture class
        EdgeGesture edgeGesture = EdgeGesture.GetForCurrentView();

        // Register event handlers for gestures
        edgeGesture.Starting += OnEdgeGestureStarting;
        edgeGesture.Completed += OnEdgeGestureCompleted;
        edgeGesture.Canceled += OnEdgeGestureCanceled;
    }
    // This event is raised when the user initiates a show or hide action.
    private void OnEdgeGestureStarting(EdgeGesture eg, EdgeGestureEventArgs args)
    {
        // Application logic
    }

    // This event is raised when edge-based gesture has successfully completed.
    private void OnEdgeGestureCompleted(EdgeGesture eg, EdgeGestureEventArgs args)
    {
        // Application logic
    }

    // This event is raised when the user cancels a show or hide action.
    private void OnEdgeGestureCanceled(EdgeGesture eg, EdgeGestureEventArgs args)
    {
        // Application logic
    }
}
```

Creating custom gesture recognizers

The support for gestures and manipulations available in the Windows platform provides developers with methods to build gesture-friendly Windows Store apps. In some cases, you might need to customize and enhance your app's interaction experience by extending the built-in set of gestures. For example, you need to support a gaming mouse with extra keys for invoking commands in your game when the user is playing a specific level or stage in the game. In such cases, you can use the low-level pointer events and implement your own application logic along with the events available from the *GestureRecognizer* class.

The Windows Runtime platform provides a number of application programming interfaces (APIs) to help you build custom gesture recognizers:

- **Windows.UI.Xaml**   This namespace provides classes such as *UIElement*, a base class for most user interface elements with a visual appearance that can process basic input.

- **Windows.UI.Xaml.Input** This namespace provides classes, delegates, and enumerations required for input support in apps and UI elements.

- **Windows.Devices.Input** This namespace provides the infrastructure for identifying the connected input devices and their properties.

- **Windows.UI.Input.Inking** This namespace provides support for the Windows 8 inking system.

Before you proceed with the development of a custom gesture recognizer, consider whether customizing the behavior of user interaction with the commonly available input modes will lead to confusion and inconsistency in the experience. For example, in a contacts manager app, you feel that users want to multi-select items in *a GridView* with a single custom gesture. It might cause confusion, however, because the Start screen and other Windows Store apps use the cross-slide gesture to select an item individually and perform operations on them.

If you decide to develop your own gesture recognizer, you should derive your own gesture recognizer class from *GestureRecognizer* or use it to process the pointer and other gesture events. In the event handlers of the pointer events, you can carry out your own processing and invoke one of the methods of the *GestureRecognizer* class to complete an action. For example, when the pointer is pressed, your app can do some processing on the data available from the event arguments and pass the event to the *GestureRecognizer*, as shown in Listing 4-20.

LISTING 4-20 Event handler for the *PointerPressed* event of the *GestureRecognizer* class

```
private void OnPointerPressed(object sender, PointerRoutedEventArgs args)
{
    // Check the device type; if a mouse, check if it is a horizontal mouse wheel.
    Pointer currentPointer = args.Pointer;
    if (currentPointer.PointerDeviceType == PointerDeviceType.Mouse)
    {
        PointerPoint currentPoint = args.GetCurrentPoint(parentElement);
        if (currentPoint.Properties.IsHorizontalMouseWheel)
        {
            // Custom processing for application logic
        }
    }

    // Route the event to the gesture recognizer. Note that _gestureRecognizer is a
    // page level variable of the type Windows.UI.Input.GestureRecognizer.
    this._gestureRecognizer.ProcessDownEvent(
                    args.GetCurrentPoint(parentElement));

    // Capture the pointer associated to this event. _target is the element being
    // manipulated. Once the pointer is captured, only the element that has the pointer
    // will raise the pointer-related events.
    this._target.CapturePointer(args.Pointer);

    // Mark event handled, to prevent execution of default event handlers
    args.Handled = true;
}
```

Listening to mouse events or touch gestures

Windows provides a set of events that are generic for input devices such as a mouse or stylus, or for touch. You can implement input features in your Windows Store apps without writing code for each input device. You can choose to implement code to take into account special features of a device such as a mouse with a horizontal wheel.

To use pointer events in your application, you should provide event handlers for the pointer events originating from the *UIElement* you are interested in and handle manipulation of that *UIElement* in the event handlers. A sample scenario is a Windows Store app that enables users to draw figures on the screen by selecting a color. You can set up a *Canvas* control and provide event handlers for its *PointerPressed* and *PointerReleased* events. The XAML code in Listing 4-21 sets up a *Canvas* and *TextBox*.

LISTING 4-21 Providing pointer event handlers in XAML

```
<Grid Grid.Row="1">
    <Grid.ColumnDefinitions>
        <ColumnDefinition Width="*" />
        <ColumnDefinition Width="200" />
    </Grid.ColumnDefinitions>
    <Canvas x:Name="DrawingCanvas" Margin="120,0,0,0"
            Grid.Column="0" Background="White" />
    <TextBlock Style="{StaticResource BasicTextStyle}" Grid.Column="1" Margin="5,5,0,0"
            x:Name="EventName" HorizontalAlignment="Left" TextWrapping="NoWrap"/>
</Grid>
```

In the code-behind, the *PointerPressed*, *PointerMoved*, and *PointerReleased* events are used to draw a stroke when the user moves the pointer after pressing on the screen. The code in Listing 4-22 shows the event handlers for these events.

LISTING 4-22 Providing pointer event handlers in the code-behind

```
public sealed partial class PointerEventsSamplePage : LayoutAwarePage
{
    public PointerEventsSamplePage()
    {
        this.InitializeComponent();

        DrawingCanvas.PointerPressed += new
                        PointerEventHandler(DrawingCanvas_PointerPressed);
        DrawingCanvas.PointerMoved += new PointerEventHandler(DrawingCanvas_PointerMoved);
        DrawingCanvas.PointerReleased += new
                        PointerEventHandler(DrawingCanvas_PointerReleased);
```

```
    }

    // PointerPressed event handler (code removed for brevity)
    privatee void DrawingCanvas_PointerPressed(object sender, PointerRoutedEventArgs e)
    {
        Windows.UI.Input.PointerPoint pt = e.GetCurrentPoint(DrawingCanvas);

        // Pointer pressed by user, record position

        e.Handled = true;
    }

    // PointerMoved event handler (code removed for brevity)
    private void DrawingCanvas_PointerMoved(object sender, PointerRoutedEventArgs e)
    {
        Windows.UI.Input.PointerPoint pt = e.GetCurrentPoint(DrawingCanvas);

        // Draw a line with a color

        e.Handled = true;
    }

    private void DrawingCanvas_PointerReleased(object sender, PointerRoutedEventArgs e)
    {
        Windows.UI.Input.PointerPoint pt = e.GetCurrentPoint(DrawingCanvas);

        // Finished with drawing
        e.Handled = true;
    }
}
```

Figure 4-17 shows two lines being drawn on the *Canvas* and the associated events.

FIGURE 4-17 Windows Store app that enables users to draw lines on a canvas and the associated pointer events

In the simple application shown in Figure 4-17, the pointer is not captured by the application when the user draws the stroke on the *canvas*. In some apps, you might want to ensure that the pointer remains captured while the user executes the action (dragging a card in a game, for example). If the user moves a finger very fast, the pointer can be separated from the element. You can use the *CapturePointer* method to capture the pointer in the *PointerPressed* event handler and call *ReleasePointerCapture* to release the pointer after the user completes the action in the *PointerReleased* event handler.

Managing stylus input and inking

A Windows Store app can use the extensive support for stylus input through the pointer classes discussed previously, such as *Pointer*, *PointerDevice*, *PointerPoint*, and *PointerPointProperties*. Your app can use a stylus to capture handwritten notes, diagrams, and annotations in existing documents. In devices with a screen that supports input from a stylus, a digitizer is embedded beneath the screen. The digitizer translates various actions of the stylus into data—such as pressure, angle, and velocity—into a data structure available in Windows Store apps.

Although you can use the pointer events discussed previously in applications that accept input from a stylus, some of the properties in the *PointerPointProperties* class are specifically made available for the stylus input:

- **IsBarrelButtonPressed**   This property is *True* if the user presses the button along the side of the pen's body. Some apps use this property to open a context menu as a pop-up.

- **IsEraser**   This property is *True* if the user is using the eraser at the back of the stylus on the screen.

- **IsInRange**   This property is *True* if the stylus is close to the digitizer but has not touched the screen.

- **IsInverted**   This property is *True* if the rear of the stylus is being used instead of the front.

- **Pressure**   This property is a float value (in the range 0.0 to 1.0) that indicates the force exerted by the stylus on the digitizer.

- **Twist**   This property is a float value that represents an angle in degrees that indicates the amount of rotation of the stylus by the user in the clockwise direction along the major axis, for example, when the user is rotating it by spinning it in their fingers.

- **Orientation**   This property is a float value that represents the angle in degrees at which the stylus is being held perpendicular to the surface of the digitizer.

- **XTilt**   This property is a float value that represents the angle in degrees at which the stylus is tilted toward the left or right of the screen's surface.

- **YTilt**   This property is a float value that represents the angle in degrees at which the stylus is tilted to the top or bottom of the screen's surface.

The *Windows.UI.Input.Inking* namespace provides inking support for Windows Store apps. It provides the infrastructure for managing data structures used while an app is using the stylus of a device for tasks such as drawing or handwriting recognition.

The *InkStroke* class represents a single ink stroke, the fundamental unit represented on the screen when the stylus is in touch with the digitizer and the user is drawing on the screen. The *InkStrokeBuilder* class is used to build ink strokes from the raw input of a stylus. It provides methods such as *BeginStroke*, *CreateStroke*, *AppendToStroke*, and *EndStroke* to create *InkStroke* objects from the user's actions with the stylus. The *InkStrokeContainer* class provides support for input, processing, and manipulation of one or more *InkStroke* objects.

Inking in Windows supports handwriting recognition through the *InkRecognizer* class. The *InkRecognitionResult* class provides properties and methods to manage one or more *InkStroke* objects used for handwriting recognition. The *GetStrokes* method of the *InkRecognitionResult* class retrieves the *InkStroke* collection for handwriting recognition; the *GetTextCandidates* method retrieves the potential matches for each word returned by handwriting recognition.

The *InkManager* class provides the core features for inking support in Windows Store apps that are used for obtaining input from the digitizer and their manipulation and processing. It also provides methods for handwriting recognition. Some methods that are important for inking support in Windows Store apps are these:

- **AddStroke**   This method adds one or more *InkStroke* objects to a collection managed by *InkManager*.
- **DeleteSelected**   This method deletes a selected *InkStroke* from a collection managed by the *InkManager*.
- **MoveSelected**   This method moves one or selected ink strokes in a bounding rectangle to a new position.
- **ProcessPointerUp** and **ProcessPointerDown**   These methods process information about the position and features of the contact point of the stylus with the digitizer, such as pressure and tilt when the stylus is taken up after an initial contact and when the stylus is placed on the digitizer, respectively.
- **ProcessPointerUpdate**   This method processes the position, pressure, and tilt for a stylus from the last pointer event up to and including the current pointer event.
- **SaveAsync**   This method is used to asynchronously save all *InkStroke* objects managed by the *InkManager* in a specified stream.
- **LoadAsync**   This method is used to asynchronously load all *InkStroke* objects from a specified stream to a collection of *InkStroke* objects managed by the *InkManager*.

The *InkManager* class has an important property called *Mode*. The value of this property determines whether the *InkManager* is doing the following:

- Appending *InkStroke* objects to its collection
- Checking for *InkStroke* objects to be removed from its collection or an *InkStrokeContainer*
- Checking whether all the points are being selected for the creation of a polyline

Thought experiment
Creating an app for touch, gestures, and inking

In this thought experiment, apply what you've learned about this objective. You can find answers to these questions in the "Answers" section at the end of this chapter.

The mathematics curriculum of a primary school has a module in which children learn about geometric shapes and how to draw them. Students are often encouraged to identify a geometric shape and write their name next to it.

Each classroom has several PCs with touch-enabled screens for students as well as a handheld tablet for the teacher. The school board supports the idea of implementing a Windows 8 application that fulfills the requirements of the mathematics curriculum. List three features of touch, gestures, and inking support in Windows 8 that you can use to build the app.

Objective summary

- Windows Runtime APIs abstract input devices into pointers and provide events that do not depend on the type of input device. The *Pointer* class and its associated classes can be used by developers in a Windows Store app for gestures provided by the system.
- Gesture and manipulation events should be used instead of low-level pointer events for a consistent experience across all applications.
- Custom gesture recognizers can be created for implementing gestures that are not available in the standard set of gestures.
- Pointer events can be used with touch gestures and a mouse to implement application logic.
- Windows provides extensive inking support that includes drawing of geometric shapes and handwriting recognitions.

Objective review

Answer the following questions to test your knowledge of the information in this objective. You can find the answers to these questions and explanations of why each answer choice is correct or incorrect in the "Answers" section at the end of this chapter.

1. You are building a simple proof-of-concept for your Windows Store app that will help young artists learn how to draw. In your proof-of-concept app, you want to show how easy it is to draw a stroke on a canvas. Which pointer events should you use to build this proof-of-concept application? (Choose all that apply.)

   A. *PointerExited*

   B. *PointerPressed*

   C. *PointerMoved*

   D. *PointerCanceled*

   E. *PointerReleased*

2. You are developing a card game application for the Windows Store. You have built the functionality that enables users to pause a game they are playing and then refer to previous games and strokes they used. What is the correct way to implement this feature without requiring them to leave the game?

   A. Use the swipe-from-left gesture to open a pop-up dialog box and display the history in it.

   B. Use the swipe-from-right gesture to open a pop-up dialog box and display the history in it.

   C. Use the tap-and-hold gesture to open a dialog box to display the history; dismiss it with a button provided within the dialog box.

   D. Use a tap gesture to open a dialog box to display the history; tap in the dialog box to close it.

3. In a Windows Store app, users can use a stylus to draw simple shapes after choosing a color and thickness for the stroke. A feature request from many users is to be able to store shapes present in the drawing canvas and load them in the future for editing. How will you implement this feature in the app?

   A. As soon as an *InkStroke* object is added to a collection in the *InkManager* class, save it to a stream. When the user requests saved data to be loaded, use the *Ink-Stroke* objects to re-create the shapes.

   B. Use the *SaveAsync* and *LoadAsync* methods of the *InkManager* class to save and load the *InkStroke* objects from and to a stream.

   C. Whenever pointer events are raised, save the shape into a stream. Shapes can then be loaded on demand.

   D. Convert the drawing canvas into a bitmap and save it. Load the bitmap into the canvas to enable the user to continue drawing shapes on it.

Objective 4.4: Design and implement navigation in an app

In its simplest form, a Windows Store app consists of a single page with a number of controls. All the functionality is embedded within the single page. However, many Windows Store apps consist of multiple pages with well-defined navigation architecture. The user navigates through such apps using shortcuts and buttons present in the pages and, in some cases, using a navigation control in the top app bar.

Microsoft provides guidance for implementing navigation in Windows Store apps to ensure consistency in the experience as well as to leverage the navigation framework built in the system. Developers can use the hub design to implement hierarchical navigation or use the flat system when there are no hierarchical levels in their app. The hub design is often combined with app bar navigation to help the user navigate through sections in the hierarchy. Visual Studio provides application templates with support for the hierarchical pattern of navigation.

In a hierarchical navigation design, the main page can contain a number of categories and a large number of items in every category. This makes browsing through the categories and selecting an item of interest difficult for the user. To help with the navigation, Semantic Zoom can be implemented in the main page to navigate through categories, enabling the user to select a category of interest and browse to the category page.

> **This objective covers how to:**
> - Design navigation to meet app requirements.
> - Handle navigation events, check navigation properties, and call navigation functions by using the navigation framework.
> - Use Semantic Zoom in your app.

Designing navigation to meet app requirements

One of the key principles in the Microsoft design style is the importance of content in an app. Presentation of content using a clean layout and typography, animations, and carefully selected UI elements are some key features of great Windows Store apps. For apps that consist of multiple pages, it is very important to design and implement a navigation pattern that matches well with other important features of a great app.

In most Windows Store apps, a hierarchical pattern with a number of levels is used to implement navigation. In this pattern, there is a main page with a set of groups, each containing a number of items. In the next level, there are number of pages, each representing a group. Each page in this level contains a list of items belonging to a group. Finally, there is a page for an individual item. The user can navigate through the hierarchy of pages in an app by clicking the back button that appears in the top-left corner of the screen. An example of hierarchical navigation in the Store app in Windows 8 is shown in Figure 4-18.

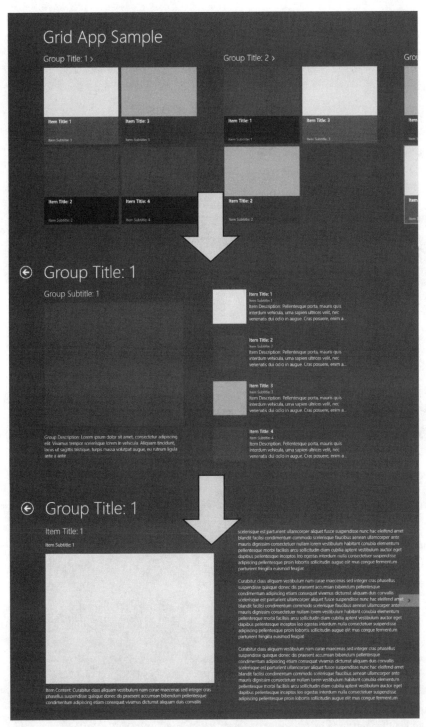

FIGURE 4-18 Hierarchical navigation in a Windows Store app built with the Grid App template in Visual Studio

In hierarchical navigation, the main page (also called the *hub page* or the *hub*) has items laid out in a virtually wide page that users can view only if they swipe or scroll to explore the items. To make it easy for users to navigate through the various groups of items, Semantic Zoom can be used to zoom in or zoom out of a page with lots of items. Sematic Zoom supports the pinch-to-zoom gesture, as well as the Ctrl+ and Ctrl- key combinations to zoom in and out, respectively. In addition, Semantic Zoom supports the Ctrl and mouse wheel scroll for zooming in and out of the page. Alternatively, the user can click the zoom icon on the bottom-right corner of the screen to apply Semantic Zoom to the visible items in the page. The Weather app in Windows 8 uses Semantic Zoom in the main page to list the various sections of the app, as shown in Figure 4-19.

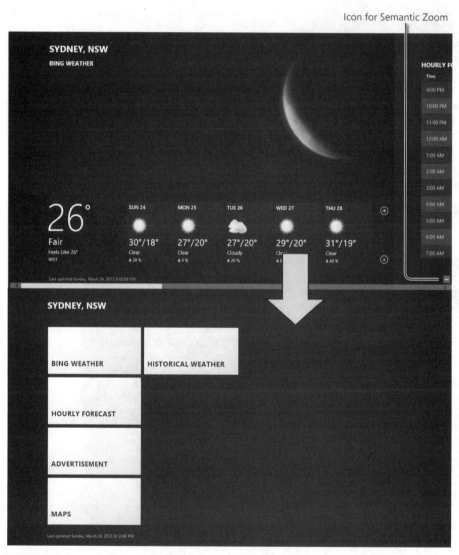

FIGURE 4-19 Semantic Zoom in the Weather app in Windows 8 is used to list various sections of the app in the zoomed-out view

In many Windows Store apps—such as games, browsers, and utility apps such as Weather—a flat system of navigation is used, in which where all the pages reside in the same hierarchical level. This pattern of navigation is useful for apps that require quick switching between a few pages. An example of this type of navigation is seen in the Weather app, shown in Figure 4-20.

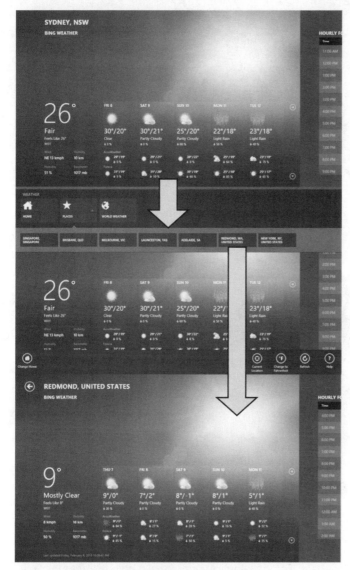

FIGURE 4-20 Flat navigation pattern implemented in the Weather app

Visual Studio provides developers with Windows Store application templates that contain the infrastructure required to implement hierarchical navigation. You can use these templates as the starting point of your app, and later enhance or modify the default navigation to implement your app's requirements. For example, you can use the top app bar in addition to the Semantic Zoom for navigating between categories and subcategories if they all fit in the app bar. Figure 4-21 shows a Windows Store app created with the Grid App template provided by Visual Studio.

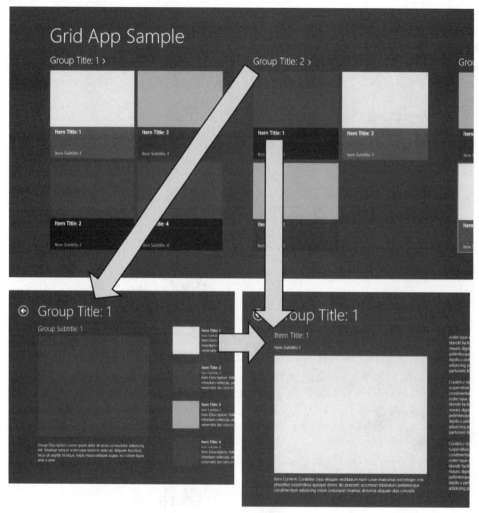

FIGURE 4-21 Hierarchical navigation implemented in a Windows Store app created using the Grid App template provided by Visual Studio

In some Windows Store apps, all the items in a group are displayed in a group details page, and there is no item details page. For such applications, Visual Studio provides the Split App template with navigation support, as shown in Figure 4-22.

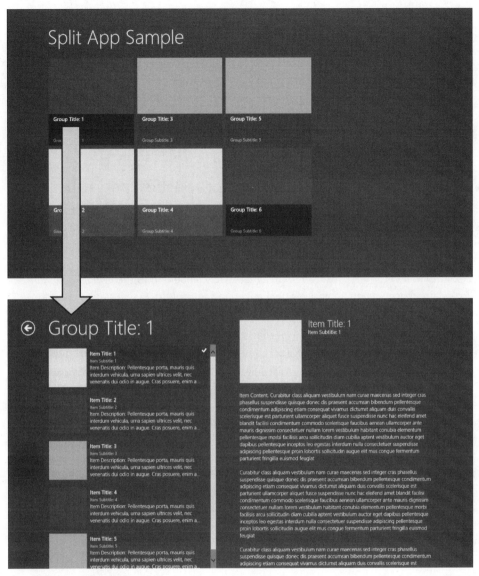

FIGURE 4-22 Hierarchical navigation implemented in a Windows Store app created using the Split App template provided by Visual Studio

The templates discussed provide support for state management for the application's lifecycle, the included pages are built with a layout that supports different visual states and orientation, and they have a sample data source to help with designing through the Visual Studio XAML designer.

MORE INFO LAYOUT AND NAVIGATION IN APPS

There are articles prepared by Microsoft for developers requiring guidance and inspiration in developing Windows Store apps. You can read these articles on designing great productivity apps (*http://msdn.microsoft.com/en-us/library/windows/apps/hh868273.aspx*) and designing great news apps (*http://msdn.microsoft.com/en-au/library/windows/apps/hh868272.aspx*) to understand how you can build Windows Store apps using the templates provided by Visual Studio.

Working with navigation events, properties, and functions

When building a Windows Store app, you have the option to add any number of pages necessary to implement its business requirements. An app is composed of a *frame* used to host multiple pages and help with the navigation between these pages. A page consists of XAML used to define its layout and code-behind for implementing logic. A page derives from the *Page* control that in turn derives from a *UIElement* (they all belong to the *Windows.UI.Xaml. Controls* namespace). When an app is launched, an instance of the *Frame* class is created, which is then used to host one or more pages.

The *Frame* class has a number of properties and methods that are useful for navigation among pages in a Windows Store app. The *CanGoBack* and *CanGoForward* properties are commonly used with navigation buttons to enable or disable them (through the *Button's Is-Enabled* property) based on whether a page is available in the requested direction of navigation. The *Navigate* method of the *Frame* class is used to navigate to a specific page in an app. You can optionally provide a parameter to this method, which is passed to the page being navigated to. This is helpful in cases when your app is launched through a toast notification or a search result. You can use the *Background* property to specify the brush used to set an image, or a pattern or a solid color as the background of the *Frame*. In Windows Store apps, a page is created every time you navigate to it and destroyed when you navigate away from it. In some cases, you might need to use the same instance of a page multiple times. The *Frame* class has the capability to cache a number of pages set via the *CacheSize* property. The value of the *CacheSize* property indicates the total number of pages that will be cached by the *Frame* class.

Use the *Page* class to compose a Windows Store app that requires support for navigation among the pages. You can create a number of pages in your application and navigate to those pages from the frame. The *Page* class has a number of properties and methods you can use in your app. If you expect users to navigate to the same page instance multiple times, you should set the *NavigationCacheMode* property of the *Page* object to either *Enabled* or *Required*. When the *NavigationCacheMode* property is set to *Required*, the page is cached even if the cache size of the *Frame* specified through its *CacheSize* property is exceeded. Figure 4-23 shows how three pages are hosted in a single frame and navigation is carried out between them.

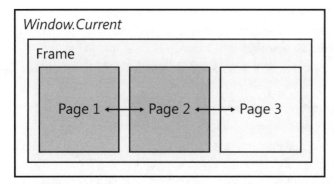

FIGURE 4-23 A *Frame* object is used to host three pages in a Windows Store app

When a Windows Store app is launched by the user, a new instance of the *Frame* class is created. The *Navigate* method of the *Frame* class is used to navigate to the default initial *Page* of an application, and the content of the app window is set to the new *Frame*. This is usually carried out in the *OnLaunched* event of the application, as shown in the C# code in Listing 4-23.

LISTING 4-23 Creating the *Frame* class for navigation

```
sealed partial class App : Application
{
    protected override void OnLaunched(LaunchActivatedEventArgs args)
    {
        Frame rootFrame = Window.Current.Content as Frame;
        if (rootFrame == null)
        {
            // Create a Frame to act as the navigation context and navigate
            // to the first page
            rootFrame = new Frame();
            SuspensionManager.RegisterFrame(rootFrame, "AppFrame");

            // Code removed for brevity

            // Place the frame in the current Window
            Window.Current.Content = rootFrame;
        }
        if (rootFrame.Content == null)
        {
            if (!rootframe.Navigate(typeof(MainPage), "AllGroups"))
            {
                throw new Exception("Failed to create initial page");
            }
        }

        // Ensure current window is active
        Window.Current.Activate();
    }
}
```

When the *Navigate* method of the *Frame* class is used to navigate between pages in a Windows Store app, a series of events is raised both by the *Frame* class and by the page being navigated to. The *Frame* class raises two events:

- **Navigating**   This event is raised when a new navigation is initiated by the system or user.

- **Navigated**   This event is raised when the page being navigated to is available, although the page might not have finished loading.

The *Page* class provides a set of virtual methods that can be used to implement application logic when the page is being navigated and when the user is navigating away from the page. These methods are useful for initializing the page or performing operations to save data when the user navigates away from it. The three virtual methods of the *Page* class that are useful for navigation are the following:

- **OnNavigatedFrom**   This method is invoked when the user has navigated away from the page and the page is no longer visible in the screen.

- **OnNavigatingFrom**   This method is invoked when the user has initiated an action to navigate away from the page, but the page is still visible in the screen.

- **OnNavigatedTo**   This method is invoked when the page is loaded and is visible in the screen.

The events raised by the *Frame* object in a Windows Store app and the methods invoked by a *Page* object when it participates in navigation are all arranged in a certain order. Figure 4-24 shows the events raised in an app with two pages with the user clicking a navigation link in Page 1 that leads her to Page 2.

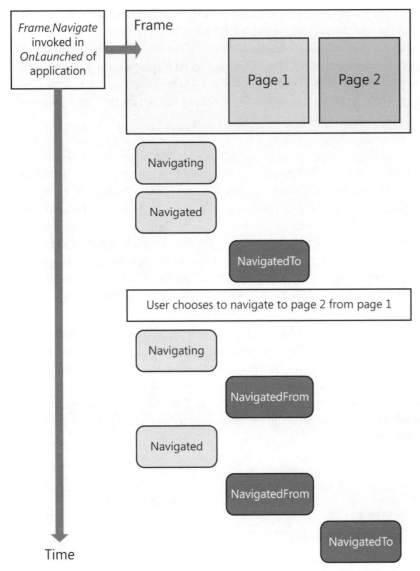

FIGURE 4-24 Sequence of events raised by the *Frame* class and methods invoked by the *Page* class in a Windows Store app

Your app might need to pass data while navigating between pages. The *Navigate* method of the *Frame* class has an overload that accepts a *System.Object* parameter. This parameter can be used to pass data between pages. The target page receives this parameter through the *OnNavigatedTo* method in its *NavigationEventArgs* instance (the value passed during navigation is available in its *Parameter* property).

In some situations, your app might need to cancel the navigation to avoid loss of data or avoid aborting an upload operation. The *NavigatingCancelEventArgs* instance available in the

Navigating event of the *Frame* class has a property called *Cancel* that cancels the navigation when set to *True*. If the navigation is not canceled by the user, any one of the three events is raised in the *Frame*. If the navigation completes successfully, the *Navigated* event is raised. If the navigation fails, the *NavigationFailed* event is raised; and if *Navigate* is invoked before the current navigation completes, the *NavigationStopped* event is raised. Within a page, the *On-NavigatingFrom* method can be used to cancel the navigation by setting the *Cancel* property of the *NavigatingCancelEventArgs* instance to *True*.

While navigating through pages, *Page* instances are created as the user moves forward or backward in the navigation. If you need to maintain state within a page in your app, you must remember to do it manually. The system provides a way to change this behavior to suit your app's requirements via the *NavigationCacheMode* property of the *Page* class. *Caching* is defined page by page, and the default behavior for a page is that it is never cached. You can change this behavior to either *Required*, which keeps the instance in the cache irrespective of the size of the cache; or *Enabled*, which caches the page but it is discarded as soon as the size of the cache for the frame is exceeded. The default limit of the number of pages a *Frame* can cache is 10; it can be changed by setting the *CacheSize* property to a different value. You should note that increasing the *CacheSize* can cause the consumption of memory to increase, and the system can shut down your app.

Pages in a Windows Store app are added and removed from the navigation history as the user navigates in the app. The *Frame* class provides two methods to navigate among pages in the navigation history. The *GoBack* method navigates the user to the previous item in the navigation history; the *GoForward* method navigates to the next item in the navigation history. The following code checks the value of the properties *CanGoBack* and *CanGoForward* to determine whether there are pages in the navigation history with respect to the current position in the navigation history:

```
private void GoBack()
{
    if (this.Frame != null && this.Frame.CanGoBack)
    {
        this.Frame.GoBack();
    }
}

private void GoForward()
{
    if (this.Frame != null && this.Frame.CanGoForward)
    {
        this.Frame.GoForward();
    }
}
```

There is no support for passing data when navigating backward or forward through the navigation history using the *GoBack* or *GoForward* methods. You should implement your own solution to store data in a shared place so that both pages can access this data.

The *NavigationEventArgs* instance available in the *OnNavigatedTo* and *OnNavigatedFrom* virtual methods of the *Page* class has a property called *NavigationMode* that tells you the direction of movement during navigation. *NavigationMode* has one of the values from the *NavigationMode* enumeration, as described in Table 4-1.

TABLE 4-1 *NavigationMode* enumeration members

MEMBER	VALUE	DESCRIPTION
New	0	Navigation is being carried out to a new instance of a page.
Back	1	Navigation is being carried out toward the back of the navigation stack.
Forward	2	Navigation is being carried out toward the front of the navigation stack.
Refresh	3	Navigation is being carried out to the current page, perhaps with a different set of data.

In Visual Studio, if you choose the Grid App template or the Split App template to create a Windows Store app, the pages contained in the app use the *LayoutAwarePage* class as their base class. This class extends the *Page* class, which is the default class that a page in a Windows Store app extends to override the virtual methods. The *LayoutAwarePage* provides developers with a number of features:

- It provides a *GoHome* method that a page can use to return to the first item in the navigation stack while traversing backward.

- It implements the *GoBack* and *GoForward* methods with the logic to check *CanGoBack* and *CanGoForward*, respectively.

- It overrides the *OnNavigatedTo* method to check the value of the *NavigationMode* property of the page being navigated to. If a new page is loading, the *LayoutAwarePage* class clears any session state stored by the *SuspensionManager* and adds the new page to the navigation stack.

- It overrides the *OnNavigatedFrom* method to save the session state for the page being navigated away from.

In Windows Store apps, you should implement utility functions, such as *GoBack* and *GoForward*, in a base class for every page. When you add a new page to a Windows Store app using Visual Studio, the page automatically derives from the *LayoutAwarePage* class. These pages are highlighted in the Add New Item dialog box of Visual Studio, shown in Figure 4-25.

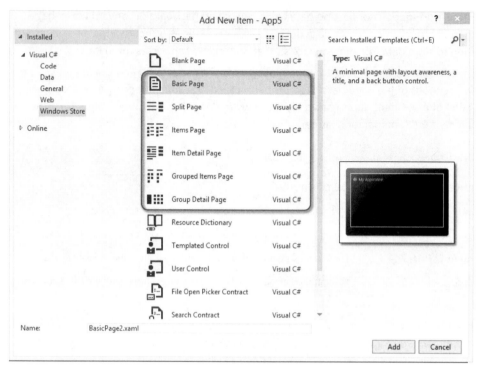

FIGURE 4-25 Pages that derive from the *LayoutAwarePage* class and are available in Visual Studio for Windows Store projects

Using Semantic Zoom in your app

In many Windows Store apps that employ hierarchical navigation, there are several categories with a variable number of items in each category. The user is expected to swipe horizontally to reveal more categories and items. This action is common in most apps and in the Start screen. When the number of categories and items is large, it can deter the user from swiping on the screen and finding items of interest. In such cases, Semantic Zoom can be used to combine a zoomed-out summary view of the hub page and a zoomed-in detailed view of the hub page. Windows supports pinch-to-zoom gestures, the Ctrl with Plus Sign (+) and Minus Sign (-) keys in the keyboard to zoom in and out, and Control+scroll wheel action to switch between the two views. For example, the zoomed-out view could be a list of movie categories with thumbnails of top-rated movies, whereas the zoomed-in view can contain top-rated movies as well as new titles.

Support for Semantic Zoom in Windows Store apps is available through the *SemanticZoom* control. To use it in your application, you need to provide a data control (for example, a *Grid-View* or a *ListView*) for the *ZoomedOutView* and one for the *ZoomedInView*. The data controls are then bound to their *CollectionViewSource*. The following is XAML for the *SemanticZoom* control:

```
<SemanticZoom>
    <ZoomedOutView>
        <!-- Zoomed out view content -->
    </ZoomedOutView>
    <ZoomedInView>
        <!-- Zoomed out view content -->
    </ZoomedInView>
</SemanticZoom>
```

MORE INFO   SEMANTICZOOM SAMPLE

You can learn more about the *SemanticZoom* control and how it can be used in a Windows
Store app in the *SemanticZoom* sample available at *http://code.msdn.microsoft.com/win-
dowsapps/GroupedGridView-77c59e8e*.

When using *SemanticZoom* in your app, you might be restricted by the limitation of using
the *GridView* and *ListView* controls for displaying data semantically. However, you can add
semantic behavior in controls such as *Grid* by implementing the *ISemanticZoomInformation*
interface and using it as a data control in the *ZoomedInView* and *ZoomedOutView* properties. You do not need to implement all the methods of the interface except the *IsActiveView*,
IsZoomedInView, and *SemanticZoomOwner* properties, for which the default implementation
added by Visual Studio is sufficient. The code in Listing 4-24 shows an example of a user control that implements the *ISemanticZoomInformation* interface.

LISTING 4-24 Implementing the *ISemanticZoomInformation* interface

```
using Windows.UI.Xaml.Controls;

namespace Appreciate.Controls
{
    public class SemanticGrid : Grid, ISemanticZoomInformation
    {
        #region ISemanticZoomInformation interface

        public void CompleteViewChange()
        {
            // Provide your own implementation
        }

        public void CompleteViewChangeFrom(SemanticZoomLocation source,
                        SemanticZoomLocation destination)
        {
            // Provide your own implementation
        }

        public void CompleteViewChangeTo(SemanticZoomLocation source,
                        SemanticZoomLocation destination)
        {
            // Provide your own implementation
        }
```

```csharp
        public void InitializeViewChange()
        {
            // Provide your own implementation
        }

        public bool IsActiveView
        {
            get;
            set;
        }

        public bool IsZoomedInView
        {
            get;
            set;
        }

        public void MakeVisible(SemanticZoomLocation item)
        {
            // Provide your own implementation
        }

        public SemanticZoom SemanticZoomOwner
        {
            get;
            set;
        }

        public void StartViewChangeFrom(SemanticZoomLocation source,
                        SemanticZoomLocation destination)
        {
            // Provide your own implementation if the source view is the
            // implementing view and destination view is the a different view
        }

        public void StartViewChangeTo(SemanticZoomLocation source,
                        SemanticZoomLocation destination)
        {
            // Provide your own implementation if the source view is a different
            // and destination view is the implementing view
        }

        #endregion
    }
}
```

Thought experiment
Following best practices for app navigation

In this thought experiment, apply what you've learned about this objective. You can find answers to these questions in the "Answers" section at the end of this chapter.

You have been asked to build a Windows Store app as a reference for other apps that your colleagues will design and develop. What are the top three best practices you will highlight while implementing navigation in your reference app?

Objective summary

- A great Windows Store app provides a smooth, simple, and intuitive navigation experience. You should follow one of the navigation patterns recommended by Microsoft design style.

- Visual Studio provides Windows Store app templates that contain support for hierarchical navigation.

- The *Frame* class hosts one or more pages, and provides events and the *Navigate* method to help in navigation. The *Page* class provides methods that are useful in passing data during navigation.

- Pages in an app can be cached or created afresh every time the app navigates to a page. The *Frame* class can cache a number of pages that can be configured in the app.

- In Windows Store apps with number of categories and items, the *SemanticZoom* control can be used to provide a summary view, making it easier for users to navigate among categories.

Objective review

Answer the following questions to test your knowledge of the information in this objective. You can find the answers to these questions and explanations of why each answer choice is correct or incorrect in the "Answers" section at the end of this chapter.

1. A Windows Store app lists the latest movies playing in all the theaters in a city (determined via the ZIP code or the user's location). The hub page consists of a grouped list of items with the title of each item set to the name of the theater. Each grouped item also contains thumbnails of the movies currently being screened. The local theaters are complaining about users not being able to browse the list and select a movie of their choice. How can you enhance the app so the user can view all the theaters at a glance and navigate to any theater to view the movies currently playing? (Choose all that apply.)

   A. Display the list of all theaters in a *GridView* and let the user tap an item that opens the theater's show times page.

   B. Use the top app bar to display all the theaters; when the user taps a theater, open the theater's show times page.

   C. Use the *SemanticZoom* control with two *GridView* controls, one for the existing view and the other for a summary view in which all the theaters are listed. Tapping an item in the summary view opens the theater's show times page.

   D. After the user is on a theater's show times page, use the top app bar to show the start times of movies, thereby enabling the user to select a time that lists all the movies that start at that time and display them in a list within the same page.

   E. Enable users to mark a theater as their favorite, with a maximum of up to 10 theaters. Use the top app bar in the hub screen to show this list of favorites to enable users to navigate to their favorite theaters.

2. You have recently enhanced an app that helps users learn about the medicinal values of plants commonly found by implementing search and toast notifications (when new information about plants you have already read is available). Users have reported that they cannot bookmark a page when the app is opened through search or a search notification. You have found the problem to be the missing name of the plant from the page used for bookmarking it. What should you do to solve the problem?

   A. Whenever the app is launched, save a copy of the data in the local settings; use the data in the page used for bookmarking.

   B. Pass the data received through the *OnLaunched* method to the page used for bookmarking by using the *Navigate* method of the *Frame* class.

   C. Implement a data-caching mechanism to store the data available through the *OnLaunched* method; use the caching mechanism in the page used for bookmarking to retrieve the data.

   D. Remove the bookmarking feature from the application.

3. You have built an app that is used by your customers to upload photos for their custom manufacturing orders. In a typical session, a user uploads two or more high-resolution photos and fills a number of details of the order they are about to place. You need to ensure that they do not navigate away before the order is complete. What is the best way to implement a feature in your app that prevents users from losing their order details by navigating away from the page by mistake?

   A. Check to see whether an order is still in process and prevent users from navigating away by canceling the navigation.

   B. Check to see whether is still in progress; if users navigate away from the page, show a dialog box and ask for their confirmation before navigating away from the page.

   C. When users navigate away, complete the order on their behalf, assuming they want to carry on with their order.

   D. Save a copy of the order and list them all in the hub page prominently. This will help the user remember the orders they are yet to complete.

Chapter summary

- Live tiles and badges in a Windows Store app helps with the popularity of the application. Live tiles can be updated regularly by your app or by using push notifications to deliver fresh content.

- Secondary tiles enable users to launch your app for a specific purpose; they can be enhanced by live tile updates, thereby making them very attractive and useful.

- Badges can provide a summary of new items available or the status from an app. Badges can be displayed on the lock screen, which helps with communication from your app with the users.

- Toast notifications deliver transient messages to the user, even when your app is not running. Toast notifications can be configured for the duration in which they are visible and the sound played when they arrive.

- Windows Runtime provides a combination of low-level pointer events and higher-level gesture and manipulation events that can be used in Windows Store apps.

- Inking and handwriting support is available for Window Store apps.

- Microsoft provides design guidelines for implementing a great navigation experience in Windows Store apps. Windows Store project templates provided by Visual Studio have built-in hierarchical navigation.

- Navigation events can be used to implement features that help with the user experience such as warning a user before they navigate away from a page.

Answers

This section contains the solutions to the thought experiments and answers to the lesson review questions in this chapter.

Objective 4.1: Thought experiment

1. **Live tile updates for the highest scores**   Whenever you finish a game and post a high score, the five highest scores can be displayed in the live tile as a queue.

2. **Badge updates for player invitations**   If a friend sends an invitation to you for a game they want you to join, the app displays a number that indicates pending invitations. Badge updates can be shown on the lock screen if enabled by the user, so the user has the latest information about invitations.

3. **Push notifications to update tiles**   Push notifications can update tiles and deliver information on new games that are available for download (or for high scores achieved by friends, for example).

Objective 4.1: Review

1. **Correct answer:** B

   A. **Incorrect:** Although push notifications can deliver this information, infrastructure requirements might be prohibitive to deliver the data to a large number of users. The complexity in the infrastructure includes the requirement of preparing content based on each user's preference and delivering content through push notifications.

   B. **Correct:** Periodic notifications can be configured to download data based on recommendations available from a server considering the user's interests; or if users have specific categories of music they like, this information can be used to fetch the data.

   C. **Incorrect:** New information m not be available every hour, which can cause an unnecessary load on the server.

   D. **Incorrect:** If live tiles are updated with the latest information, such as artists or albums, whenever the app is run, the updates will stop after three hours, and no updates will be available until the app is run again.

2. **Correct answers:** A, B, D

   A. **Correct:** Live tile updates can be delivered to secondary tiles in addition to primary tiles, so weather updates for a specific city can be delivered through a secondary tile.

   B. **Correct:** When the user taps a secondary tile, it launches the app and the user is taken to the page that was bookmarked. This makes it easy for the user to open a specific page in the app.

   C. **Incorrect:** Although the primary tile of the app can be removed from the Start screen, the user can always add it back from the All apps view.

   D. **Correct:** When a secondary tile is created, it can be configured so that whenever the same user signs in on a different device and installs the app, the associated secondary tiles are also available.

   E. **Incorrect:** Secondary tiles can be resized to either wide or narrow; users cannot resize them to arbitrary dimensions.

3. **Correct answer:** B

   A. **Incorrect:** A stock's price usually changes frequently, so push notifications have to be delivered to several users for a variety of stocks several times within a short duration. This procedure causes issues with infrastructure requirements and is not a valid solution.

   B. **Correct:** Periodic updates help balance the load over time and across requests. Therefore, multiple users can issue periodic updates for stock prices from different PCs without causing scalability issues.

   C. **Incorrect:** Stock prices change frequently, so downloading updates for stock prices at a specific time of day is not very useful.

   D. **Incorrect:** Although a Windows service can download the latest stock prices, local live tile updates are issues only when the application runs, and they expire after 3 hours.

   E. **Incorrect:** Scheduled updates can be created for intervals that are no shorter than 30 minutes. If users are forced to open the app, they do not have a good user experience.

Objective 4.2: Thought experiment

1. **Reminders for workouts**   The user or the user's trainer can create reminders for upcoming workout sessions. This helps the user avoid missing any workout sessions.

2. **New fitness report available**   When a trainer prepares a report for a user, the user can be notified through a toast notification of the availability of the report. Clicking the toast opens the application, which then displays the report.

3. **User joining a training session**   When the user signs in at the fitness center, the trainer can be notified through a toast notification and can proceed to the session.

Objective 4.2: Review

1. **Correct answer:** B

   A. **Incorrect:** Although cloud services can deliver reminders, you would ideally like the user to use your app as much as possible. Therefore, you should implement reminders within your app.

   B. **Correct:** Scheduled toast notifications delivered by your app help users to manage their tasks and other activities. It is the best option to implement reminders in your app.

   C. **Incorrect:** Similar to option A, if the reminders are created by the user through your app but delivered via cloud services, your app is never involved in the delivery of reminders.

   D. **Incorrect:** A Windows Store app occupies the whole screen when it is running, so, you cannot assume that the user will keep the app running all the time.

2. **Correct answer:** B

   A. **Incorrect:** A toast notification cannot remain on the screen for longer than 25 seconds, and the sound file should be chosen from the toast template audio catalog.

   B. **Correct:** The payload in a toast notification can contain the name of the file and the URL where it is available. It can be downloaded by the Windows Store app and played. The user can choose to save the voice mail file in the app for future reference.

   C. **Incorrect:** A MP3 file cannot be embedded in the payload of a push notification. It can only contain text, for example, the URL and name of the file with the voice mail.

   D. **Incorrect:** Voice mail for a user might not be delivered frequently, so a Windows service polling the server for voice mail causes an unnecessary load on the server. A toast notification can be created locally only with a Windows Store app.

3. **Correct answers:** B, C, E

   A. **Incorrect:** A toast notification, when tapped or clicked on by the user, opens the Windows Store app that it is supposed to activate; it cannot be used to launch just any app.

   B. **Correct:** Toast notifications can be scheduled for events to remind users of those events.

   C. **Correct:** Toast notifications can be created and dispatched by the WNS. If a message is available for the user, a push notification can be used to deliver the message as a toast.

   D. **Incorrect:** Toast notifications can contain audio only from the toast notification template audio catalog.

E.   **Correct:** Launch parameters can be embedded in the XML used to set up the toast notification. The type or name of the page can be extracted from the parameters available through the *OnLaunched* event and used for navigating to the desired page.

Objective 4.3: Thought experiment

1.   **Stylus input**   Stylus input can be used to implement drawing of shapes on a screen with a digitizer. This feature of a stylus can be used to draw various shapes on the screen by the students and the teacher.

2.   **Handwriting recognition**   Students can write their answers for questions during a practice session or test, and teachers can writes notes about their students using the stylus. Handwriting can be used to recognize the text and convert it into text.

3.   **Saving drawings**   As a teacher aid, diagrams drawn by students can be saved as *InkStrokes* for help with assessment and preparation of progress reports.

Objective 4.3: Review

1.   **Correct answers:** B, C, E

   A.   **Incorrect:** *PointerExited* is raised when the pointer exits the canvas. For the purpose of the proof-of-concept app, there is no need to use this event.

   B.   **Correct:** The *PointerPressed* event is used to detect when the input device is on the digitizer surface and initialize the app to prepare for drawing on the canvas.

   C.   **Correct:** The *PointerMoved* event is used to detect movement of the input device after drawing on the canvas has commenced. This event is useful for drawing the stroke on the canvas.

   D.   **Incorrect:** *PointerCanceled* is raised when the pointer loses contact with the canvas abnormally; for example if the mouse is disconnected when the left key is pressed on the *canvas*. Because this is a proof-of-concept application, you do not need to use this event.

   E.   **Correct:** The *PointerReleased* event is raised when the input device loses contact with the digitizer. It can be used to finalize the drawing on the canvas.

2. **Correct answer:** C

   A. **Incorrect:** This gesture is reserved by the system and used for switching apps, so it cannot be used in any app.

   B. **Incorrect:** This gesture is reserved by the system and used for opening the charms bar, so it cannot be used in any app.

   C. **Correct:** Windows provides an event for this gesture, and it can be used to open a dialog box. The tap-and-hold gesture is distinct from a single tap, which should be avoided because the user can tap the pause button.

   D. **Incorrect:** The user might accidentally tap the pause button and restart the game.

3. **Correct answer:** B

   A. **Incorrect:** Although *InkStroke* objects can be saved and retrieved independently of *InkManager,* custom code needs to be written that might be error-prone and provide an experience different from other apps.

   B. **Correct:** The *SaveAsync* method can be used to save a collection of *InkStrokes,* and the *LoadAsync* method can be used to load a collection of *InkStrokes.*

   C. **Incorrect:** You need to write fair amount of application logic to react to the pointer events and capture the data, followed by its serialization.

   D. **Incorrect:** A drawing can be saved into a bitmap, but it cannot be converted back into *InkStrokes*. Therefore, if a bitmap is used to save the *InkStrokes*, the app cannot edit the saved *InkStrokes*.

Objective 4.4: Thought experiment

1. **Simple, intuitive navigation is fundamental in an excellent user experience**   If users feel comfortable using an app after the first few times, it means they are likely to continue using it.

2. **Semantic information about data**   Providing semantic information helps the user decide which section of data to browse if there is a lot of data present in the user interface.

3. **Leveraging the navigation framework**   Features such as page caching, forward/backward navigation, and passing navigation parameters using the navigation framework help to implement navigation in a great Windows Store app.

Objective 4.4: Review

1. **Correct answers:** C, D, E

   A. **Incorrect:** A *GridView* can display only a limited number of items in the visible area of the screen, so this is not an ideal solution.

   B. **Incorrect:** A top app bar might not be adequate to accommodate all the theaters in a city, so this is not an ideal solution.

   C. **Correct:** A *SemanticZoom* control provides semantic information about the data, so it should be used to display the list of theaters in a city with minimal details. The user can tap an item to browse the movies being screened.

   D. **Correct:** The top app bar can be used very effectively to list a set of buttons, one for each start time. Whenever the user taps a button, the list of movies is automatically scrolled to the point that lists the movies starting at the selected time.

   E. **Correct:** Unless users travel to a different city or a faraway location to watch a movie, they will prefer to visit a specific theater. Adding support for shortcuts helps with navigation to the specific theater.

2. **Correct answer:** B

   A. **Incorrect:** This is not an efficient way of passing data to the page concerned. It is recommended that parameters should be passed around pages using the methods provided in the *Frame* and *Page* classes.

   B. **Correct:** The launch event arguments contain the parameter that the user should know. This parameter can be passed to the page for bookmarking the information.

   C. **Incorrect:** Caching is not an efficient way of passing data across pages.

   D. **Incorrect:** The requirements of the app do not permit this.

3. **Correct answer:** B

   A. **Incorrect:** This solution is likely to annoy users because they might use the back button to navigate away from the page and cancel their order in the process.

   B. **Correct:** A dialog box prevents navigation until it is closed. Therefore, the app enables users to decide whether they indeed want to discard the order and return to the previous page.

   C. **Incorrect:** This solution is likely to annoy users because they might use the back button to navigate away from the page without approving the app to process their order.

   D. **Incorrect:** Every time an order is discarded, adding it to a list in the hub page will annoy the user. The app can provide this as an option.

Manage security and data

An important aspect of the design and implementation of a Windows Store app is how it handles data in various forms, such as its own settings, user-specific data, and, data from remote services. Many apps depend on a remote source of data to be fully functional, whereas some apps require data to be persisted locally. Data access in a Windows Store app can be implemented based on its requirements. The WinRT application programming interface (API) provides support for both local and remote data storage for Windows Store apps.

Some Windows Store apps depend on data from remote web-based services. Such apps require a connection over the network to access the web services. Modern web services are designed using Representational State Transfer (REST) architecture, which requires apps to use the appropriate HTTP verb while sending a request for data or to invoke an operation on the data.

Windows Store apps that display and manipulate data can utilize data binding, a flexible yet powerful technique. Data binding can connect a data model with the app's presentation layer using declarations in XAML instead of code. Dependency properties can be used in the data model to support data binding.

Securing data access by Windows Store apps is important to prevent data from being compromised by third parties. It is particularly important to protect the user's credentials. The WinRT APIs provide methods to secure sensitive data within a Windows Store application. Windows Store apps should use single sign-on (SSO) whenever an authentication provider is available.

Objectives in this chapter:

- Objective 5.1: Choose an appropriate data access strategy.
- Objective 5.2: Retrieve data remotely.
- Objective 5.3. Implement data binding.
- Objective 5.4: Manage Windows authentication.
- Objective 5.5: Manage web authentication.

Objective 5.1: Choose an appropriate data access strategy

Choosing a data access strategy is an important step in the development of a Windows Store app. An app might need to store its own settings as well as settings configured by its users. It might also need to connect to the Internet and download data to present to the user, or upload user information to a remote web service. If the user has your app installed on multiple devices, each instance of the app might need to synchronize the data and present the settings as updated by the user.

You have a wide range of data access options available to help develop your app. You should consider extensibility of your app for enhancements in the future so that your app does not need to be modified heavily to support new requirements. Your app can use the local, roaming, or temporary data store for settings and application-specific data; it can use file access APIs for storing and retrieving files on the device; and it can connect to remote services for downloading data and displaying it.

> **This objective covers how to:**
> - Choose the appropriate data access strategy (file based, web service, remote storage, including Windows Azure storage) based on app requirements.

Choosing the appropriate data access strategy based on app requirements

Storage and retrieval of data is a fundamental feature in most Windows Store apps. Windows Store apps can interact with data in a variety of ways. In some cases, the user is involved in this interaction; in other cases, the app stores and retrieves data. The choice of a data access strategy depends on the type of data and data storage available to your app, and the way users create and access their data.

When users interact with a Windows Store app, the app usually requires one or more of the following types of data:

- Settings that are created by the app and are not controlled by the user. These are often specific to the device (for example, the last time the app was launched).
- Settings that are created by the app and are not controlled by the user; however, these settings need to be synchronized across multiple devices.
- Settings that are configured by the user according to their preferences. Your application provides a set of default values, and the user has the option to change these values, usually through the Settings charm. These settings might need to be synchronized across multiple devices of the user.

- Data created by the app on a device while it is being used. This includes cached data stored between application sessions to support situations when the device is not connected to the Internet.

- Data created by the app and cached temporarily on a device to help with the performance of the application. This type of data usually has a lifetime of its own and it can be deleted by the app.

- Data created by the user and imported in your application and saved in the local device or a remote service. An example is an app used to manipulate photos and store them afterwards.

WinRT APIs provide a number of options for developers to work with data in their Windows Store apps. These options relate to the pattern of interaction between the data and the app or the user, and they can be broadly classified into the following types:

- **Local application data**   This option should be used to store settings and device-specific temporary files—data that does not affect the app's operations on other devices and will not be required by the user on other devices. There is no restriction on the size of data that can be stored in the local application data store.

- **Roaming application data**   When users configure your application's settings to suit their preferences, they expect the settings to be available across all their devices. The roaming application data store automatically synchronizes such data across multiple devices for the same user account. There is a restriction on the size of data that can be stored in the roaming application store.

- **Temporary application data**   The temporary application data store can be used to store transient data that can be deleted by the system at any time. This might include data created by the user or from a remote web service that is not likely to change frequently and does not affect the functionality of the app.

- **Local and remote files**   Your app can store data in a file and save it in one of the folders it has access to. A folder in the user's Microsoft SkyDrive account can also be used to save files. In addition, an app can access files in the device or in a remote service, manipulate them, and save them.

The application data store is available to an app on a per-user basis for storing settings and files. The *Windows.Storage* namespace provides a number of classes that are useful for data management in the application data store as well as for file storage. The *ApplicationData* class provides events, methods, and properties that Windows Store apps can use to incorporate the application data store.

Local application data

A Windows Store app should store information locally that is required whenever the application is running and need not be available across multiple devices. This includes settings internal to the app as well as any files created by the app. There is no size restriction on the local data store.

The *LocalSettings* property of the *ApplicationData* class provides an instance of the *ApplicationDataContainer* class, which represents a container for the application's settings. The *ApplicationDataContainer* class helps in the creation, deletion, and updates of settings for a Windows Store app. The *Locality* property of the *ApplicationDataContainer* class can be used to obtain the type of data store (local, roaming, or temporary) associated with the container. The value of the *Locality* property is a member of the *ApplicationDataLocality* enumeration. The *CreateContainer* method is used to create a container to store values for settings with a unique name along with a creation option. The creation option is specified using the *ApplicationDataCreateDisposition* enumeration. Table 5-1 describes the *ApplicationDataCreateDisposition* enumeration members.

TABLE 5-1 *ApplicationDataCreateDisposition* enumeration members

Member	Value	Description
Always	0	This value indicates the data container should be created if it does not exist. If the container exists, a new container is not created.
Existing	1	This value indicates the data container should be opened if it already exists. If the requested container does not exist, it will not be created.

The C# code in Listing 5-1 shows how to save a simple setting, a composite setting, and a setting in a container, and then retrieve them.

LISTING 5-1 Storing settings locally

```csharp
using Windows.Storage;

public sealed partial class LocalSettingsSamplePage : LayoutAwarePage
{
    private void SaveApplicationSettings()
    {
        ApplicationDataContainer localSettings = ApplicationData.Current.LocalSettings;

        // Store simple setting
        localSettings.Values["simpleSetting"] = "Simple Settings Example";

        // Store composite setting
        ApplicationDataCompositeValue compositeSetting = new
                                    ApplicationDataCompositeValue();
        compositeSetting["intVal"] = 44;

        // You can use the Add method to add a setting
        compositeSetting.Add("strVal", "Composite Settings Example");
        localSettings.Values["compositeSetting"] = compositeSetting;

        // Store settings in a container, create container if it doesn't exist
        ApplicationDataContainer container =
                    localSettings.CreateContainer("localSettingsContainer",
                        ApplicationDataCreateDisposition.Always);
        if (localSettings.Containers.ContainsKey("localSettingsContainer"))
        {
```

```
        localSettings.Containers["localSettingsContainer"].Values["containerSetting"]
                = "Hello Windows";
    }
}

private void ReadApplicationSettings()
{
    ApplicationDataContainer localSettings = ApplicationData.Current.LocalSettings;

    // Read data from simple setting
    object simpleSetting = localSettings.Values["simpleSetting"];
    if (simpleSetting == null)
    {
        // Settings not found
    }
    else
    {
        // Settings found, read it
    }

    // Remove simple setting
    localSettings.Values.Remove("simpleSetting");

    // Read data composite settings
    ApplicationDataCompositeValue compositeSettingValue =
      (ApplicationDataCompositeValue)localSettings.Values["compositeSetting"];
    if (compositeSettingValue == null)
    {
        // No data
    }
    else
    {
        // Access data in compositeSettingValue["intVal"] and
        //          compositeSettingValue["strVal"]

        // Remove a specific key/value pair
        compositeSettingValue.Remove("intVal");
    }

    // Read settings from container
    bool hasContainer =
            localSettings.Containers.ContainsKey("localSettingsContainer");

    if (hasContainer)
    {
        bool hasSetting =
            localSettings.Containers["localSettingsContainer"].Values.ContainsKey(
                        "containerSetting");

        if (hasSetting == true)
        {
            // Read the setting
        }
```

```
        // Delete the container
        localSettings.DeleteContainer("localSettingsContainer");
      }
   }
}
```

Application settings require a string key and support many different types of values, such as Boolean, byte, integer, unsigned integer, double, float, and string, and others. If your app needs to store binary data or it generates large amount of data, you should consider writing it to a file in the local application data folder. The *LocalFolder* property of the *ApplicationData* class provides the *StorageFolder* that can be used to create, save, and retrieve files from the local storage folder. Listing 5-2 shows an example of how to create a file in the local application data folder, write to it, and read the data from the file.

LISTING 5-2 Creating, writing to, and reading from a file in the local application data folder

```
using Windows.Storage;
public sealed partial class LocalFolderSamplePage : LayoutAwarePage
{
    private async void SaveApplicationDataInLocalFolder()
    {
        StorageFolder localFolder =
                        ApplicationData.Current.LocalFolder;

        try
        {
            // Create a new file and store data
            StorageFile lastRunFile = await localFolder.CreateFileAsync("dataFile.bin",
                          CreationCollisionOption.ReplaceExisting);
            if (lastRunFile != null)
            {
                await FileIO.WriteBufferAsync(lastRunFile, GetBufferToWrite());
            }
        }
        catch (Exception)
        {
            // Handle any exception
        }
    }

    // Use the WriteBuffer method of the DataWriter class to prepare the buffer
    private IBuffer GetBufferToWrite()
    {
        return null;
    }

    private async void ReadApplicationFromLocalFolder()
    {
        StorageFolder localFolder =
                ApplicationData.Current.LocalFolder;
        try
        {
            StorageFile lastRunFile = await localFolder.GetFileAsync("dataFile.bin");
            if (lastRunFile != null)
```

```
        {
            IBuffer buffer = await FileIO.ReadBufferAsync(lastRunFile);
            using (DataReader dataReader = DataReader.FromBuffer(buffer))
            {
                // Use the data to perform additional tasks
            }
        }
    }
    catch (Exception)
    {
        // Handle any exception
    }
}
}
```

Roaming application data

In some Windows Store apps, data created by the app or by the user while interacting with the apps needs to be available on all the devices where the app is installed. Windows provides support for synchronizing this data across multiple devices of the user without the need of building an online data synchronization service. Windows provides a roaming application data store that is synchronized across all a user's devices on which the app is installed. If your app relies on a critical setting that is roamed, you can receive a notification of any changes to this data by creating an event handler for the *DataChanged* event of the *ApplicationData* class and refreshing the data in your app. Your app can signal a change in the data stored in the roaming data store by invoking the *SignalDataChanged* method of the *ApplicationData* class.

Although the roaming data store makes it easy for developers to implement synchronization of important data across all a user's devices, the system does not guarantee that this data is synchronized instantaneously. When the user is offline or is on an unreliable Internet connection, synchronization of roamed data can be delayed. Windows provides a setting that can be configured so that the data stored in the setting is synchronized with a higher priority. You can mark this setting with a key of *HighPriority* and set the value so it is not larger than 8 kilobytes (KB). You can even add a composite setting with this key so that more than one setting is available across all devices.

Windows limits the amount of data that can be stored in the roaming data store by an app. This is to ensure synchronization is quick and does not fail unless there is a loss of Internet connectivity from a device. After a Windows Store app reaches the limit on the amount of data that can be stored in the roaming data store, synchronization of data is halted until the total size of the roamed data is less than the limit. Therefore, you should use the roaming application data store to store user preferences and small files only. You can use the *RoamingStorageQuota* property of the *ApplicationData* class to obtain the maximum size of data that can be synchronized to the cloud from the roaming data store.

The system preserves the roaming data of an app for a specific period of time. If the user does not launch the app or uninstalls the app within this period of time, the data is still preserved. If the user reinstalls the app within this period, the roaming data is synchronized from the cloud. This period is set to 30 days by the system.

If the roaming data of an app is updated to a new version when the user installs an update, the updated data is copied to the cloud. However, the updated roaming data is not synchronized with the application running on other devices until the user updates the app to the current version.

The roaming settings are again an instance of the *ApplicationDataContainer* class and are accessed using the *RoamingSettings* property of the *ApplicationData* class. Listing 5-3 shows how to write settings to the roaming application data store, including a *HighPriority* setting, and read them from the store.

LISTING 5-3 Writing settings to the roaming application data store

```
using Windows.Storage;
public sealed partial class RoamingSettingsSamplePage : LayoutAwarePage
{
    public RoamingSettingsSamplePage()
    {
        this.InitializeComponent();

        // Subscribe to the DataChanged event
        ApplicationData.Current.DataChanged +=
                    new TypedEventHandler<ApplicationData, object>(OnDataChanged);
    }

    private void OnDataChanged(ApplicationData appData, object o)
    {
        // Roaming data has changed, refresh your data
    }

    private void SaveRoamingSettings()
    {
        ApplicationDataContainer roamingSettings =
                        ApplicationData.Current.RoamingSettings;

        // Store simple setting
        roamingSettings.Values["simpleSetting"] = "Roaming Settings Example";

        // Store a high priority setting, for example, the last
        // newsitem read by the user
        roamingSettings.Values["HighPriority"] = "itemId=344";

        // Store composite setting
        ApplicationDataCompositeValue compositeSetting = new
                    ApplicationDataCompositeValue();
        compositeSetting["intVal"] = 44;

        // You can use the Add method to add a setting
        compositeSetting.Add("strVal", "Composite Settings Example");
        roamingSettings.Values["compositeSetting"] = compositeSetting;

        // Store settings in a container, create container if it doesn't exist
        ApplicationDataContainer container =
                        roamingSettings.CreateContainer("roamingSettingsContainer",
                            ApplicationDataCreateDisposition.Always);
```

```
    if (roamingSettings.Containers.ContainsKey("roamingSettingsContainer"))
    {
        roamingSettings.Containers["roamingSettingsContainer"].
                    Values["containerSetting"] = "Hello Windows";
    }
}

private void ReadRoamingSettings()
{
    ApplicationDataContainer roamingSettings =
                    ApplicationData.Current.RoamingSettings;

    // Read data from simple setting
    object simpleSetting = roamingSettings.Values["simpleSetting"];
    if (simpleSetting == null)
    {
        // Settings not found
    }
    else
    {
        // Settings found, read it
    }

    // Remove simple setting
    roamingSettings.Values.Remove("simpleSetting");

    // Read the high priority value
    object highPriorityValue = roamingSettings.Values["HighPriority"];

    // Read data composite settings
    ApplicationDataCompositeValue compositeSettingValue =
        (ApplicationDataCompositeValue)roamingSettings.Values["compositeSetting"];
    if (compositeSettingValue == null)
    {
        // No data
    }
    else
    {
        // Access data in compositeSettingValue["intVal"] and
        //       compositeSettingValue["strVal"]

        // Remove a specific key/value pair
        compositeSettingValue.Remove("intVal");
    }

    // Read settings from container
    bool hasContainer =
        roamingSettings.Containers.ContainsKey("roamingSettingsContainer");

    if (hasContainer)
    {
        bool hasSetting =
                roamingSettings.Containers["roamingSettingsContainer"].
                Values.ContainsKey("containerSetting");
        if (hasSetting == true)
```

```
        {
            // Read the setting
        }

        // Delete the container
        roamingSettings.DeleteContainer("roamingSettingsContainer");
    }
  }
}
```

The roaming application data folder can be used to store files that are synchronized across multiple devices. Due to the limited space available in this store, you should store files that are essential in the operation of the app across multiple devices. For example, if the profile picture of the user is available from a location on the Internet, you should not store it in the roaming app data store because the file can be downloaded from the Internet. You can store the message being composed or the steps in a game in a file and roam it across multiple devices. The *RoamingFolder* property of the *ApplicationData* class provides the *StorageFolder* which can be used to create, save, and retrieve files in the roaming data folder. Listing 5-4 shows how you can use the roaming application data store to create files, store them, and retrieve data from them.

LISTING 5-4 Creating, writing to, and reading from a files in the roaming application data store

```
using Windows.Storage;

public sealed partial class RoamingFolderSamplePage : LayoutAwarePage
{
    private async void SaveApplicationDataInRoamingFolder()
    {
        StorageFolder roamingFolder = ApplicationData.Current.RoamingFolder;

        // Create a new file and store data
        try
        {
            StorageFile lastMovesFile = await
                roamingFolder.CreateFileAsync("lastMoves.xml",
                        CreationCollisionOption.ReplaceExisting);
            if (lastMovesFile != null)
            {
                await FileIO.WriteBufferAsync(lastMovesFile, GetBufferToWrite());
            }
        }
        catch (Exception)
        {
            // Handle any exception
        }
    }

    // Use the WriteBuffer method of the DataWriter class to prepare the buffer
    private IBuffer GetBufferToWrite()
    {
        return null;
    }
```

```
private async void ReadApplicationFromRoamingFolder()
{
    StorageFolder roamingFolder =
            ApplicationData.Current.RoamingFolder;
    try
    {
        StorageFile lastMovesFile = await
                        roamingFolder.GetFileAsync("lastMoves.xml");
        if (lastMovesFile != null)
        {
            IBuffer buffer = await FileIO.ReadBufferAsync(lastMovesFile);
            using (DataReader dataReader = DataReader.FromBuffer(buffer))
            {
                // Use the data to perform additional tasks
            }
        }
    }
    catch (Exception)
    {
        // Handle any exception
    }
}
}
```

Temporary application data

The temporary application data folder is used to store transient data in files. Files stored in this location are not roamed and they can be removed at any time by the system. Alternatively, the user can clear files from this folder by running the Disk Cleanup utility. This data store should be used to store data used during an application session, such as caching photos and video clips in a social event sharing application. This helps with the responsiveness of the application because the data is readily available after it is downloaded once.

The *TemporaryFolder* property of the *ApplicationData* class provides the *StorageFolder*, which can be used to create, save, and retrieve temporary files. This is shown in Listing 5-5.

LISTING 5-5 Creating, saving, and retrieving temporary files

```
using Windows.Storage;

public sealed partial class TemporaryFolderSamplePage : LayoutAwarePage
{
    private async void SaveApplicationDataInTemporaryFolder()
    {
        StorageFolder temporaryFolder =
                ApplicationData.Current.TemporaryFolder;

        try
        {
            // Create a new file and store data
            StorageFile profilePictureFile = await
                    temporaryFolder.CreateFileAsync("ProfilePicture-Large.png",
                        CreationCollisionOption.ReplaceExisting);
```

```
            if (profilePictureFile != null)
            {
                await FileIO.WriteBufferAsync(profilePictureFile, GetBufferToWrite());
            }
        }
        catch (Exception)
        {
            // Handle any exception
        }
    }

    // Use the WriteBuffer method of the DataWriter class to prepare the buffer
    private IBuffer GetBufferToWrite()
    {
        return null;
    }

    private async void ReadApplicationFromTemporaryFolder()
    {
        StorageFolder temporaryFolder =
                ApplicationData.Current.TemporaryFolder;
        try
        {
            StorageFile profilePictureFile = await
                        temporaryFolder.GetFileAsync("ProfilePicture-Large.png");
            if (profilePictureFile != null)
            {
                IBuffer buffer = await FileIO.ReadBufferAsync(profilePictureFile);
                using (DataReader dataReader = DataReader.FromBuffer(buffer))
                {
                    // Use the data to perform additional tasks
                }
            }
        }
        catch (Exception)
        {
            // Handle any exception
        }
    }
}
```

Managing application data

Your application can load files that are packaged with the app by specifying a uniform resource identifier (URI) and it can load files created in the application data folder by specifying
a URI. The *StorageFile* class provides the *GetFileFromApplicationUriAsync* method to load files
using URIs. Listing 5-6 shows an app loading files from within the app package as well from
the local, roaming, and temporary settings folders.

```
using Windows.Storage;
using Windows.Foundation;

public sealed partial class FolderUriSamplePage : LayoutAwarePage
{
    private async void ReadFileFromApplicationPackage()
    {
        // data.xml is packaged with the application
        Uri uri = new Uri("ms-appx:///Assets/data.xml");

        // Load the file
        StorageFile file = await StorageFile.GetFileFromApplicationUriAsync(uri);
        if (file != null)
        {
            var stream = file.OpenReadAsync();

            // Deserialize the XML
        }
    }

    private async void ReadFileFromApplicationDataStore()
    {
        // Read a file from the local application data store
        StorageFile lastRunFile = await StorageFile.GetFileFromApplicationUriAsync(
                    new Uri("ms-appdata:///local/dataFile.bin"));

        // Read a file from the roaming application data store
        StorageFile detailedSettingsFile = await
                StorageFile.GetFileFromApplicationUriAsync(
                    new Uri("ms-appdata:///roaming/lastMoves.xml"));

        // Read a file from the temporary application data store
        StorageFile cachedImageFile = await StorageFile.GetFileFromApplicationUriAsync(
                    new Uri("ms-appdata:///temp/images/ProfilePicture
                            -Large.png"));
    }
}
```

The *StorageFile* class also provides a *GetFileFromPathAsync* method that loads a file from the specified path. Be careful when using this method with the local, temporary, and roaming stores because the user can move the file from the location you specify.

Windows Store apps sometimes need to clear all the data stored in the local, roaming, and temporary data stores. For example, if your app is launched after a prolonged period, it will initialize by clearing stored data. You can use the *ClearAsync* method of the *ApplicationData* class to remove all the data stored by your app in the local, roaming, and temporary application data store. If your app selectively needs to clear data from only one store, you can use the *ApplicationDataLocality* enumeration to specify the type of application data store to clear. Table 5-2 describes the *ApplicationDataLocality* enumeration members.

TABLE 5-2 *ApplicationDataLocality* enumeration members

Member	Value	Description
Local	0	The data stored in the local application data store
Roaming	1	The data stored in the roaming application data store
Temporary	2	The data stored in the temporary application data store

To avoid any conflict between currently stored data and the data stored by future releases of your app, you can use data versioning, which enables future versions of the app to change the format of application data and avoid compatibility problems. If the version of data detected by the updated app is an older version, the app should update the application data to the new format and store the version number. You can use the *Version* property of the *ApplicationData* class to obtain the version number of the application data and the *SetVersionAsync* method to set the version number of the application data.

Application data is stored in the package folder of the app, with a clear hierarchy separating the local, roaming, and temporary application data stores. The local, roaming, and temporary data stores are located in the *LocalState*, *RoamingState*, and *TemporaryState* folders. The root directory of these data store folders is located in *%userprofile%\AppData\Local\Packages\{PackageFamilyName}*. The *PackageFamilyName* of the app is available from the Packaging tab of Visual Studio's package manifest editor from the field named Package family name. Your application does not have permission to access the data store of other applications and it cannot access other folders on the user's device unless it is granted permissions through the capabilities declaration in the app's package manifest.

Local and remote files

When adding to settings and files stored in the application data stores, a Windows Store app can interact with files that are present on a device or PC and is managed by other Windows Store apps. For example, a photo viewer app should be able to access the user's Pictures library, or an app might download videos from a remote location and save them in the user's Videos library.

A Windows Store app can access the user's Downloads folder, application data folders, and some locations in the file system. Apps can access additional locations with the file open picker and file save picker, and by declaring capabilities in the package manifest. An app can access the following locations by default:

- **User's Downloads folder**   Your app can programmatically access the folders and files it created in the user's Downloads folder. In addition, it can access other folders and files in the Downloads folder by using a file picker so the user can navigate through them for access within the app. The system prevents programmatic access to folders and files created by other apps or by the user in the Downloads folder. The *DownloadsFolder* class provides the *CreateFolderAsync* and *CreateFileAsync* methods for creating a new subfolder and a new file, respectively, in the Downloads folder located at *%user-profile%/Downloads*.

- **Application data locations**   Whenever an app is installed, the system creates the local, roaming, and temporary application data stores. It can access files and folders in these locations by using the properties of the *ApplicationData* class. The methods provided by the *StorageFolder* object returned for the app's folders can be used to work with folders and files. Alternatively, your app can access a file in its data folders by using the *ms-appdata:///* prefix in the URI and the *GetFileFromApplicationUriAsync* method of the *StorageFile* class. The prefix of the *LocalFolder* folder URI is *ms-appdata:///local*, the prefix for the *RoamingFolder* URI is *ms-appdata:///roaming,* and the prefix for the *TemporaryFolder* URI is *ms-appdata:///temp*. Your app does not have access to the data folders for other Windows Store apps.

- **Application install location**   Your app can access its install location and obtain a *StorageFolder* object using the *Windows.ApplicationModel.Package.Current.InstalledLocation* property. It can access files and folders with methods and properties provided by the *StorageFolder* object. Alternatively, your app can access a file using the *ms-appx:///* prefix in the URI, which refers to the app's install directory, and the *GetFileFromApplicationUriAsync* method of the *StorageFile* class. The app's install location provides read-only access to your app and the file picker cannot be used to access this location. In addition, your app cannot access the install location of other Windows Store apps.

A Windows Store app can access folders and files on removable devices, such as a USB drive or a camera, using a file picker. If your app uses the AutoPlay extension, it can be launched automatically whenever an external device is connected. An app is restricted to file types that are specified through the File Type association declaration in its package manifest.

Your app can access additional locations for files and folders by declaring capabilities in its package manifest. The *KnownFolders* class provides read-only access to these locations through its properties, described as follows:

- **DocumentsLibrary**   This is used to access the Documents library in the user's device. The app must be configured with the Documents Library capability in the package manifest.

- **PicturesLibrary**   This is used to access the Pictures library in the user's device. The app must be configured with the Pictures Library capability in the package manifest.

- **MusicLibrary**   This is used to access the Music library in the user's device. The app must be configured with the Music Library capability in the package manifest.

- **VideosLibrary**   This is used to access the Videos library in the user's device. The app must be configured with the Videos Library capability in the package manifest.

- **HomeGroup**   This is used to access the HomeGroup folder on the user's device. The app must be configured with the Music Library, Pictures Library, or Videos Library capability in the package manifest.

- ***RemovableDevices*** This is used to access the Removable Devices section in My Computer of the user's device and includes devices such as USB flash drives and external portable drives. The app must be configured with the Removable Storage capability.

- ***MediaServerDevices*** This is used to access the media server devices folder on the user's device or PC. The app must be configured with the Music Library, Pictures Library, or Videos Library capability in the package manifest.

Figure 5-1 shows the list of capabilities available in the package manifest of a Windows Store app.

FIGURE 5-1 Options available in the package manifest of a Windows Store app to configure file and folder and file access

File pickers

In addition to programmatically accessing the folders and files, your app can use the *FileOpenPicker* and *FileSavePicker* to access files in the system. You should add the File Open Picker and File Save Picker declarations (as well as the File Type Associations declaration if your app accesses files in removable devices and UNC locations) for your app to be able to use the pickers. This is shown in Figure 5-2.

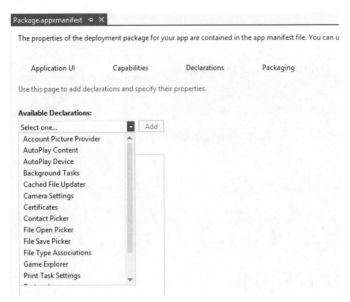

FIGURE 5-2 Options available in the package manifest of a Windows Store app to configure declarations for file pickers and file type associations

A *StorageFolder* object returned by the *DocumentsLibrary*, *MusicLibrary*, *PicturesLibrary*, or *VideosLibrary* property of the *KnownFolders* class can be used to obtain a list of all items (folders and files) in a folder, or it can be used to obtain a list of all the files or the folders stored in a location. Listing 5-7 shows how to access the items in the *DocumentsLibrary* of the device and save a new text file.

LISTING 5-7 Accessing items in *DocumentsLibrary* and saving a text file

```
using Windows.Storage;
public sealed partial class FileAccessSamplePage : LayoutAwarePage
{
    private async void ReadAllItemsInDocumentsLibraryAsync()
    {
        StorageFolder documentsFolder = KnownFolders.DocumentsLibrary;
        StringBuilder outputText = new StringBuilder();

        IReadOnlyList<IStorageItem> itemsList = await documentsFolder.GetItemsAsync();

        foreach (var item in itemsList)
        {
            if (item is StorageFolder)
            {
                outputText.Append(item.Name + " folder\n");
            }
            else
            {
                outputText.Append(item.Name + "\n");
            }
        }
    }
```

```
        // Display the list
        itemsListTextBlock.Text = outputText.ToString();
    }

    private async void ReadAllFilesInDocumentsLibraryAsync()
    {
        StorageFolder documentsFolder = KnownFolders.DocumentsLibrary;
        StringBuilder outputText = new StringBuilder();

        IReadOnlyList<IStorageItem> filesList = await documentsFolder.GetFilesAsync();

        foreach (var item in filesList)
        {
            outputText.Append(item.Name + " file\n");
        }

        // Display the list of files
        filesListTextBlock.Text = outputText.ToString();

        IReadOnlyList<IStorageItem> foldersList = await
                    documentsFolder.GetFoldersAsync();

        foreach (var item in foldersList)
        {
            outputText.Append(item.Name + " folder\n");
        }

        // Display the list of folders
        foldersListTextBlock.Text = outputText.ToString();
    }

    private async Task<string> ReadFriendsListFromDocumentsLibraryAsync()
    {
        StorageFolder storageFolder = KnownFolders.DocumentsLibrary;
        StorageFile friendsListFile =
            await storageFolder.GetFileAsync("friends-list.txt");
        string text = await FileIO.ReadTextAsync(friendsListFile);
        return text;
    }

    private async void WriteFriendsListIntoDocumentsLibraryAsync(string friendsList)
    {
        StorageFolder storageFolder = KnownFolders.DocumentsLibrary;
        StorageFile friendsListFile =
            await storageFolder.CreateFileAsync("friends-list.txt");
        await FileIO.WriteTextAsync(friendsListFile, friendsList);
    }
}
```

In certain cases, your app might need to apply a filter on a folder to group the folders and files in blocks. A folder can be queried with a filter set to one of the members of the enumeration *CommonFolderQuery* after checking whether filtering is allowed on that folder with the specified filter. As an example of filtering, Listing 5-8 shows how to group pictures by their creation month.

LISTING 5-8 Grouping pictures by using a filter

```
using Windows.Storage;

public sealed partial class FileAccessSamplePage : LayoutAwarePage
{
    private async void ListItemsInPicturesLibraryByMonth()
    {
        StorageFolder picturesFolder = KnownFolders.PicturesLibrary;
        if (picturesFolder.IsCommonFolderQuerySupported(CommonFolderQuery.GroupByMonth))
        {
            StorageFolderQueryResult queryResult =
                    picturesFolder.CreateFolderQuery(CommonFolderQuery.GroupByMonth);

            StringBuilder outputText = new StringBuilder();
            IReadOnlyList<IStorageItem> folderList = await
                                         queryResult.GetFoldersAsync();

            foreach (StorageFolder folder in folderList)
            {
                IReadOnlyList<StorageFile> fileList = await folder.GetFilesAsync();

                // Print the month and number of files in this group.
                outputText.AppendLine(folder.Name + " (" + fileList.Count + ")");

                foreach (StorageFile file in fileList)
                {
                    // Print the name of the file.
                    outputText.AppendLine("    " + file.Name);
                }
            }

            // Display the list
            itemsListTextBlock.Text = outputText.ToString();
        }
    }
}
```

> **MORE INFO** **MEMBERS OF THE *COMMONFOLDERQUERY* ENUMERATION**
>
> A list of members of the *CommonFolderQuery* enumeration is available at *http://msdn.microsoft.com/en-us/library/windows/apps/xaml/windows.storage.search.commonfolderquery.aspx.*

Your app might need to provide an option to users to pick a location for importing files into your app or for saving files created using your app. File pickers let users pick folders and files from within your app if it is set up with the appropriate permissions. The *Folder-Picker* presents a user interface (UI) element to the user for picking a folder to save a file. The *FileOpenPicker* class is used to present a UI element to the user for choosing and opening one or more files, and the *FileSavePicker* class is used to specify the name and location where they will save content from your app. An important thing to note for file pickers is they cannot be opened when your app is in the snapped state. Therefore, it is important to check the current view state of an app and attempt to unsnap it. Listing 5-9 shows how to use the *FileOpen-Picker* to open a photo from the *PicturesLibrary* and the *FileSavePicker* to save text in a file in the user's *DocumentsLibrary*.

LISTING 5-9 Using the *FileOpenPicker* and *FileSavePicker*

```
using Windows.Storage;
using Windows.Storage.Pickers;

public sealed partial class FilePickerSamplePage : LayoutAwarePage
{
    // FilePicker APIs will not work if the application is in a snapped state.
    // If an app wants to show a FilePicker while snapped, it must attempt
    // to unsnap first
    private bool EnsureUnsnapped()
    {
        bool unsnapped = ((ApplicationView.Value != ApplicationViewState.Snapped) ||
                          ApplicationView.TryUnsnap());
        if (!unsnapped)
        {
            // Inform the user the application cannot be unsnapped
        }

        return unsnapped;
    }

    // Note: Your app must declare "Pictures Library" in the capabilities
    // of your app's package manifest
    private async void OpenPhotoFromPicturesLibraryAsync()
    {
        if (this.EnsureUnsnapped())
        {
            FileOpenPicker openPicker = new FileOpenPicker();
            openPicker.ViewMode = PickerViewMode.Thumbnail;
            openPicker.SuggestedStartLocation = PickerLocationId.PicturesLibrary;
            openPicker.FileTypeFilter.Add(".jpg");
            openPicker.FileTypeFilter.Add(".jpeg");
            openPicker.FileTypeFilter.Add(".png");

            StorageFile file = await openPicker.PickSingleFileAsync();
            if (file != null)
            {
                // Application now has read/write access to the picked file
            }
            else
            {
                // User canceled the operation

            }
        }
    }
}
```

```csharp
// Note: Your app must declare "Documents Library" in the capabilities
// of your app's package manifest
private async void WriteTextToFileAsync(string text)
{
    if (this.EnsureUnsnapped())
    {
        FileSavePicker savePicker = new FileSavePicker();
        savePicker.SuggestedStartLocation = PickerLocationId.DocumentsLibrary;

        // Dropdown of file types the user can save the file as
        savePicker.FileTypeChoices.Add("Plain Text", new List<string>() { ".txt" });

        // Default file name if the user does not type one in
        // or select a file to replace
        savePicker.SuggestedFileName = "New Document";

        // Show the picker
        StorageFile file = await savePicker.PickSaveFileAsync();
        if (file != null)
        {
            // Prevent updates to the remote version of the file until
            // the app finishes making changes and call CompleteUpdatesAsync.
            CachedFileManager.DeferUpdates(file);

            // write to file
            await FileIO.WriteTextAsync(file, text);

            // Let Windows know that the app is finished changing the file
            // so the other app can update the remote version of the file.
            // Completing updates might require Windows to ask for user input.
            FileUpdateStatus status = await
                    CachedFileManager.CompleteUpdatesAsync(file);
            if (status == FileUpdateStatus.Complete)
            {
                // File was saved
            }
            else
            {
                // File couldn't be saved
            }
        }
        else
        {
            // File save operation was canceled
        }
    }
}
```

Most recently used and future access lists

A Windows Store app can track a list of files it accesses frequently by adding them to the most recently used (MRU) list or the future access list. The MRU list can hold up to 25 items and is automatically managed by Windows for the app. The future access list can hold up to 1,000 items and is managed by the app.

You can use the *MostRecentlyUsedList* property of the *StorageApplicationPermissions* class (in the *Windows.Storage.AccessCache* namespace) to access the most recently accessed list of files and folders. Files and folders can be added for tracking and items can be retrieved from the list. An item already in the list can be updated with a more recent version; for example, a file accessed recently by the user and updated. A file or folder can be added to this list with optional metadata. A token is available after the file is added to the MRU list, which is used later to retrieve the item.

The *FutureAccessList* property of the *StorageApplicationPermissions* class provides support for Windows Store apps to add files to the future access list and remove them. You should use this list in your app when you do not want the system to remove items from the list.

Listing 5-10 shows how to add and remove items from both the lists.

LISTING 5-10 Adding and removing items from the recently accessed list and the future access list

```
using Windows.Storage;
using Windows.Storage.Pickers;
using Windows.Storage.AccessCache;

public sealed partial class FilePickerSamplePage : LayoutAwarePage
{
    string profilePicToken = string.Empty;
    string futureAccessListToken = string.Empty;

    // FilePicker APIs will not work if the application is in a snapped state.
    // If an app wants to show a FilePicker while snapped, it must
    // attempt to unsnap first
    private bool EnsureUnsnapped()
    {
        bool unsnapped = ((ApplicationView.Value != ApplicationViewState.Snapped) ||
                                ApplicationView.TryUnsnap());
        if (!unsnapped)
        {
            // Inform the user the application cannot be unsnapped
        }

        return unsnapped;
    }

    // Note: Your app must declare "Pictures Library" in the capabilities
    // of your app's package manifest
    private async void OpenPhotoFromPicturesLibrary()
    {
        if (this.EnsureUnsnapped())
        {
```

```
            FileOpenPicker openPicker = new FileOpenPicker();
            openPicker.ViewMode = PickerViewMode.Thumbnail;
            openPicker.SuggestedStartLocation = PickerLocationId.PicturesLibrary;
            openPicker.FileTypeFilter.ReplaceAll([".jpg", ".jpeg", ".png"]);
            StorageFile file = await openPicker.PickSingleFileAsync();
            if (file != null)
            {
                // Application now has read/write access to the picked file

                // Add the picked file to the MRU list and store token for future access
                profilePicToken =
                StorageApplicationPermissions.MostRecentlyUsedList.Add(file, file.Name);

                // Add the picked file to the future access list and
                // store token for future access
                futureAccessListToken =
                    StorageApplicationPermissions.FutureAccessList.Add(file, file.Name);
            }
            else
            {
                // User canceled the operation
            }
        }
    }


    private async void OpenProfilePhotoFromMRUListAsync()
    {
        StorageFile profilePicFile = await
      StorageApplicationPermissions.MostRecentlyUsedList.GetFileAsync(profilePicToken);
        if (profilePicFile != null)
        {
            // Use it in your app
        }
        else
        {
            // File not in MRU list, pick a file from the Photos library
            OpenPhotoFromPicturesLibrary();
        }
    }


    private async void OpenProfilePhotoFromFutureListAsync()
    {
        StorageFile profilePicFile = await
      StorageApplicationPermissions.FutureAccessList.GetFileAsync(futureAccessListTok
en);
        if (profilePicFile != null)
        {
            // Use it in your app
        }
        else
        {
            // File not in future access list, pick a file from the Photos library
            OpenPhotoFromPicturesLibrary();
        }
    }
}
```

Storing and retrieving data from a remote location

Application data of a Windows Store app is removed whenever it is uninstalled by the user. Therefore, your app should not use the application data store for storing valuable and irreplaceable information. This includes the roaming store, which is also removed after a period of time when the user removes the app from all his devices. A web service or remote data store can be one of the following:

- The user's SkyDrive account
- Windows Azure blob storage
- Windows Azure Mobile Services
- Any other service that provides an API or your own application that stores data from the Windows Store app

When you use file pickers in your application, users are given the option to open files from their SkyDrive account and select a location in SkyDrive to save files created with your application. The files accessed by your app and saved in the user's SkyDrive account are not deleted even after the app is removed.

> **MORE INFO** **SKYDRIVE API AND SOFTWARE DEVELOPMENT KIT (SDK)**
>
> You can read more about the SkyDrive API at *http://msdn.microsoft.com/en-us/library/live/hh826521*. Learn how to reference the Live Connect APIs at *http://msdn.microsoft.com/en-us/library/live/hh826551.aspx*. Download the sample Windows 8 application published by the Microsoft Live Services team at *https://github.com/liveservices/LiveSDK/tree/master/Samples/Windows8/XAML*.

Windows Store app developers can use Windows Azure to build their own data storage and retrieval service. Windows Azure provides blob storage for apps to store files of any type and size. Blob storage can be programmatically accessed using classes in the *Microsoft.WindowsAzure.Storage* namespace.

> **MORE INFO** **WINDOWS AZURE BLOB STORAGE**
>
> A walkthrough of how you can create, download, and delete blobs is available at *http://www.windowsazure.com/en-us/develop/net/how-to-guides/blob-storage/*.

Windows Azure supports storage and manipulation of structured nonrelational data with its table storage service. If your app needs to store large amounts of structured data, you should consider using Windows Azure table storage. A table consists of one or more entities that represent a row in a traditional database, except that tables do not enforce a schema on them. An entity is a set of properties of up to 1 megabyte (MB) in size, and a property is a name-value pair. Each entity holds up to 252 properties to store data. Table storage can be programmatically accessed using classes in the *Microsoft.WindowsAzure.Storage* namespace.

> **MORE INFO**   **WINDOWS AZURE TABLE STORAGE**
>
> A walkthrough of how you can use Windows Azure table storage in Windows Store apps is available at *http://www.windowsazure.com/en-us/develop/net/how-to-guides/table-services/*.

Windows Azure Mobile Services is a Windows Azure service providing Windows Store apps to rapidly and easily include storage, push notifications, and integration with other cloud services. You can use Windows Azure Mobile Services in your app to store structured, nonrelational data using classes available in the *Microsoft.WindowsAzure.MobileServices* namespace.

> **MORE INFO**   **USING MOBILE SERVICES TO STORE DATA**
>
> A detailed walkthrough of storing data in a table using Mobile Services is available at *http://www.windowsazure.com/en-us/develop/mobile/tutorials/get-started-with-data-dotnet/*.

Thought experiment
Developing a data access strategy for a Windows Store app

In this thought experiment, apply what you've learned about this objective. You can find answers to these questions in the "Answers" section at the end of this chapter.

An application deployed in a rugged laptop is used by technicians to analyze faults in data centers. The technicians use the app to refer to a knowledge base of previous faults and their remedies, and use the app to write reports of the faults they find and fix while onsite. The technicians occasionally copy data using the application on a USB flash drive and use the app on the servers. In some cases, log files are copied to a flash drive and uploaded to a central repository using the app.

You have been asked to investigate the feasibility of developing a Windows Store app to incorporate the current set of features and possibly enhance them. What data access strategy would you develop for this app?

Objective summary

- A well-planned data access strategy implemented in a Windows Store app helps with the overall quality and usability of the app.
- Windows Store apps can use local and roaming application data stores for storing settings and files and the temporary data store for caching files.
- WinRT provides APIs for creating and accessing files on the users' devices and their SkyDrive accounts. Windows Store apps can use file and folder pickers to select the location where files can be stored and accessed.
- A set of capabilities and declaration must be configured in the package manifest for an application to access the folders in the user's device.
- Windows Azure provides blob storage for various types of files and table storage for structured, nonrelational data. Windows Store apps can use Windows Azure APIs to store data in the cloud storage.
- Windows Azure Mobile Services can be used to easily integrate table storage, push notifications, and integration with other cloud services in Windows Store apps.

Objective review

Answer the following questions to test your knowledge of the information in this objective. You can find the answers to these questions and explanations of why each answer choice is correct or incorrect in the "Answers" section at the end of this chapter.

1. You are developing a Windows Store app that enables users to download their photos from social networking sites; manipulate them; and share them with friends through email, Twitter, and Facebook. Your app shows a list of photos that the user viewed recently as well as their modified versions. Which file storage options should you use? (Choose all that apply.)

   A. Use the roaming application data store to save the processed files so that they are available on all devices.

   B. Use the temporary application data store to save a copy of the original and processed files.

   C. Use Windows Azure to store processed files and access these files on other devices owned by the user.

   D. Use the roaming application data store to store the list of files accessed recently.

   E. Use your application's install location to store all the files.

2. You have developed a Windows Store app for authors to help them publish their books using various publication services. An author has one or more titles under development at any time. In your application's hub page, a list of recently accessed files is displayed. They are optionally grouped by title and date. What should you implement in your app so that users can quickly access their work?

   A. Use a local database with your application to store the list of files recently accessed.

   B. Use the MRU list and the future access list to store the list of files recently accessed.

   C. Use the roaming application data store to store the list of files recently accessed.

   D. Use the temporary application data store to store the list of files recently accessed.

3. You have developed a Windows Store app that enables a user to read news items. The app uses a subscription-based news feed to fetch news items after the user provides his or her credentials for the service. What is the correct way to use the roaming application data store in such an app?

   A. Store the user's credentials in a file so the app can use it across multiple devices.

   B. Store the most recently read article so that it opens if the reader closed the application while reading the article.

   C. Store the ID of the article being read currently so the ID can be accessed on any other device to open the news item.

   D. Store the top news articles for the day so they are available in all the user's devices.

Objective 5.2: Retrieve data remotely

Many Windows Store apps require content from the web to be available for various features. A connected behavior is important in presenting regular updates from social networks, for example, or for downloading new items from a subscription site.

The *HttpClient* class is useful in implementing features that require data to be transferred in to and out of a Windows Store app. The class supports web services that expect REST verbs to be used in the requests as well as the standard set of HTTP status codes. The *HttpClient* class can be used for secure connections to protect the data being transferred. Windows Communication Foundation (WCF) provides a runtime environment for web services that expose business logic. Simple Object Access Protocol (SOAP) is often used as the communications protocol with these services. WinRT APIs provide support for applications to integrate with such web services. WebSockets provide a mechanism for transporting messages and binary data over HTTP. The protocol implements a two-way handshake which makes it suitable for use in Windows Store apps. WebSockets can be used for server-application communication that involves a simple exchange of data. The *HttpClient* class provides methods for data transfers as well as cancelling all ongoing transfers. For transferring large files and chunks of data that consume significant amount of time, background transfers can be used in Windows Store apps.

Using *HttpClient* to retrieve data from web services

WinRT APIs provide networking features for Windows Store apps with the *HttpClient* class, which is in the *System.Net.Http* namespace. You can use this class to retrieve data from servers located on the Internet or in an intranet. *HttpClient* has a number of methods that help with the implementation of features in Windows Store. In its simplest form, *HttpClient* can be used to read a string, a stream, or an array of bytes from a remote location whose address is specified through a URI. Listing 5-11 shows the *GetStringAsync* method being used to retrieve a string from a remote location.

LISTING 5-11 Using the *GetStringAsync* method with *HttpClient* to retrieve a string remotely

```
using System.Net.Http;

public sealed partial class HttpClientSamplePage : LayoutAwarePage
{
    private async void ReadStringFromRemoteSite(string url)
    {
        try
        {
            // Prepare a HttpClient and issue a request
            HttpClient httpClient = new HttpClient();
            string response = await httpClient.GetStringAsync(url);

            // Display the string
            responseTextBlock.Text = response;
        }
        catch (catch (HttpRequestException hEx)
        {
            statusTextBlock.Text = hEx.ToString();
        }
        catch (Exception ex)
        {
            statusTextBlock.Text = ex.ToString();
        }
    }
}
```

The code does not check for the status of the response received from the remote location. The *HttpResponseMessage* class provides a number of properties and methods that can be used to examine the status of the response received from the remote site. If a failure occurs, you can find out more about it by examining the HTTP status code and reason phrase. The *HttpResponseMessage* object obtained as a result of an HTTP request contains a number of properties that can be used to examine the metadata of the response:

- **Content** This property represents an object of type *HttpContent*. It provides properties to read the content as an array of bytes, a stream, or a string.

- **Headers** The HTTP response headers can be examined with this property.

- **StatusCode** This property indicates the HTTP status code of the HTTP response. Its value is set to a member of the *HttpStatusCode* enumeration.

- **IsSuccessStatusCode** This property indicates whether the HTTP request was successful.

- **ReasonPhrase** This property is used to send the reason for a failure of the HTTP request along with the appropriate status code.

Listing 5-12 shows how the *StatusCode* and *ReasonPhrase* properties of the *HttpResponseMessage* class can be used with the *HttpClient* class to download data from a remote location.

LISTING 5-12 Using *HttpResponseMessage* and *HttpClient* to download remote data

```
using System.Net.Http;

public sealed partial class HttpClientSamplePage : LayoutAwarePage
{
    private async void ReadStringFromRemoteSite(string url)
    {
        try
        {
            // Prepare a HttpClient and issue a request
            HttpClient httpClient = new HttpClient();
            HttpResponseMessage response = await httpClient.GetAsync(url);

            // Raise an exception if the remote server returned an
            // HTTP error status code.
            response.EnsureSuccessStatusCode();

            // Display the status code and reason phrase
            statusTextBlock.Text = response.StatusCode + ", " +
                        response.ReasonPhrase;

            string responseBody = await response.Content.ReadAsStringAsync();

            // Display the string
            responseTextBlock.Text = responseBody;
        }
        catch (HttpRequestException hEx)
        {
            statusTextBlock.Text = hEx.ToString();
        }
        catch (Exception ex)
```

```
        {
            statusTextBlock.Text = ex.ToString();
        }
    }
}
```

In many situations, requests for fetching from remote servers require customizations before they can be sent using the *HttpClient* class. An overload of the constructor of the *Http-Client* class accepts an object of the type *HttpMessageHandler*. Some of the message handlers that can be used with the *HttpClient* class are:

- **HttpClientHandler**   This is the default message handler used by *HttpClient*.

- **MessageProcessingHandler**   This class is used as a base type for HTTP message handlers and should be used to create custom message handlers.

- **DelegatingHandler**   This class is used as a base type for HTTP handlers that are used to delegate the processing of HTTP response messages to another handler. These types of handlers are useful for testing.

The *HttpClientHandler* class, which is in the *System.Net.Http* namespace, has a number of useful properties:

- **Proxy**   This property is used to specify a proxy present in the network that all HTTP requests should use. If specified, the requests bypass the proxy set in the local computer or application's configuration file.

- **Credentials**   This property specifies the authentication information if the remote server requires authentication.

- **UseDefaultCredentials**   This property (a Boolean) is used to force the default credentials to always be sent to the remote server.

- **CookieContainer**   This property provides an instance of the *CookieContainer* class that contains the cookies associated with the handler. The app can set custom cookies through this property before the request is sent to the server.

- **UseCookies**   This property (a Boolean) is used to indicate whether the handler uses the *CookieContainer* property to store server cookies and use them when it sends requests. The default value is *True*.

- **SupportsAutomaticDecompression**   This property (a Boolean) is used to specify whether the handler supports automatic decompression of the content in the response.

- **AutomaticDecompression**   This property is used to specify the decompression method used by the handler for automatic decompression of the content in the HTTP response. The value of this property is set to a member of the *DecompressionMethods* enumeration. The *DecompressionMethods* enumeration enables a bitwise combination of the values *None*, *GZip*, and *Deflate*. The default value of *AutomaticDecompression* property is set to *None*.

- **AllowAutoRedirect**   This property is specified if the handler follows the request from the remote service for redirection. The default value is *True*.

In addition to the properties available in the *HttpClientHandler* class, some properties of the *HttpClient* class can be used to further customize an HTTP request:

- **DefaultRequestHeaders**   This property is used to specify the HTTP request headers in the request sent with the *HttpClient*. A user-agent header can be added using this property to avoid errors when the remote server expects a user-agent header to be set in the HTTP request.

- **MaxResponseContentBufferSize**   This property is used to specify the maximum number of bytes to buffer when reading the content in the HTTP response message. The default value is 2 gigabytes (GB).

- **Timeout**   This property is used to specify the duration in milliseconds that the HTTP request waits before it times out. The default value is 100 seconds.

Listing 5-13 shows how properties of the *HttpClientHandler* and *HttpClient* are used to configure an HTTP request.

LISTING 5-13 Using *HttpClientHandler* and *HttpClient* to configure an HTTP request

```
using System.Net.Http;
public sealed partial class HttpClientSamplePage : LayoutAwarePage
{
    private async void ReadStringFromRemoteSite(string url,
                           string username, string password)
    {
        try
        {
            // Prepare an HttpClientHandler
            HttpClientHandler httpHandler = new HttpClientHandler();
            httpHandler.Credentials = new NetworkCredential(username, password);
            httpHandler.UseDefaultCredentials = false;
            httpHandler.AllowAutoRedirect = false;

            // Prepare an HttpClient and issue a request
            HttpClient httpClient = new HttpClient(httpHandler);

            // Set a timeout of 60 seconds
            httpClient.Timeout = new Timespan(0, 0, 60);

            // Set up the request header
            httpClient.MaxResponseContentBufferSize = 256000;

            // Add a user-agent header
            httpClient.DefaultRequestHeaders.Add("user-agent",
                "Mozilla/5.0 (compatible; MSIE 10.0;
                    Windows NT 6.2; WOW64; Trident/6.0)");

            HttpResponseMessage response = await httpClient.GetAsync(url);

            // Raise an exception if the remote server returned an
            // HTTP error status code.
            response.EnsureSuccessStatusCode();
```

```
            // Display the status code and reason phrase
            statusTextBlock.Text = response.StatusCode + ", " +
                        response.ReasonPhrase;

            string responseBody = await response.Content.ReadAsStringAsync();

            // Display the string
            responseTextBlock.Text = responseBody;
        }
        catch (HttpRequestException hEx)
        {
            statusTextBlock.Text = hEx.ToString();
        }
        catch (Exception ex)
        {
            statusTextBlock.Text = ex.ToString();
        }
    }
}
```

A Windows Store app that uses the *HttpClient* class to connect to a remote server must declare network capabilities in its package manifest. If the app connects to a remote server on the Internet, it must declare the Internet (Client) capability in the manifest. In addition, if the app connects to web services on the home or corporate network, it needs to declare the Private Networks (Client & Server) capability in the manifest. Figure 5-3 shows how to declare the capabilities in Visual Studio.

FIGURE 5-3 Capabilities required for supporting *HttpClient* in a Windows Store app

Setting the appropriate HTTP verb for REST

Representational State Transfer (REST) is an architectural style based on HTTP for exposing data in the web where they can be consumed by a variety of clients on different platforms. REST uses common HTTP verbs such as GET, POST, PUT, and DELETE to access resources on a server and interact with them. An HTTP web service designed in a RESTful way consists of a collection of URIs, each representing a resource with a set of actions defined on them. These actions are specified with an HTTP verb in the outgoing request. Unlike SOAP and other web service implementations, a RESTful web service does not require XML in the request messages.

The *SendAsync* method of the *HttpClient* class can be used to send an HTTP request to a remote web service that implements a RESTful interface. This method requires an *HttpRequestMessage* object that specifies the HTTP verb to use with the request as well as the HTTP headers configured with various items, such as the user-agent. The verb used for preparing the *HttpRequestMessage* is specified as one of the static properties of the *HttpMethod* class:

- **Get**   This represents the HTTP GET verb and is used with HTTP requests to obtain an object from the remote service.

- **Head**   This represents the HTTP HEAD verb and is used to obtain the details of an object with only the headers in the response.

- **Delete**   This represents the HTTP DELETE verb and is used to delete an existing object in the remote service.

- **Post**   This represents the HTTP POST verb and is used to create an object that does not exist in the remote service.

- **Put**   This represents the HTTP PUT verb and is used to update an existing object in the remote service.

- **Options**   This represents the HTTP OPTIONS verb and is used to obtain a list of methods the remote service supports.

- **Trace**   This represents the HTTP TRACE verb and is used to echo the request received by the remote service so that a client can see whether any changes have been made to the original request by servers on the path of the request.

In most cases, you will be working with the GET, POST, PUT, and DELETE HTTP verbs. You should remember that RESTful interfaces define their API for resources. Therefore, if your app must obtain an object from the resource, it should use an HTTP request with the GET verb. If it needs to update an existing object, it has to issue an HTTP request with the PUT verb to a URI that is the location of the object on the server. Listing 5-14 shows an HTTP request with the GET verb used to obtain an item from the recipes collection of a remote service.

LISTING 5-14 Using GET in an HTTP request

```
using System.Net.Http;

public sealed partial class HttpClientSamplePage : LayoutAwarePage
{
    private async void GetRecipeForRecipeIDAsync(string url, string ID)
    {
        try
        {
            // The URL is http://www.contosorecipes.com/recipes/,
            // the ID needs to be appended
            HttpRequestMessage httpRequestMessage = new
                    HttpRequestMessage(HttpMethod.Get, url + ID);

            // Prepare an HttpClient and issue a request
            HttpClient httpClient = new HttpClient();

            // Set up the request header
            httpClient.MaxResponseContentBufferSize = 256000;

            // Add a user-agent header
            httpClient.DefaultRequestHeaders.Add("user-agent",
                "Mozilla/5.0 (compatible; MSIE 10.0; Windows NT 6.2; WOW64;
                        Trident/6.0)");
            HttpResponseMessage response = await
                    httpClient.SendAsync(httpRequestMessage);

            // Raise an exception if the remote server returned an
            // HTTP error status code
            response.EnsureSuccessStatusCode();

            // Display the status code and reason phrase
            statusTextBlock.Text = response.StatusCode + ", " +
                        response.ReasonPhrase;

            string responseBody = await response.Content.ReadAsStringAsync();

            // Display the recipe
            responseTextBlock.Text = responseBody;
        }
        catch (HttpRequestException hEx)
        {
            statusTextBlock.Text = hEx.ToString();
        }
        catch (Exception ex)
        {
            statusTextBlock.Text = ex.ToString();
        }
    }
}
```

WinRT APIs provide a number of utility methods in the *HttpClient* class that can be used for HTTP GET, POST, PUT, and DELETE requests:

- **GetAsync**   This method is used to send an HTTP GET request.

- **DeleteAsync**   This method is used to send an HTTP DELETE request.

- **PostAsync**   This method is used to send an HTTP POST request.

- **PutAsync**   This method is used to send an HTTP PUT request.

These methods make it simpler to prepare and send the most common HTTP requests to RESTful web services. There are several overloads for each of these methods. Listing 5-15 shows how the *GetAsync* method is used to obtain a recipe from a remote service.

LISTING 5-15 Using the *GetAsync* method to retrieve remote data

```
using System.Net.Http;

public sealed partial class HttpClientSamplePage : LayoutAwarePage
{
    private async void GetRecipeForRecipeIDAsync(string url, string ID)
    {
        try
        {
            // Prepare an HttpClient and issue a request
            HttpClient httpClient = new HttpClient();

            // Set up the request header
            httpClient.MaxResponseContentBufferSize = 256000;

            // Add a user-agent header
            httpClient.DefaultRequestHeaders.Add("user-agent",
                "Mozilla/5.0 (compatible; MSIE 10.0; Windows NT 6.2; WOW64;
                        Trident/6.0)");

            // The URL is http://www.contosorecipes.com/recipes/,
            // the ID needs to be appended
            HttpResponseMessage response = await
                    httpClient.GetAsync(url + ID);

            // Raise an exception if the remote server returned an
            // HTTP error status code.
            response.EnsureSuccessStatusCode();

            // Display the status code and reason phrase
            statusTextBlock.Text = response.StatusCode + ", " +
                        response.ReasonPhrase;
```

```
            string responseBody = await response.Content.ReadAsStringAsync();

            // Display the recipe
            responseTextBlock.Text = responseBody;
        }
        catch (HttpRequestException hEx)
        {
            statusTextBlock.Text = hEx.ToString();
        }
        catch (Exception ex)
        {
            statusTextBlock.Text = ex.ToString();
        }
    }
}
```

Consuming SOAP/WCF services

WCF is a framework for developing web services that can be located in the Internet or within an intranet. WCF services use SOAP to exchange messages usually formatted in XML over HTTP or Transmission Control Protocol (TCP) with their interface described in a Web Services Description Language (WSDL) file. Windows Store apps can send asynchronous requests over HTTP to WCF service endpoints.

Visual Studio makes it simple to consume WCF services in Windows Store apps. You can right-click your app, select Add Service Reference from the menu, and add the location of the WCF service, as shown in Figure 5-4.

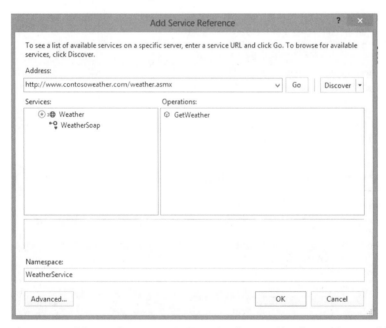

FIGURE 5-4 Adding a reference to a WCF service that provides the weather conditions for a city

After the reference to the WCF service is added successfully, Visual Studio adds the code required to invoke the web service in the Service References folder. The following code queries the weather for a city and displays it in the XAML:

```
protected override async void OnNavigatedTo(NavigationEventArgs e)
{
    WeatherService.WeatherSoapClient client = new WeatherService.WeatherSoapClient();
    WeatherService.GetWeatherResponse response =
                await client.GetWeatherAsync("New York");
        Response.Text = response.Body.GetWeatherResult;
}
```

The response received from the weather service is shown in Figure 5-5.

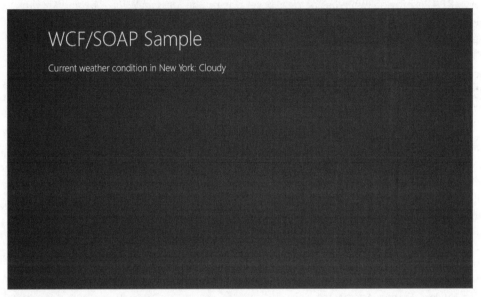

FIGURE 5-5 A Windows Store app showing the weather prediction received from a WCF service

The code generated by Visual Studio when the service reference is added supports only asynchronous requests to the remote service. This ensures the UI remains responsive while data is being fetched.

Using WebSockets for bidirectional communication

In traditional Windows applications requiring network connectivity with a server that stays alive, transporting data over sockets used to be the popular mechanism. With the increasing popularity of web services and the use of HTTP with REST for developing clients to access them, the WebSocket protocol was created to use HTTP to set up the initial connection and use sockets for exchanging data over TCP. Although accessing remote servers over HTTP using a RESTful interface is easier than other options, it does not guarantee that a large amount of data can be reliably delivered to the client or to the server.

The WebSocket protocol specifies a method to exchange data over a fast and secure two-way communications channel in the network between a client and a server. Data can be transferred between the client and server in real time over a single socket in both directions. Examples of Windows Store apps that benefit from WebSockets are games and dashboards displaying stock quotes or weather information.

In the setup stage of the connection between the client and a server, an HTTP-based handshake is exchanged between the two parties. If the handshake is successful, WebSockets is used as the application protocol instead of HTTP using the same TCP connection. After the WebSockets connection is established, HTTP is no longer involved. Either party can close the WebSockets connection at any time. To use WebSockets, the server must support WebSockets.

WinRT APIs provide two types of WebSocket classes: the *MessageWebSocket* and *StreamWebSocket* in the *Windows.Networking.Sockets* namespace. The *MessageWebSocket* class is useful when the data exchanged is not large, and the message can be either in the UTF-8 or binary format. It also provides a notification that an entire WebSocket message has been received. The *StreamWebSocket* class is useful when a large amount of data, such as photos or movies, needs to be transferred. It supports messages in the binary format only, and sections of a message can be read with each read operation.

The WebSocket protocol specifies two URI schemes: *ws:* for all unencrypted communications, and *wss:* for all secure communications that should be encrypted. The *ConnectAsync* method of both the WebSocket classes expect the URI of the remote server to be specified with the *ws:* as the URL prefix for unencrypted connections and *wss:* as the URL prefix for encrypted connections. The C# code in Listing 5-16 shows how the *MessageWebSocket* class can be used to send data to the server and be notified that the message sent was received by the server.

LISTING 5-16 Using the *MessageWebSocket* class to send data to a server and receive confirmation

```
using Windows.Networking.Sockets;
using Windows.Storage.Streams;
using Windows.Web;

public sealed partial class WebSocketsSamplePage : LayoutAwarePage
{
    private MessageWebSocket messageWebSocket;
    private DataWriter messageWriter;

    private async void SendMessageToRemoteServer(string url, string message)
    {
        try
        {
            // Make a local copy to avoid races with Closed event. This avoids the
            // socket from being closed when the app is trying to send a message
            // to the server.
            MessageWebSocket webSocket = messageWebSocket;

            if (webSocket == null)
            {
                // Set up connection
```

```
                Uri server = new Uri(url);
                webSocket = new MessageWebSocket();

                // Set up the MessageWebSocket to UTF-8 format
                webSocket.Control.MessageType = SocketMessageType.Utf8;

                // Set up callbacks
                webSocket.MessageReceived += MessageReceived;
                webSocket.Closed += Closed;

                // Connect and store a copy of the websocket
                await webSocket.ConnectAsync(server);
                messageWebSocket = webSocket;

                messageWriter = new DataWriter(webSocket.OutputStream);
            }

            // Buffer the data being sent
            messageWriter.WriteString(message);

            // Send the data as one complete message
            await messageWriter.StoreAsync();
        }
        catch (Exception ex)
        {
            WebErrorStatus status =
                WebSocketError.GetStatus(ex.GetBaseException().HResult);
            // Handle the error
        }
    }

    private void MessageReceived(MessageWebSocket sender,
            MessageWebSocketMessageReceivedEventArgs args)
    {
        try
        {
            using (DataReader reader = args.GetDataReader())
            {
                reader.UnicodeEncoding = Windows.Storage.Streams.UnicodeEncoding.Utf8;
                string read = reader.ReadString(reader.UnconsumedBufferLength);
            }
        }
        catch (Exception ex) // For debugging
        {
            WebErrorStatus status =
                WebSocketError.GetStatus(ex.GetBaseException().HResult);

            // Handle the error
        }
    }

    private void Closed(IWebSocket sender, WebSocketClosedEventArgs args)
    {
        // This is invoked on another thread so use Interlocked.Exchange
        // to avoid race conditions with the Start/Close/Reset methods.
```

```
            MessageWebSocket webSocket = Interlocked.Exchange(ref messageWebSocket, null);
            if (webSocket != null)
            {
                webSocket.Dispose();
            }
        }
    }
}
```

The *StreamWebSocket* class can be used to exchange large files in the binary format. It provides a *Closed* event when a close packet is received as part of closing the socket after the exchange. Listing 5-17 shows how a *StreamWebSocket* class is used to exchange data with the server.

LISTING 5-17 Using the *StreamWebSocket* class to exchange data with a server

```
using Windows.Networking.Sockets;
using Windows.Web;

public sealed partial class WebSocketsSamplePage : LayoutAwarePage
{
    private StreamWebSocket streamWebSocket;
    private byte[] readBuffer;

    private async void SendMessageToRemoteServer(string url, string message)
    {
        try
        {
            // Make a local copy to avoid races with the Closed event. This avoids the
            // socket from being closed when the app is trying to send a message
            // to the server.
            StreamWebSocket webSocket = streamWebSocket;

            if (webSocket != null)
            {
                // Set up connection
                Uri server = new Uri(url);
                webSocket = new StreamWebSocket();
                webSocket.Closed += Closed;

                // Connect and store a copy of the websocket
                await webSocket.ConnectAsync(server);
                streamWebSocket = webSocket;

                readBuffer = new byte[2048];

                // Start a background task to continuously read for incoming data
                Task receiving = Task.Factory.StartNew(ReceiveData,
                                    webSocket.InputStream.AsStreamForRead(),
                                    TaskCreationOptions.LongRunning);

                // Start a background task to continuously write outgoing data
                Task sending = Task.Factory.StartNew(SendData,
                            webSocket.OutputStream, TaskCreationOptions.LongRunning);
            }
        }
```

```
        catch (Exception ex)
        {
            WebErrorStatus status =
                    WebSocketError.GetStatus(ex.GetBaseException().HResult);
            // Handle the error
        }
}

// Send data to the server
private async void SendData(object state)
{
    int dataSent = 0;
    byte[] data = new byte[] { 0x00, 0x01, 0x02, 0x03, 0x04,
                               0x05, 0x06, 0x07, 0x08, 0x09 };

    try
    {
        IOutputStream writeStream = (IOutputStream)state;

        // Send until the socket gets closed/stopped
        while (true)
        {
            // using System.Runtime.InteropServices.WindowsRuntime;
            await writeStream.WriteAsync(data.AsBuffer());

            dataSent += data.Length;

            // Display the data in the DataSentField TextBlock
            MarshalText(DataSentField, dataSent.ToString(), false);

            // Delay so the user can watch what's going on.
            await Task.Delay(TimeSpan.FromSeconds(1));
        }
    }
    catch (ObjectDisposedException)
    {
        // Display a message that the write has stopped, or take a specific action
    }
    catch (Exception ex)
    {
        WebErrorStatus status =
            WebSocketError.GetStatus(ex.GetBaseException().HResult);

        // Handle the error
    }
}

// Read data received from the server
private async void ReceiveData(object state)
{
    int bytesReceived = 0;
    try
    {
        Stream readStream = (Stream)state;
        while (true) // Until closed and ReadAsync fails.
        {
```

```
                int read = await readStream.ReadAsync(readBuffer, 0, readBuffer.Length);
                bytesReceived += read;

                // Display the data in the DataReceivedField TextBlock
                MarshalText(DataReceivedField, bytesReceived.ToString(), false);

                // Do something with the data.
            }
        }
        catch (ObjectDisposedException)
        {
            // Display a message that the read has stopped, or take a specific action
        }
        catch (Exception ex)
        {
            WebErrorStatus status =
                    WebSocketError.GetStatus(ex.GetBaseException().HResult);

            // Handle the error
        }
    }

    private void Closed(IWebSocket sender, WebSocketClosedEventArgs args)
    {
        // This is invoked on another thread so use Interlocked
        // to avoid races with the Start/Close/Reset methods.
        StreamWebSocket webSocket = Interlocked.Exchange(ref streamWebSocket, null);
        if (webSocket != null)
        {
            webSocket.Dispose();
        }
    }

    // When operations happen on a background thread, need to
    // marshal UI updates back to the UI thread.
    private void MarshalText(TextBox output, string value, bool append)
    {
        var ignore =
         output.Dispatcher.RunAsync(Windows.UI.Core.CoreDispatcherPriority.Normal, () =>
        {
            if (append)
            {
                output.Text += value;
            }
            else
            {
                output.Text = value;
            }
        });
    }
}
```

Exceptions raised during data exchange by either the *MessageWebSocket* or *StreamWeb-Socket* class can be examined to determine the type of error. The *WebSocketError* class (in the

Windows.Networking.Sockets namespace) provides the method *GetStatus*, which returns a member of the *WebErrorStatus* enumeration to indicate the type of error.

MORE INFO   **MEMBERS OF THE *WEBERRORSTATUS* ENUMERATION**

The list of members of the *WebErrorStatus* enumeration is available at *http://msdn. microsoft.com/en-au/library/windows/apps/windows.web.weberrorstatus.*

Some Windows Store apps require secure WebSocket connections with Transport Layer Security (TLS)/Secure Sockets Layer (SSL) for exchanging data. To encrypt a WebSocket connection, you should use the *wss:* URI scheme as shown in the following C# example:

```
private async void SendDataToServer(string message)
{
    webSocket = new MessageWebSocket();
    await WebSocket.ConnectAsync("wss://www.example.com");
}
```

Both the *MessageWebSocket* and *StreamWebSocket* classes have companion classes (*MessageWebSocketControl* and *StreamWebSocketControl*, respectively) that provide properties for advanced configuration of the WebSocket classes such as the size of the buffer to be used for sending data, the credential to use for authentication with a proxy and the credential to use for authentication with the server. You can use the *Control* property in the WebSocket classes to access and set these properties to the values you require.

MORE INFO   **ADVANCED CONTROL OF THE WEBSOCKET CLASSES**

You can read more about advanced control of the WebSocket classes at *http://msdn.microsoft.com/library/windows/apps/hh994400.*

To use either the *MessageWebSocket* class or the *StreamWebSocket* class in your Windows Store app, you must ensure that the right set of capabilities is declared in the package manifest file. The capabilities required for WebSocket communications are *Internet (Client & Server)* for bidirectional communications with servers in the Internet, and *Private Networks (Client & Server)* for bidirectional communications with servers located in the user's trusted places, such as home and work.

Handling the progress of data requests

Some Windows Store apps need to control the progress of data requests sent to remote web services. Whereas some apps examine the HTTP response headers before they use the content in them, other apps cancel, HTTP requests before any response is received.

An overload of the *GetAsync* and *SendAsync* methods of the *HttpClient* class accepts a parameter of type *HttpCompletionOption*. *HttpCompletionOption* is an enumeration with the following members:

- **ResponseHeadersRead** This specifies that the *HttpClient* object will return a response as soon as the HTTP headers have been read before the payload is read.

- **ResponseContentRead** This specifies that the *HttpClient* object will return a response as soon as the HTTP headers and the payload are both available.

By adding the *ResponseHeadersRead* option in the *HttpClient* object, an *HttpResponseMessage* is available as soon as the HTTP readers have been read before the payload is available. You can examine the HTTP headers for the content type and size before consuming the payload. An app can start preparing for the content to be displayed after the headers have been examined. Listing 5-18 shows how the *HttpCompletionOption* is used with the *GetAsync* method in C#.

LISTING 5-18 Using the *GetAsync* method with the *HttpCompletionOption*

```
using System.Net.Http;

public sealed partial class HttpClientSamplePage : LayoutAwarePage
{
    private async void ReadMessageFromServer(string url)
    {
        try
        {
            // Prepare a HttpClient and issue a request
            HttpClient httpClient = new HttpClient();

            // Add a user-agent header
            httpClient.DefaultRequestHeaders.Add("user-agent",
                "Mozilla/5.0 (compatible; MSIE 10.0;
                    Windows NT 6.2; WOW64; Trident/6.0)");

            HttpResponseMessage response = await httpClient.GetAsync(url,
                    HttpCompletionOption.ResponseHeadersRead);

            // Raise an exception if the remote server returned an
            // HTTP error status code.
            response.EnsureSuccessStatusCode();

            // You can prepare the UI for displaying the content

            // Payload is available now
            string responseBody = await response.Content.ReadAsStringAsync();

            // Display the string, content is available
            responseTextBlock.Text = responseBody;
        }
        catch (HttpRequestException hEx)
        {
            statusTextBlock.Text = hEx.ToString();
        }
        catch (Exception ex)
        {
```

```
            statusTextBlock.Text = ex.ToString();
        }
    }
}
```

The *HttpClient* class provides the *Timeout* property, which can be used to set a timeout on the outgoing HTTP request, the default being 100 seconds. An instance of *HttpClient* can cancel all pending requests with the *CancelPendingRequests* method, and the same instance can still create and send new HTTP requests. The *GetAsync*, *DeleteAsync*, *PostAsync*, *PutAsync*, and *SendAsync* methods can be provided with a *CancellationToken* that enables calling objects to receive a notification if an HTTP request is canceled.

MORE INFO   **CANCELLATION OF ASYNCHRONOUS OPERATIONS**

You can read more about cancellation of asynchronous operations in the article at *http://msdn.microsoft.com/en-au/library/dd997364.aspx*.

Thought experiment
Designing an enterprise app's architecture

In this thought experiment, apply what you've learned about this objective. You can find answers to these questions in the "Answers" section at the end of this chapter.

A digital media publications company with multiple offices around the world is developing a Windows Store app. It will be used by employees in their offices as well as from temporary locations.

Employees create digital media and store them in the server. They can access the work of their colleagues by browsing the internal collaboration site. A user in the system is authenticated over a secure connection before they can perform any activities. The server fully supports WebSockets for communications and exposes a RESTful HTTP web services for access to the resources.

What are your recommendations for implementing the following features in the organization's Windows Store app?

1. Users must be authenticated with the system over a secure connection to the server.

2. Users can examine the media created by their colleagues by browsing through various lists.

3. Users can upload and download media files over a secure connection to the server.

Objective summary

- You can use the *HttpClient* class to retrieve data from remote servers. You can set additional properties in the request to control its behavior.
- HTTP verbs such as GET, POST, PUT, and DELETE can be used to retrieve and update resources in a remote server.
- Windows Store apps can reference WCF services and use methods exposed by the services to carry out operations such as requesting data.
- WebSockets provide a simple yet powerful method of communications between a Windows Store app and a server that supports WebSockets.
- You can use MessageWebSockets in scenarios where relatively small messages in either UTF-8 or binary format are exchanged between the client and server.
- You can use StreamWebSockets for exchanging large messages in the binary format between the client and the server.
- The progress of data requests can be controlled by examining the HTTP headers first and then reading the payload; requests can be canceled if necessary.

Objective review

Answer the following questions to test your knowledge of the information in this objective. You can find the answers to these questions and explanations of why each answer choice is correct or incorrect in the "Answers" section at the end of this chapter.

1. You are developing a Windows Store app that requires data to be downloaded from a remote server. The server enables secure connections from browsers and other clients only with the user-agent present in the request header. The data is a string never exceeding 1 KB. What is the best way to implement this requirement in your app?

   A. Use Windows sockets over TCP to create and send requests to the server.

   B. Create a request, encrypt it, and send it to the server using Windows sockets over TCP.

   C. Use an *HttpClient* with its user-agent set in its *DefaultRequestHeaders* property and a URL with *https://* prefix.

   D. Use a *StreamWebSocket* to send the request to a URL with the *https://* prefix.

2. A Windows Store app requires data to be downloaded from a remote server and displayed as content. The app has to be responsive while content is being downloaded. The server can send various types of messages with varying sizes on a connection that is prone to timeouts. It uses HTTP response headers to provide the meta information on the payload contained in the response. How will you implement this requirement in your app? (Choose all that apply.)

   A. Use the *HttpCompletionOption* of the *HttpClient* class set to *ResponseHeadersRead*, read the headers, and then decide whether the expected content type is present in the payload.

   B. Use the *MaxResponseContentBufferSize* in the *HttpClient* object to set a maximum size on the buffer while reading the payload.

   C. Use sockets over TCP for an always-on connection. This will allow your app to parse every response from the server and use the ones that are required.

   D. Set a timeout value to control the time your app needs to wait before the request times out.

   E. Use MessageWebSockets to receive data from the server. Parse the data in the *MessageReceived* handler and use it in your app.

3. A popular multi-player game available in other platforms is being ported to Windows 8. You are asked to implement the features that will enable the app to exchange various kinds of data with a high-performance gaming server. Which options will you use to implement this requirement in the app? (Choose all that apply.)

   A. Use the *HttpClient* with a long timeout to download all data after authentication.

   B. Use sockets over TCP with data encrypted by your app.

   C. Use *HttpClient* to authenticate the user over SSL using a URL with an *https://* prefix.

   D. Use a *MessageWebSocket* to exchange player moves and scores with the server.

   E. Use a *StreamWebSocket* to download updates for the game whenever they are available on the server.

Objective 5.3: Implement data binding

Data binding is a powerful technique that simplifies the process of adding data to the presentation layer of a Windows Store. Traditionally, applications would iterate through a collection of data items and add each item to a control in the UI using code. This meant regular updates to code as requirements of the UI changed or the dataset itself changed. Data binding decouples the data model from the view, enabling updates in the data to appear in the view and vice versa.

WinRT APIs support data binding in common controls through markup extensions in XAML. The connection between a control and its data source is expressed as a declaration in the XAML of the user interface. Data binding enables data from controls within the same page to be bound to other controls. It also supports binding of a control to a specific property or path within a collection or data context. Item controls enable a collection of items to be bound so that they are displayed as a list in the user interface. *ItemsControl* can be used to bind collections and customize the way the data is displayed in the user interface. *ItemsControl* provides a good starting point to create your own data controls for Windows Store apps.

Items in a data collection that are bound to a data control can be modified using value converters. In addition, values entered by a user in a data control can be converted to suit the format supported by the data source. Typically, a class is created by implementing the *IValueConverter* interface to convert the format of data between the source and the target. Value converters are handy for modifying data for specific source-target pairs, such as the visibility of a control based on the value of a Boolean.

Dependency properties are central in the data binding mechanism. A dependency property is a special type of property, the value of which is obtained from other sources. These sources can include values of controls, user input, values from parent-child relationships in the user interface, and similar items. Dependency properties extend basic properties by providing a property wrapper instead of a private field that usually backs a basic property. You can create your own dependency properties and use them in data binding of controls through XAML.

Validation of data entered by the user is an important step before the data is used in the data model. Validation is typically implemented in the viewmodel in the Model-View-ViewModel (MVVM) architecture. The *INotifyDataErrorInfo* interface can be used to implement custom synchronous and asynchronous validation for user input. Filtering, grouping, and data sorting can be implemented through the data collection that is bound to a data collection in the user interface. The *CollectionViewSource* class supports filtering, grouping, and data sorting for presentation in the user interface.

This objective covers how to:

- Choose and implement data-bound controls.
- Bind collections to items controls.
- Implement the *IValueConverter* interface.
- Create and set dependency properties.
- Validate user input.
- Enable filtering, grouping, and sorting data in the user interface.

Choosing and implementing data-bound controls

Data binding is a method available for Windows Store apps to display and interact with data. It provides a connection between a binding source, usually a data source, and a binding target, which is a UI element in the presentation layer. The connection is made with an object of the type *Binding*, which implements the logic to move data between the target and source, and is modified with an optional converter.

A binding source can be a simple common language runtime (CLR) object including the target element as well as other UI elements. Classes defined in C# and Visual Basic produce CLR objects, so they can act as the binding source. In addition, WinRT objects that implement the *ICustomPropertyProvider* or have a *BindableAttribute* can be a source for data binding.

A binding target is a *DependencyProperty* of a *FrameworkElement*, a class that helps with the behavior and layout of UI elements. The dependency property framework provides a way to express the value of a property of an object that depends on the value of one or more other properties. In WinRT, classes that participate in the dependency property system must derive from the *DependencyObject* base class. Classes that derive from the *DependencyObject* class can define one or more dependency properties that help in data binding.

The data binding framework obtains information from the *Binding* object about the source and target objects; the direction of the data flow between the source and target; and a value converter, if used. Data binding is commonly set up in XAML or with the *SetBinding* method of the *FrameworkElement* class.

The *Binding* class provides a number of properties commonly used to declare the data binding in a UI element through XAML:

- **ElementName**   This property is used to set the source for the binding to an element in the UI.
- **Source**   This property is used to set the data source for the binding.
- **RelativeSource**   This property is used to set the source for the binding, specifying a location that is relative to the location of the binding target.
- **Path**   This property is used to specify a property in the data source as the binding's source. For example, if the data source is specified with the *Source* property in the binding, the *Path* property can be used to refer to a property in the data source. You can omit this in the XAML declaration of the binding, as shown in Listing 5-19.
- **Converter**   This property is used to specify a converter object that is used by the binding framework to modify the data as it flows between the target and the source.
- **ConverterParameter**   This property is used to specify a parameter used by the converter specified for the binding.
- **ConverterLanguage**   This property is used to specify a language for the converter object, if specified for the binding with the *Converter* property. The default value of this property is the current language of the application context.

- **Mode**   This property is used to specify the direction of the data flow in the binding. The value of the property is set to one of the members of the *BindingMode* enumeration.

Setting up the data binding in the UI of a Windows Store app requires the details of the data source as well as the direction of the flow of data. In some UI elements, you expect data to be presented as a read-only value; in other elements, you expect the user to interact with the data and update it. The direction of data flow in binding is specified with the *BindingMode* enumeration, which has the following members:

- **OneWay**   In this mode, the target property is set with the value from the source when the binding is created and updated when the source changes. This is the default value for the *Mode* property of a *Binding* object.

- **OneTime**   In this mode, the target property is set with the value from the source when the binding is created. The target property is not updated after the binding is created.

- **TwoWay**   In this mode, the target property is set with the value from the source when the binding is created. Data binding updates the target or the source when either the source or target changes.

The XAML code in Listing 5-19 shows the *Text* property of a *TextBlock* control set to the *FirstName* property of a binding object in the default *OneWay* binding mode. It also shows the *Foreground* property set to the *UserName* property of a *Binding* object with the mode set to *OneTime*.

LISTING 5-19 Using the default *OneWay* and *OneTime* binding modes

```
<TextBlock x:Name="FirstNameTextBlock" Text="{Binding FirstName}"
           Foreground="{Binding UserNameBrush, Mode=OneTime}"/>
```

An important concept in data binding is data context. If a data source is set as the data context of a UI element, all its children inherit the data context. In Listing 5-19, the *Binding* object is set in the code-behind through the data context. The data context of a *FrameworkElement* is specified using an object of the type *DataContext*. The children and descendants of the *FrameworkElement* inherit the value of the *DataContext*. For example, in a grid with a number of controls, their *DataContext* property is set to the data context of the grid. Setting a value in the *DataContext* is particularly useful when a collection of objects needs to bind to a control.

Changes in the source of a data-bound control are propagated to the target if the direction of the data flow is either *OneWay* or *TwoWay*. For the changes in the source to propagate to the target, the source must implement the *INotifyPropertyChanged* interface. The *INotifyPropertyChanged* interface has a single event: *PropertyChanged*. This event is used by the source to notify targets that the value of the property has changed. Listing 5-20 shows a sample implementation of the *INotifyPropertyChanged* interface.

LISTING 5-20 Implementing the *INotifyPropertyChanged* interface

```
using System.ComponentModel;
using Windows.UI.Xaml.Media;

// Create a class that implements INotifyPropertyChanged.
public class ForegroundColorBrush : INotifyPropertyChanged
{
    private SolidColorBrush _userNameBrush;

    // Declare the PropertyChanged event.
    public event PropertyChangedEventHandler PropertyChanged;

    // Create the property that will be the source of the binding.
    public SolidColorBrush UserNameBrush
    {
        get { return _userNameBrush; }
        set
        {
            if (_userNameBrush != value)
            {
                _userNameBrush = value;

                // Call NotifyPropertyChanged when the source property
                // is updated.
                NotifyPropertyChanged("UserNameBrush");
            }
        }
    }

    // NotifyPropertyChanged will raise the PropertyChanged event,
    // passing the source property that is being updated.
    private void NotifyPropertyChanged(string propertyName)
    {
        if (PropertyChanged != null)
        {
            PropertyChanged(this,
                new PropertyChangedEventArgs(propertyName));
        }
    }
}
```

An instance of the *ForegroundColorBrush* class can be used as the data source for the *Foreground* property of a *TextBlock,* as shown in the XAML. The data context for the *TextBlock* is set up in the code-behind of the page where the UI element is laid out. This is shown in the following C# code:

```
using Windows.UI.Xaml.Media;

public sealed partial class XAMLBindingDemoPage : LayoutAwarePage
{
    public XAMLBindingDemoPage()
    {
        ForegroundColorBrush textBlockBrush = new ForegroundColorBrush();
        textBlockBrush.UserNameBrush = new SolidColorBrush(Colors.Blue);
```

```
        FirstNameTextBlock.DataContext = textBlockBrush;
    }
}
```

In addition to binding to objects that implement the *INotifyPropertyChanged* interface, UI elements can bind to properties of other UI elements in a page of a Windows Store app. In the following XAML code, a text block's *Text* property is bound to the *Value* property of a *Slider* control:

```
<StackPanel Orientation="Vertical">
    <Slider x:Name="sliderTwoWayDataSource" Width="180"
            Minimum="1" Maximum="100" Value="50" />
    <TextBox x:Name="tbTwoWayDataBound" Width="150"
            Text="{Binding ElementName=sliderTwoWayDataSource,
                    Path=Value, Mode=TwoWay}" />
</StackPanel>
```

Binding collections to items controls

In addition to the controls that can be data bound to a dependency property of a *FrameworkElement*, WinRT APIs provide controls that can be bound to a collection of data. The data source in such cases is a list that implements the *IEnumerable* interface. These controls are commonly called items controls. They derive from the *ItemsControl* class.

The *ItemsControl* can be used in XAML as a control to display a list of items. You can use its *Items* property to specify a collection of objects that contains text blocks and buttons, for example. The following sample XAML shows the *Items* property of an *ItemsControl* used to arrange collection of other UI elements:

```
<ItemsControl Width="400" HorizontalAlignment="Left">
    <ItemsControl.Items>
        <TextBlock Text="Collection of items" Style="{StaticResource
                                                GroupHeaderTextStyle}" />
        <Rectangle Height="40" Width="360" Fill="Red" Margin="0,20,0,0"
                                        HorizontalAlignment="Left"/>
        <TextBox Text="Input here" Margin="0,20,0,0" FontSize="28" Height="50"
                                Width="360" HorizontalAlignment="Left"/>
        <Button Content="Submit" FontSize="22" Margin="0,20,0,0"
                                HorizontalAlignment="Center" />
    </ItemsControl.Items>
</ItemsControl>
```

Figure 5-6 shows the UI elements laid out in the *ItemsControl* control as set up in the XAML sample.

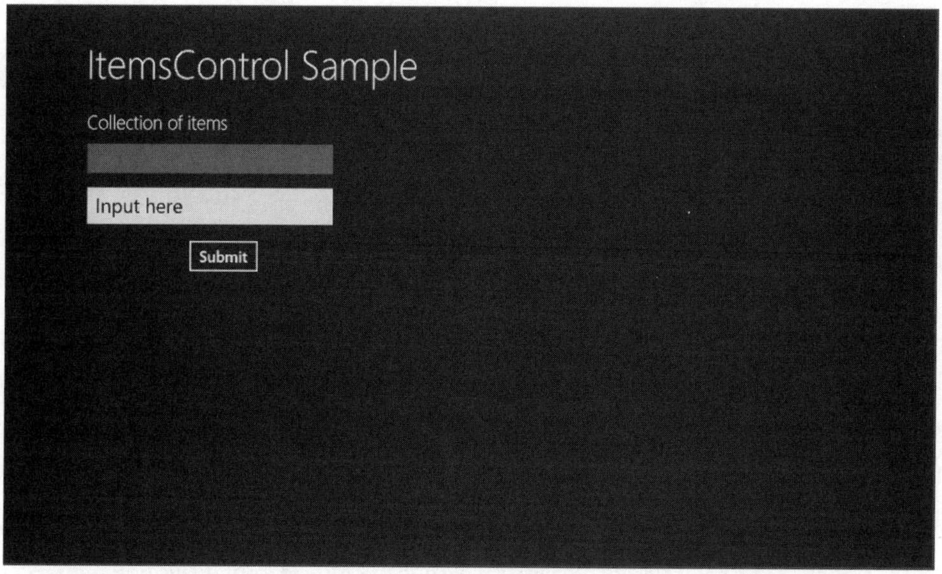

FIGURE 5-6 A Windows Store app with a list of UI elements laid out in an *ItemsControl*

The *Items* property of the *ItemsControl* class specifies the collection of items used to generate the content of the control. The *Items* property is of the type *ItemCollection* class, which holds a list of items.

> **MORE INFO   ITEMCOLLECTION CLASS**
>
> You can read more about the *ItemCollection* class at *http://msdn.microsoft.com/en-us/library/windows/apps/xaml/windows.ui.xaml.controls.itemcollection.aspx*.

You can use the *ItemsSource* property of the *ItemsControl* class to set a collection of data as the data source for the control. The collection is an instance of a class that implements the *IEnumerable* interface. Note that you can use either the *Items* property or the *ItemsSource* property only. If you use the *ItemsSource* property, you cannot modify the collection using the *Items* property. When you bind a control to a whole object in the code-behind, there is no need to specify a value for the *Path* property. A simple example of an *ItemsControl* used to display a list of persons is shown in the following XAML code:

```
<ItemsControl x:Name="PersonsList" ItemsSource="{Binding}" />
```

ItemsControl is a useful control that can display a static collection of items. In many Windows Store apps, you want the user to interact with the items in a collection. For example, a user can select one or more items from a collection and mark them as favorite items. Users can also choose an item from a collection to view details typically displayed in a details page. In such cases, controls that derive from the *Selector* class are used to display a collection of items. The *Selector* class derives from the *ItemsControl* class and adds the *SelectionChanged* event. This event is raised whenever the user selects an item from the collection.

There are a number of controls that bind to a collection and enable users to select one or more items from the collection:

- **ComboBox**   This control displays a list of items in a collection, with only one item visible at any time. The user can select a single item from the collection.

- **ListBox**   This control displays items in a collection to fill its dimensions. If all the items cannot be displayed within the bounds of the control, the user can scroll and view the collection. The *ListBox* control supports multiple selections of items from the displayed list. Users can use the Shift key on their keyboard to select multiple items in sequence or the Control key to select multiple items from anywhere within the list.

- **ListView**   This control is similar to the *ListBox* control. It is friendlier for touch-based devices with the support for the cross-slide gesture as well as the right-tap to select an item from the list. Items in a *ListView* are laid out vertically with a scrollbar visible in certain conditions.

- **GridView**   This control is identical to the *ListView* control, except it lays out items in a horizontal direction. They both derive from the *ListViewBase* class.

- **FlipView**   This control is designed to show one item at a time from a collection. The *FlipView* control provides users with the effect of flipping through the collection, similar to reading a book or viewing a photo album.

The *ItemsControl* class provides a number of properties to customize the layout and display of items in the item controls listed previously:

- **ItemContainerStyle**   This property sets the style for rendering an item in the collection. The value of this property is set to a style that is used to customize the visual properties of the item container. For example, the *Style* property of a *GridView* control is set through the *ItemContainerStyle*, which is meant to customize each *GridViewItem* that displays an item from the collection.

- **ItemContainerStyleSelector**   This property sets the logic to select a specific *ItemContainerStyle* based on the characteristics of the item being displayed from the collection.

- **ItemsPanel**   This property sets the panel that is used to lay out the items from the collection. The value of this property is an *ItemsPanelTemplate* object, which can have one or more child elements that define the panel layout.

- **ItemTemplate**   This property sets the data template to display an item from the collection. A *DataTemplate* object has one or more child elements that are used to define the visual appearance of an item. For example, in a *GridView* that binds to a collection of movies, it can consist of an *Image* control for the thumbnail and a *TextBlock* control to display the title of the movie.

- **ItemTemplateSelector**   This property sets the logic to select a specific *DataTemplate* data template based on the characteristics of the item being displayed.

To bind a collection to an *ItemsControl* object, you should use the *ItemTemplate* property to specify the data template used in binding of each piece of data from the binding source and the *ItemsPanel* property to specify the layout of items in the user interface. The following XAML code shows a *GridView* control used to display a collection of items with its *ItemTemplate* and *ItemsPanel* properties used to configure the data binding of each item and their layout:

```xml
<GridView ItemsSource="{Binding}" MaxHeight="500">
    <GridView.ItemTemplate>
        <DataTemplate>
            <StackPanel Margin="20">
                <TextBlock Text="{Binding Name}" FontWeight="Bold" />
                <TextBlock Text="{Binding BirthDate}"/>
            </StackPanel>
        </DataTemplate>
    </GridView.ItemTemplate>
    <GridView.ItemsPanel>
        <ItemsPanelTemplate>
            <WrapGrid ItemWidth="145" ItemHeight="70"
                    MaximumRowsOrColumns="1"
                    VerticalChildrenAlignment="Center" />
        </ItemsPanelTemplate>
    </GridView.ItemsPanel>
</GridView>
```

The data source of an item control can change over time. The user expects the UI to update automatically instead of having to click a refresh button on the app bar or on the screen. In such cases, instead of binding to a collection that implements the *IEnumerable* interface, the item control should bind to an *ObservableCollection* or an object that implements the *IList* and *INotifyCollectionChanged* interfaces. The *CollectionChanged* event of the *ObservableCollection* class can be used to inform the user when an item is added, removed, changed, or moved; or if the collection is refreshed.

In some data sources, items can be added progressively or, to optimize the loading process, the business logic of a Windows Store app can request data to be loaded in the collection incrementally. In such cases, the *ObservableCollection* class can be extended with your own class that implements the *ISupportIncrementalLoading* interface. For example, the response from a remote web service can contain a certain number of items as well as a flag to indicate whether there are more items available. In addition, you have to implement the *HasMoreItems* property that returns a Boolean to indicate whether there are more items to load and the *LoadMoreItemsAsync* method to load the specified number of items from the source, for the *ISupportIncrementalLoading* interface. The item control uses the *HasMoreItems* property to find out whether there are more items to be loaded. If this property is *False*, it does not invoke the *LoadMoreItemsAsync* method to load more data.

Implementing the *IValueConverter* interface

Think of data binding as the glue that binds the source of data with a target. In some cases, there is a need to control the connection between the source and the target (for example, when the value of a data member crosses a threshold, the control bound to the data member can show a different color). Although it seems that the connection between the source and the data is very rigid, there is a way to control this connection.

WinRT APIs provide the *IValueConverter* interface that, when implemented in a class, enables the conversion of data between the source and the target. The *IValueConverter* interface defines two methods that must be implemented in a converter class:

- **Convert** This method is called before the data from the source is passed to the target for displaying it in the user interface.

- **ConvertBack** This method is called before the data from the UI is passed to the source for storage or updates. This method is called only in *TwoWay* data bindings.

Using the *ConverterParameter* XAML binding property for a converter, you can provide a parameter for both the *Convert* and *ConvertBack* methods. This parameter is useful when the conversion requires an additional value such as the format of a date for the target or a value such as a threshold to compare the source with.

Listing 5-21 shows a converter class that converts a *DateTime* object to a value displayed in the user interface.

LISTING 5-21 Using a converter class to implement the *IValueConverter* interface

```
public class BirthDateFormatter : IValueConverter
{
    // This method converts the date of birth of the user to
    // a format specified by the ConverterParameter in XAML.
    public object Convert(object value, Type targetType,
                    object parameter, string language)
    {
        // Retrieve the format string and use it to format the value.
        string formatString = parameter as string;
        if (!string.IsNullOrEmpty(formatString))
        {
            return string.Format(
                new CultureInfo(language), formatString, value);
        }

        // If the format string is null or empty, simply call ToString()
        // on the value.
        return value.ToString();
    }

    // Implementing one-way binding, no need to implement this method
    public object ConvertBack(object value, Type targetType,
        object parameter, string language)
    {
        throw new NotImplementedException();
    }
}
```

The converter class in Listing 5-21 formats the date of birth of employees in the language of the app's context. This value is not modified, so the *ConvertBack* method is not implemented. The format of the string displayed in the UI is specified in XAML in Listing 5-22.

LISTING 5-22 Formatting a string in an app using a converter class

```
<Grid x:Name="LayoutRoot">
    <Grid.Resources>
        <!-- "local" is the namespace of value converter class -->
        <local:BirthDateFormatter x:Key="birthDateFormatter" />
    </Grid.Resources>
    <ListView x:Name="EmployeeList">
        <ListView.ItemTemplate>
            <DataTemplate>
                <StackPanel>
                    <TextBlock Text="{Binding Path=Name}" Mode="OneWay"
                    Style="{StaticResource BasicTextStyle}"
                            HorizontalAlignment="Center" />
                    <TextBlock Text="{Binding Path=DateOfBirth, Mode=OneWay,
                            Converter={StaticResource birthDateFormatter},
                            ConverterParameter=\{0:d\}}"
                            Style="{StaticResource BasicTextStyle}"
                            HorizontalAlignment="Center" />
                    <TextBlock
                </StackPanel>
            </DataTemplate>
        </ListView.ItemTemplate>
    </ListView>
</Grid>
```

In addition to a parameter, you can specify a language for the conversion, which is important when the conversion is applicable for a specific region and language. You can also specify the data type of the target for which the data is being converted.

Creating and setting dependency properties

WinRT APIs provide a dependency property framework that helps in data binding of a UI element with a data source. A dependency property is a special kind of property that depends on multiple providers for determining its value at any time. It provides a notification to interested parties whenever its value changes. Consider a dependency property as an extension of the concept of a class property.

Unlike the traditional properties of a class that use a private member as their backing store, dependency properties use a property store that backs the property. A property store consists of a set of property identifiers and associated values that exist for an object. A property in this store is identified by an instance of *DependencyProperty* instead of its name. A dependency property is registered and owned by an object of the type *DependencyObject*. The *DependencyObject* class is located high in the class hierarchy, and most classes that are used in the UI of a Windows Store app inherit from the *DependencyObject* class.

Dependency properties are important in custom controls where they are used to implement features required in the user interface. The base class of a custom control (such as the *Control* class) inherits from *DependencyObject*. The *DependencyObject* class provides the following wrapper methods that are used with dependency properties:

- **SetValue** This method is used to set the local value of a dependency property to the value provided.

- **GetValue** This method is used to get the current value of a dependency property.

- **ReadLocalValue** This method is used to read the local value of a dependency property if a local value is set.

- **ClearValue** This method is used to clear the local value of a dependency property.

You can set a local value for a dependency property to an attribute or property element in XAML. When you set a current value to a dependency property, it enables you to change the value of the property without overwriting the source of a previous value; that is, the binding is left as is.

To create a *DependencyProperty* in a custom control, the property needs to be registered with the dependency property framework using the static *Register* method. You can provide metadata for the dependency property or specify it as null. A *DependencyProperty* identifier as a public static read-only member of the custom control is also required. A wrapper property with the name set to the value used with the *Register* method is required. You can implement the *get* and *set* accessors to connect the wrapper property with the dependency property it wraps. Listing 5-23 shows C# code for a custom control that uses an image with a label.

LISTING 5-23 Creating a *DependencyProperty* in a custom control

```
using Windows.UI.Xaml;
using Windows.UI.Xaml.Controls;
using Windows.UI.Xaml.Media;

public sealed class ImageWithLabelControl : Control
{
    public ImageWithLabelControl()
    {
        this.DefaultStyleKey = typeof(ImageWithLabelControl);
    }

    // Wrapper property
    public ImageSource ImagePath
    {
        get { return (ImageSource)GetValue(ImagePathProperty); }
        set { SetValue(ImagePathProperty, value); }
    }

    // Using a DependencyProperty as the backing store for ImagePath.
    // This enables animation, styling, binding, etc.
    public static readonly DependencyProperty ImagePathProperty =
        DependencyProperty.Register("ImagePath", typeof(ImageSource),
            typeof(ImageWithLabelControl), null);
```

```
    // Wrapper property
    public string Label
    {
        get { return (string)GetValue(LabelProperty); }
        set { SetValue(LabelProperty, value); }
    }

    // Using a DependencyProperty as the backing store for Label.
    // This enables animation, styling, binding, etc.
    public static readonly DependencyProperty LabelProperty =
        DependencyProperty.Register("Label", typeof(string),
            typeof(ImageWithLabelControl), null);
}
```

The custom control is declared in XAML as shown in Listing 5-24.

LISTING 5-24 Declaring a custom control with a *DependencyProperty*

```
<common:LayoutAwarePage
    x:Class="DPSample.DPSample"
    xmlns=http://schemas.microsoft.com/winfx/2006/xaml/presentation
    xmlns:x=http://schemas.microsoft.com/winfx/2006/xaml
    xmlns:local="using:DPSample"
    xmlns:common="using:SDKTemplate.Common"
    xmlns:d=http://schemas.microsoft.com/expression/blend/2008
    xmlns:mc=http://schemas.openxmlformats.org/markup-compatibility/2006
    mc:Ignorable="d">
    <Grid x:Name="LayoutRoot">
        <Grid.Resources>
            <Style TargetType="local:ImageWithLabelControl">
                <Setter Property="Template">
                    <Setter.Value>
                        <ControlTemplate TargetType="local:ImageWithLabelControl">
                            <Border Background="LightBlue" BorderBrush="Black"
                                    BorderThickness="2" HorizontalAlignment="Center"
                                    Width="140" Height="150">
                                <StackPanel HorizontalAlignment="Center">
                                    <Image Stretch="Uniform" Width="100" Height="100"
                                            Source="{TemplateBinding ImagePath}"
                                            Margin="5" />
                                    <TextBlock TextAlignment="Center"
                                            Text="{TemplateBinding Label}"
                                            FontFamily="Seqoe UI" FontWeight="Light"
                                            FontSize="26.667" Foreground="Black" />
                                </StackPanel>
                            </Border>
                        </ControlTemplate>
                    </Setter.Value>
                </Setter>
            </Style>
        </Grid.Resources>
        <StackPanel Orientation="Horizontal">
            <local:ImageWithLabelControl ImagePath="Assets/Fruit1.png"
                    Label="Orange" Margin="0,0,20,0" />
```

```
        <local:ImageWithLabelControl ImagePath="Assets/Fruit2.png"
                Label="Strawberry" />
        </StackPanel>
    </Grid>
</common:LayoutAwarePage>
```

Figure 5-7 shows the custom control in a Windows Store app.

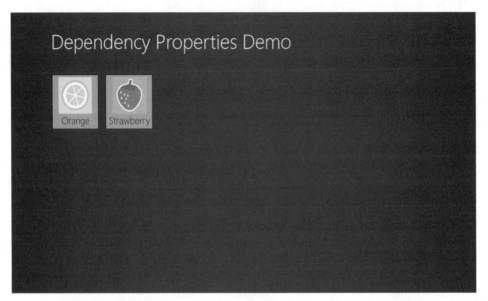

FIGURE 5-7 A Windows Store app with a custom control that has two dependency properties used to set up the visual appearance

Validating user input

Data entered by the user through the UI of a Windows Store app requires validation before its current value is updated. Data binding does not carry out the validation on behalf of the user. As a developer, you should implement user input validation of the data entered by the user. The *INotifyDataErrorInfo* interface can be used to implement custom synchronous and asynchronous validation support in data classes.

In the data class, validation is carried when the value of a property is being set. If there is an error in validating the input data, the property name is used with the *ErrorsChanged* event to notify the target about the error, and it is up to the target to display them correctly to the user. The data binding framework uses the *GetErrors* method to obtain a list of errors encountered during the validation for a specific property or the entire data entity. The *HasErrors* property indicates whether there are validation errors for the data entity.

In the C# code in Listing 5-25, a data model class implements the *INotifyDataErrorInfo* interface. The validation rule checks the age of the player and sets the value in the source only if it is in a certain range.

```csharp
using System.ComponentModel;

public class PlayerDataModel : INotifyPropertyChanged, INotifyDataErrorInfo
{
    private int age;
    private Dictionary<string, List<string>> errors =
                new Dictionary<string, List<string>>();

    public int Age
    {
        get { return age; }
        set
        {
            if (IsAgeValid(value))
            {
                age = value;
                OnPropertyChanged();
            }
        }
    }

    // Age validation
    public bool IsAgeValid(int value)
    {
        bool isValid = true;
        if (value < 18)
        {
            AddError("Age", "Too young to play this game!");
            isValid = false;
        }
        else if (value > 50)
        {
            AddError("Age", "Too old to play this game!");
            isValid = false;
        }

        return isValid;
    }

    // INotifyPropertyChanged members
    public event PropertyChangedEventHandler PropertyChanged;

    // Notifies listeners that a property has changed
    protected void OnPropertyChanged([CallerMemberName]string propertyName = null)
    {
        var eventHandler = this.PropertyChanged;
        if (eventHandler != null)
        {
            eventHandler(this, new PropertyChangedEventArgs(propertyName));
        }
    }

    // Validation error management
```

```csharp
// Adds the specified error to the collection if it is not already present.
// Raise the ErrorsChanged event if the collection changes
private void AddError(string propertyName, string error)
{
    if (!errors.ContainsKey(propertyName))
        errors[propertyName] = new List<string>();

    if (!errors[propertyName].Contains(error))
    {
        errors[propertyName].Add(error);

        // Raise the ErrorsChanged event, if available
        if (ErrorsChanged != null)
            ErrorsChanged(this, new DataErrorsChangedEventArgs(propertyName));
    }
}

// Remove an error from the collection if it is present.
// Raise the ErrorsChanged event if the collection changes
private void RemoveError(string propertyName, string error)
{
    if (errors.ContainsKey(propertyName) &&
        errors[propertyName].Contains(error))
    {
        errors[propertyName].Remove(error);
        if (errors[propertyName].Count == 0) errors.Remove(propertyName);

        // Raise the ErrorsChanged event, if available
        if (ErrorsChanged != null)
            ErrorsChanged(this, new DataErrorsChangedEventArgs(propertyName));
    }
}

// INotifyDataErrorInfo members
public event EventHandler<DataErrorsChangedEventArgs> ErrorsChanged;

public System.Collections.IEnumerable GetErrors(string propertyName)
{
    if (String.IsNullOrEmpty(propertyName) ||
        !errors.ContainsKey(propertyName)) return null;

    return errors[propertyName];
}

public bool HasErrors
{
    get { return errors.Count > 0; }
}
}
```

Enabling data filtering, grouping, and sorting in the user interface

When data-binding controls to collections, many Windows Store apps display data grouped into categories or types. For example, a collection of photos in a photo sharing app can be grouped by date taken, tags, or the location where the photos were taken. In addition, users can choose to filter their photos by a data range or by selecting only a set of tags. Filtering limits the data that is displayed in the screen, enabling users to easily select the items they are interested in. The user can choose to sort the data so that the items are displayed in a certain order (for example, the most recent photos are displayed first).

In many cases, altering the format of the data obtained from a source to make it suitable for binding is not feasible. Creating a custom view of the data and using it between the data source and the target data-bound control is often the best solution. The *ICollectionView* interface supports manipulation of the data before it is presented to the user.

> **MORE INFO**   **THE *ICOLLECTIONVIEW* INTERFACE**
>
> You can read more about the *ICollectionView* interface at *http://msdn.microsoft.com/en-us/library/windows/apps/windows.ui.xaml.data.icollectionview*.

If your Windows Store apps needs to display data in groups with headers for each group clearly highlighted, you can use the *GridView* control because it supports data binding with collections that contain grouped data. WinRT APIs provide the *CollectionViewSource* class that wraps a data collection and presents it in a way suitable for binding with a data control such as a *GridView*. In other words, it helps you to create a custom view for the data and have it available for binding. The main properties of the *CollectionViewSource* class are these:

- **Source**   This property is used in the code-behind to set the collection that provides the data for the view. The collection can be a list of items retrieved from a remote web service or local database, for example.

- **IsSourceGrouped**   This property is used to indicate whether the source of data is grouped.

- **ItemsPath**   This property specifies the path to follow in the data source to find groups within the *CollectionViewSource*.

A *CollectionViewSource* is declared in XAML and is set as the *ItemsSource* of the data control. It provides a custom view of the original data, grouped per the requirements for the app. With the *GroupStyle* property of a data control such as the *GridView*, you can customize the header, the control used for laying out items of each group, and so on. Listing 5-26 shows an example of the *CollectionViewSource* and the *GridView* control in XAML code.

LISTING 5-26 Declaring a *CollectionViewSource* in XAML

```xaml
<Page>
    <Page.Resources>
        <CollectionViewSource x:Name="employeesList" IsSourceGrouped="True"
                              ItemsPath="Employees"/>
    </Page.Resources>
    <Grid x:Name="LayoutRoot">
        <GridView ItemsSource="{Binding Source={StaticResource employeesList}}"
                  Margin="120,20,10,20">
            <GridView.ItemTemplate>
                <DataTemplate>
                    <StackPanel Margin="20">
                        <TextBlock Text="{Binding Name}" FontWeight="Bold"
                                   Style="{StaticResource ItemTextStyle}"/>
                        <TextBlock Text="{Binding Designation}" TextWrapping="NoWrap"
                                   Style="{StaticResource BodyTextStyle}" />
                    </StackPanel>
                </DataTemplate>
            </GridView.ItemTemplate>
            <GridView.GroupStyle>
                <GroupStyle HidesIfEmpty="True">
                    <GroupStyle.HeaderTemplate>
                        <DataTemplate>
                            <Grid Background="LightGray" Margin="0">
                                <TextBlock Text='{Binding Department}'
                                           Foreground="Black" Margin="30"
                                           Style="{StaticResource HeaderTextStyle}"/>
                            </Grid>
                        </DataTemplate>
                    </GroupStyle.HeaderTemplate>
                    <GroupStyle.ContainerStyle>
                        <Style TargetType="GroupItem">
                            <Setter Property="MinWidth" Value="600"/>
                            <Setter Property="BorderBrush" Value="DarkGray"/>
                            <Setter Property="BorderThickness" Value="2"/>
                            <Setter Property="Margin" Value="3,0"/>
                        </Style>
                    </GroupStyle.ContainerStyle>
                    <GroupStyle.Panel>
                        <ItemsPanelTemplate>
                            <VariableSizedWrapGrid Orientation="Horizontal"/>
                        </ItemsPanelTemplate>
                    </GroupStyle.Panel>
                </GroupStyle>
            </GridView.GroupStyle>
        </GridView>
    </Grid>
</Page>
```

In the Listing 5-26, the items in the data sources are grouped by a key (the key is the *Department* in this case) and used as the source for the *CollectionViewSource*. This is shown in C# code in Listing 5-27.

LISTING 5-27 Creating a grouped source of data

```
var employees = EmployeeService.GetEmployeesAsync();
var groupedEmployees = from employee in employees
                       group employee by employee.Department into g
                       select g;

employeesList.Source = groupedEmployees;
```

When you create a grouped source of data, as shown in Listing 5-27, a view object (of the type *ICollectionView*) is created. When set as the source of data for a *CollectionViewSource*, the data control bound to the *CollectionViewSource* updates itself. The *ICollectionView* class does not provide built-in support for data sorting and filtering. Therefore, if you need to provide data sorting and filtering in a data control such as the *GridView*, the *Source* property of the *CollectionViewSource* associated with the *GridView* needs to be updated. It is recommended you use Language-Integrated Queries (LINQ) to perform the data sorting and filtering from the source into a collection view and use it as a source for the *CollectionViewSource*.

Thought experiment
Using data binding in an app

In this thought experiment, apply what you've learned about this objective. You can find answers to these questions in the "Answers" section at the end of this chapter.

You are building a Windows Store app that will be used by tourists to explore attractions in various cities around the world. How would you use data controls, multiple layout and language format support, and value converters provided by the WinRT APIs in your app?

Objective summary

- WinRT APIs provide a data binding framework for building Windows Store apps. Data binding helps with the implementation of a presentation layer that is loosely coupled to its data model.

- The UI of an app is composed of visual elements that provide dependency properties for binding with data sources. Data binding for a visual element can be configured in XAML using various properties of the *Binding* class.

- Item controls such as *ComboBox*, *ListBox*, *ListView*, *GridView*, and *FlipView* are particularly useful for binding collections of items.

- A value converter can modify the value of a binding between a source and target through a value converter. A value converter implements the *IValueConverter* interface.

- Dependency properties can be used in custom controls to create properties that can be bound with data.

- UI input validation requires the implementation of the *INotifyDataErrorInfo* interface, which provides methods for notifying validation errors.

- The *CollectionViewSource* class provides support for data grouping. Controls such as the *ListView* and *GridView* can be styled to highlight groups of data provided through a *CollectionViewSource* object.

Objective review

Answer the following questions to test your knowledge of the information in this objective. You can find the answers to these questions and explanations of why each answer choice is correct or incorrect in the "Answers" section at the end of this chapter.

1. You are implementing a Windows Store app in which the hub details page displays a list of popular recipes. Recipes are grouped by their categories, ingredients, or popularity. You want to show the list of groups and items in each group. What is the best way to implement this feature?

   A. Use a *ComboBox* to show the list of groups and a *StackPanel* that is populated in the code-behind with controls based on the selection.

   B. Use a ListBox to show the list of groups and a *GridView* to show the items for the group selected with the *ListBox*.

   C. Use a *ComboBox* to show the list of groups and a *GridView* to show the items for the group selected with the *ComboBox*.

   D. Use a *StackPanel* to arrange the items in the list of groups and a *ListBox* to show the items for the group selected.

2. You are creating a data entity class for representing data received from a remote web service. Your app will use this class for data binding in the user interface. Some members of the entity are expected to be updated by users. Before the remote web service is updated, these entities should be validated for the data entered by the user. How will you implement the class?

   A. The data binding framework provided by the WinRT APIs support data binding including validation of the entered data. Binding the entity class in the UI is adequate.

   B. Implement the *INotifyPropertyChanged* interface for property change notifications and the *INotifyDataErrorInfo* interface for notifying the user of any errors in the entered data.

   C. Implement the *INotifyPropertyChanged* interface for property change notifications and the *INotifyDataError* interface for notifying the user of any errors in the entered data.

   D. Although data binding support provided by the WinRT APIs are adequate, the *INotifyDataErrorInfo* should be implemented for notifying the user of any errors in the entered data.

3. You have been asked to implement a data control that displays photos from an album with a grouping option selected by the user. In future releases, you are expected to support photo filtering and sorting from the user's photo collection. What are the steps required to implement this feature? (Choose all that apply.)

   A. Use a *GridView* control in the UI and bind the *GridView* with the collection of albums.

   B. Use a *GridView* control in the UI and bind the *GridView* to a CollectionViewSource object.

   C. Prepare an *ICollectionView* view by using LINQ to group items from the collection of albums, use this view as the *Source* of the *CollectionViewSource*.

   D. Set the IsSourceGrouped property of the *CollectionViewSource* to true.

   E. Create a custom *DataTemplateSelector* for the *GridView* and use the selector for displaying the items for various grouping options.

Objective 5.4: Manage Windows Authentication

Windows Store apps often require user authorization before they can carry out an action or access resources. However, the currently authenticated user might belong to a certain group of users or a domain that does not grant access to certain features of the app. An app could be used in multiple locations, including an intranet or corporate environment, in a home or public network, and so on. Therefore, user authorization based on a user name and password is not adequate. The implementation of authorization in Windows Store apps requires a technology that provides the identity of a user and roles while on the intranet of an organization or on the public Internet. Claims-based identity provides a common way to obtain the identity information of users irrespective of their location. The *ClaimsPrincipal* class provides methods to obtain users' claims and check the roles they belong to.

Windows Store apps that require users to provide their user name and password for authentication should not store them using their own implementation for storing credentials. The *PasswordVault* class can be used to securely store user credentials and retrieve them whenever required. These credentials can be removed at any time. User credentials stored with the *PasswordVault* class are available across multiple devices when the user logs in to these devices using the same Microsoft account. The *CredentialPicker* class provides a simple way to show a dialog box to obtain a user's credentials. The credentials can then be stored using the *PasswordVault* class. The dialog box provided by the *CredentialPicker* class can be customized to suit an application's requirements.

Retrieving a user's roles and claims

User authentication and authorization in Windows Store apps can be implemented in several different ways. You can implement your own mechanism within your app or as a service hosted in the cloud, for example. The process of identifying the user is an important step before an app enables the user to use various features; this is the step of authenticating users with their credentials. Users then attempt to access a set of features restricted to only a certain group of users, usually identified by a role; this is the step of authorizing users to one or more roles they belong to. An authenticated user belongs to one or more roles, with specific features assigned to each role.

Role-based access to features in a Windows Store app, including the ability to interact with online services, requires users' authorization after they are authenticated by the app. A custom method of authorization in an app is often not flexible whenever it needs to be extended to include a new set of roles or a new set of features accessible by one or more roles. To make the process of authorizing a user easier, a user authenticated by an app or service can be identified with a set of claims. Claims can carry information about the authenticated user, such as email address and full name.

A claims-based model of authorizing users is useful for decoupling user authentication and authorization for a set of roles. In addition, a user identified with a set of claims can be granted access to resources across multiple domains, provided these domains trust each other. In such cases, the need for credential synchronization does not arise at all. When the user needs to be removed from a domain, it does not require the user's account to be deleted from the domain. Instead, it is sufficient to remove the claims of the user from the domain. This model of identifying a user based on a set of claims is useful for implementing SSO in Windows Store apps. A token created as part of the sign-on process can be used to authorize the user.

A claims-based token can be obtained from a token issuer for a user providing valid credentials. During the authentication process, the token issuer determines the roles available to the user for authorization based on the user's claims. In many cases, the token issuer delegates this process to a third-party service such as Windows Live Services. Users are required to provide their Windows Live credentials and to trust the application from which they are logging on. The token is then passed to the application. In all future authentication requests, this token is used by the application to recognize the user as genuine. The process of obtaining a token with a third-party provider is shown in Figure 5-8.

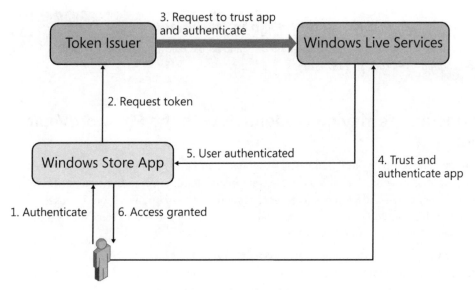

FIGURE 5-8 Steps involved in authorizing a user based on claims

In traditional Windows applications, claims-based user authentication and authorization is performed using the Windows Identity Foundation (WIF), part of the .NET Framework since version 4.5. WinRT APIs provide a set of interfaces and an enumeration in the *System.Security. Principal* namespace to help with tokens, user identification, roles, and more.

The *IIdentity* interface is used in the implementation of an identity object that represents a user in an app. It has the following properties:

- **Name** This property is used to obtain the name of the user as a string. Note that the name is not available if the user has not been authenticated yet.

- **AuthenticationType** This property is used to obtain the type of authentication used in the app as a string. For example, the app might use EncryptMessage (NTLM) or Kerberos for authenticating a user that belongs to a domain in a corporate network.

- **IsAuthenticated** This property is used to check whether the user is already authenticated.

The identity of users, along with the roles they are associated with in an app, is available as a security principal. A security principal object implements the *IPrincipal* interface. The *Identity* property of this interface provides the user's identity through an identity object associated with the principal; the identity object implements the *IIdentity* interface. In addition, a Windows Store app can check whether the user represented by the principal belongs to a certain role with the *IsInRole* method that expects a string for the role being queried. The method returns *True* if the user belongs to the role queried, otherwise, the result is *False*.

Storing and retrieving credentials with the *PasswordVault* class

A Windows Store app can obtain the user's user name and password for authentication within the app or for authentication with a remote web service. In some cases, the credentials are required every time the user needs to access a resource or carry out an action. The user can choose to run an app on multiple devices, so it is not ideal for the app to force the user to enter credentials on multiple devices.

The *PasswordVault* class in the *Windows.Security.Credentials* namespace enables Windows Store apps to securely store the credentials of a user and have them available across all the devices where the app is installed and accessed with the user's Microsoft account. You can add a credential with a resource name that your app can later use to retrieve the stored credential.

The *PasswordVault* class stores the credentials of a user as a *PasswordCredential* object. An instance of the *PasswordCredential* class is created with the user name and password provided by the user along with the resource name to identify the credentials. The following example shows how the *PasswordVault* and *PasswordCredential* classes are used to store user credentials:

```
using Windows.Security.Credentials;

public sealed partial class PasswordVaultSamplePage : LayoutAwarePage
{
    // Provide a resource which will be used to access the credentials later
    private void SaveUserCredentials(string username, string password, string resource)
    {
        try
        {
            PasswordVault vault = new PasswordVault();
            PasswordCredential cred = new PasswordCredential(resource,
                                            username, password);
            vault.Add(cred);
        }
        catch (Exception ex)
        {
            // Handle the error
        }
    }
}
```

The *PasswordVault* class provides the following methods to retrieve and search credentials stored in the password vault:

- **FindAllByResource** This method provides a read-only collection of *PasswordCredential* objects that are associated with a specific app matching the resource name specified. Note that the *PasswordCredential* objects in the list do not contain passwords; the password should be retrieved with the *Password* property of the *PasswordCredential* object after calling the object's *RetrievePassword* method .

- **FindAllByUserName** This method provides a read-only collection of *PasswordCredential* objects that are associated with a specific app matching the user name specified. Note that the *PasswordCredential* objects in the list do not contain passwords; the password should be retrieved with the *Password* property of the *PasswordCredential* object after calling the object's *RetrievePassword* method.

- **Retrieve** This method provides the *PasswordCredential* object associated with an app for the specified resource name and user name. The returned object contains all the data for the credential.

- **RetrieveAll** This method provides a read-only list of all *PasswordCredential* objects stored in the device.

Listing 5-28 shows how to retrieve the *PasswordCredential* object for a user with a specified resource using the *FindAllByResource* method of the *PasswordVault* class.

LISTING 5-28 Retrieving credentials using the *PasswordVault* class

```
using Windows.Security.Credentials;

// This method shows how to use the FindAllByResource method. To retrieve the
// credentials of a single user, you can use the Retrieve method too.
public sealed partial class PasswordVaultSamplePage : LayoutAwarePage
{
    // Find the PasswordCredential for a user with a specified resource
    private PasswordCredential FindCredentialsForResourceAndUsername(string resource,
                                                    string username)
    {
        try
        {
            PasswordVault vault = new PasswordVault();
            IReadOnlyList<PasswordCredential> credentials =
                                            vault.FindAllByResource(resource);
            foreach (var credential in (IEnumerable<PasswordCredential>)credentials)
            {
                if (credential.UserName.Equals(username))
                {
                    return credential;
                }
            }
        }
        catch (Exception ex)
        {
            // Handle the error
```

```
        }

        return null;
    }
}
```

A Windows Store app might need to delete all the credentials saved in the password vault. The *PasswordVault* class provides the *Remove* method to remove a *PasswordCredential* object from the password vault. Listing 5-29 shows the *Remove* method being used to clear the password vault.

LISTING 5-29 Using the *Remove* method in the *PasswordVault* class to clear passwords

```
using Windows.Security.Credentials;

public sealed partial class PasswordVaultSamplePage : LayoutAwarePage
{
    // Remove all the credentials stored in the password vault
    private void RemoveAllCredentials()
    {
        try
        {
            PasswordVault vault = new PasswordVault();
            IReadOnlyList<PasswordCredential> credentials =
                                            vault.RetrieveAll();
            foreach (var credential in credentials)
            {
                vault.Remove(credential);
            }
        }
        catch (Exception Error)
        {
            // Handle the error
        }
    }
}
```

Implementing the *CredentialPicker* class

Windows Store apps often require users to submit their credentials to access resources or interact with data obtained from remote sources that require authentication with credentials. In traditional desktop apps, the typical approach for enabling users to enter their credentials is through a custom dialog box with fields chosen by the developer. While building a Windows Store app, you can use a custom dialog box to enable users to submit their credentials. Ideally, you want the user experience of your custom dialog box to be similar to other apps.

To provide a consistent experience to users submitting their credentials for authentication, WinRT APIs provide the *CredentialPicker* class in the *Windows.Security.Credentials.UI* namespace. This class has a single method, *PickAsync*, that shows a dialog box in which users can enter their credentials. Although the dialog box can be customized to a certain extent, the overall user experience is consistent wherever it is used.

In its simplest form, the *PickAsync* method accepts two parameters: a target name used to identify the application or service for which the credentials are required, and a message that is displayed in the dialog box. An overload of the *PickAsync* method accepts a third parameter that can be used to display a caption in the dialog box. A further overload of the *PickAsync* method can be used with an object of the type *CredentialPickerOptions* that enables additional customization of the dialog box. For example, the Save Credentials check box can be selected when the dialog box is shown. The properties of the *CredentialPickerOptions* class that you will typically use in Windows Store apps are as follows:

- **Caption**   This property is used to set the caption of the dialog box to be visible to the user.

- **Message**   This property is used to set a message to the user in the dialog box.

- **CredentialSaveOption**   This property is used to configure the Remember My Credentials option shown in the dialog box and it is used to indicate whether the user wishes to save the credentials. The value of this property is set to a member of the *CredentialSaveOption* enumeration, such as *Hidden* to hide the option, *Selected* to show the check box as selected, and *Unselected* to show the check box cleared. The default value of the *CredentialSaveOption* property is *Unselected*.

- **CallerSavesCredential**   This property is used to specify whether the application will save the credential of the user if the user has opted through the Remember My Credentials check box. The default value of the *CallerSavesCredential* property is *False*.

- **AuthenticationProtocol**   This property is used to specify the type of authentication protocol that will be used with the credentials for user authentication. The value of this property is set to a member of the *AuthenticationProtocol* enumeration. The default value for this property is *Negotiate*.

- **CustomAuthenticationProtocol**   This property is used to specify the name of the custom authentication protocol that will be used with the credentials for user authentication. To use a custom authentication protocol, you must set the value of the *AuthenticationProtocol* property to *AuthenticationProtocol.Custom*.

- **PreviousCredential**   This property is used to specify the credential of the user previously stored by the application and to prefill the fields in the *CredentialPicker* dialog box.

MORE INFO   AUTHENTICATIONPROTOCOL ENUMERATION

You can read about the *AuthenticationProtocol* enumeration at *http://msdn.microsoft.com/en-us/library/windows/apps/windows.security.credentials.ui.credentialpickeroptions.authenticationprotocol.aspx*.

The *PickAsync* method returns an object of the type *CredentialPickerResults*. This class has the following read-only properties:

- **Credential**   This property contains the credentials entered by the user using the dialog box in a buffer of bytes. If the user canceled the authentication, a valid but empty *IBuffer* object is returned in this property.

- **CredentialDomainName**   This property contains the domain name of the user logged on to the device. If a domain name is not available, this property contains an empty string.

- **CredentialUsername**   This property contains the user name entered by the user in the dialog box. If the user cancels authentication or does not provide a user name, this property contains an empty string.

- **CredentialPassword**   This property contains the password entered by the user. If the user does not enter a password or cancels authentication, this property contains an empty string.

- **CredentialSaved**   This property indicates whether the credentials of the user were saved successfully.

- **CredentialSaveOption**   This property indicates whether the Remember My Credentials check box, if visible, was set by the user to save the credentials. The value of this property is a member of the *CredentialSaveOption* enumeration. If the dialog box was configured to hide the option, the value of this property is *Hidden*.

- **ErrorCode**   This property contains the value of the error code returned from the credential input operation. If the operation completed with the user adding credentials, the value of this property is zero. A nonzero value indicates a failure.

The result from the credential input operation can be saved as buffer in the roaming store, usually after it is encrypted. Alternatively, the recommended approach for roaming credentials is through the *PasswordVault* class. A new *PasswordCredential* object is created using the credentials obtained using a *CredentialPicker* dialog box, and it is added to the password vault. Listing 5-30 illustrates this process.

LISTING 5-30 Adding passwords to a vault using the *CredentialPicker* class and *PasswordCredential* object

```
using Windows.Security.Credentials;
using Windows.Security.Credentials.UI;

private async void Button_Click(object sender, RoutedEventArgs e)
{
    CredentialPickerOptions options = new CredentialPickerOptions()
    {
        CallerSavesCredential = true,
        AlwaysDisplayDialog = true,
        AuthenticationProtocol = AuthenticationProtocol.Ntlm,
        TargetName = "MyApp",
        Message = "Please login to Awesome App",
        Caption = "Awesome App"
    };
```

```
var credPickerResults = await CredentialPicker.PickAsync(options);
if (credPickerResults.ErrorCode == 0)
{
    string username = credPickerResults.CredentialUserName;
    string password = credPickerResults.CredentialPassword;

    // Authenticate the user here.

    // If the username and password are available and the user was authenticated
    // successfully, store the credentials in the
    // password vault
    if (!string.IsNullOrEmpty(username) && !string.IsNullOrEmpty(password))
    {
        PasswordVault vault = new PasswordVault();
        PasswordCredential credential = new PasswordCredential("MyApp", username,
                    password);
        vault.Add(credential);
    }
}
}
```

The *CredentialPicker* dialog box produced by Listing 5-30 is shown in Figure 5-9.

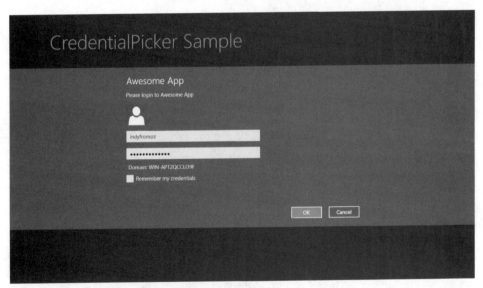

FIGURE 5-9 Dialog box shown to request the user's credentials

If the user enters enterprise credentials, they can't be roamed across devices for the user.

Thought experiment

Implementing credentials and role management in a Windows Store app

In this thought experiment, apply what you've learned about this objective. You can find answers to these questions in the "Answers" section at the end of this chapter.

A large organization has employees located in multiple offices around the world. To access the organization's intranet, employees must use their credentials to log on. The organization is planning to invest in employee productivity by building a Windows Store app, and the app will require employees to use their intranet logon credentials to access the app.

For confidential data, employees use a smart card that contains their credentials. Access to various resources is usually based on the roles assigned to employees. What are your recommendations for the organization to implement credential and role management in its Windows Store app?

Objective summary

- Windows Store apps can use identity providers such as Windows Live Services to authenticate and authorize users. A user identified with claims is issued a token whenever the user needs to be authenticated.
- The *PasswordVault* class can be used to securely store the credentials of a user in an app and have it roam across all devices for the same user. The *PasswordVault* contains *PasswordCredential* objects identified by their resource name.
- Windows Store apps should use the *CredentialPicker* class to retrieve user credentials. The *CredentialPicker* class provides a dialog box that is consistent with the user experience across Windows Store apps.

Objective review

Answer the following questions to test your knowledge of the information in this objective. You can find the answers to these questions and explanations of why each answer choice is correct or incorrect in the "Answers" section at the end of this chapter.

1. You need to implement user authentication in your Windows Store app that enables messaging between logged-on users and their friends. A user expects to be logged on to the app and have access to messages from multiple devices. How should you implement this feature?

   A. Show a dialog box to request credentials every time the user needs to check the account for messaging.

   B. Authenticate the user when the app is installed and save the credentials in the roaming app data store.

C. Use the *CredentialPicker* to retrieve the credentials if the credentials are not available in the *PasswordVault*. Save the credentials in the *PasswordVault* whenever the user enters them.

D. Authenticate the user when the app is installed and save the credentials in the temporary app data store.

2. In the next release of your Windows Store app, you will include user authentication after users register for premium access. You will provide the option to your users to save their credentials and to log out from the app. A fully featured desktop version of the app is already available and it uses a simple dialog box for obtaining the credentials. How should you implement the authentication dialog box for your Windows Store app? (Choose all that apply.)

A. Create a custom control that embeds a dialog box in which users enter their credentials.

B. Use the Settings charm to log on users with simple text fields to obtain their credentials.

C. Use the CredentialPicker class with the *CredentialSaveOption* property set to Selected.

D. Use the *PasswordVault* class to store user credentials if the user opted to have them saved.

E. Use the Settings charm to provide an option to the user to log out from the app. When the user logs out, remove the credential from the password vault.

3. The owner of a popular wholesale coffee bean store has a website that enables users to order beans. Regular customers are rewarded for their loyalty when they sign in using their Windows Live account. Signed-in users can view their orders and participate in forum discussions, for example. Some users can act as moderators. You have been asked to implement the authentication and authorization portion of the Windows Store app being built for the business. How should you implement this feature? (Choose all that apply.)

A. Use the *CredentialPicker* class to obtain the user's Facebook credentials and use it to sign in the user.

B. Use the *PasswordVault* object to save the credentials because users shouldn't sign out of the application again.

C. Obtain a token from the Facebook identity property based on the claims of the user.

D. Examine the users' roles while enabling them to access various sections of the app, including moderation of forum posts.

E. Provide an option in the Settings pane that enables the user to revoke access to the app and delete the saved token.

Objective 5.5: Manage web authentication

Windows Store apps can implement a custom authentication and authorization mechanism for users to log on and access resources as well as to interact with specific content. With the popularity of online services many users access every day—such as Windows Live, Twitter, Facebook, Flicker, and others—Windows Store apps can authenticate users using these services. This is more relevant when the content from these services is being accessed with the Windows Store app. An app should be able to log on the user without requiring them to provide their credentials in the app itself.

WinRT APIs provide the *Windows.Security.Authentication.Web* namespace for supporting authentication of Windows Store apps with remote web services. The *WebAuthentication-Broker* class helps with the authentication of a Windows Store app with a remote web service without requiring the user to leave the application.

The *WebAuthenticationBroker* class can be used to connection to identify providers on the web using protocols such as OAuth and OpenID. Most modern web services use the OAuth2 protocol for authenticating applications. The same class can used to implement SSO, a process of authenticating the user within multiple Windows Store apps without users having to enter their credentials for the remote web service.

The *CredentialPicker* class can be used to retrieve the credentials with a consistent user experience across Windows Store apps. It provides a number of options for the developer to configure the standard dialog box in which users insert their credentials. When used with the *PasswordVault* class, the user credentials can be roamed across multiple devices for the same Microsoft account.

> **This objective covers how to:**
> - Use the *Windows.Security.Authentication.Web* namespace.
> - Implement the *WebAuthenticationBroker* class.
> - Set up OAuth2 for authentication.
> - Set up single sign-on (SSO).
> - Implement the *CredentialPicker* class.
> - Implement credential roaming.

Using the *Windows.Security.Authentication.Web* namespace

Windows Store apps that require content from remote web services often require the user to be authenticated. Instead of implementing authentication using traditional methods, apps can utilize authentication protocols such as OAuth, which in many cases is the only acceptable option. Most web services expect the user to enter their credentials in an area that is provided by the service itself. The user authentication process might consist of a number of steps the user needs to perform before access is granted to the Windows Store app.

The *Windows.Security.Authentication.Web* namespace provides the *WebAuthenticationBroker* class that sets up the authentication of a Windows Store app with a remote web service. This class provides two methods for carrying out authentication in a Windows Store app with a remote web service:

- **AuthenticateAsync**   This method sets up the authentication process with the remote web service specified with a URI. In its simplest form, this method accepts a set of options specified through a *WebAuthenticationOptions* object and the URI of the web service. An overload of this method accepts a third parameter, which is the callback URI used to extract the access token returned by the remote service as a result of successful authentication. The URI for the *AuthenticateAsync* method should use the *https://* prefix; otherwise, the method fails to start the authentication process with an invalid parameter error.

- **GetCurrentApplicationCallbackUri**   This method is used to obtain the app's implicit callback URI and register with the remote web service for SSO support. The URI is of the form *ms-app://[application package SID]*.

The response from the *AuthenticateAsync* method is an object of type *WebAuthentication-Result*. It has the following read-only properties:

- **ResponseData**   This property contains the data, including the entire URL returned by the remote web service after the authentication completes.

- **ResponseStatus**   This property contains the result of the authentication operation. The value is a member of the *WebAuthenticationStatus* enumeration.

- **ResponseErrorDetail**   This property contains the HTTP status code if the authentication failed with the remote service.

The status of the authentication process with the *AuthenticateAsync* method is represented in the *WebAuthenticationResult ResponseStatus* property with the *WebAuthenticationStatus* enumeration. Table 5-3 describes *WebAuthenticationStatus* enumeration members.

TABLE 5-3 *WebAuthenticationStatus* enumeration members

Member	Value	Description
Success	0	The authentication was successful, and the result is available in the *ResponseData* property.
UserCancel	1	The user canceled the authentication.
ErrorHttp	2	The authentication failed because an HTTP error was encountered. The *ResponseErrorDetail* property contains the HTTP status code indicating the type of error.

The *AuthenticateAsync* method that carries out the authentication with the remote web service can be configured using the *WebAuthenticationOptions* enumeration. Table 5-4 describes *WebAuthenticationOptions* enumeration members.

TABLE 5-4 *WebAuthenticationOptions* enumeration members

Member	Value	Description
None	0	There are no options specified for the method.
SilentMode	1	This option is used to set up the *WebAuthenticationBroker* without showing the UI. It is used in apps in which SSO is implemented.
UseTitle	2	This option is used to specify that *WebAuthenticationBroker* should return the title of the webpage at the end of the authentication process in *ResponseData* property.
UseHttpPost	4	This option is used to specify that *WebAuthenticationBroker* should return the body of the webpage at the end of the authentication process in *ResponseData* property. This option is used in apps in which SSO is implemented.
UseCorporateNetwork	8	This option is used to set up the *WebAuthenticationBroker* for accessing an authentication provider within a corporate network. The app should be set up with the Internet (Client & Server), Enterprise Authentication, and Shared User Certificates capabilities in the package manifest.

Implementing the *WebAuthenticationBroker* class

A Windows Store app can incorporate authentication with a remote web service with the *WebAuthenticationBroker* class. The following steps are required to use the *WebAuthenticationBroker* class for authenticating a user in a Windows Store app:

1. Register your app for a client ID and, optionally, a redirect URL where the remote web service will redirect your app at the end of a successful authentication process.

2. Use the *WebAuthenticationOptions* to provide any options to the *WebAuthenticationBroker* based on your app's requirements.

3. Set up the URI for the *AuthenticateAsync* method to send the authentication request.

4. When the *AuthenticateAsync* method returns a *WebAuthenticationResult* object, examine its *ResponseStatus* property to check whether the authentication was successful.

5. If authentication was successful, use the *ResponseData* property of the *WebAuthenticationResult* object to obtain the access token.

6. Requests to access content from the remote service should contain the access token obtained as a result of the authentication.

The following C# code sample illustrates how to set up the *WebAuthenticationBroker* to authenticate users to their Facebook account:

```csharp
private async void Button_Click(object sender, RoutedEventArgs e)
{
    try
    {
        string facebookAppID = "426372210771029";
        string redirectUrl = "https://www.facebook.com/connect/login_success.html";

        // This is a basic example of setting up a URL for Facebook authentication
        // of the user. Refer the Facebook API to request specific permissions in the
        // URL to post updates on the user's timeline, for example.
        string facebookUrl = "https://www.facebook.com/dialog/oauth?client_id=" +
                            Uri.EscapeDataString(facebookAppID) +
                            "&redirect_uri=" + Uri.EscapeDataString(redirectUrl) +
                            "&display=popup&response_type=token";

        Uri startUri = new Uri(facebookUrl);
        Uri endUri = new Uri(redirectUrl);

        WebAuthenticationResult result = await
            WebAuthenticationBroker.AuthenticateAsync(WebAuthenticationOptions.None,
                                                startUri, endUri);

        if (result.ResponseStatus == WebAuthenticationStatus.Success)
        {
            // Parse the ResponseData property for the access token
        }
        else if (result.ResponseStatus == WebAuthenticationStatus.ErrorHttp)
        {
            // Parse the ResponseErrorDetail property to obtain the HTTP status code
        }
        else if (result.ResponseStatus == WebAuthenticationStatus.UserCancel)
        {
            // User canceled authentication
        }
    }
    catch (Exception ex)
    {
        // Handle the exception
        // Note: If an HTTPS URL is not used for the authentication, an invalid
        // parameter error is raised
    }
}
```

Figure 5-10 shows a Windows Store app set up for authentication with Facebook.

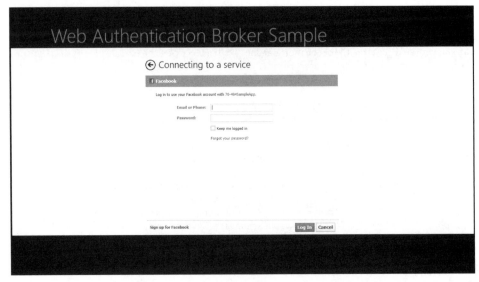

FIGURE 5-10 Windows Store app with *WebAuthenticationBroker* used for authenticating the user with Facebook

> **MORE INFO** **HOW THE WEB AUTHENTICATION BROKER WORKS**
>
> You can read about the details of the web authentication broker works at *http://msdn. microsoft.com/library/windows/apps/Hh750286.aspx*.

Setting up OAuth2 for authentication

The *WebAuthenticationBroker* class is useful for Windows Store apps planning to use OpenID- and OAuth-based online identity providers. The authentication mechanism in the app is delegated to a third-party service that the user already has access to and has a valid set of credentials with the service.

The OAuth2 open standard provides a simple mechanism to authenticate a user with an identity provider and authorize the requesting application to gain access to resources such as social media updates and blog posts. An access token is provided at the end of a success- ful authentication to the app, which is used in all future requests from the app to the remote service. The OAuth2 standard does not provide backward compatibility with the OAuth1 standard, which implemented a complex mechanism of authenticating a user and authorizing the user for access to resources.

You can use OAuth2 in your Windows Store app to authenticate users with an identity provider that implements the OAuth2 standard. Most modern web services implement the OAuth2 standard. The following steps are required to set up the *WebAuthenticationBroker* class for OAuth2 authentication:

1. Register a new application with the remote web service that enables applications to authenticate users with the OAuth2 standard. Most services provide an application or client ID along with a client secret key when you register a new application. The client secret key is not required during the authentication process. Some web services require you to register a redirect URI, which is used to redirect your application at the end of a successful authentication. The access token is added to the URI in a query parameter.

2. Prepare a URI required for authentication with the base URI from the remote service. This URI will specify the client ID as well as the redirect URI and, optionally, the requested scope of access for resources by the user logging on.

3. Use the *AuthenticateAsync* method of the *WebAuthenticationBroker* class with the URI prepared for authentication along with the redirect URI.

4. If the response from the web service is successful (the user was authenticated successfully), the redirect URI can be retrieved using the *GetCurrentApplicationCallbackUri* method of the *WebAuthenticationBroker* class.

5. The redirect URI contains the access token that should be used for accessing the user's resources on the remote service.

The access token issued by the remote service usually has a finite lifetime; the duration is dependent on the service implementing the OAuth2 standard. The user can revoke the rights granted by the remote service to your application, which will cancel all access tokens granted to your app.

The remote service can provide a URI that your application can use to determine if the access token can still be used. If the access token has expired, your app can request a new token without going through the authentication process again by sending a request to the remote service to refresh the token by providing the client ID and, in some cases, the client secret key.

Setting up single sign-on (SSO)

User authentication with OAuth and OpenID in Windows Store apps enables users to log on with an online identity provider. Users remain authenticated for a session or as long as the access token obtained from the remote service is valid. Users have to log on to an app in their PC or device whenever the apps require the user to be authenticated. SSO enables a user to log on to an app using an online identity provider and remain logged on across multiple devices. It usually provides an option to the user through a check box in the logon dialog box to enable them to remain logged on to the service.

SSO requires cookies to be stored in an application. Although the default behavior of the *WebAuthenticationBroker* class does not allow cookie storage, when the *WebAuthenticationBroker* class is set up for SSO authentication, cookies received during the authentication steps can remain in a special SSO application container. To support SSO, the online identity provider must allow the registration of URLs with the format *ms-app://[Application SID]*. The application's package ID (also called the SID) can be obtained from the application's page in the Windows Store.

The following steps are required to set up SSO with *WebAuthenticationBroker* in Windows Store apps:

1. Register your application with the identity provider and obtain a client ID and secret key. Request the provider to register a redirect URL of the form *ms-app://[Application SID]*.

2. Use the *SilentMode* and *UseHttpPost* members of the *WebAuthenticationOptions* enumeration in the *AuthenticateAsync* method; do not specify the redirect URL.

3. If authentication was successful, the online identity provider redirects the app to the redirect URL configured with an access token as a query parameter.

4. If the redirect URL matches with the application's SID, the *WebAuthenticationBroker* class returns the token to the app. The whole URL is kept in a cookie stored in a special app container so that future authentication requests do not require the user to log on with the credentials.

The cookies used for SSO in a Windows Store app are not shared with Internet Explorer, other browsers, or other apps. If an app attempts to misuse a cookie for an app in which the user is already logged on, it will fail authentication because the redirect URL of the two apps will never match.

> **MORE INFO   SINGLE SIGN-ON WITH MICROSOFT LIVE SERVICES**
>
> You can read more about implementing SSO with the Live Software Development Kit (SDK) for Microsoft accounts in the article at *http://blogs.msdn.com/b/windowsappdev/ archive/2012/03/14/bring-single-sign-on-and-skydrive-to-your-windows-8-apps-with-the-live-sdk.aspx*. The Microsoft Live Services team provides an interactive portal in which you can explore the Live SDK at *http://isdk.dev.live.com/isdk.aspx*.

Implementing the *CredentialPicker* class

Windows Store apps can use the *CredentialPicker* class in the *Windows.Security.Credentials.UI* namespace to implement a logon dialog box. The *CredentialPicker* class provides a consistent user experience for authentication of Windows Store apps with remote web services. The dialog box presented by the *CredentialPicker* class can be customized with the *CredentialPickerOptions* class.

> **MORE INFO   CREDENTIALPICKER CLASS**
>
> For details about the implementation of the *CredentialPicker* class in Windows Store apps, refer to Objective 5.4.

Implementing credential roaming

After a user logs on to a Windows Store app on a device, the user can access the same app on a different device. If the app expects the user to log on again with their credentials, it results in a poor user experience. The *PasswordVault* class provides support for credential roaming. One or more *PasswordCredential* objects with the user's credentials can be stored in the *PasswordVault* of an app and the credentials of the user are synchronized for a user logged on to multiple devices with the same Microsoft account.

> **MORE INFO** **CREDENTIAL ROAMING IN WINDOWS STORE APPS**
>
> For details on credential roaming in Windows Store apps, refer to Objective 5.4.

Thought experiment
Improving the authentication experience

In this thought experiment, apply what you've learned about this objective. You can find answers to these questions in the "Answers" section at the end of this chapter.

You have developed a Windows Store app that is popular among your users. You regularly receive feature requests from your users, and a common one concerns improving the authentication experience.

Several users have requested access to their Facebook and Flickr accounts through your app so that they can post their photos. How can you enhance your app to address the requests from your users?

Objective summary

- The *Windows.Security.Authentication.Web* namespace enables developer to implement user authentication in the Windows Store apps through online identity providers.
- The *WebAuthenticationBroker* class supports authentication in Windows Store apps with identity providers such as Windows Live Services.
- The *WebAuthenticationBroker* class supports the OAuth2 standard for user authentication in Windows Store apps.
- The *WebAuthenticationBroker* class also supports SSO by enabling the access token to be stored with the redirect URL in a special container.

Objective review

Answer the following questions to test your knowledge of the information in this objective. You can find the answers to these questions and explanations of why each answer choice is correct or incorrect in the "Answers" section at the end of this chapter.

1. By popular demand, you have decided to implement sharing photos using your photo mosaic Windows Store app with Facebook. You need to allow users to post photos to their Facebook timeline. What are the steps required to implement this feature? (Choose all that apply.)

   A. Authenticate the user by requesting Facebook credentials in a custom dialog box.

   B. Register your app with Facebook to obtain a client ID; configure a redirect URL to obtain an access token.

   C. Set up the *WebAuthenticationBroker* with a URL that contains the client ID, redirect URL, and the permissions requested.

   D. Use the *AuthenticateAsync* method of the *WebAuthenticationBroker* class to authenticate the user and use the access token from the result for posting photos to Facebook using the recommended APIs.

   E. After the user is logged on, post photos to Facebook using the methods available for desktop apps.

2. You are investigating the feasibility of implementing OAuth2 authentication using an online identity provider. To provide a consistent user experience to your users, you decide to use the *WebAuthenticationBroker* class in your app. Which of the following is a correct statement for the WebAuthenticationBroker about OAuth2 support?

   A. The *WebAuthenticationBroker* class supports OAuth2 authentication with only those identity providers that are located in the domain in which the user has joined with the app.

   B. The *WebAuthenticationBroker* class supports OAuth2 authentication with online identity providers that implement the OAuth2 standard and it also supports SSO.

   C. The *WebAuthenticationBroker* class must be used every time the user wishes to log on because it does not support SSO.

   D. The *WebAuthenticationBroker* class is suitable for use with online identity providers that support only the *http://* prefix.

3. To improve the employee productivity in an organization that provides a Windows Store to its employees, you recommend it uses SSO in the app. Which of the following is true of SSO?

   A. Implementation of SSO requires the application's SID to be present in a URL that is used as the redirect URL.

   B. Every time an update for the app is released, users need to log on again because the cookie is no longer available as the SID changes with every update.

   C. SSO works with both *http://* and *https://*. Therefore, if the employee is logged on to the corporate network through VPN, they do not require *http://* for the authentication.

   D. A user can use SSO to log on to any app along with the organization's app using the same set of credentials; this is one of the major benefits of using SSO.

Chapter summary

- WinRT APIs provide developers with local, roaming, and temporary data stores for data storage and manipulation. In addition, when configured with the appropriate capabilities and declarations, apps can access files and folders on users' devices.

- Windows Azure can be used to store files such as photos and documents; as well as structured, nonrelational data in tables. Windows Azure Mobile Services provides a simple way to integrate Windows Azure storage in Windows Store apps.

- The *HttpClient* class can be used to retrieve data from remote servers. Common HTTP verbs can be used in these requests to perform operations such as create, restore, update, and delete on resources in the remote server.

- Windows Store apps can use WebSockets to exchange short messages and stream large messages with a server that supports WebSockets.

- WinRT APIs provide a data binding framework that is used to data-bind UI elements with their data source. Most controls support data binding with item controls providing support for binding with collections.

- Value converters can be used to modify the data exchanged between the source and the target to modify the data format.

- Dependency properties are used in custom controls for data binding with data sources.

- The *INotifyDataErrorInfo* interface can be used to implement user input validation in a data entity class.

- The *CollectionViewSource* class provides a view for a data source that can be bound with item controls such as the *ListView* and *GridView*. Data in the view can be sorted, filtered, and grouped with LINQ.

- Windows Store apps can use online identity providers to authenticate users based on their claims. User roles provide the authorization required to access various resources and carry out actions.

- The *PasswordVault* class can be used to securely store a user's credentials and have them available across multiple devices where the user is logged on with the same Microsoft account.

- The *Windows.Security.Authentication.Web* namespace provides developers with APIs to implement authentication via OpenID and OAuth identity providers.

- The *WebAuthenticationBroker* class can be used to implement OAuth2 authentication along with SSO in Windows Store apps.

Answers

This section contains the solutions to the thought experiments and answers to the lesson review questions in this chapter.

Objective 5.1: Thought experiment

A Windows Store app can use a number of options to store and retrieve data based on its requirements. For an app used in the field requiring access to a document repository, or data transferred in and out of removable USB flash devices, for example, there are a number of options that can be implemented:

- **Windows Azure Storage for log files**   When a technician copies a log file for diagnosis and analysis, it can be saved into Windows Azure Storage. These files can be accessed from any location at any time by any technician.

- **Temporary application data store for knowledge base**   While in the field, the technician might need to refer to knowledge base articles several times. The technician can download these articles and save them in the temporary store for quick access.

- **MRU and future access list for reports created**   The technician might spend a considerable amount of time writing a report, and refer to previously written reports frequently. Using the MRU list and future access list for providing the most recently accessed files helps improve the technicians' productivity.

- **Accessing removable devices**   The app can be configured so that data can be copied and saved to a removable USB flash device.

Objective 5.1: Review

1. **Correct answers:** B, C, D

   A. **Incorrect:** The roaming application data store has restrictions on the amount of data that can be stored in it. It is meant to be used for storing data that can be rapidly synchronized with other devices.

   B. **Correct:** The temporary application data store can be used to cache files while the application is running. The system periodically removes files from this store, so an app doesn't need to manage the data stored in a temporary store.

   C. **Correct:** The photos modified and saved by the user need to be available across multiple devices. Therefore, the photos can be stored as blobs in Windows Azure and accessed from any device.

   D. **Correct:** The roaming application data store can be used to store a list of recently accessed files with the files stored in Windows Azure or any other remote store. Because this list is available across multiple devices, the app can use the list to access the files from a remote service from any device.

E. Incorrect: Although the install location is available to all applications, when the app is removed by the user, all the files in the install location are deleted. Therefore, the install location is not suitable for storing files.

2. **Correct answer: B**

   A. Incorrect: An app requires a custom implementation to use a local database for storing the MRU list. It is better to use the WinRT APIs instead of maintaining custom code for the feature.

   B. Correct: The MRU and future access lists can be easily used to implement the feature. The future access list can hold up to 1,000 items, which is adequate for such an app.

   C. Incorrect: The roaming application data store has limitations on its size, and the same file cannot be accessed by the user on multiple devices. Therefore, this is not a valid option.

   D. Incorrect: Files stored in the temporary application data store can be removed by the system at any time. There is a risk of the file with the most recently accessed items being deleted, so it is best not to use the temporary store for such data.

3. **Correct answer: C**

   A. Incorrect: It is not a good practice to store the credentials of a user in a file in any data store.

   B. Incorrect: An article saved in the roaming data store can cause issues with synchronization because changes in the store are propagated across multiple devices. An article can be downloaded on any device if the user accesses it.

   C. Correct: The ID of the article can be used to download it and have it ready for viewing by the user. Therefore, roaming the ID of the last read article helps with improved usability.

   D. Incorrect: Use the roaming store to store data required by the app to function properly, such as the ID of the article being read or a list of IDs of the top news articles.

Objective 5.2: Thought experiment

1. **User authentication over a secure connection** The Windows Store app can use *HttpClient* with a URL that has an *https://* prefix to authenticate users of the organization over a secure connection.

2. **HTTP verbs for RESTful requests** The app can use HTTP verbs such as GET to browse through various items in the system. When they need to upload a new piece of work, a new item can be created with an HTTP request with its verb set to POST. They can delete their work by sending an HTTP request with its verb set to DELETE and also update an item with an HTTP request in which the verb is set to PUT.

3. **StreamWebSocket for uploading and downloading media**   StreamWebSockets help with the exchange of binary data between the client and server over a secure connection when the URL begins with a prefix *wss://*. Because the server supports WebSockets, the app should use StreamWebSockets for exchanging media created by the members of the organization.

Objective 5.2: Review

1. **Correct answer:** C

   A. **Incorrect:** Although sockets can be used to create a client to exchange data with the server, it requires a fair amount of work to implement such a client.

   B. **Incorrect:** Similar to option A, encrypting the traffic manually requires effort and the server might not be able to decrypt the data.

   C. **Correct:** The *DefaultRequestHeaders* property is used to set up the HTTP headers, and a request is sent over SSL if the remote server supports it through an *https://* prefix.

   D. **Incorrect:** A server supporting StreamWebSockets accepts only a *ws://* or *wss://* prefix.

2. **Correct answers:** A, B, D

   A. **Correct:** Your app can decide whether to use the payload or discard it without processing it. This helps to improve client performance.

   B. **Correct:** This helps with buffering content while the response is being read by the client. This helps to improve client performance.

   C. **Incorrect:** An always-on connection might be useful for receiving data continuously, but the client has no control over the type of the data it expects to parse and use.

   D. **Correct:** Setting a realistic timeout ensures that the app does not have to wait until the server times out the connection. This helps to improve client performance.

   E. **Incorrect:** MessageWebSockets are used to exchange small amounts of data between the client and the server. Because the data from the server can vary in size, MessageWebSockets is not a suitable option.

3. **Correct answer:** C, D, E

   A. **Incorrect:** Although the *HttpClient* can be used for secure authentication using a URL with a *https://* prefix, setting a long timeout to download all data will make the game unresponsive while it waits for the data to arrive in scenarios where it takes long for the data to arrive.

   B. **Incorrect:** Sockets over TCP can be used to implement the requirements, but it will require fair amount of work to manually authenticate, control the download requests, and so on.

   C. **Correct:** The user can be securely authenticated using a URL with an *https://* prefix before any data is exchanged between the client and the server.

   D. **Correct:** MessageWebSockets are useful in exchanging small amounts of data between the server and the client. The client can use a URL with a *wss://* prefix for SSL security.

   E. **Correct:** StreamWebSockets are useful for downloading large amounts of binary data such as game content from a server. The client can use a URL with a *wss://* prefix for SSL security.

Objective 5.3: Thought experiment

WinRT APIs provide developers with a number of features that can be used to develop Windows Store apps that target multiple geographies, and they can be used in any location in the world. Windows Store apps can benefit from these features as follows:

1. **Data controls**   Tourists can view information about a destination or an attraction in various ways. If similar items are grouped together, data controls along with the *CollectionViewSource* can be used to group, sort, and filter them. This provides a convenient feature in such an app.

2. **Multiple layout and language format support**   Data controls support right-to-left layouts as well as right-to-left languages. This feature helps users from anywhere in the world to use the app.

3. **Value converters**   Value converters are very useful for customizing data presentation to a specific category of users. The language parameter available in the converter methods can be used to specify the language for the data conversion. This is useful when formatting data specific to the geography in which the app is being used.

Objective 5.3: Review

1. **Correct answer:** C

    A. **Incorrect:** A *StackPanel* is used to arrange a list of items in a layout, so it is not ideal to use it for displaying a collection of items.

    B. **Incorrect:** A *ListBox* is used to show a list of items with a scrollbar visible that exceeds its bounds. A *ListBox* is not ideal for showing a small fixed list of items.

    C. **Correct:** A *ComboBox* is ideal for showing a fixed list of items with only one item visible at any time. A *GridView* is suitable for displaying a collection.

    D. **Incorrect:** Although a *StackPanel* can be used to display a small fixed list of items, a *ListBox* is not ideal to display a collection that the user can interact with, such as selecting a recipe.

2. **Correct answer:** B

    A. **Incorrect:** The data binding framework does not provide support for validating data; you need to implement the *INotifyDataErrorInfo* interface in the data entity class.

    B. **Correct:** The *INotifyPropertyChanged* interface enables property changed notifications to update the target of data binding whenever the source changes. The *INotifyDataErrorInfo* interface adds support for validating user input.

    C. **Incorrect:** *INotifyDataError* interface is not supported by the WinRT APIs. Instead, you should use the *INotifyDataErrorInfo* interface.

    D. **Incorrect:** To update the target of data binding with any changes in the source, the *INotifyPropertyChanged* interface should be implemented.

3. **Correct answers:** B, C, D

    A. **Incorrect:** Any updates in the collection are not visible in the *GridView* when it is bound to the collection. A *CollectionViewSource* or an *ObservableCollection* should be used.

    B. **Correct:** The *GridView* control supports displaying grouped items present in a *CollectionViewSource* object. Therefore, the *ItemsSource* property of the *GridView* should be set to the *CollectionViewSource* object.

    C. **Correct:** You should group items from the data source using LINQ and use the view as the source of data for the *CollectionViewSource* object.

    D. **Correct:** Setting the *IsSourceGrouped* to *True* indicates that the data in *CollectionViewSource* is grouped and adequate for display in groups in a *GridView*.

    E. **Incorrect:** A *DataTemplateSelector* is useful for customizing individual items in a data control such as a *GridView*; it is not adequate for displaying items in groups.

Objective 5.4: Thought experiment

WinRT APIs support secure credentials storage, credential roaming, and claims-based authentication. The *CredentialPicker* and *PasswordVault* classes can be used along with claims-based authentication to implement these requirements:

- **Use the *CredentialPicker* class for a consistent user experience**   Because employees of an organization can use the app on a desktop PC or on a handheld device, it is important that a consistent user experience is considered for retrieving the users' credentials. The *CredentialPicker* class should be used to show the dialog box in which users can enter their credentials.

- **Support multiple sources of credentials**   Users need their smart cards to provide their credentials for accessing specific resources, and the *CredentialPicker* class can be used for this feature. When a removable device such as a smart card is available in the device, the *CredentialPicker* class shows a list of options available for obtaining the credentials including the smart card.

- **Consider using claim-based authentication**   If the infrastructure enables an identity provider to be available, the app should consider using claims-based authentication for the user wherever possible. Users can be authorized for a set of roles based on their claims available through a token issued by the identity provider. These roles can be used to grant user access to resources and sections of the intranet.

Objective 5.4: Review

1. **Correct answer:** C

   A. **Incorrect:** If users often access your app, requesting their credentials results in a poor user experience. In addition, incorporating a custom dialog box in a Windows Store app does not provide a consistent experience compared with other apps.

   B. **Incorrect:** Although the roaming data store is restricted for access and tampering, it is not a good option when security and data synchronization are considered. Roaming might stop if the quota for the roaming storage available for the app exceeds the limit.

   C. **Correct:** The *CredentialPicker* class provides a consistent user experience for retrieving a user's credentials when compared with other apps. The *PasswordVault* class can be used to save the user credentials and have them roamed.

   D. **Incorrect:** The temporary app data store can be cleared at any time by the system, so credentials saved in the temporary store can be deleted.

2. **Correct answers:** C, D, E

   A. **Incorrect:** A custom control with a dialog box used for entering credentials does not provide consistent user experience compared with other apps. Custom controls are created for reusability across apps.

   B. **Incorrect:** Using a Settings pane accessible via the Settings charm is not the correct way to obtain the user's credentials. The Settings charm should be used with default values for most settings, but this is not the case for logging on the user. The Settings charm can be used for providing a link to log off the user.

   C. **Correct:** The *CredentialPicker* class provides a consistent user experience for retrieving the credentials of the user. Users can opt for their credentials to be saved.

   D. **Correct:** The *PasswordVault* class provides a secure way of storing a user's credentials and having them roam across multiple devices.

   E. **Correct:** The Settings charm can be used for actions that require minimal user interaction, such as clicking a button. The user can log off of the app through a button placed in the Settings charm.

3. **Correct answers:** C, D, E

   A. **Incorrect:** Users probably will not provide their Facebook account credentials in your app because they might not trust your app to use their credentials properly. Therefore, the app should not request their Facebook credentials.

   B. **Incorrect:** The *PasswordVault* class should be used to save the credentials of the user, but the user should be able to log off of the app, which should remove the saved credentials from the *PasswordVault*.

   C. **Correct:** A token obtained from an online identity provider identifies the user and provides the roles. The app does not have to authorize the user separately to obtain these roles.

   D. **Correct:** Moderating forum posts requires users to belong to a specific role. Therefore, by examining the roles of the user, the app should be able to grant the user access to various features.

   E. **Correct:** The Settings charm should be used to provide an option for the user to revoke access to the app.

Objective 5.5: Thought experiment

WinRT APIs help developers easily incorporate authentication with online identity providers through APIs in the *Windows.Security.Authentication.Web* namespace. Several features of the app can be enhanced with these APIs:

- **Improve the authentication experience** The *WebAuthenticationBroker* class can be used with an online identity provider to authenticate users in your app. The dialog box presented for authentication provides a consistent user experience among other Windows Store apps.

- **Request the correct set of permissions from the remote service**   Your app can request a set of permissions in the scope during the authentication process. These permissions are attached to the access token obtained at the end of authentication process. Your app can use these permissions to access the remote web service and post items on behalf of the user.

- **Implement SSO in your app**   The *WebAuthenticationBroker* can be used to implement SSO if the remote identity provider supports SSO. With SSO, users do not need to authenticate through your app every time they use various devices. This improves the authentication experience of your app.

Objective 5.5: Review

1. **Correct answers:** B, C, D

   A.   Incorrect: Users might never enter their user names and passwords from third-party sites into an app's custom dialog box due to lack of trust and the fear of having their credentials compromised.

   B.   Correct: Registration of a new app with a remote service provides your app with a client ID, secret key, and option to set up the redirect URL.

   C.   Correct: The URL used by the *WebAuthenticationBroker* class needs to contain the client ID, redirect URI, and in most cases the scope for the permissions requested.

   D.   Correct: If the *AuthenticateAsync* is successful in authenticating the user, the response contains the access token. The app is expected to use the access token with all future requests.

   E.   Incorrect: An app is expected to use well-defined APIs for accessing resources on the user's behalf and carrying out actions such as posting photos. These require an access token that is available only through authentication using OAuth2.

2. **Correct answer:** B

   A.   Incorrect: The *WebAuthenticationBroker* class supports identity providers that implement the OAuth2 standard and are located on an intranet or the Internet.

   B.   Correct: The *WebAuthenticationBroker* can be configured for SSO with OAuth2 providers. SSO requires a redirect URL containing the app's SID to be set up with the identity provider.

   C.   Incorrect: The *WebAuthenticationBroker* supports SSO for Windows Store apps.

   D.   Incorrect: The *WebAuthenticationBroker* can only be used with URLs that support the *https://* prefix.

3. **Correct answer:** A

  A. **Correct:** The *WebAuthenticationBroker* class uses a custom URL that contains the SID of the app to ensure the access token contained in a cookie in the SSO app container is belongs to the app.

  B. **Incorrect:** The SID of an application does not change with updates, so the user will be automatically signed in after the app has been updated.

  C. **Incorrect:** The *WebAuthenticationBroker* can be used only with URLs that support the *https://* prefix.

  D. **Incorrect:** SSO enables users to log on to an app on a device and automatically log on to the same app on different devices, provided they are logged on to the device with the same Microsoft account.

Index

A

M

O

P

U

About the Author

INDRAJIT CHAKRABARTY, MCP, is a software architect and developer living in Sydney, Australia. Indrajit started programming with Fortran 77 and assembly language in high school, and progressed to C and C++ in college. Since 1998, he has worked with various Microsoft technologies, most recently with Windows Phone, Windows 8, and Windows Azure. Indrajit specializes in mobile application design and development on various platforms, as well as the architecture that powers mobile services, such as push notifications, data synchronization, and security.

Indrajit runs Liana Solutions (*http://www.lianasolutions.com.au*), a boutique software consultancy firm in Sydney that delivers professional software design and development services. You can learn more about Indrajit by visiting his personal website at *http://www.indyfromoz. com* and following him on Twitter (*@indyfromoz*).

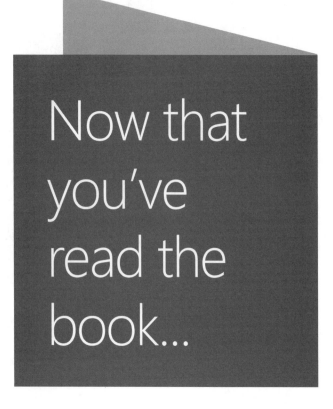

Now that you've read the book...

Tell us what you think!

Was it useful?
Did it teach you what you wanted to learn?
Was there room for improvement?

Let us know at http://aka.ms/tellpress

Your feedback goes directly to the staff at Microsoft Press,
and we read every one of your responses. Thanks in advance!

 Microsoft